Web Programming Languages Sourcebook

Gordon McComb

with contributions by

Marty Bower and

Mark Robinson

WILEY COMPUTER PUBLISHING

John Wiley & Sons, Inc.

New York • Chichester • Weinheim • Brisbane • Singapore • Toronto

Executive Publisher: Katherine Schowalter
Editor: Phil Sutherland
Assistant Editor: Pam Sobotka
Managing Editor: Carl Germann
Electronic Products, Associate Editor: Mike Green
Text Design & Composition: Benchmark Productions, Inc., Boston, MA

This text is printed on acid-free paper.

Library of Congress Cataloging-in-Publication Data:

McComb, Gordon, 1957– .
Web programming languages sourcebook / Gordon McComb ; with contributions by Marty Bower and Mark Robinson.
p. cm.
Includes index.
ISBN 0-471-17576-5 (pbk. : CD-ROM : alk. paper)
1. Internet programming. 2. Programming languages (Electronic computers) 3. World Wide Web (Information retrieval system)
I. Bower, Marty. II. Robinson, Mark, 1955– . III Title.
QA76.625.M35 1997
005.2'76--DC21 97–3988
CIP

Printed in the United States of America

10 9 8 7 6 5 4 3 2 1

Contents

Dedication

To my dad, for keeping his faith in me.

Acknowledgments

This book turned out to be much more difficult than I had imagined because it's not just on one language, but many. It's a book many of us believed needed to be written, in answer to the endless calls from lost souls who are just getting their feet wet with the Web and programming for it.

I am indebted to the abled assistance of a number of professional programmers who contributed to this book. Marty Bower contributed the chapters on Web programming using Perl and C; Mark Robinson took over the reins on the chapters on Java. Both helped me make my deadlines and greatly enhanced the usefulness of this book.

On the business side, an avalanche of huzzahs for my agent, Matt Wagner, for going out of his way to get the best deal possible, and for Phil Sutherland, Pam Sobotka, Bob Ipsen and Katherine Schowalter of Wiley Computer Books, for being so enthusiastic and supportive of this project.

Finally, had my family—wife Jennifer and children Mercie and Max—not been so understanding, there is no way I could work 'til 2:00 a.m., then sleep until 7:00! I love you all!

Introduction

The World Wide Web comes to life when it's interactive—when it adjusts and conforms based on user input. There are many ways to achieve this interactivity, but in almost all cases, interactivity involves programming of some type. The programming reacts to the user's input and responds accordingly.

Programming requires writing in a language that the computer can understand. A number of programming languages have been developed over the years, with many of them now out of use, either because the computer system they were designed for is archaic or because the language has been replaced by something newer and better.

One reason for the popularity of the World Wide Web is that it does not require the use of any single type of computer. At least three major operating systems provide Web pages. These operating systems are UNIX, Windows, and Macintosh, and different programming languages are available for each. While the choice of computers and operating systems offers variety to those who design and maintain Web pages, it also complicates the issue of programming for the Web.

Web publishers are currently bombarded with a dizzying array of programming language choices. Should you use Perl? Or will a bash or Korn shell script do? Can JavaScript, VB Script, or Java do the job?

This is where the *Web Programming Languages Sourcebook* comes in. This book is your one-step guide to all the popular languages used for Web programming. This unique book describes the important facets of *the most common languages used for publishing on the Internet and World Wide Web*. Each language is covered in enough detail so that you can use that language to build a functional program—even if you are not a professional programmer.

What's Inside the *Web Programming Languages Sourcebook*

This book is about the popular programming languages used for the Internet and the World Wide Web. It is designed to meet the needs of programming "newbies" and those with intermediate experience in programming. You don't need to know anything about programming to benefit from this book, but if you do, you'll be able to jump to those chapters of most interest to you. All of the most widely used languages are covered in this book, including:

- UNIX bash shell language
- Perl (under UNIX, Windows, and Macintosh)
- Java
- JavaScript
- VB Script
- C

Why this book is special:

- It takes a unique approach to Web programming by covering all the popular languages.
- It includes chapters on programming fundamentals, in case you're a relative newcomer to the programming scene.
- It details Web progamming for CGI, server-side processes (like counters, shopping carts, user authentication, server maintenance, and databases).
- It covers client-side scripting using the latest versions of JavaScript and VB Script.
- It comes with plenty of examples to show you neat tips, tricks, and secrets that can jazz up your Web pages.

Is This Book for Me?

The *Web Programming Languages Sourcebook* is written for the person already somewhat familiar with the Internet, as well as the general process of electronic publishing of HTML documents on the World Wide Web. But no other special skill or knowledge is assumed. This book can be used by those with little or no programming experience. Of course, the more programming experience you have, the faster you'll be able to learn and use the programming fundamentals covered in this book. The chapters of this book are organized so that if you already know programming fundamentals you can go straight to learning about the programming language you are interested in. I don't assume you already know programming topics such as expressions, conditionals, variables, and arrays, so I explain these concepts when first introduced. Skip these pages if these topics are familiar to you.

This book is *not* for the Internet newbie. If you don't know what the Web is and if you've never seen a document in HTML format, let alone created one, this book isn't for you. Pick up some good introductory books on the Internet and the Web. Then come back to this one.

This book is for you if:

- You are intrigued by the notion of programming for the Web, but don't have the programming experience to know which language is best suited for what you want to do.
- You want to take advantage of enhanced Web page capabilities, like forms and visit counters.
- You'd like to use an existing program someone else wrote and adapt it to your needs, but you don't understand the programming language that was used to be successful at revising it.
- You want to make your pages dynamic—changing day-to-day or even hour-to-hour!—all on their own.

Where Do I Start?

If you wish you may read this book cover to cover, but it is not necessary. Early chapters lead you through the basics of the Web, CGI, and programming fundamentals. Then additional sections of the book deal with specific programming languages. The final section of the book provides advanced information on integrating languages and adopting existing scripts. Throughout this book you'll find lots of *tips, tricks, and great ideas*—plus plenty of working examples—that will help you on the road to becoming a Web programming master; read the partd that are of interest to you and that match your knowledge level.

I	Start Here
Am new to Web programming, CGI, and other topics	Chapter 1
Am somewhat familiar with the Web, no programming experience	Chapter 3
Want to learn how to program with UNIX shell scripts	Chapter 8
Want to learn how to program in Perl	Chapter 10
Want to learn how to program in Java	Chapter 13
Want to use JavaScript or VB Script	Chapter 15
Want to learn how to program in C/C++	Chapter 17
Am interested in additional programming topics	Chapter 19

Where Do I Learn More About Web Programming?

This book teaches you the *fundamentals* of a dozen of the Web's most popular programming languages. Expect to learn enough about a language to write or revise a basic program, but don't expect to learn everything about the language.

The *Web Programming Languages Sourcebook* Web site provides up-to-date information on Web languages, plus scores of free examples and other goodies. You'll also find additions and corrections for this book. Visit us at: http://gmccomb.com/languages/

If a programming language strikes your fancy, you'll find plenty of additional information on it in your local bookstore and on the Web. The *sources.htm* file included on the CD-ROM that accompanies this book lists a number of source for learning more about Web programming languages. If you're looking for printed books, the publisher would like to recommend the following:

- *The JavaScript Sourcebook* by Gordon McComb
- *C and UNIX* by M. Barrett
- *Developing CGI Applications with Perl* by John Deep

- *The HTML Sourcebook Third Edition* by Ian S. Graham
- *The Java Sourcebook* by Ed Anuff
- *Object-Oriented Programming with REXX* by Tom Ender
- *UNIX System Administrator's Companion* by Michael R. Ault
- *Visual Basic Internet Programming* by William Horton
- *World Wide Web Database Programming for Windows NT* by Brian Jepson

These books are published by Wiley Computer Publishing and are probably just a foot or two away from the shelf where you found this one.

An additional source of information on UNIX programming topics (*bash*, *Tkl* and *Tk*, *Perl*, *sed* & *awk*, and others) is the Nutshell book series, published by O'Reilly & Associates.

Copyright Information

By its nature the Internet is a sharing medium. It's always been that way, and it likely will remain so. This book continues in that spirit. You are welcome to incorporate all or parts of the code you find in this book in your Web pages, for whatever purpose—private or commercial—under the following conditions.

- If you use a program from this book in its entirety, please retain the copyright notice that accompanies it (if any). This goes for programs I (or my contributors) wrote and copyrighted, as well as freeware programs contributed by others.
- You may use portions of programs and make revisions to the code in any way you wish, without including the copyright notice as stated above.
- Redistribution of the programs carrying the copyright of the author is prohibited unless you first get written permission from the publisher and author. So, *don't post these programs on your Web or FTP site, include them in your book, or stuff them away on your BBS unless you check with us first.*
- Programs under the GNU copyright (these are so indicated) may be freely distributed in any form, as long as you adhere to the GNU copyright provisions.

Though certainly not a requirement for using the examples in this book, feel free to provide a link on your page to my Web page at http://gmccomb.com/languages/.

Stuff You Can Probably Skip

Book introductions are notorious for overstating the obvious, and I've probably done that enough already. But it's a good place to put all the "housekeeping chores" necessary when presenting a book. If you're itching to start learning Web programming, then by all means stop reading now and proceed directly to Chapter 1. Otherwise, for the interminably curious here's some semi-useful information you may want to know.

Conventions Used in This Book

Example code is displayed in a special type style, like this:

```
var CurrentRoom = 0;
var TextFrame = parent.frames["text"];
var ResultFrame = parent.frames["result"];
var CtrlFrame=parent.frames["ctrl"];
var Doc = ResultFrame.document;
var RoomVisited = new Array(5);
```

A Note About the CD-ROM

This book comes with a CD-ROM. It contains all the example files and applications detailed in this book, as well as a number of useful Internet tools and utilities. See the Appendix for full details on using the CD-ROM.

Chapter

1

Programming for the World Wide Web

Technology has a way of changing business. As an example, in the middle 1800s the technology of the train and the Transcontinental Railroad expanded commerce across America. The train connected distant parts of the country, and that link increased the markets for companies that had concentrated until then on only business east of the Mississippi.

With rail service came towns, many of which existed only to service the trains passing through the area. The new towns created local businesses—there were the saloons, of course, but also the village blacksmith, the innkeeper, the livery owner, and more.

Technology once again changed business in the early twentieth century with the advent of the automobile. By the 1940s, cars were commonplace, used for commuting, vacationing, and shopping. More and more roads were built to handle the increased traffic. The United States quickly became a country totally dependent on the automobile and the many businesses it created, including the manufacturing of the car itself, automobile service, gas stations, and road building and maintenance—in short, tens of thousands of new kinds of businesses that hadn't existed before.

You've probably heard this before, but it's likely true: The Internet is poised to change business—and our entire way of living—just as the train and automobile have done. Using the train and automobile as metaphors for the Internet is not accidental. Both the train and automobile are a means of transportation—a way of getting something (goods, produce, people)—from one place to another. Likewise, the Internet is a means of getting something from one place to another. Only this "something" is data. This data can take many forms, all the way from simple text to images, sounds, and movies. There is no piece of information that cannot be transported by the Internet.

Aiding the importance of the Internet is its global reach. The Internet currently uses the telephone network to connect computers from all around the world. This network ensures that almost anyone with phone access can connect to the Internet. (I say almost anyone: because there are still countries in the world where the phone service is too poor to accommodate the high-speed data transfer the Internet requires. Additionally, some countries, for one reason or another, restrict or forbid Internet access to most or all of its citizens.)

The Internet is not one single means of transporting data, but many. E-mail is one of the Internet's most important data transport methods. Every day, millions of electronic messages are shuttled through the Internet's connections. In fact, e-mail has become such a staple of Internet life that in 1996, more e-mails were delivered via the Internet than first-class letters delivered by the United States Post Office!

Another important Internet data transfer method is the World Wide Web, or the Web for short. This relatively recent innovation permits users from all over the world to view documents containing text, graphics, and other multimedia content. People can view "pages" using a Web browser program, such as Netscape Navigator or Microsoft Internet Explorer.

The Web is a virtual magazine or book. Everything is electronic, so no paper, ink, or trucks are needed to deliver heavy books or magazines. Publishers can update their works at a moment's notice, so nothing has to become outdated. Already, the Web has begun to change the way print media are produced and distributed. In the very near future, for example, newspapers and magazines may blur—the traditional role of the newspaper having been overtaken by the almost immediate dissemination of news possible with the Web.

Publishing is only one business opportunity of the Web. Others include catalog sales, real estate sales, visitor or business information, and much, much more. In short, there is no limit to the potential of the Web because it serves a very fundamental purpose: to get information to lots of people in a very short period of time, and for very little money.

All of which brings us to this book. In the beginning, producing Web content (we'll call it "publishing on the Web," even though the content may not be book- or magazine-like material) involved static documents—documents that stayed the same once they were created by some human. Though the Web is only a few years old, it has matured at a very fast pace. Today, people expect more from sites that support Web pages. In the early days of the Web (1994 or 1995), simply printing the phone number of a company for customers to call for more information was acceptable. Now, people want to access that information directly through the Web.

This interactive, or dynamic, element of the Web requires programming of some type to process the user's request and provide the information he or she has asked for. As with all computer programming, programming for the Web involves using a programming language.

Since its beginning, the Internet—and the Web itself—has predominately relied on computers running the UNIX operating system. Even though the Windows operating system is making inroads, currently the majority of Internet Web sites use UNIX computers. If you want to program for the Web, you have to know a programming language for UNIX (or Windows 95 or NT if you have a Web server computer that runs under Windows). Not everyone has experience writing programs for either UNIX or Windows, but everyone does want to create dynamic Web pages.

This book will cover the basics of Web programming, including primers on the six most popular programming languages used on the Web:

- Perl
- UNIX shell
- Java
- C/C++
- JavaScript
- VBScript

To put these languages into perspective, let's first discuss the role of Web programming in further detail. Programming for the Web is not a particularly easy task (nor is it painfully difficult), so you want to save it for just those jobs that really need it. You must understand what needs to be programmed in Web pages and what doesn't. You'll learn about this topic in this chapter as we review some alternative methods of creating dynamic Web pages that do not requires hands-on programming. You'll also discover realistic and useful applications of Web programming, like shopping carts, forms processing, and user authentication. Finally, you'll read about what you need to program for the Web, including skills, development systems, and software.

Applications for Web Programming

You already know that you're interested in Web programming, but you may not have a full grasp of exactly what kinds of programs are used on the Web. We'll cover that here. If you are familiar with Web programming applications, such as shopping carts and forms processing, feel free to skip to the next section.

Recall that one main, if not the main, aim of Web programming is to create dynamic Web pages. Web pages interact with the user in some ways, much like a computer program such as a word processor interacts with its user.

> **NOTE** Some forms of Web programming are not designed to interact with users directly. These programs are commonly referred to "back-end" systems. A typical back-end Web program is one that analyzes the activity log of a site and uses this log to create a review of the the number of times each page and other element (image, sound file, whatever) have been accessed in a given day, week, or month. Another example of a back-end program is a database management system that connects a Web page to the large database maintained by your company. These kinds of programs are beyond the scope of this book because they require intimate knowledge of Web servers and all the individual software programs that run on them.

Web Programs for Forms Processing

Perhaps the premier application of Web programs is processing user forms. The form is part of the HTML of the Web page, and it allows users to send data—

name, address, phone number, credit-card information, or whatever—to the Web server. A program running on the server snatches up this data and processes it in some way. For example, if the user has just submitted a credit-card order for a product, the server program might log the order and format the data so that a human assistant could actually fill the order.

> **NOTE** Very elaborate forms processing programs are even capable of validating the credit card immediately; these require extensive programming and database interfacing. They are well beyond the scope of this book, and even beyond the capabilities of some professional programmers. It's nice to know, though, that a Web program can be used for this task.

The benefit of forms processing is that it allows interactivity with the user, typically without any human intervention. The credit-card example above eventually relies on a person to take the information collected and do something with it. Lots of forms processing, however, never involves a person at all. A Web search program that looks through a collection of text files for matching words and phrases is a good example of this. With a surprisingly minimal amount of programming, you can devise a form that allows users to enter a search word or phrase. That word or phrase is then used in a text lookup program running on the Web server. Files that contain the word or phrase are then displayed for the user.

Another common and useful application for forms processing is the "comments form," which allows users to write comments and e-mail them to a specific recipient. The form contains one or more entry blanks and other form controls (check boxes, radio buttons, list boxes, and so forth), and the user's response is formatted in a convenient mail message. One such comments form is shown in Figure 1.1; the resulting e-mailed form is shown in Figure 1.2. The program that translates the form contents to the e-mail message is surprisingly simple. An example of such a program is found in Chapter 11.

Shopping Cart

In the world of the Web, a shopping cart is a specialized program for processing orders, such as orders for books, videotapes, or software. The user is allowed to browse through the Web site and examine the various offerings within it. When he or she encounters something of interest, it can be added to the shopping cart by clicking on a button, as shown in Figure 1.3. The shopping cart remembers each

Figure 1.1 A comment form is a typical application of a Web program. Users may fill in the form, which is automatically e-mailed to a specific recipient.

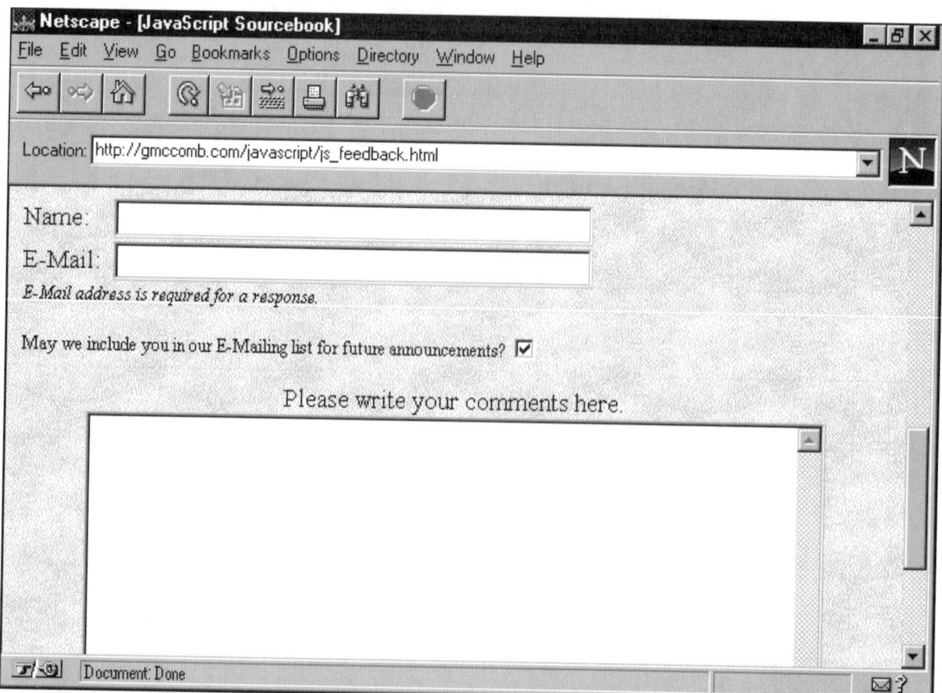

item that the user selects, so that when it's time to check out and pay the bill, the items can be totaled and displayed.

Shopping carts do more than meets the eye. The standard Web server uses what's known as "stateless" connections—that is, each time you connect with the Web site, it's a new connection to the server. The server ordinarily has no knowledge of any requests you might have made before. A shopping cart application must store previous choices using some type of temporary file. When the user checks out and pays the bill (or leaves the store and doesn't return), the temporary file is deleted.

A number of techniques have been developed for creating shopping carts. These days, the most common technique uses a temporary file that's stored on the client computer, not the server. In that way the server doesn't have to juggle numerous temporary files at once. It also doesn't have to worry about matching each customer with the right file. The temporary file on the client computer is called a

Figure 1.2 The output of the e-mailed form is formatted for appearance.

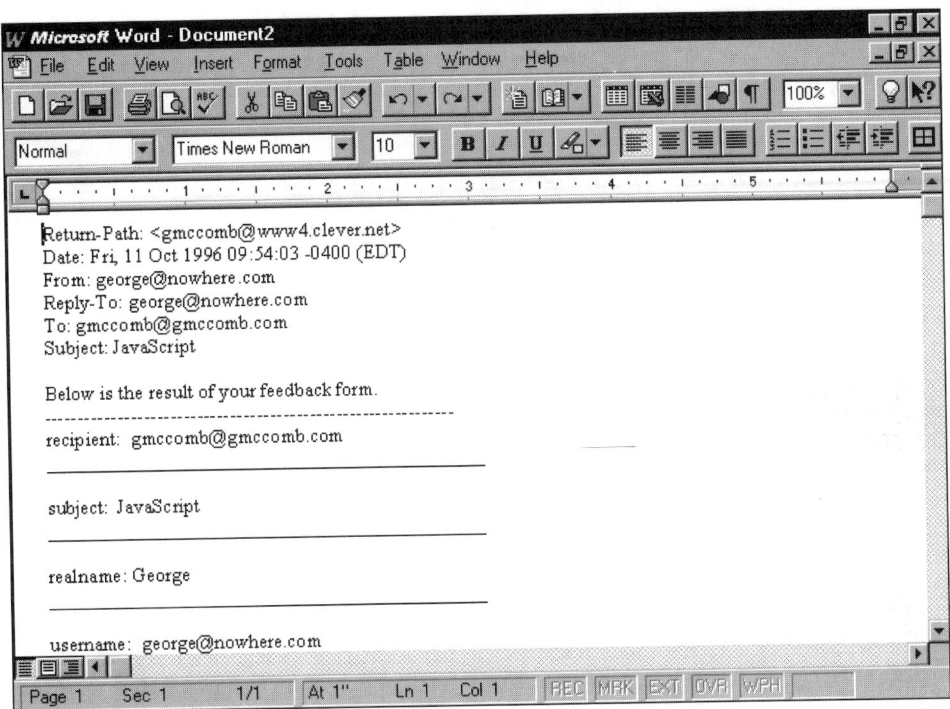

cookie, and the browser controls the text that is stored within it. The contents of the cookie file can be read only by the site that put it there. This feature helps ensure privacy and security.

With the cookies file recording all purchases, it's a rather simple matter to read back all the items at the checkout stand, total the charges, and display the result.

Not all browsers support cookies, however, and the latest versions of Netscape Navigator and Microsoft Internet Explorer allow users to disable the cookies feature (or at least specify when writing or reading a cookie value is acceptable). Because of this, a preferred method of creating shopping carts involves using forms and hidden text fields. The contents of the text fields are not displayed on the page, but they can be read by the server when the user finally reaches the checkout stand. Although the hidden fields approach is a little messier to implement, it can be used with all modern Web browsers. Because this technique doesn't pose even a hint of a security hole, there is no need to provide users with the means to turn it off.

Figure 1.3 A shopping cart application allows users to select items in various pages of a site, then have those items totaled for "checkout."

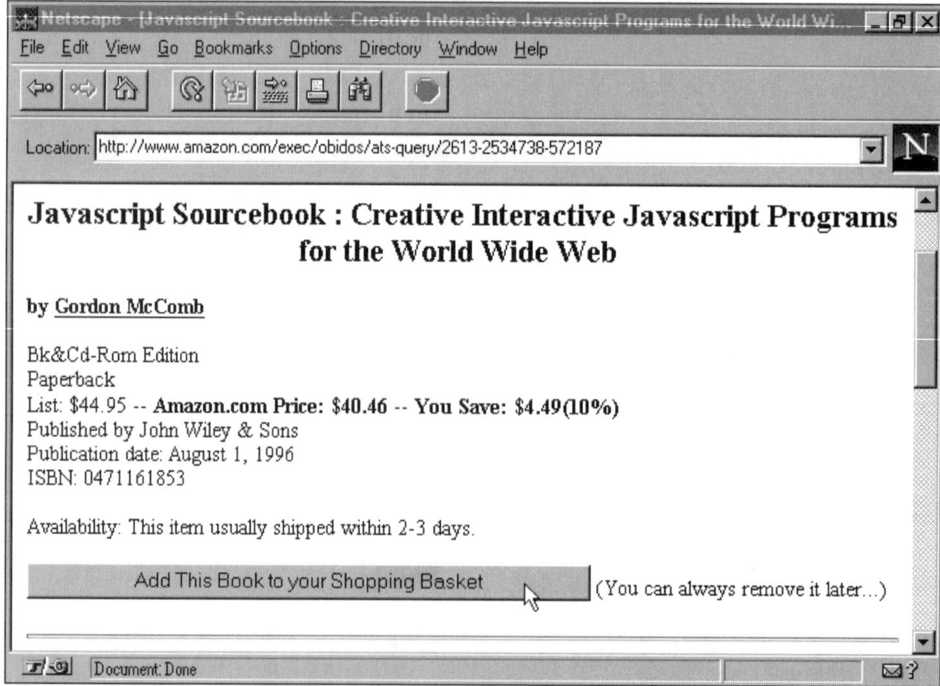

User Authentication

Third in the list of popular applications for the Web is user authentication, sometimes better known as password protection. A Web program is used to prevent unauthorized access to a page, all of the pages within a directory, or even an entire site. To gain access the user must provide a name and password. If the name and password match the information stored in a password file, the user is allowed in. If the name and password don't match, the user is tossed out, and access is denied.

Most server software includes its own password scheme, which is designed to work in concert with the user authentication feature built into most browsers. With this feature, a pop-up box appears that asks for the user name and password. Software already provided by the server determines if the user name and password match what is stored in a password file. If there's a match, the server allows access. If there isn't a match, the server displays an error page.

Even though no extra Web programs are typically required for user authentication, some Web administrators prefer their own password protection scheme. The usual approach for server-provided user authentication restricts access to specific directories at a site (see Figure 1.4). Some applications require users to be able to access certain files in the directory and not others. This is where a Web program specifically engineered to allow access to certain pages comes in handy. In this scenario, the server does not provide the page unless the proper password is given.

Dynamic Pages

The fourth and final common use of Web programs is to create dynamic pages. A dynamic page is anything in which all or some of its content is determined by the server. A good example is a server displaying the current local time along with the rest of the document.

Figure 1.4. User authentication keeps unwanted trespassers from visiting sensitive pages at your site.

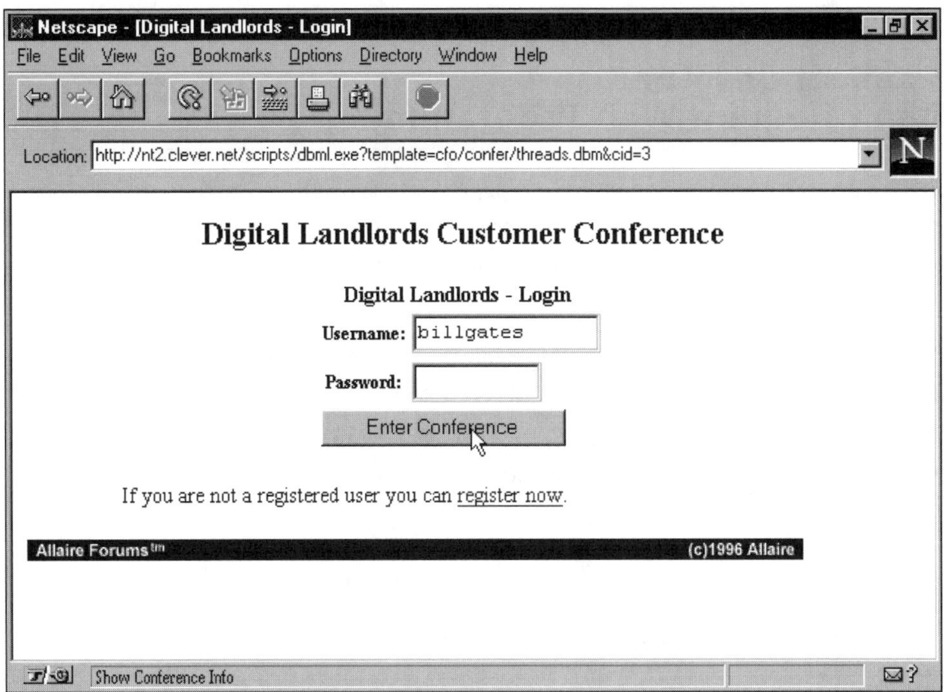

A more esoteric—but still highly useful—application for dynamic page construction is displaying content based on the capabilities of the browser. Among the data the browser sends to a server when it connects is the name and version of the browser software. The server can then use this information and construct a page specifically designed for that browser. For instance, if the browser is the latest version of Netscape Navigator or Microsoft Internet Explorer, the server can respond by sending pages that use the frame feature supported by both of these browsers. If the browser is an earlier version of these products that does not support frames (or it's another browser that lacks frame capabilities), the server can provide a frameless version instead.

Depending on the application and the server being used, dynamic pages can be created using a specialized Web program, or they can be created using something called server-side includes. Server side includes are special instructions included with the rest of the HTML in a Web page. These instructions are then interpreted as the page is transferred from the server to the client. For example, one such instruction displays the date the file being served was created (so that the date of last modification doesn't have to be hard-coded into the document).

Applications That Don't Require Web Programming

Just because you want a dynamic Web page doesn't mean you have to write a program. Each new version of Web browser software brings with it new features for enhancing Web pages, which serves to reduce the need to write specialized Web programs.

The latest versions of Netscape Navigator, Internet Explorer, and other popular browsers now support four common tasks that used to require Web programming. If you're looking to do any of these, odds are you won't need to create a specialized Web program for it (instead, save the programming for when you really need it!). These tasks are as follows:

- Clicking on parts of one image to display different pages
- Displaying animation or moving graphics

- Automatically reloading a page after a period of time
- Sending users to another page, either immediately after loading your page or after a time delay

> **NOTE** It isn't the intention of the following sections to explain how to implement each of these techniques. Use the information that follows as a drawing board for considering alternative approaches.

Clicking on an Image

An image that you can click on to display different pages uses a technique called *mapping*. When the Web was born, mapping an image required help from the Web server computer. The user would click on a portion of the image, and the browser program would tell the server where to open the image on which the mouse had clicked. This location took the form of X and Y coordinates. With this information, a program on the server would determine which new page to display in the browser. This technique, still used by some, is called *server-side image mapping* because the logic for determining which page to display is handled by the server.

Browsers such as Netscape Navigator (version 2.0 and higher) support what's known as *client-side image maps*, so called because the logic for determining which page to display is handled by the browser, which is technically referred to as the *client*. Client-side image mapping is much easier to implement because it does not involve any programming at all.

Creating Animation

Everyone likes a pictures that moves. Because Web browsers can display images with text, the next logical step is to have those images move. For example, the image might be a picture of a spinning globe, ideal for a company with offices in different parts of the world. The early Web browsers were not, in themselves, capable of producing this animation, so a program running on the server provided the animation. A number of techniques were developed to accomplish this, including one rather awkward approach developed by Netscape called server push. Few people, if any, now use this technique because there are much better and simpler ways of accomplishing the same thing.

One method that involves no programming or even special HTML tags in the Web document uses a relatively little known feature of the GIF 89a file specification: frame animation. The normal GIF file contains a single "frame" or image; this is the image shown when it is displayed in a Web browser or other graphics program. A GIF file for animation includes many frames, which are displayed one after the other, as in a motion picture. The frames in most GIF files are set to repeat over and over again, so the image appears to constantly move.

Animated GIFs require special software to link the frames of the image into one file. These programs also allow you to specify options, including whether you wish the animation to repeat and the speed of the repeat. Most animated GIF files are set to auto-repeat. For best results, the speed of the animation should not be too fast, or else some browsers may have trouble updating the image while the remainder of a page is loaded. This can cause pages to "jam" as they load.

Once the animation file has been created, it is used like any other GIF image. For example, to display an image called myworld.gif (a spinning globe, no doubt), you'd include the following HTML <IMG> tag in the Web document:

```
<IMG SRC="myworld.gif">
```

When a browser like Netscape loads this image, it automatically starts the animation. If the file is set for auto-repeat animation, the browser will continue to display the animation until the page is unloaded.

Automatically Reloading a Page

Say your Web page contains a link to the U.S. weather map provided by a satellite. This map is not at your site, but located at some other site that provides it for free or for a fee. The map is updated once every five minutes. This updating, however, occurs only when your page is reloaded into the browser. The updating does not occur if the page is not reloaded.

Ordinarily, a task like this would require a program that would set up some sort of time delay, count when five minutes' time is up, and reload the page. Fortunately, this capability is built into most Web browsers, where you can quickly and easily specify a time delay as short as none at all (not too useful!) or many hours and even days in the future.

The reload feature uses the little known <META> tag, and a technique Netscape (and others) call client-pull. Client-pull is supported by Netscape Navigator 2.0 and above, as well as Microsoft Internet Explorer 2.0 and above (other browser programs are beginning to support it as well). The <META> tag is officially used for a number of tasks, but one of its most common is with the HTTP-EQUIV="Refresh" attribute. This tells the browser to "refresh"—that is, reload—the page. A second parameter lets you specify the number of seconds for the delay.

To add client-pull to your page you insert a <META> tag into the head of the document, like so:

```
<META HTTP-EQUIV="Refresh" CONTENT="5">
```

This tag tells Netscape to refresh (reload) the document after a five-second wait.

Automatically Redirecting to a Different Page

The <META> tag has a number of useful applications. You've already read about one: reloading the same page after a given period of time. Another useful application of the <META> is directing the browser to a completely different page from the current one. This can be done simply by specifying a different page along with the time delay. Here is an example that loads a page at the URL http://mydomain.com/page.html after a five-second delay.

```
<META HTTP-EQUIV="Refresh" CONTENT="5;
URL=http://mydomain.com/page.html">
```

The Refresh directive is a one-shot deal, so that when the browser loads the page at http://mydomain.com/page.html, the reloading is considered done, and the browser stays at that page. The exception occurs when you have a <META> tag in the page.html document as well, possibly redirecting the browser to yet another page.

In fact, you can use this technique to create a "slide show." The user starts out at the first page and is automatically taken to different pages at predetermined time delays. Each <META> tag merely redirects the browser to a new page. For instance, the <META> tag in the first document—let's call it "page1.html"—might be:

```
<META HTTP-EQUIV="Refresh" CONTENT="10;
URL=http://mydomain.com/page2.html">
```

This automatically directs the browser from page1.html to page2.html, after a 10-second delay. The <META> tag in the second document would then be:

```
<META HTTP-EQUIV="Refresh" CONTENT="12;
URL=http://mydomain.com/page3.html">
```

This tag redirects the browser from page2.html to page3.html, this time after a 12-second delay.

Note that you can also specify no delay for the redirection, in which case the page changes as soon as it is loaded by the browser. Use a value of 0 for an immediate redirection:

```
<META HTTP-EQUIV="Refresh" CONTENT="0;
URL=http://mydomain.com/gohere.html">
```

Here are some things to keep in mind when using the <META> tag to redirect the browser:

- You must provide a fully qualified path in the URL. Relative paths aren't enough.
- Notice the quoting scheme. The quote starts after CONTENT= and ends after the URL.
- Don't forget the semicolon after the CONTENT=x attribute, or you'll wind up reloading the same page instead of the new page.
- Remember that you can specify any time delay you want, including 0. When using 0 Netscape will fetch the page (either the same page or a new URL) as soon as the current one has finished loading.

Using Extension Technologies

Depending on the capabilities of your browser—and the browser you expect your users to use—some additional Web applications don't require programming. The latest versions of Netscape Navigator and Microsoft Internet Explorer support "extension" technologies that can often take the place of programming. These technologies, which include Java and ActiveX, provide "canned" solutions that most anyone can use, including nonprogrammers. The only requirement is that someone has to have developed the canned solution you're looking for.

Take the popular Java "chat" program, for example. Chat is a method that provides real-time discussions between users. For Web pages a special chat program is required that interfaces users so they can communicate with one another. The Java chat program, such as the one created by EarthWeb, lets you add chat abilities to your Web site without the need to write or administer a chat program on the server used for your Web pages. Figure 1.5 shows an example of the EarthWeb Java chat program in action.

To use the EarthWeb Java chat program, or any similar chat program, for that matter, you simply specify the name of the Java applet in your Web page. The applet, along with your Web page, is then uploaded to your Web server site. When someone visits your page, Netscape, Internet Explorer, or another Java-capable browser downloads the page itself, along with the Java chat applet. Once the chat applet has been received by the browser, the browser runs it, and the chatting can begin.

Chat is but one example of using Java and ActiveX technologies to do what specialized Web programs used to do. For instance, you can use a stock ticker ActiveX

Figure 1.5 The EarthWeb Java chat applet allows most any page on the Web to add user-to-user chat capabilities. No additional programming is required to use the applet.

component that continually fetches data and displays it in a ticker banner that scrolls within the browser window.

> **NOTE** If you have the programming expertise, you can write your own Java and ActiveX programs. Java uses its own distinct programming language, the basics of which are covered in some detail in Chapters 13 and 14 of this book. ActiveX programs use the C/C++ or Visual Basic languages, both of which are standards among programming languages. Chapters 17 and 18 of this book provide a primer on the C/C++ program, but as it relates to Web programs, not ActiveX.

Using a Client-Scripting Programming Language

Canned Java and ActiveX solutions rely on an existing application, which may or may not be available for the task that you need done. Some jobs do not require a full Web program running on your server, nor do they require the power of ActiveX or Java. Yet they are more than what can be accomplished using built-in technologies such as GIF 89a animation and client-pull. For these tasks, a client-based programming language such as JavaScript or VBScript may be the answer.

The main benefit of a client-based scripting program is that it's generally easier to write than a program designed to run on a Web server. Client-based programs are also beneficial if you are not allowed to upload programs to your Web site. The disadvantage of client-based programs is that they are not well suited for most of the jobs normally given to Web programs, which include user authentication and forms processing (except for validating the form, a job perfect for a client-based scripting program).

Though JavaScript and VBScript are not actually Web programs—they run in the client (that is, browser) and not on the server—their importance to the Web programmer is such that they merit chapters in this book. See Chapter 15 for more information about JavaScript, and Chapter 16 for more information about VBScript.

Dealing with Noncompatible Browsers

It pays to keep in mind that programming alternatives like client-side image maps, <META> tags for client-pull, Java, ActiveX, JavaScript, and VBScript are not universally supported by all browsers in use for the World Wide Web. Fortunately, the two top-dog browsers—Netscape Navigator and Microsoft Internet Explorer—claim about 80 to 85 percent of all browsers currently used. This percentage is growing as online services such as America Online, CompuServe, and Prodigy adopt one or the other product (sometimes both) as the standard browser for use by their customers.

So, too, Internet service providers such as Netcom, AT&T, and hundreds of others are supplying either Netscape Navigator or Internet Explorer to users when they join their service. Unless something quite unexpected happens, it's a fair bet that Netscape Navigator and Internet Explorer will represent close to 100 percent of the general-purpose browser market.

With this in mind, you can determine whether your use of special browser features, such as Java support or client-pull, will suit the needs of your Web page. If you absolutely, positively must ensure compatibility with as many users as possible, you cannot rely on these newer technologies because some of your visitors will not have the proper software to take advantage of your site. If you want a dynamic Web page you will need to consider creating a program that runs on your Web server.

However, if absolute compatibility with everyone is not needed (and it's usually not, at least for Web pages that do more than display text), you can consider the time and energy savings of using an alternative to devising a Web server program. This also applies to "intranets"—internal company networks that are designed around the same technology that makes the Internet work. Becaues intranets are private networks, the choice of browser can be stipulated by management, and that makes ensuring compatibility much easier.

Purchasing an Off-the-Shelf Programming Solution

Suppose you are faced with not being able to use browser-specific technology (Java, ActiveX, client-pull, GIF 89a animation, and so forth) to make your Web pages dynamic. Does this mean you must write a custom program to do what you need to get done? Not at all. Though the Web is still fairly new and is still maturing, a number of companies have developed ready-made programming solutions that are designed to be installed and run by those with even minimal programming experience. Depending on your requirements, this approach may be more cost-effective and less time-consuming than writing your own custom program.

NOTE Of course, this doesn't mean you should never write your own Web program—that would be anathema to the purpose of this book! However, time and money are still important considerations, and they apply to the Internet as well. It never hurts to consider the alternatives.

The number and type of ready-to-go Web programming solutions increases every day, so you should look to see what's available. Your local software store is a good place to start, but also consider the magazines devoted to Web page management and publishing, such as *The Net*, *Web Developer*, and *Internet World*. These magazines, and others like them, often carry articles about ready-to-go programming packages. And, of course, keep an eye out for advertisements for these software solutions. The ads tend to come out before the editors of the magazine have a chance to write about the new products.

An example of a ready-to-go Web programming solution is Borland's IntraBuilder, which is primarily designed to help you create Web-based databases fore use on private intranets, though other applications are possible as well. IntraBuilder assumes you're using a Web server based on Windows 95 or Windows NT. To create an application with IntraBuilder you use point-and-click methods to generate the form you wish to use for entering data. You can also specify if your Web database connects to the company's database—when you want users to be able to tap into the company database via the intranet for extra information.

Before settling on any ready-to-go Web programming solution, be sure it does everything you need it to do. This may entail talking with someone else who has already used the package. Also determine what, if any, programming may be required. Even the ready-to-go solutions sometimes require programming, and the programming language may not be one you know. There is little benefit in using a ready-to-go solution if you must take time out to learn a proprietary programming language.

Using or Rewriting an Existing Program

An alternative to writing a complete program yourself—or using one of the nonprogramming methods discussed earlier in this chapter—is to use or rewrite an existing program that someone else wrote. There are literally thousands of free and mostly free Web programs available, and odds are someone has done what you're looking to do, or at least a close facsimile. Most of the best programs are found on the Web itself, in one of the many "script repositories," like the one shown in Figure 1.6. This topic is so important to the Web programmer that an entire chapter of this book is devoted to finding and using prewritten programs. See Chapter 20, "Finding and Using Script Repositories," for more information.

Whether you plan to use an existing script in its original (unaltered) form or to rewrite it, you must still know a little bit about the programming language application. It is frustrating and time-consuming to attempt to use or revise a Web program without knowing at least the basics of the language. This book will help you gain enough mastery that you should be able to successfully install existing scripts on your Web server, as well as rewrite simpler scripts to suit your needs.

Figure 1.6. An example of a script respository on the Web. Sites like this often contain example programs you can revise or use as-is.

If you plan to use a program "out-of-the-box" (in its original form), be sure to read at least Chapter 7, "Installing Your Web Program on a Server." Web programs aren't like regular HTML documents—you cannot always upload them to your Web server and expect them to work right off the bat. This is especially true if your Web server uses the UNIX operating system.

If you plan to revise an existing program and you know little or nothing about the programming language used, be sure to read the relevant chapters on that language before you proceed. Once you've read the chapter(s), you will have a clearer understanding of how a program using that language is constructed.

Bear in mind that not all existing Web programs are easy to modify. Some use more advanced programming techniques than can be addressed in the confines of this book. Others use unusual language syntax that can be hard for anyone but the original programmer to understand. And a few are badly written in the first place! These are perhaps the worst programs to attempt to revise because not only is revision difficult, but quirks in the way the program is written may prevent you from getting it to work the way you want.

Unfortunately, except through experience, it's not always easy to tell a well-written program from a badly written one. Your best bet is to use existing programs from a known and trusted source. The URLs provided in Chapter 20, the sources.htm file on the CD-ROM, and URLs cited elsewhere in this book are links to such trusted sites.

Determining the Need for a Program

If you are planning a major programming job, it pays to first determine if it is necessary to create a custom program for the application or if you can use one of the alternative methods above. To recap, here are your options, in reverse order of difficulty (hardest listed first):

- Write the Web program yourself.
- Revise an existing Web program.
- Develop the program using a ready-to-go package (for example, IntraBuilder).
- Use an already written Web program.

- Write an alterative program using a client-based language (for example, JavaScript or VBScript).
- Use an extension technology (for example, Java or ActiveX).
- Use built-in browser technology (for example, GIF 89a animation or client-pull).

Skills and Tools You Need for Web Programming

Programming for the Web is not rocket science, but neither is it child's play. You need at least a basic understanding of the programming language you wish to use. A mistake made by many "newbies" to Web programming is to rush into things too quickly—they have a job to do, and only a limited time to do it. They attempt to use the language before they know the ropes, and this almost always leads to poor results and frustration. A willingness to learn, and more importantly the time to learn, is perhaps the most important ingredient in successful Web programming.

Beyond this, you need knowledge of how to interact with the server computer that houses your programs. If you have experience uploading HTML pages to your server, you already know most of what you need to know about uploading Web programs to it. However, keep in mind that most servers place added restrictions on programs. In the case of UNIX computers, for example, you must specify that the file is an executable.

Unlike the Windows operating system, UNIX has no inherent way of detecting the type of file. If you fail to indicate that the program you've uploaded is an executable, the server will assume it's just an ordinary document. When you try to use it, the program won't run—instead you'll see the text of the program in the browser!

> **NOTE** Consult Chapter 7, "Installing Your Web Program on a Server," for more information on uploading programs and setting the file type. Much of the chapter is devoted to UNIX servers rather than Windows servers because these are currently the more common of the two. UNIX is also more picky when it comes to installing Web programs.

If you are primarily a Windows user, but your Web server runs UNIX, you should have at least a basic understanding of how to get around in UNIX. Chapter

7 provides some of the more common UNIX commands you will use, but nothing beats a little bit of experience, as well as a book on UNIX. If you don't already have a book on UNIX commands, be sure to pick up one the next time you're at the bookstore.

There are two general ways to upload files to a Web server:

- For Web servers connected to the company network, you can usually log into the server by name or drive letter. Once logged onto the server, you can transfer files to the server in the usual manner (if using Windows, for example, this is as easy as dragging files in the File Manager or Explorer).
- For Web servers connected to the regular phone lines, you must establish a dial-up connection and transfer the Web program files in one of three ways: via Telnet, via FTP, or via the upload feature of your browser (not all browsers support this last feature). When using a UNIX server, Telnet is the recommended choice: Once connected via Telnet you interact with the computer as if you were sitting behind a terminal. As UNIX is primarily a command-based operating system, you must interact with the computer by typing commands (now you know why you need a book on UNIX commands!). FTP is a second choice, but most FTP programs do not allow for setting the file type to executable, something that is absolutely required for Web programs on UNIX machines.

Some programming languages require a software development kit, which at the very minimum includes a "compiler." The compiler transforms your program file to a form more readily understood by the server. A compiler is needed if you plan on programming with either Java or C/C++. In the case of C/C++, you can obtain free compilers from many sources on the Internet, or you can purchase a commercial C/C++ compiler from almost any computer software store.

In the case of Java, a full software development kit (SDK) that contains an assortment of additional files and libraries is needed; a compiler alone is not enough. You can purchase a Java SDK at almost any computer software store, but one is also available free from Sun, the creators of the Java language. The benefit of the commercial Java SDKs is that they are generally easier to install and configure than the Java SDK from Sun.

The other programming languages described in more detailed in this book are "interpreted," which means that no compiling is necessary. So, when using Perl, a

UNIX shell, JavaScript, or VBScript, you need nothing more than what's already included with your server or browser.

Perl and UNIX shell scripts require the proper interpreter program on the server. It's highly unusual for a UNIX server to not have both Perl and at least one UNIX shell installed. Windows servers don't use a UNIX shell (obviously), and not all provide a Perl interpreter. Both JavaScript and VBScript are supported by the browser (specifically Netscape Navigator and Microsoft Internet Explorer), so no special server software is required.

Chapter

2

Web Servers and CGI at Work

Nothing strikes fear in the heart of a Web publisher more than the letters "C-G-I." Yet there's little reason for this fear. In actuality, CGI—which stands for *common gateway interface*—is a relatively simple concept.

CGI is a mechanism for safely transporting data from a client (a browser like Netscape Navigator or Internet Explorer) to a server. CGI requires a program or script, much like a batch file on a PC, running on the server to accept data from the client and process it. Although most all of us work with programs on our local computer—running them, feeding them data, and more—for some reason CGI programs seem more difficult and troublesome and ornery.

CGI can be scary stuff (though unnecessarily so), but it's also awe-inspiring for what it can do. It can process forms, it can display "hit" counters, it can search databases and return a result, and it can do much, much more.

A number of client-based programming languages—notably JavaScript and VBScript—are designed to reduce the reliance on CGI for advanced Web work. Client-based programming languages work with the browser and function entirely on the client's computer, rather than the server. However, CGI remains the primary application for Web programming, and it is the main focus throughout this book.

To fully understand CGI it's necessary first to explore the world of Web servers. Like CGI, Web servers tend to be mysterious and frightening to those just learning about them. And like CGI, the basic technology behind Web servers is actually very simple. This chapter first covers Web servers, then discusses how CGI works within the Web server framework.

How Web Servers Work

At its basic level, a Web server is an ordinary computer connected to a network. Instead of expecting the bulk of its input via a keyboard, the Web server expects the bulk of its input to be data coming over the network communications lines. (Similarly, instead of displaying its results on a monitor attached directly to it, the Web server is designed to transfer its output back through the network. More about this later.)

Software running on the server—called a *daemon*—continually checks for data coming through the network lines. This data is in the form of requests from other users connected to the server. These requests take the form of simple text commands. The vast bulk of the requests for a Web server start with the word GET, followed by the name of a file desired on the server. For example, if a user wants to view a file named index.html, the GET request (shown simplified) looks like this:

```
GET index.html
```

In response, the Web server fetches the file index.html and sends it back to the user via the network connection. This is 99 percent of what Web servers do.

Web servers follow a world-standard protocol so that they all function in the same way. In this manner a user in New York can connect with a Web server in Bombay, India—even through there are thousands of miles and a different spoken language between them. This standard protocol is known as HTTP, which stands for *hypertext transfer protocol.*

Displaying a Web Page

As you can see, a Web server is actually a simple piece of hardware—an ordinary computer attached to a network—running a simple piece of software—a daemon

NOTE As a point of interest, the daemon software running on the Web server that catches all the requests coming over the network lines is known as an HTTPd program—the lowercase "d" denotes daemon. (As used in computer circles, a daemon is an "attendant," or helper.)

that reacts whenever a user's request comes over the network. One of the benefits of the Web is that its underlying structure is so simple.

The typical Web page, complete with text, graphics, Java applets, and perhaps even multimedia content such as movies and virtual reality images, is composed of nothing more than files fetched individually from a server, as shown in Figure 2.1. The files are combined in a browser program, such as Netscape Navigator or Microsoft Internet Explorer, and the appearance is formatted in a somewhat consistent manner. The apparent complexity of some Web pages belies their simple construction.

To display a page a Web browser first fetches a primary document. This is most commonly done by typing the Universal Resource Locator (URL) address of the Web server, along with the page desired, such as http://www.myserver.com/ index.html.

In this case, the server is www.myserver.com, and the page is index.html, which is located on the www.myserver.com server. (Note the http: "protocol" used at the beginning of the URL. This tells the browser what kind of protocol to use to fetch the page, and it is necessary as the Internet supports several different ways to access data from remote computers.)

The index.html document may contain only text, in which case the Web server delivers just the one document. The standard format of documents delivered over the Web is HTML, otherwise known as *hypertext markup language*. Like HTTP, HTML is a worldwide standard and ensures that users the world over can access the same pages, without the need for proprietary software.

A typical text-only HTML document file looks like this:

```
<HTML>
<HEAD>
<TITLE>This is a sample document</TITLE>
</HEAD>
<BODY>
<H1>Sample document</H1>
```

Figure 2.1 An HTML page is composed of individual files, collected by the browser and displayed as a whole.

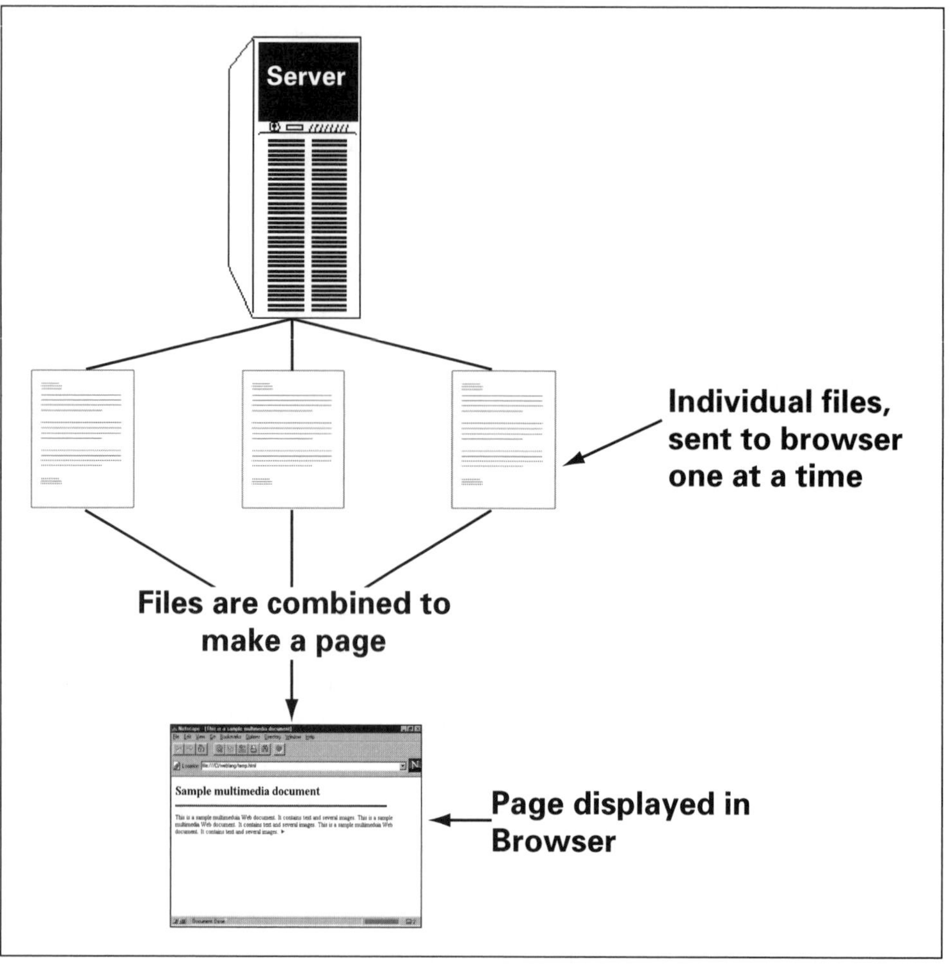


```
This is a sample Web document. It contains only text. This is a sample Web doc-
ument. It contains only text. This is a sample Web document. It contains only
text.
</BODY>
</HTML>
```

When viewed in a browser program such as Netscape Navigator, the HTML document is formatted for readability and appears as in Figure 2.2. The text between the < and > markers is a *tag*; HTML makes heavy use of tags.

Figure 2.2 The Web browser uses simple text markup (HTML) and formats it for appearance.

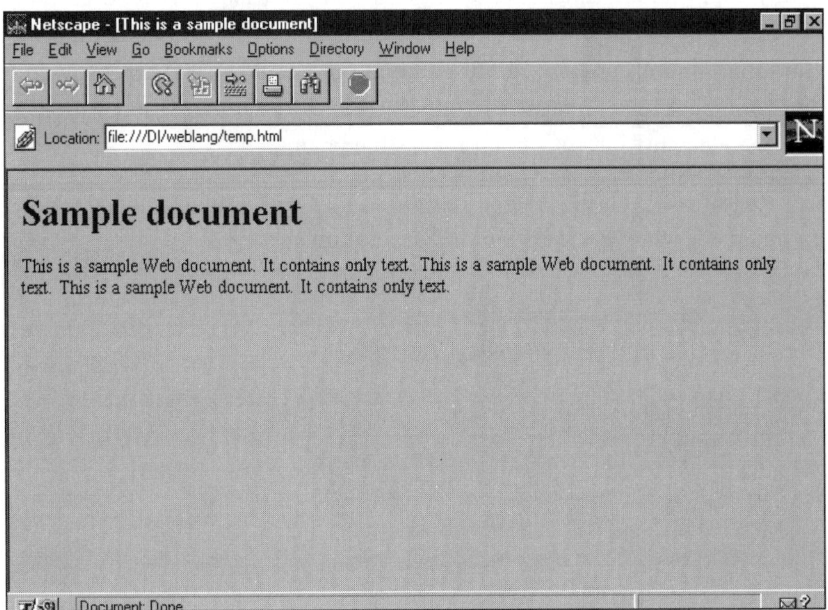

> **NOTE** If HTML is a new document concept for you I recommend you read the *HTML Sourcebook, Third Edition* by Ian Graham (Wiley Computer Publishing, 1997). This book details how HTML works and what all the tags mean. Also see Chapter 22, "An HTML Primer," in this book for some additional information on HTML.

To retrieve a document from a Web server, the user types its URL into the browser software—say, http://www.myserver.com/sample.html. The browser then connects to the server over the Internet and sends the following GET request:

```
GET /sample.html
```

The server responds by returning the file sample.html, and the browser displays it for the user.

Multimedia Content

The Web readily supports multimedia content, and you can easily mix text, graphics, and other elements on the same page. This is done merely by adding additional tags for the graphics and other elements. It is the job of the Web server to provide each element of the page as a separate file; it is the job of the browser software to combine all of the elements into one comprehensible page.

The typical multimedia HTML page might look like the following. This page contains text against a white background and several images.

```
<HTML>
<HEAD>
<TITLE>This is a sample multimedia document</TITLE>
</HEAD>
<BODY TEXT="black" BGCOLOR="white">
<H1>Sample multimedia document</H1>
<IMG SRC="image1.gif">
This is a sample multimedia Web document.  It contains text and
several images. This is a sample multimedia Web document.
It contains text and several images. This is a sample multimedia
Web document.  It contains text and several images.
<IMG SRC="image2.gif">
</BODY>
</HTML>
```

The appearance of this page in Netscape Navigator is shown in Figure 2.3.

Notice the two images identified in the HTML document as image1.gif and image2.gif. These are separate GIF graphics files and are provided by the Web server separately from the HTML document itself. Instead of just one GET request for the HTML document, there are three:

```
GET /sample.html
GET /image1.gif
GET /image2.gif
```

To render this page, the browser displays the text of sample.html, then inserts the images in their proper locations—as indicated by the <IMG> tags in the sample.html document.

The previous example shows how images are rendered as part of an HTML document. Other forms of content are requested from the server in a similar manner

Figure 2.3 Text and graphics are merged into one unit when an HTML page is rendered in a browser.

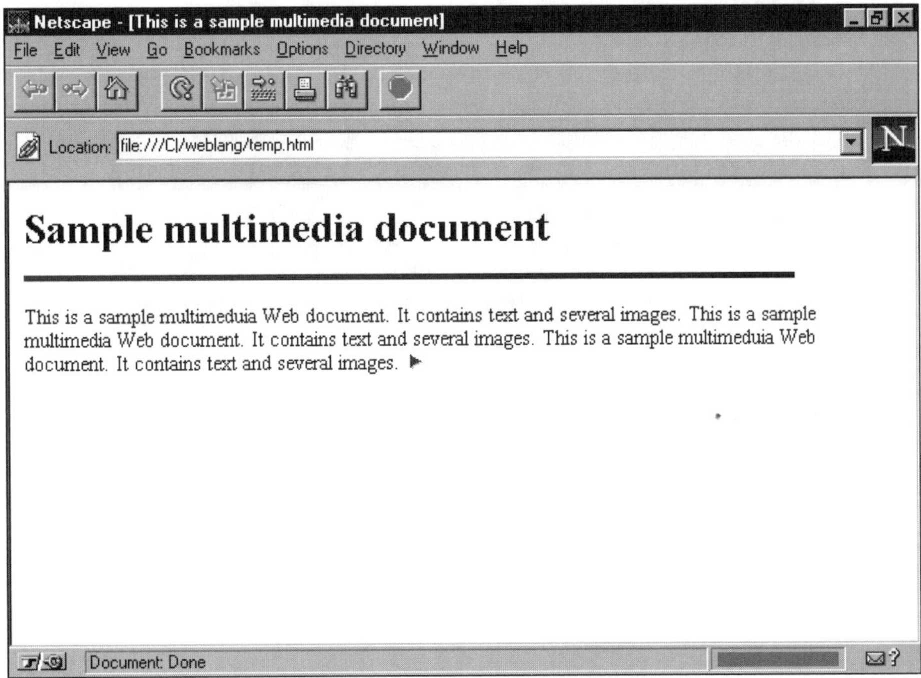

and are returned to the browser accordingly. For example, if the HTML page contains a tag for a Java applet—the tag appears as <APPLET> in the HTML document—the server fetches the applet and delivers it to the browser along with all other parts of the page. In this way, the actual content of the file sent is inconsequential to the server. It merely provides the files as requested.

Web Servers and CGI

The HTTP protocol used by the Web is mostly a one-way street: from server to client. The vast bulk of data on the Web travels down this one-way street: all the text, graphics, sound effects, VRML Java applets, movies, and other data you see in a browser. But there's also a narrow back alley that allows traffic in the other direction, as shown in Figure 2.4. This is the *requester path*, where the browser can ask the server to display this or that file. It is this path to which the GET requests between client and server are sent.

Figure 2.4 The two-way street of the Web is more like a main highway for the data you receive, and a little back alley is available for the data sent to the server.

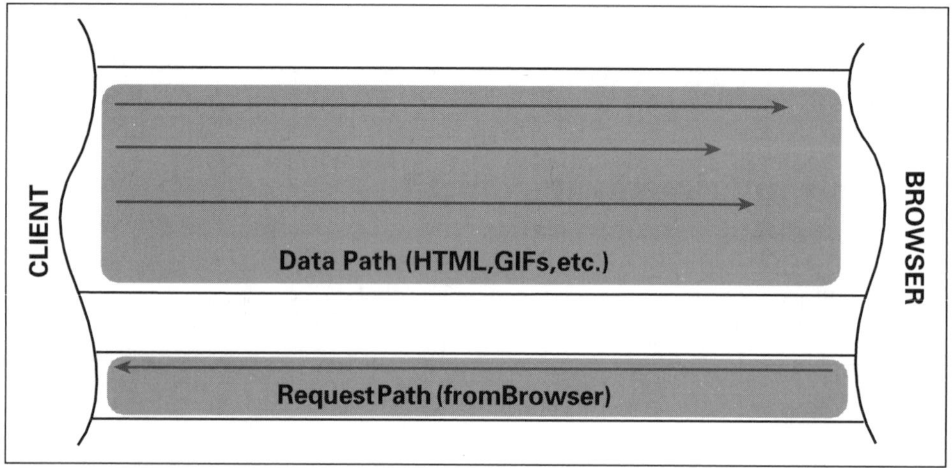

In addition to GET requests, additional data flows in this requester path, including your identification (at least your domain, if not also your e-mail), your "user agent" (the kind of browser you have), and other variables such as a list of file types that your browser can render. When the server gets this data it can decide what kind of data to send you, based on the information it has received. And, of course, it also receives a URL of the page you want to view.

Where CGI Fits In

It is the requester path that CGI also functions. CGI has two means of passing data from the client to the server: one is URL-based and you can readily see it; the other is hidden away, as part of the requester data.

The URL approach is accurately called the *GET* method. You've probably seen it at work if you've ever seen a URL like this one: http://mydomain.com/cgi-bin/program.cgi?subject=goodies.

The text beyond the ? question mark is data accessed by the server, ostensibly to be used with a CGI program. The program itself is the basic URL: http://mydomain.com/cgi-bin/program.cgi.

The rest is treated like a "command-line option" like that used in DOS, Windows, and UNIX. The server fetches the command-line option as the data and processes it so it knows what information the user has requested.

> **NOTE** The GET method is also sometimes referred to as URL encoding because the CGI portion of the string is part of the URL. It is also encoded to contain only valid URL characters—that is, no spaces and almost no other punctuation. These characters are encoded using *%nn* number sets—for example, a space is encoded as %20.

The other method used by CGI is called *POST*. It leaves the URL alone and instead passes its data completely via the requester path. The CGI program is activated merely by specifying it in an URL: http://mydomain.com/cgi-bin/program.cgi.

This passes a series of data structures from the browser to the client through the back-alley requester path and arrives at the CGI program running on the server. The data received by the server is accessed by the CGI program *environment variables* and/or something called STDIN (which stands for "standard input"). With the POST method, the CGI program sifts through these environment variables or the STDIN to collect the data.

The Path of the CGI Request

Technically the Web server and a CGI program running on it are two separate entities, and many books on CGI programming make a distinction between the two. I'll be a little more lax and for the bulk of this book I will lump the CGI programs and the Web servers that run them in a single group.

But before doing so, let's review what really happens between client, server, and CGI program. Figure 2.5 shows how data is sent from client to server and back again, both with and without CGI in the mix. Note that CGI is handled as a separate process. When a server gets a request to run a CGI program, it collects the necessary data sent from the client and passes this information to the CGI program (by either filling in one or more environment variables or preparing an STDIN virtual file), where it is then acted upon.

Figure 2.5 When a CGI program is called, data is routed from the server to it. The CGI program is never directly accessed by the browser.

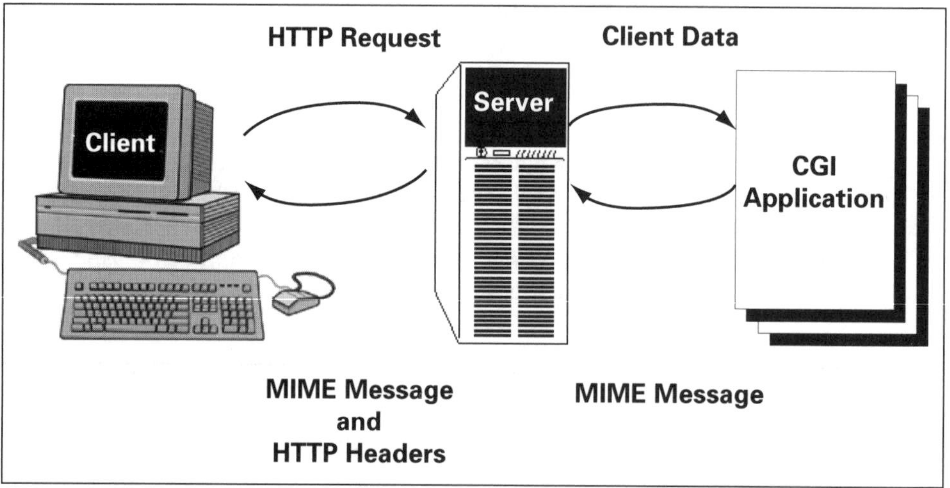

When the CGI program is finished, it sends its output back to the Web server, via something called STDOUT (which stands for "standard output"). In turn, this data is usually relayed as an HTML document, which is sent back to the client browser.

> **NOTE** In this section, and in the remainder of the sections in this chapter, different Web servers sometimes behave differently and use alternate means of accessing and outputting information. What follows applies to the typical Web server such as Apache, NCSA, CERN, or Netscape.

The data path between client and server, and from server to CGI program, differs depending on the method used to interact with the server. Recall the two methods of sending CGI data, GET and POST. There is actually a third, little used method called ISINDEX that can also be used to process data from client to server to CGI program. Table 2.1 summarizes how the three methods—GET, POST, and ISINDEX—interrelate with the Web server and CGI program.

Note that for all three methods the server passes data it has received from the client to the CGI program using the QUERY_STRING environment variable.

Table 2.1 Server Interaction Methods

CGI Request	How the data gets from/to Client to Server	Server to CGI Program
ISINDEX	URL	Command line or QUERY_STRING
GET	URL	QUERY_STRING
POST	Requester path	STDIN

Additionally, the ISINDEX method allows you to pass data from the server to the CGI program via the command line.

Note that ISINDEX is an older, now deprecated method for sending data to a server via CGI. Though many servers continue to support ISINDEX, the GET and POST methods offer the same flexibility, typically with less programming hassle (and usually with greater security). For this reason, we'll discuss only the GET and POST methods in this chapter.

Understanding GET

The GET method, which is the default used by browsers, passes data from the client to the server via the URL. Once the data arrives at the server, the server packs it into one or more environment variables held in memory. The server then starts the CGI program, which, in turn, looks in these environment variables for the data it needs to run.

The most common environment variable used with GET is QUERY_STRING. QUERY_STRING contains all the text after the ? character in the URL. Quite often, the QUERY_STRING data needs to be "picked apart" by the CGI program to determine all of the options the user has selected. This is actually easier than it sounds, with ready-made code routines for this available for all the popular Web programming languages. When using Perl, for example, it's possible to pick apart—or *parse*—any number of individual pieces of information in QUERY_STRING with just a few short lines of code.

Understanding POST

With the POST method, data is transferred from client to server in the form of user-defined environment variables, and no data is passed as part of the URL. Once the server collects the data in the environment variables, it passes the information to the CGI program in the form of STDIN, or standard input, a UNIX term describing the default method of inputting data to a program. As with GET, the CGI program is required to pick apart this standard input and obtain meaningful information from it.

Understanding CGI Environment Variables

CGI makes heavy use of environment variables, which is data sent from client to server, as well as information derived from the server itself, such as the current date and time. If you are familiar with UNIX, the environment variables used in CGI programming will likely also be a familiar sight to you. Table 2.2 covers the most common environment variables used with CGI programming (environment variables never or seldom used with CGI programming are not included). Note that some Web servers provide more environment variables and some less. You learn which variables your server supports only by reading its documentation.

Also note that by convention, all environment variables are spelled with uppercase letters and are single words only, with an underscore used to join multiple words.

Table 2.2 Environment Variable Quick Reference

Environment Variable	What It's For
AUTH_TYPE	Access authentication type
CONTENT_LENGTH	Length of the data to follow
CONTENT_TYPE	The MIME type of the data to follow
GATEWAY_INTERFACE	CGI version running on the server
HTTP_ACCEPT	Accept list of MIME types
HTTP_USER_AGENT	Name/ID of client browser
PATH_INFO	"Extra path" information
PATH_TRANSLATED	Virtual to physical mapping of file on server
QUERY_STRING	Query portion (part of ? character) of URL
REMOTE_ADDR	IP address of client
REMOTE_HOST	Domain name of client
REMOTE_IDENT	Identify data about client

Table 2.2 *Continued*

Environment Variable	What It's For
REMOTE_USER	USER ID of client (now rarely provided)
REQUEST_METHOD	Request method by client (i.e., POST or GET)
SCRIPT_NAME	URL path of CGI program
SERVER_NAME	Name of server
SERVER_PORT	Server port where request was received (typically 80)
SERVER_PROTOCOL	Name and version of request protocol
SERVER_SOFTWARE	Name and version of server software

AUTH_TYPE

The AUTH_TYPE environment variable provides rudimentary server-access restrictions. Example: AUTH_TYPE=Basic.

CONTENT_LENGTH

The CONTENT_LENGTH environment variable indicates the length in bytes of the STDIN virtual file. (Recall that STDIN is used only with the POST method.) Example: If the data in STDIN is 72 bytes, then CONTENT_LENGTH contains 72.

CONTENT_TYPE

The CONTENT_TYPE environment variable indicates the type of data being requested if that information is important. The data type is specified using a standard MIME description, which takes the form type/subtype. The most common MIME types used with CGI Web programming are CONTENT_TYPE=text/html, which specifies that the data is in text format and includes HTML tags. Other MIME types are used for binary graphics, binary application programs, and other data.

GATEWAY_INTERFACE

The GATEWAY_INTERFACE environment variable is used to hold the version number of the CGI protocol in use. Example: CGI/1.1.

HTTP_ACCEPT

The HTTP_ACCEPT environment variable provides a list of MIME types (separated by commas) that are acceptable by the browser. The server and/or CGI program can use this information to determine the type of content the browser should receive in return. Example: HTTP_ACCEPT=image/gif, image/x-bitmap, image/jpeg, */*. Note the final */*, which tells the server/CGI program that any content is acceptable. The MIME types are preferred.

HTTP_USER_AGENT

The HTTP_USER_AGENT environment variable contains the name, version, and other descriptor of the browser making the request. The format of the user agent information is variable and depends entirely on the whim of the browser maker. Example: Netscape/3.0 (Win95; I).

PATH_INFO

The PATH_INFO environment variable contains extra information supplied as part of the URL for a CGI program. The CGI program can then use this information as a list of command-line parameters. For example, if the URL is http://myserver.com/cgi-bin/cgiprog.pl/extradir/special, it indicates a CGI program named cgiprog.pl contained in the cgi-bin directory of myserver.com. The PATH_INFO environment variable contains the text /extradir/special.

QUERY_STRING

The QUERY_STRING environment variable is, by far, the most commonly used. This variable contains any text following the ? "search" character in the URL. The data following the ? character is in the format of name/data pairs, where information is defined by name, then by value. The name and data are separated by an equal sign. Additional name/data pairs can be appended simply by adding an & (ampersand) character between them.

The most common source of the name/data pairs is from an HTML form. If the form is submitted using the GET method, the browser automatically appends the URL specified in the ACTION= statement of the <FORM> tag with the name/data pairs for each control in the form.

For example, if the URL is http://myserver.com/cgi-bin/cgiprog.pl?name=George &birthmonth=May, then the QUERY_STRING environment variable contains the string

```
name=George&birthmonth=May
```

It is the job of the CGI program to break this query string apart. The first job is to split apart the two name/data pairs (name=George and birthmonth=May). The next job is to separate the name and data values.

REMOTE_ADDR

The REMOTE_ADDR environment variable contains the IP address of the client browser making the request. The data is in the format xxx.xxx.xxx.xxx, where the xxx's denote numbers for a real IP address.

REMOTE_HOST

The REMOTE_HOST environment variable contains the resolved domain name used by the client browser making the request. This data is not always available, depending on how the client connected with the server. In addition, many Web server administrators disable this environment variable because it causes extra work for the server. Example: mydomain.com refers to a domain named mydomain.com.

REMOTE_IDENT

The REMOTE_IDENT environment variable contains the identification string (usually e-mail name) used by the client browser making the request. Example: me@myself.com. While this environment variable exists, it is usually blank, having been squelched by the browser for privacy reasons. And when it's not blank, there is no assurance that the information is accurate because this information can be set by the user.

REMOTE_USER

The REMOTE_USER environment variable contains the user name, as set in the client browser making the request. This environment variable is typically used for user authentication (password) purposes. The server is able to fetch the user name and request just the password, thereby saving the user some time.

REQUEST_METHOD

The REQUEST_METHOD environment variable supplies the information by which a CGI program was invoked, typically GET or POST. This information is useful if the CGI program is designed to work with either GET or POST requests (and, quite often, the better-written CGI programs are).

SCRIPT_NAME

The SCRIPT_NAME environment variable contains the name of the CGI program being invoked. Example: /cgi-bin/cgiprog.pl.

SERVER_NAME

The SERVER_NAME environment variable contains the Web server's host name, alias, or IP address. For example, if your server is named www.myserver.com, then that's what is in the SERVER_NAME environment variable. This variable is useful when you want to restrict your CGI program and execute it only from your or some other server. If the SERVER_NAME variable doesn't match the one(s) in the script, the program doesn't run. For best results, be sure to check for at least domain name and IP address.

SERVER_PORT

The SERVER_PORT environment variable contains the port used to access the Web site. The default port number for Web pages is 80, but it can be set to nearly anything.

SERVER_PROTOCOL

The SERVER_PROTOCOL environment variable is used to contain the name and version of the server protocol. Example: HTTP/1.0.

SERVER_SOFTWARE

The SERVER_SOFTWARE environment variable is used to contain the name and version of the software used for the Web server. Example: Apache/1.1.

An Example of CGI

Here's an example of a CGI program written in Perl for the typical Unix server. It's a public domain, generic, "use-it-anywhere" form mail processor. The file name is called formmail.cgi: It collects data filled into an HTML form, then mails the data—nicely formatted—off to your e-mail address. This script is shown here as an example because it is widely used on the Web; you're likely to encounter it as you troll for useful CGI programs to learn from and adopt.

For the most part, the formmail.cgi program does not need customization. You tell it the e-mail address to which you want to send mail, and the rest is done for you. However, you may need to alter the script a bit to suit the requirements of your server. For example, the script assumes the Perl interpreter program is found on a root directory of the server named /usr/local/bin/perl (this is, by far, the most common location). However, if the Perl interpreter is in another directory on your server you will need to modify this line. The formmail.cgi program also assumes your server uses the (fairly) standard sendmail program. You'll need to modify the script if your server uses something different.

```
#! /usr/local/bin/perl
######################
# General Mail Form To Work With Any Fields
# Created 6/9/95                 Last Modified 6/11/95
# Version 1.0
# http://mydomain.com/cgi-bin/formmail.cgi?http://mydomain.com/mypage.html
# Define Variables
$mailprog = '/usr/lib/sendmail';
$date = 'date'; chop ($date);

######################
# Necessary Fields in HTML Form:
# recipient = specifies who mail is sent to
# username = specifies the remote users email address for replies
# realname = specifies the remote users real identity
# subject = specifies what you want the subject of your mail to be

# Print the Initial Output Heading
print "Location: ";
print  $ENV{'QUERY_STRING'};
print "\n\n";

# Get the input
read(STDIN, $buffer, $ENV{'CONTENT_LENGTH'});

# Split the name-value pairs
@pairs = split(/&/, $buffer);

foreach $pair (@pairs)
{
     ($name, $value) = split(/=/, $pair);

     # Un-Webify plus signs and %-encoding
     $value =~ tr/+/ /;
     $value =~ s/%([a-fA-F0-9][a-fA-F0-9])/pack("C", hex($1))/eg;
     $name =~ tr/+/ /;
     $name =~ s/%([a-fA-F0-9][a-fA-F0-9])/pack("C", hex($1))/eg;

     # Stop people from using subshells to execute commands
```

```
    # Not a big deal when using sendmail, but very important
    # when using UCB mail (aka mailx).
    # $value =~ s/~!/ ~!/g;

    $FORM{$name} = $value;
}

open (MAIL, "|$mailprog $FORM{'recipient'}") || die "Can't open $mailprog!\n";
print MAIL "From: $FORM{'username'} ($FORM{'realname'})\n";
print MAIL "Reply-To: $FORM{'username'} ($FORM{'realname'})\n";
print MAIL "To: $FORM{'recipient'}\n";
print MAIL "Subject: $FORM{'subject'}\n\n";
print MAIL "Below is the result of your feedback form.  It was submitted by
$FORM{'realname'} $FORM{'username'} on $date\n";
print MAIL "------------------------------\n";
foreach $pair (@pairs)
{
    ($name, $value) = split(/=/, $pair);

    # Un-Webify plus signs and %-encoding
    $value =~ tr/+/ /;
    $value =~ s/%([a-fA-F0-9][a-fA-F0-9])/pack("C", hex($1))/eg;
    $name =~ tr/+/ /;
    $name =~ s/%([a-fA-F0-9][a-fA-F0-9])/pack("C", hex($1))/eg;

   $FORM{$name} = $value;

# Print the MAIL for each name value pair
  print MAIL "$name:  $value\n";
  print MAIL "__________________________________________\n\n";

}
close (MAIL);
```

Don't worry if the program itself looks like gibberish. The program is written in Perl, which is discussed in Chapter 11.

To call the script you submit a form created with standard HTML markup. Here's a basic form (using no JavaScript). It asks for the user's name and e-mail address and has form controls for a check box and a text area. Clicking the Submit Form button submits the form.

```
<FORM METHOD=POST ACTION="/cgi-bin/formmail.cgi?http://mydomain.com">
<INPUT TYPE="hidden" NAME="recipient" VALUE="me@mydomain.com">
<INPUT TYPE="hidden" NAME="subject" VALUE="Stuff">
Name: <INPUT TYPE="text" NAME="realname" SIZE=40><BR>
```

```
E-Mail: <INPUT TYPE="text" NAME="username" SIZE=40><P>
Do you like us?
<INPUT TYPE="checkbox" NAME="include" CHECKED><P>
Please write your comments here.<BR>
<TEXTAREA NAME="comments" ROWS=10 COLS=60>
</TEXTAREA><P><INPUT TYPE="subit" VALUE="Submit Form">
<INPUT TYPE="reset" VALUE=" Erase Form">
</FORM>
```

Here is a summary of what this code does:

- The form is sent to the URL specified in the ACTION parameter. This includes the path and name of the CGI program (in this case cgi-bin/formmail.cgi).
- The formmail.cgi script takes one URL parameter: the URL you want to return to when the form has been submitted. This can be a home page or a "form successfully submitted" page.
- The NAME="recipient" hidden field stores the e-mail address to send the completed form.
- The NAME="subject" hidden field stores the subject of the e-mail message (useful if you employ the formmail.cgi script for other forms on your pages).

The remainder of the form is standard HTML form markup, including text fields, a check box, a text area box, a reset button, and a submit button.

Chapter

3

Programming Fundamentals

When stripped to its essentials, computer programming is neither complex nor difficult. Most programming tasks involve problem solving, then applying the solution using a syntax the computer can understand. With even minimal programming experience and skills, you can create programs for the Web for playing games, displaying reminder calendars, running self-testing and scoring quiz games, and much more. In short, there is almost no limit to what you can do.

If you're new to programming or need a refresher course, be sure to read this chapter. It details some of the key concepts you will need to understand Web programming fundamentals. This chapter explains the basic concepts of programming, such as flow control, conditional testing, variables, expressions, and other topics.

Step One: Think Like a Programmer

Although you don't need any previous training or experience at computer programming to master most programming languages, you will find that it does help. At the very least, you should learn how to "think like a programmer," or at least think in terms of programming and problem solving. Of course, this does not mean that you must *become* a programmer. You can master programming and yet not take it up as a new career.

It is not the intent of this book to teach programming principles. Programming is a varied subject that involves many disciplines, and it would require a substantial book to do it justice. However, you can gain a good grasp of programming fundamentals by concentrating on the 11 main areas of program design:

- Objects
- Flow
- Routines
- Variables
- Expressions
- Strings
- Numeric Values
- Conditional Statements
- Looping
- Data Entry
- Data Output

Objects

Many of the languages used for Web programming are designed around the object, which is something like a virtual "black box" machine. *Objects* are predefined elements of a program with which you can interact, but only in predefined ways. For example, a typical object used in many Web languages, including Java, JavaScript, VBScript, and C++, is the string. A string object is designed to store one or more text characters. It is not designed to store numeric values or any other kind of data.

It's important to remember that objects are designed with specific tasks in mind. One object might represent the current document, another the entire window, and yet another a form within that document. Objects impose a strict compliance; you can't just manipulate any object in any way you like. This is a departure from many older programming languages, such as C or Basic, where you had complete freedom to manipulate the data in your programs in any way you wished. This freedom also comes with a price: It's rather easy to shoot yourself in the foot by making a relatively minor programming error. Objects are supposed to make programming safer and more streamlined.

Object-based programming brings with it its own object-related jargon. Here are the most important terms to learn:

- *Method*. This is something you can do with (or to) an object.
- *Property*. This is a value you can fetch from an object.
- *Event*. This is a condition that the object is trained to watch out for and will signal you when it occurs.

Note that the use of objects does not necessarily make a programming language object-oriented. The term *object-oriented* has a specific meaning in computer programming, encompassing many design elements. *Object-based* languages, such as JavaScript, VBScript, and Perl, use objects to make programming easier and more flexible. But they limit what you can do with those objects and how you can alter their internal mechanisms.

In a true *object-oriented* language—such as Java and C++—you not only use objects to create a program, but also have full control over the creation and use of those objects. As an example, with Java and C++ you can create your own object from scratch and specify exactly how other parts of your program can interact with the object. You can forbid your program to work directly with the object, for instance, and instead write the program so that only other objects can access it. Even though this may sound overly restrictive, creating objects and hierarchies in this way helps to streamline your programs and make them easier to use.

Because object-oriented programming is specific to just a few of the languages used on the Web, more details about its use can be found in Parts IV and VI, which deal with Java and C/C++, respectively.

Flow

The *flow* is the order of events your program takes to complete its task. That flow can be dictated by a strict progression from start to finish that never varies between uses. Or it can deviate depending on user input or some other condition. Flow is something you have to visualize, or your programs may become hopelessly confusing to you. You'll lose track of what they are supposed to do and when.

Simple, one-function programs can be created without a blueprint or flow chart, but you should still give extra thought and consideration to what your program is supposed to do. As you gain experience writing programs you'll do this subconsciously. At first you'll have to force yourself to think in terms of progression.

You will especially want to consider flow if the program is complex in nature. You may find it helpful to draw a programming *flow chart* that includes the basic steps of the program, such as that shown in Figure 3.1. Each box contains a complete step; arrows connect the boxes to indicate the progress of steps throughout the program.

Flow charts are particularly handy when creating programs that involve other programs as part of a complex interaction using frames. For example, suppose you're writing a JavaScript program that uses frames in Netscape Navigator or Internet Explorer. The JavaScript in one frame can control what happens in another

Figure 3.1 A flow chart helps you visualize the construction of your program.

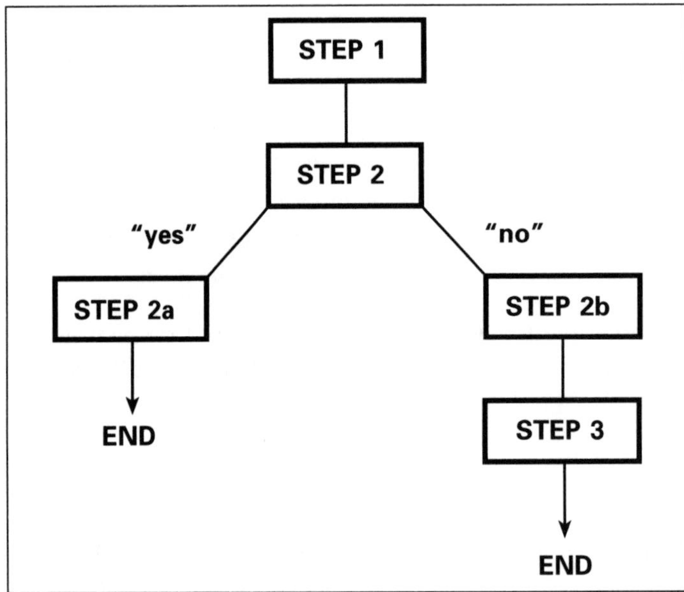

frame. By making a "map" of the JavaScript program and how it interacts with everything you can better visualize the requirements and design principles involved.

Routines

One of the first things a programmer does when he or she starts on a project is to map out the individual segments, or *routines*, that make up the software. Even the longest, most complex program consists of little more than bite-sized routines. The program progresses from one routine to the next in an orderly and logical fashion.

What exactly is a routine? A *routine* is any self-contained segment of code that performs a basic action. A routine can be a single command or character of text, or it can take up the bulk of a mammoth 200K program. Suppose your program accepts the user's entry from a form, formats it, and mails it to your e-mail address. It then displays a "thank you for responding" page. The program can be segmented into four routines:

- *Routine 1.* Accept user's data in the form and "parse" it so it can be used.
- *Routine 2.* Format the data for readability.
- *Routine 3.* Send the formatted output to your e-mail address.
- *Routine 4.* Display the "thank you" screen

There's no need to separate these routines within a program physically, but it helps to think of the program as being composed of these more basic parts. If the program doesn't work properly, you can analyze the problem more easily if you can narrow it down to a specific segment of the code. For example, if the program is not formatting the text properly, then you can reasonably narrow the problem to the number 2 routine.

The bulk of the programs you'll create or revise for use on the Web simply start at the beginning and advance one step at a time to the end, taking each instruction in turn and acting on it. This is the approach taken by the example program just cited. Better program design calls for segmenting the routines into something called *functions*. That way, the functions can be used in any order and even repeated. For example, your program could easily be revised to repeat Routine 1 (formatting the document) after the user has successfully picked an item from the list and the response is shown on the screen.

There is another benefit to working with discrete routines: Because the code for a particular task is all contained in a routine, it can be transported more easily to other programs. This lets you share code so you don't have to write everything from scratch.

If you're familiar with older versions of Basic, you've probably seen numbers at the beginning of each line. One purpose of these numbers is to help you reference parts of your code in other areas of the program. No modern programming language uses line numbers. Rather, they all use *labels*, which help you identify routines by area or function name. You merely provide the name of the label you want to execute. This makes it extremely easy to revise your program, as you don't need to worry about changing line numbers as you add and remove contents.

Variables

A *variable* is a special holding area for information. All Web languages use named variables, and in most cases the names can be any length (but for your benefit, variable names should be kept under 15 characters and should be easy to type and remember). You make up the name of the variable as you write the program. The contents of the variable is specified by one of the following:

- You, when you write the program
- The browser, when the program is run
- The server, which houses your program and Web page
- The user, who enters some data or makes a selection

The information in the variable is kept so that it can be used elsewhere in the program (see Figure 3.2). This information can take many forms and includes numbers and text. In the case of programs that run on the server, variables normally last only as long as the program runs. When the program is over, the variable is deleted from the computer's memory. In the case of JavaScript and VBScript, both of which run on the client, the variable is deleted only when the page that contained it is removed from the viewing window.

Web languages follow two types of variable construction: loose typing and strict typing.

Figure 3.2 Variables store information for later retrieval in a program.

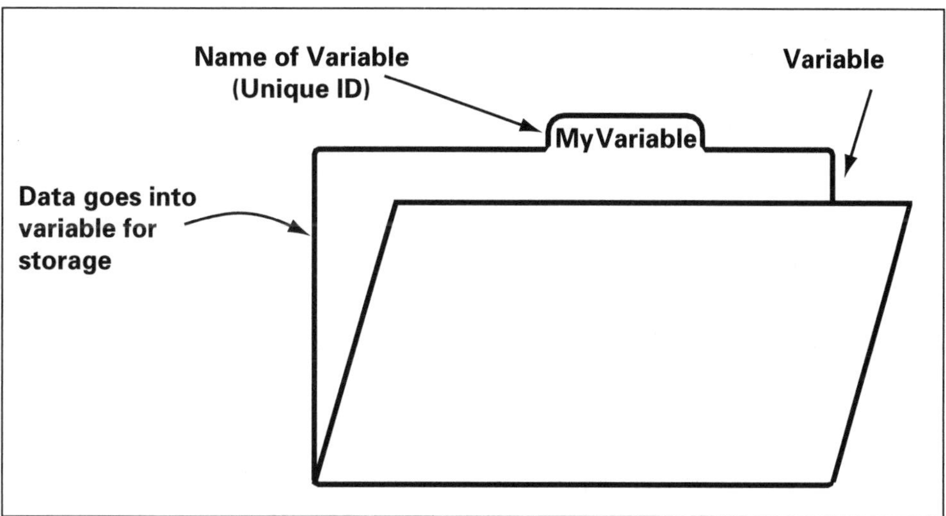

- JavaScript, VBScript, Perl, and the UNIX shell languages use the loose typing method, This essentially means that the contents of variables are not tightly controlled, and any variable can contain any type of data. For example, you can put a text value into a variable, then replace it with a number value. The programming language will cope by automatically figuring out what kind of data is being stored, and it will adjust its internal memory handling requirements to suit.

- Java, C, and C++ use the strict typing method, where you must define the type of variable you want when you create it. Variables cannot be "mixed and matched"; you cannot put data for one kind of variable into another. With strict typing you "declare" a variable type, such as

  ```
  int MyInteger;
  ```

  to define a variable named MyInteger that will contain an integer (whole number) value.

Expressions

An *expression* is a process a program must follow to complete a task you've given it. Sometimes the expression is a simple math problem: "Take the contents of this variable and apply it to that value." Often, the expression is a little more complex: "Take this number from this variable, add 15 to it, and compare it to the value in this other variable."

When you ask a program to perform some type of calculation or thinking process, you're asking it to *evaluate an expression*. For example, if the expression reads "1+1," then the program must first evaluate it (add 1 and 1 to make 2) before proceeding.

Some more advanced expressions may appear exotic, but you'll have plenty of chance to use them. The most common is evaluating if a statement is *true* or *false*. Here's a good example of a *true/false* expression that must be evaluated by a program:

```
if Number equals10, then alert ("the number is ten");
```

In reading the expression (which is not in acceptable programming notation, but that's not important now), it reads "if the contents of the Number variable is equal to 10, then display a message." Before proceeding with the remainder of the program, the program must pause, take a peek inside the Number variable, and apply it to the logical expression. If the result is *true*, then the program displays a message that reads, "the number is ten." If it's *false* (the Number variable has a number other than 10), then something else happens.

Strings

A common term in programming circles is the *string*. A string is simply a sequence of alphabetic or numeric characters, as shown in Figure 3.3. These characters are stored within the computer's memory one right after the other, like beads on a string. Therein lies the root of the word *string*.

In the context programming languages used for the Web, strings are most used in variables. Once stored in a variable, the string can be acted upon by the program. For example, if the string is text, you can compare it with another string to see if the two are the same. The concept of comparing string comes in handy when designing interactive programs.

Strings are also used to display messages to the user and display text in the browser. For instance, you use a string to display a paragraph of text generated by the program. Strings are especially important in Web programming because an HTML document is nothing but text. This includes images, sounds, Java applets,

Figure 3.3 Strings are composed of one or more characters—letters, numbers, or symbols—strung one after the other.

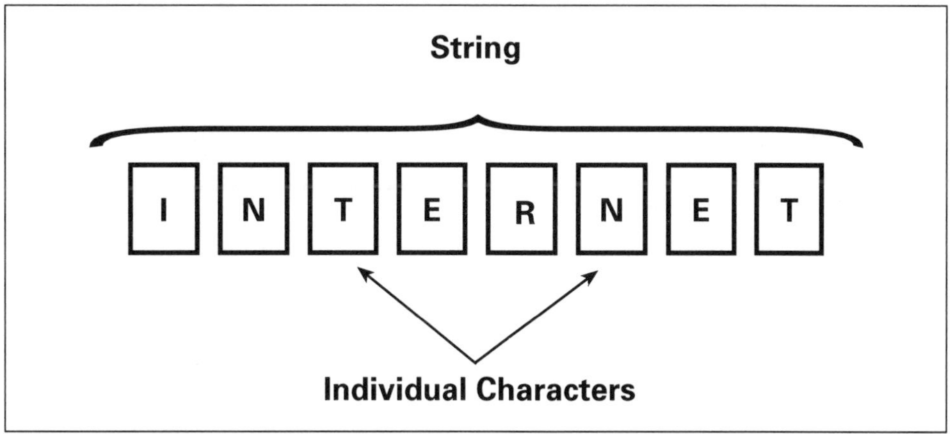

plug-ins, and more—all of these elements are stored in an HTML document as textual tags.

Numeric Values

Computers are designed from the ground up to work with *numeric values* (numbers). The size of the number is inconsequential and is entirely up to the application running on the computer. In fact, most programs for the Web can deal with numbers as large as 1e+308—that's 1 with more than 300 zeros after it! Unless you're having an argument with an astronomer over the number of stars in the known universe, you'll probably never have a reason to use a number that large. As with strings (see above), numerical values are most often used in variables.

Numbers differ from strings in one important area: The computer can perform math calculations on two numbers and give you the result. Calculations are not possible with strings because you can't multiply or divide strings.

Note that programs can store digits as numbers or as strings. It can sometimes be difficult to tell when a "number" (like 1 or 263) is a numeric value and when it's a string. For the sake of clarity, we'll refer to numbers stored as digits in the computer's memory as a *numeric value*. And we'll refer to numbers stored as text characters as a *number string*. This is by no means standard notation in programming books, but it works for our needs.

Conditional Statements

Computer programs can be constructed so that they perform certain routines in one instance and other routines in another. The program responds to specific conditions, set by the user, by the browser, by information from the server, or by some other source.

A *conditional statement* is a fork in the road with a choice of two directions to take, depending on the response to a simple true/false question. All Web programming languages provide many ways to create conditional statements, but they all have one thing in common: to activate a certain routine (or group of routines) depending on external data.

Here's an example of a conditional statement. "If it's cold outside, I'll wear my jacket. Otherwise, I'll leave the jacket at home." The statement can be broken down into three segments:

- The condition to be met (if it's cold).
- The result if the condition is *true* (wear the jacket).
- The result if the condition is *false* (leave the jacket at home).

Obviously, this isn't the kind of conditional statement you'll write for your Web page. But you may design a conditional statement, for instance, that loads one document depending on one type of user input or another document depending on other types of user input.

All conditional statements have a condition that must be met and a specified action if the condition is *true* or *false*—there is no other possible outcome. Not all conditional statements specify an action for both a *true* and a *false*, but most do.

Spend some time learning all the ropes of conditional statements because this is the element of programming that gives your program true intelligence. Although your programs may never have a life of their own—though you may sometimes think they do!—conditional statements endow them with limited smarts to perform the action you want.

Looping

A *loop* is a command or routine that repeats two or more times. A typical loop used in some programming languages is a "keyboard scan" in which the program checks the keys you press. If you press the key the loop routine is looking for, the program breaks out of the loop (usually just momentarily) and continues with some other routines. If the key isn't the one that the loop is looking for, the routine is restarted.

Keyboard scans are not applicable for Web programs because Web programs are not intended to take control of the user's computer. In the realm of the Web, you might construct a routine that insists the user respond to a prompt by providing valid data. The loop is repeated until valid data is entered.

Another common use of loops in Web programming is sifting through all the text boxes of a form and formatting them for output in an e-mail message. The program is written generically, so it can be used with any form—whether it has one text box or many. The program executes the same pieces of code, as a loop, until it has processed all of the text boxes in the form.

In many ways loops are really specialized versions of conditional statements. Instead of stopping to provide a choice of two directions, the program is designed to continue the loop until a certain condition, which may be internal or external, is met. Web programming languages contain many sophisticated ways to construct loops, including the for loop and the while loop—both of which will be familiar to you if you've done any programming.

Data Input

The basic Web program is merely a series of commands. You can also devise programs to stop and wait for *user input*. Once the user has entered the data, the program uses the information—be it text, a number, or some other value—to complete its task.

For example, you might have a JavaScript or VBScript program prompt the user for her real name or e-mail name, or some other variable information. Your program may then use that information to create a personalized page. Input data can be entered directly into the document or can be temporarily stored in a variable. The program can then extract the contents of the variable and use it in a conditional statement, a branch, or a loop—or even save it for use later.

For Web programs running on a server, user input typically takes one form: an HTML form, where you enter text or make a selection. User input is restricted on the Web to prohibit unauthorized access to the Web server computer. Therefore, only the HTML form, which confines user input to a fairly narrow response, is used. Another fairly common data input source for server-side programs is a disk file on the Web server. The file can contain a counter value, a database, or any other collection of data. The program is designed to open this file and sift through it to get the data it needs.

For programs running on the client (JavaScript and VBScript, or perhaps Java), user input can be through an HTML form or in response to a pop-up message box or other prompt (see Figure 3.4). For security reasons, neither JavaScript nor VBScript offer anything more than simple prompt-box data input.

Data Output

Most programs that run on the server output their data in HTML format, so that the result is seen on the user's browser. The output of the program is sent to the Web server, which, in turn, delivers the HTML document to the browser. To the browser, the page it has just received is no different from a regular "static" HTML document. That is, the browser has no way to tell that the page was generated by a Web program.

Some server-based programs are also designed to output data to a disk file on the server computer. A typical example of this is a counter program, which keeps track of the number of visitors to a site. As each new visitor arrives, a number stored in a counter file is incremented by 1. The Web program reads this value (data input), adds 1 to it, then writes a new value into the file (data output).

For programs running on the server, data output is restricted to the browser window—it is not possible to use a client-side program to write data directly in a file on the server for reasons of security. JavaScript and VBScript are restricted to displaying text and graphics in the browser's main window or in messages boxes, but neither can output data to a file on the user's computer. The appearance of the data is completely up to your unique JavaScript or VBScript program. You can display

Figure 3.4 Message boxes prompt for user input.

plain text or add special formatting and imaging, as desired. Any Web document you can create using HTML commands you can duplicate with JavaScript or VBScript—hence the popularity of these languages.

Programming Considerations

Keep these considerations in mind when developing Web programs.

Commands or Entities

Programs are constructed by stringing together commands. The use and order of these commands dictate what the program is doing. For example, the command may be a simple print statement as used in Perl to output text.

Not all programming languages call a command a "command." Many languages refer to their commands in a more specific manner, which may better describe what the command really does. For example, the typical object-based language breaks down "commands" into several subgroups, including properties, methods, events, and statements. Each type of "command" is used in a unique way.

One common way of describing this collection of "commands" is to refer to them as *entities*. Unlike the term *command*, which usually connotes some action, the term *entity* is generic. It does not refer only to those elements of a programming language that invoke some action. Another common word for command used by some programmers is *construct*.

Arguments or Parameters

Most commands (or entities or constructs) are not complete unless you tell them what you want to do. For example, the *if* statement needs to have an expression to evaluate. Without the expression, the *if* statement has nothing to do. To complete these commands you provide one or more arguments, also commonly referred to as *parameters*. Arguments are variable pieces of information you provide as needed.

Here's a concrete example. Take the Perl print command. Perl expects you to provide the text you want to print as part of the command. Therefore, you follow the print command with the text you want to output. This text is the *argument* for the print command.

```
print "<H1>Output this header</H1>\n\n";
```

Syntax

To properly construct a program in any language you must first understand the syntax of that language. Syntax is the unique way parts of a program are assembled, much like the way words are put together in defined ways to create complete sentences. Without proper syntax, the computer will not know how to execute the program, regardless of the commands you've used. Imagine the sentence "Go desk before I." These are simply words strung together that have no contextual meaning.

Comments

A common element of all programs is programmer comments. These are short snippets of text that serve as explanatory notes or instructions. Comments are not interpreted by the computer; they are merely for the benefit of its human operator.

Comments are not strictly required, but they can come in handy to remind you of work you did months ago. As you become more involved with Web programming, you'll find yourself forgetting the tricks and techniques you've used. Should you revisit an old program, you may find some of your work alien, unless you provide some comments to remind you of what you did. Comments are also particularly handy when adapting other people's programs to your own. A well-commented program includes its own instruction manual.

Comments are defined in a program by using a sequence of special characters. A common sequence, //, is used by Javascript, C, C++, and Java. The two slashes mean any text following, and up to the first hard return, is to be treated as a comment.

In Perl, comments are defined by the # character; in VBScript, comments are defined by the ' character or the words REM.

Sources of Programs and Program Routines

It is unlikely that you will be the original author of all the Web programs you create. Programming is a collaborative effort, and you are encouraged to "borrow" from those who have solved the same problem. There is no need to reinvent the wheel for each task you must accomplish unless you are more interested in the challenge of coming up with a new way of doing things, rather than simply getting the job done.

The Web itself is a vast repository of free and nearly free examples you can use for your own Web programming jobs. Odds are, someone has already done something at least remotely similar to the project you have to get done, and that script might be available as an example on the Web.

Before embarking on any new programming task, first check the various sources on the Web to determine if there are one or more examples you can use to begin your work. The sources.htm file on the CD-ROM that accompanies this book lists a number of script repositories you should visit. Many of the repositories are language-specific—you'll find only Perl scripts in a Perl repository, for example. If you've already decided on the programming language to use, you can narrow your search by concentrating on only those repositories that contain examples written for the language you are using.

Alta Vista, Yahoo!, and the other search engines of the Web are invaluable in helping you find new and updated program examples. Type perl+example at the Alta Vista prompt, for instance, and you get thousands of entries (you'll probably want to refine your search to return fewer hits, of course).

Repositories on the Web are there as a means to share Web programs. Seldom do you need to pay a royalty or use fee, though this is requested at some script repositories. Still, most of the better examples you will find are copyrighted, which means the original author still retains control over how the program is to be used. Read any accompanying note about use restrictions and requirements, which include retaining the copyright notice of the original author.

There is much debate over the amount of a program a person can copyright. In general, small chunks (one or two lines) are not copyrightable in themselves. These chunks represent ideas you can use and adapt to your own program, without fear of stepping on copyright toes. It's only when you use a larger portion of a program that copyright becomes a factor.

As you develop your Web programs keep an eye out for chunks you can reuse. It's not unusual for professional programmers to assemble a program using only generic routines, piecing them together to form a new program. Reuse of code helps to save time and energy.

Chapter

4

Understanding Variables, Expressions, and Statements

This chapter details the use of variables in a JavaScript program. You will learn how to assign variables and how to use the values contained within variables. We'll cover both "regular" variables and array variables.

Understanding Variables

Variables are the means a program uses to store information for later use. This information can come from the program itself ("hard coded" into the program itself), or it can come from some other source, including the user, the computer running the program, the browser, and a number of others.

One common use for variables in Web programming is retrieving and storing "environment" settings, which are created by the server. These so-called environment variables provide such information as the current date, the name of the file currently being processed, the kind of browser used by the user to access the server, and more.

Variables are temporary holders of information—they hold the information as long as a program is running. A variable can hold numeric values ("numbers"), character strings, true/false values, and—depending on the language used—"objects" that define special kinds of data:

- *Numeric values* are numbers that can be added together. Example: 2 + 2 results in 4.
- *Character strings* are a collection of text, such as "Internet" or "My name is Mudd." Strings can contain number characters, but they are not treated as numbers. Adding 2 + 2 when the numbers are strings results in "22."
- *True/false values* are the Boolean true and false.

Placing a value in a variable is referred to as *assigning* or *assigning a value to a variable*. When you see a phrase such as, "Assign the value of 10 to variable *Num*," you know that it means to store the number 10 in a variable referred to as *Num*.

With few exceptions, Web programming languages use a small and consistent set of symbols to create and store variables within a program. The basic way to assign content (number, string, and so on) to a variable is with the equal (=) assignment operator. The basic syntax is:

```
VariableName = value
```

The structure of a variable is as follows:

- *The first argument is the name of the variable.* All the Web languages discussed in this book let you use very long names for variables, but you are often restricted by the characters you may use. See "Variable Name Limits," later in this chapter, for more information on valid variable names.
- *The second argument is the contents of the variable.* You can put all sorts of stuff into a variable, including a number, a string, a math expression (such as 2 + 2), and various other things that we'll get to in a bit.

Web programs allow you to store an almost unlimited number of variables. The maximum number of variables you can create and use in a program depends on what kind of information the variable contains, and the amount of available memory in your computer. Most of the Web programs you create will use a dozen or two variables. Even if all of these are filled with fairly long strings, there should not be a worry of running out of memory.

However, it is possible to write a program that creates so many variables that the computer runs out of memory. This is actually quite common in scripts written by "newbies" who have not learned all the ins and outs of a language. Rather than writing the program that uses one variable and refills it with different content, for example, a faulty program might create new variables for each change of content.

If this program is allowed to run long enough memory could run out. While this may be an extreme example that you may or may not do yourself, it pays to remember that computers have a limited amount of information they can store. This is particularly important if you plan on writing Web programs that manage lots of data.

Understanding Data Types

Computers deal with specific forms of data, even though it may look all the same to us. A number is composed of digits from 0 to 9, but to a computer, those digits are not *really* numbers unless they are true numeric values. It's entirely possible to give a computer a set of digits as a string ("12345") rather than as a true number (12345). This distinction is important because a computer—and, by extension, a programming language—can do some tasks with numbers that it can't do with strings, and vice versa.

Perhaps more importantly, some programming languages used for the Web (namely Java and C/C++) impose very strict rules and limitations on what kinds of data you can apply to variables.

For this reason, it's a good idea to have a clear understanding of how different data types are used with variables and the tasks that can be accomplished with each type. For the sake of discussion, we'll use generic examples to show how data might be assigned in a program. Bear in mind that not all programming languages use the same syntax. You'll want to consult the individual chapters on each language for specific information on how to construct variables and variable assignments.

Numbers in Variables

A number is one or more digits stored in the computer in such a way that JavaScript can perform math calculations with them. Web programs can store extraordinarily large numbers, typically from 1.7×10^{-308} to $1.7 \times 10^{+308}$. Spreadsheet users may know this span of numbers as "scientific" values with 15-digit precision. That is, the numbers are precise up to 15 digits to the right of the decimal point. Programmers familiar with other computer languages may know this span of numbers as "double precision floating point."

To place a number in a variable, just provide the variable name, the equal sign—this is the variable assignment operator—and the value you want to use. For example, to place the number 10 in a variable named MyVar, do this:

```
MyVar = 10;
```

Strings in Variables

A string is one or more text characters arranged in memory in a single file. Strings can contain numbers (digits), letters, punctuation, or a combination of these. Math calculations cannot be performed on strings. In all languages strings are assigned to variables by enclosing them in a set of single or double quotation marks, like this:

```
"I am a string"
```

Why are the quotes necessary? Without the quotes, JavaScript will mistake each word in *I am a string* as the name of a function or variable. When you try to play the program JavaScript will respond with an error message. Here's a working example of placing a string into a variable:

```
MyVar = "This is JavaScript";
```

> **NOTE** In some languages (such as Perl and JavaScript), you can use single quotation marks instead, such as
>
> ```
> 'I am a string'
> ```
>
> However, keep in mind that in Perl there is a subtle difference between those strings assigned with single quotation marks and those assigned with double quotation marks. See Chapter 11 for more information on Perl string variables.

Boolean Values in Variables

There are two Boolean values: *true* and *false*. Some programming languages don't have a separate set of Boolean values and instead use 0 for false, and 1 or –1 (or any other nonzero value) for true. Web programming languages can also use these numbers to represent true and false, but several languages (for example, JavaScript and VBScript) also reserve the words *true* and *false* to mean Boolean *true* and *false*. You can think of the Boolean *true* and *false* values as being equivalent to on/off or yes/no.

To assign a Boolean value to variable provide just the word true or false, without quotes. Example:

```
MyVar = true;
```

Objects in Variables

Many Web programming languages support objects, which are variables that contain data specific to a program. Most often an object isn't one individual piece of information, but lots of pieces of information packed together in one homogenous unit. For example, a programming language might define an object to maintain information about the Web browser window.

This information can include the size of the window, the name of the document displayed in the window, the URL of the document in the window, and much more. In fact, a window object is defined and supported by both JavaScript and VBScript. You will become quite familiar with the object if you do any programming in either JavaScript or VBScript because objects are central to just about everything you do in the language.

Other Things You Can Assign to a Variable

There are a few other things you can assign to a variable as well. The following techniques can come in handy when using most Web programming languages.

Strings That Look Like Numbers

You will want the program to treat some numbers as a string of text, not as a numeric value, for example, your phone number or your Zip code.

```
Phone = "555-1212";
Zip = "09876";
```

This technique is handier than you may think, as you'll discover in the next section on expressions. If you assign a numeric value to the Phone variable, as in

```
Phone = 555-1212;
```

most programming languages will take it upon themselves to "evaluate" the assignment, and the result stored in the Phone variable will be -675, which is the result of subtracting 1212 from 555. By assigning the variable as a string, the program does not evaluate the assignment, and the phone number remains intact.

Contents of Other Variables

These are the innards of one variable assigned to the innards of another. Example (both contain the same string, "This is a test"):

```
OriginalVar = "This is a test";
CopyCatVar = OriginalVar;
```

Expressions

An expression—as you'll learn later in this chapter—is some formula you want your program to calculate. The "formula" is usually a math expression of some type. Expressions are used quite heavily in assigning variables:

```
Result=2+2            // Add 2+2; value stored in variable is 4;
Count=Count+1         // Add 1 to value in Count; store it back in Count;
MyName=FirstName+LastName    // Add contents of these variables
                               to MyName;
```

Variable Name Limits

All of the programming languages discussed in this book provide a great deal of latitude when it comes to the names you can give variables. Variables can be almost unlimited in length, though for practical reasons you'll probably keep your variable names under 10 or 15 characters. Shorter variable names usually help your program run faster.

Keep the following in mind when naming your variables. These rules may or may not apply to all of the Web programming languages detailed in this book. However, for the sake of consistency, these rules are good to follow whether or not the language provides for additional flexibility in naming variables.

- Variable names should consist of letters only, without spaces. You can use numbers, as long as the name doesn't start with a digit. For example, MyVar1 is acceptable, but 1MyVar is not.

- Don't use punctuation characters in variable names. Exception: the underscore character. That is, the variable My_Var is acceptable, but My*Var is not. Variables can begin with the underscore character.
- For most Web languages, *variable names are case sensitive*! The variable MyVar is a distinctly different variable from myVar, myvar, and other variations. (This applies to C/C++, Java, JavaScript, and the UNIX shell scripts, but not to VBScript, which is not case sensitive).

The following are valid variable names:

```
MyVar
myvar
MyVar1
My_Var
_MyVar
```

(Note that not all languages support an initial underscore, but most do. When in doubt, don't use it.)

These are not valid variables for most Web programming languages—all will result in an error:

```
1MyVar
MyVar^
My*Var
```

These cause an error because either the name contains an invalid character or the first character is invalid. For example, 1MyVar is invalid because it starts with a numeric, and MyVar^ and My*Var are invalid because they contain unsupported characters.

> **NOTE** Perl uses many symbol characters to define special kinds of data. These characters include the $, @, and % symbols. For this reason it's a good idea to use only letter characters for Perl variable names. Read more about Perl variable naming conventions in Chapter 11.

Capitalization of Variable Names

None of the Web programming languages discussed in this book requires a specific capitalization scheme for variables. It is perfectly acceptable to use myvar, MYVAR, MyVar, or any other variation. However, you will note that most programmers use a consistent capitalization scheme. This scheme is usually part convention and part habit, and it varies from programmer to programmer.

Generally, professional programmers tend to use all uppercase for variables that are designed to be set once in a program (usually at the beginning) and left at the same value. These variables are known as constants. By using all uppercase, the programmer can easily see that the variable is a constant and that it should not be changed elsewhere in the program. For example, the following assigns the string value "This is a variable constant" to a variable named CONST_STRING:

```
CONST_STRING = "This is a variable constant"
```

Using all uppercase for constants is not a universal approach, however. It is a common technique to use uppercase for nearly all variables in Perl. Perl can accept variables of any capitalization.

Conversely, variables that are meant to be changed throughout the course of the program are given either all lowercase or mixed case. The choice of which format to use is up to you—the only important consideration is that once you spell a variable with a given capitalization, that you spell it the same way throughout the rest of the program. Otherwise, an error will result (again, this does not apply to VBScript, which is not a case-sensitive language).

While all lowercase seems to be somewhat common among professional programmers, a mixed-case technique may be the all-around better choice for most users. The mixed-case approach makes it a little easier to use (and later understand!) compound words that have been joined together to make a variable name.

For example, suppose you need a variable to hold the current date. You combine the words "current" and "date," and use the variable name "currentdate." But the one word can be hard to discern in a program because it's all one case. Instead, use initial caps to help delineate the two words used to create the variable name. You might use one of the following alternatives:

```
CurrentDate
```

or

```
currentDate
```

Among professional programmers, the latter of the alternatives—currentDate—is the most commonly used, so it will be the form you may see in existing programs. Recognizing the capitalization scheme used in an existing program is important if you plan to modify it for your use. With the exception of VBScript, you will need to ensure that any modifications you make to the program adhere to the variable name capitalization scheme used by the original author. If you don't take this precaution, you run the risk of using a different capitalization, and the program will fail.

Understanding "Loose" versus "Strict" Data Types

Some Web programming languages don't care what kind of data you provide to a variable; others do. VBScript, JavaScript, Perl, and the UNIX shell languages use what's known as *loose data typing*. Java and C/C++ use what's known as *strict data typing*. Both approaches have their advantages and disadvantages.

With loose data typing, you can assign any kind of value to a variable, and you do not need to "declare" the type of variable ahead of time. If you're familiar with older versions of Basic, for example, you probably encountered the use of variables like MyVar$—the dollar sign is used to denote a string variable. These older versions of Basic had to be told whether the variable was to hold a numeric value or a string; hence the need to differentiate between the two using a special symbol.

Languages that support loose data typing also allow you to mix and match variable content. That is, a variable can start out holding a string, and later on in the program that string can be replaced by a numeric value. And later on still, the numeric value can be replaced by a Boolean value. This flexibility means that you never have to worry that a variable is of the correct type before you assign a value to it.

With strict data typing, you must specify the type of data that the variable will hold. Once specified, the variable cannot be changed. Specifying the variable type is done by declaring it, which must be performed before the variable is first used. In both Java and C/C++, variables are declared using the syntax:

```
type varname;
```

where type is one of several supported variable types, and varname is the name of the variable. For example, a commonly used variable type is "int," which stands for integer—an integer is a whole number. To declare a variable named myvar, you'd write:

```
int myvar;
```

You can then assign an integer value—and only an integer value—to myvar:

```
myvar = 100;
```

Note that both Java and C/C++ also support a combination declaration/assignment syntax where you can declare the variable type and assign a value to it in one step. This syntax takes the form:

```
int myvar=100;
```

While strict data typing is more restrictive (hence the name!), it does have its advantages. For one, the compiler used to create machine-ready programs from Java and C/C++ code knows to watch for mistakes in mismatched variables. For example, the compiler will issue an error message if you try something like this:

```
int myvar;
myvar = "My name is Mudd";
```

This is not allowed because myvar has been declared to be an integer variable (referred to in programming parlance as "of type integer"), yet the second line attempts to assign a string to it. Because of this error checking, there is less chance of making a mistake that might otherwise go unnoticed until the program is "in the field" and already in use.

Understanding the "Scope" of Variables

The "scope of a variable" determines the extent to which a variable is visible to other parts of a program. Depending on the language, variables defined in one area of the program are not "visible" to other parts of the program. This can cause a rude awakening for neophyte programmers if they are expecting that a variable defined one place in the program can be used anywhere within the program.

With few exceptions, Web programming languages follow these rules of variable scope:

- Variables defined outside of a user-defined function are available to any function within the program. These are referred to as *global variables.*
- Variables defined inside of a function are "local" to that function only. These are referred to as *local variables.*

Do note that not all Web programming languages adhere to these rules. For example, with JavaScript, variables defined in functions are also global—unless the variable is prefixed using the *var* keyword. Although these rules usually hold, there can be subtle differences, depending on the language. The scoping rules are defined in their respective chapters for each of the Web programming languages covered in this book.

The difference between local and global variables is an important one to keep in mind. Local variables are treated as if they don't exist outside of the function where they are defined. That way, you can use the same variable name inside a function, and that variable won't "collide" with the same-named variable elsewhere in the program.

Following is an example that demonstrates this. Two functions are defined, and each one contains a variable named myvar. But because the variables are assigned within their own functions, they are treated as distinct entities by the program. For this example, we'll use JavaScript because it is easy to test as the JavaScript interpreter is built into both Netscape Navigator and Internet Explorer. Note that the example uses the var keyword to ensure that JavaScript creates local variables in each function.

```
<HTML>
<HEAD>
<TITLE>This is a test</TITLE>
<SCRIPT LANGUAGE="JavaScript">
function firstFunction ()  {
   var MyVar = 1;
   alert ("firstFunction: " + MyVar);
   secondFunction();
   alert ("firstFunction: " + MyVar);
}

function secondFunction () {
   var MyVar = 2;
   alert ("secondFunction: " + MyVar);
}
```

```
</SCRIPT>
</HEAD>
<BODY>
<FORM NAME="testform">
<INPUT TYPE="button" NAME="button1" VALUE="Start" onClick="firstFunction()"><P>
</FORM>
</BODY>
</HTML>
```

Here's how this example works. Click on the form button, and JavaScript calls the firstFunction() function. This function assigns a value of 1 to a variable named MyVar. The value of the MyVar variable is displayed in an alert box. A second function—appropriately called secondFunction—is called, which also assigns a value (2) to MyVar. Likewise, this value is displayed in an alert box. Finally, the program returns to firstFunction, where it displays a third alert box. The value of MyVar is shown to be back to 1 because JavaScript has kept two versions of MyVar in its memory: one for firstFunction, and another for secondFunction.

Understanding Variable Arrays

All of the Web programming languages described in this book support *arrays* of variables. For the uninitiated, a variable array is one variable, but with many "compartments." Each compartment stores a different value, like that shown in Figure 4.1. The compartments in a variable array are called *elements*. The benefit of the variable array is that it allows you to store many values, but you can access these values using a common name.

The syntax for creating and using arrays varies somewhat between languages. However, the basic concepts behind arrays are the same, and that's what we'll concentrate on here. Where appropriate, the individual chapters on each language provide additional information on the syntax and use of arrays.

Each element of the array is referenced by number. This number is called the *subscript* or *index*. In most languages, the index is separated from the rest of the variable name by enclosing it in brackets, as in *MyVar[1]*. Remember the qualifier *most*; for example, in the case of VBScript the index is defined within parentheses, as in *MyVar(1)*. For simplicity and consistency, we'll stick with the VarName[1] syntax throughout the remainder of this section.

The [1] identifies a particular element of the variable *MyVar*. Additional elements of the *MyVar* variable have different index numbers:

Figure 4.1 Arrays are a single variable, but with multiple "pockets"; each pocket can store a separate piece of information.

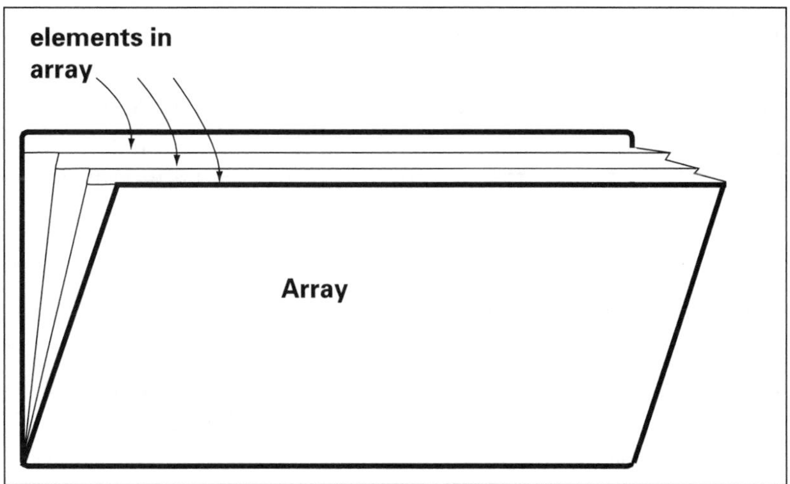


```
MyVar[1]  // Element number 1
MyVar[2]  // Element number 2
MyVar[3]  // Element number 3
//... and so forth
```

> **NOTE** In Perl, JavaScript, and VBScript, variable arrays can contain a mix of data types. You are not limited to restricting a particular array to a certain type of data, such as only numbers or only strings. Further, if the array contains strings, the strings can all be of different lengths. Conversely, restrictions are placed on arrays created in Java and C/C++, where you must use a consistent data type for all of the elements of the array.

Variable arrays are most often used when you want to store values that go together. For example, you might use the variable *Customer* to store five different pieces of information: the customer's name, company, address, phone number, and age. The five array elements might be used as follows:

- *Customer[1]*. Contains the customer's name (a string)
- *Customer[2]*. Contains the customer's company (a string)
- *Customer[3]*. Contains the customer's address (a string)

- *Customer[4].* Contains the customer's phone number (a numerical string)
- *Customer[5].* Contains the customer's age (a number)

Arrays are also useful when you don't know the number of variables you may need to contain the information collected from the user or from the program itself. You merely create the array and go about stuffing data into it. You don't even need to consider making the array "large enough" to hold all the data, as you do in many other programming languages. The size of the array can be dynamically increased.

Understanding Expressions

An *expression* tells a program what to do with the data you provide. Along with variables, they form the basic building blocks for creating useful programs. For example, an expression can be used in an *if* statement to test for a certain condition—if the user's name is Fred, for instance, the script displays a personalized message just for him. Everyone else gets a standardized greeting.

Expressions are also used to perform basic math functions using a programming language. For example, a typical expression adds a value to another value stored in a variable. In this way, the program can keep track of what's going on around it, storing important information it might need later. Let's delve into expressions in this section and discover what they are and how they are used.

Creating Expressions

An expression specifies what you want a program to do with information given to it. An expression consists of two parts:

- One or more values, called *operands*
- An *operator* that tells the program what you want to do with these values

Expressions are typically used when defining the contents of variables, as in

```
Test1 = 1+1;
Test2 = (15*2)+1;
Test3 = "This is" + " a test";
```

The program processes the expression and places the result in the variable.

Expressions can also be part of a more elaborate scheme using other program constructs called *statements* (covered in more detail later in this chapter). A typical statement is the *if* command, which determines if a particular expression is true or false. If the expression is true, the program can be told to do one thing; if it's false, the program can be told to do another. Used in this way, expressions provide a way for your programs to think on their own (although they may seem to act on their own more than you'd like them to).

Following is a list of operators supported by almost all the Web programming languages detailed in this book and how they are used to construct expressions. Most of the operators work with numbers only, but some can also be used with strings. The list is divided into three parts:

- *Assignment* operators, which assign values to variables
- *Math* operators, which apply to number values only, with one exception
- *Relational* operators, which apply to numbers and some of which apply to strings

In all cases, you substitute the operands *v1* and *v2* as your values or variables.

Using the = (Equals) Assignment Operator

Use the = (equals sign) assignment operator whenever you wish to assign a new value to a variable. If the variable previously contained a value, that value is replaced. For example, the following assigns the value 5 to a variable named version:

```
version = 5;
```

Math Operators

These operators shown in Table 4.1 perform math calculations with one or more numbers.

Table 4.1 Math Operators

Operator	Function
– *value*	Treats the *value* as a negative number.
v1 + *v2*	Adds values *v1* and *v2* together. Can also be used to connect (concatenate) two or more strings together.

Continued

Table 4.1 ***Continued***

Operator	Function
v1 – v2	Subtracts value *v2* from *v1*.
v1 * *v2*	Multiplies values *v1* and *v2*.
v1 / *v2*	Divides value *v1* by *v2*.
v1 % *v2*	Divides value *v1* by *v2*. The result is the floating-point remainder of the division.
v1++	Adds 1 to *v1*.
v1––	Subtracts 1 from *v1*.

For example, you use the + operator to add two numbers together. This can be done when assigning a value to a variable, as in:

```
addedNumbers = 1+1+2;
```

The result, as stored in the addedNumbers variable, is 4.

Relational Operators

Relational operators, listed in Table 4.2, compare two values to see if they are equal, not equal, greater than, or less than (and sometimes a combination of these).

Table 4.2 Relational Operators

Operator	Function
v1 == *v2*	Tests that *v1* and *v2* are equal (note the two equal signs are used in most Web languages).
v1 = *v2*	Tests that *v1* and *v2* are equal (alternative format for VBScript and Perl).
v1 <> *v2*	Tests that *v1* and *v2* are not equal.
v1 > *v2*	Tests that *v1* is greater than *v2*.
v1 >= *v2*	Tests that *v1* is greater than or equal to *v2*.
v1 < *v2*	Tests that *v1* is less than *v2*.
v1 <= *v2*	Tests that *v1* is less than or equal to *v2*.
! *value*	Evaluates the logical NOT of *value*. The logical NOT is the inverse of an expression: *true* becomes *false*, and vice versa.

Table 4.2 *Continued*

Operator	Function
v1 && *v2*	Evaluates the logical AND of *v1* and *v2*.
v1 || *v2*	Evaluates the logical OR of *v1* and *v2*.

Relational operators are also known as Boolean or *true/false* operators. Whatever they test, the answer is either yes (*true*) or no (*false*). For example, the expression 2==2 would be *true*, but the expression 2==3 would be *false*.

The typical use of relational operators is with the *if* statement, covered in more detailed later in this chapter. Following is an overly simplistic example, but it gets the point across:

```
if ((2+2) == 4)
   print "true";
else
   print "false";
```

In this example, the program first adds 2 + 2 and arrives at 4. The program then compares the result of the addition with the value 4 to see if they are equal. Of course they are, so the program prints "true." Had the *if* expression read if ((2+2) == 5), then the program would have printed "false."

Operators and Strings

Recall that in a program a string is any assortment of text characters. You can't perform math calculations with text, but you can compare one string of text against another.

With the exception of && (AND) and || (OR), the relational operators can be used with strings for the purpose of comparing them. For instance, you may want to see if two strings are the same, as in:

```
if ("MyString" == "StringMy");
```

This results is *false* because they are not the same. In a working script, no doubt you'd construct the string comparison to work with variables, as in

```
if (StringVar1 == StringVar2);
```

The program compares the *contents* of the two variables and reports *true* or *false*, accordingly.

In all languages, the program considers the case of the characters when you compare strings. The strings must match exactly, including the case of the string. Examples are shown in Table 4.3.

The == (or =) operator is used extensively in comparing strings, but you can use !<, !>, <, >, <=, and >= as well. The != (not equal) operator is an obvious choice—you can use it to check if one string is not equal to another. But why the others? Don't they check if one value is greater or lesser than the other? How can one string have "less" or "more" value than the other?

The < and > operators do indeed test for greater than and less than, and while they will work with strings, they don't work in exactly the way you may think. Strings—whether they are composed of one character or many—have a numeric value in all programming languages. Here's how they typically work:

- If there is one character in the string, the value is the ASCII equivalent of the character. For example, the ASCII equivalent of the letter "A" is 65.
- If there is more than one character in the string, the value is a composite of the ASCII equivalents of all the characters.

Multiple Operators

All modern programming languages, including those used for Web programming, can handle more than one operator in an expression. This allows you to string three or more numbers, strings, or variables together to make complex expressions, such as 5+10/2*7.

With this feature of multiple operators comes a penalty: You must be careful of the *order of precedence*, the order in which the program evaluates an expression.

Table 4.3 String Comparison

String 1	String 2	Result
hello	hello	Match
Hello	hello	No match
HELLO	hello	No match

Like many programming languages and electronic spreadsheet programs, the program doesn't merely start at the left side of the expression and calculate to the other side. Rather, it calculates multiplication and division first, then addition and subtraction, and so forth, following a general left-to-right progression.

The actual order of precedence for expression operators differs between languages. Refer to the chapters on each of the programming languages discussed in this book for a table of operator precedence.

Understanding Statements

All computer languages use *statements* (also sometimes called commands) for controlling the flow and operation of the program. Not all languages support the same statements, but they all support the same basic ones; we'll discuss these basic statements in this section.

Here is a list of the most commonly used statements:

- for
- function
- if...else
- return
- while

In addition, all languages support a means to add comments to a program. These comments are designed to be ignored by the program and serve only as reminders and notes for the programmer. Comments are defined using a special word or symbol, which varies depending on the language, as shown in Table 4.4.

Table 4.4 Web Languages and Their Comment Symbols

Language	Comment Symbols
JavaScript, Java, C/C++	// for single-line comments /* ... */ for multiline comments
Perl, UNIX shell	#
VBScript	' or REM

Take the // comment characters used by JavaScript, Java, and C/C++, as an example. The // characters tell the program that you want to include explanatory comments in your program, from the start of the // characters to the first hard return.

```
// This is a simple comment
```

You can place the // comment characters anywhere on the line. The program will treat *all* the text on that line after the // as a comment.

```
MyVariable="This is a test"  // assigns text variable MyVariable
```

> **NOTE** When using JavaScript, Java, and C++, you can use the /* and */ comment markup syntax for multiple-line commands. It's ideal for copyright and version notices, like this:
>
> ```
> /*----------------------
> JavaScript Magic!, Version 1.0
> (c) Copyright 2001, by John P. Doe.
> All Rights reserved.
> Copy this and die!!
> ------------------------*/
> ```

for

The *for* statement repeats a block of instructions one or more times. The number of iterations is controlled by values supplied as arguments. The syntax of the *for* statement usually takes the following form. (Be sure to read the individual chapters on each Web language discussed in the book for specific details on how the *for* statement is structured for that language.)

```
for (InitVal; Test; Increment)
```

Here is how the three arguments of the for statement are used:

- *InitVal* is the starting value of the for loop and is often 0 or 1, but it can be any number. *InitVal* is an expression that establishes the initial value and assigns that value to a variable. For example, *Count=0* or *i=1*.
- *Test* is the expression used by the *for* statement to control the number of iterations of the loop. As long as the *Test* expression is *true*, the loop continues.

When the *Test* expression proves *false*, the loop ends. Example: Count<10 is *true* as long as the value in the Count variable is less than 10.

- *Increment* indicates how you want the *for* loop to count, by 1s, 2s, 5s, 10s, and so on. This is also an expression and usually takes the form of *CountVar++*, where *CountVar* is the name of the variable first assigned in the *InitVal* expression. Example: Count++ increases the value in the Count variably by 1 for each iteration.

Here's an example of a *for* loop that counts from 1 to 10, stepping 1 digit at a time. At each iteration the script inserts some text and begins a new line. The code you wish to repeat is enclosed in { and } characters following the *for* statement—this forms the *for statement block*. You can provide one line or many within the { and } characters.

```
for (Count=1; Count<=10; Count++) {
        document.write ("Iteration: "+Count+"<BR>");
}
```

Count is the variable name used to store the *for* loop counter. The *for* loop starts out with 1 and proceeds to 10. The test expression is Count<=10 which reads:

```
Count is less than or equal to 10
```

As long as this expression is *true*, the *for* loop continues. Do note that the *Increment* argument is also an expression and in the example uses the Count variable to increment the *for* loop by 1 for each iteration. There's no law that says you must increment the *for* loop by 1s. Here's just one of the many alternatives:

```
for (Count=1; Count<101; Count+=10) {
        document.write ("Iteration: "+Count+"<BR>");
}
```

This example counts by 10s, from 10 to 100.

function

The *function* statement allows you to create your own user-defined functions for your programs. Functions are self-contained routines that can be "called" elsewhere within your program code. That way, if you need to reuse some code many times over in your program, you only have to write it once and "call" it as a function each time you need it.

For example, if you have a function named writeMyName, which displays your name in headline text, you can activate it merely by referring to the name writeMyName someplace within your code. Here's a short test that shows how this might work, using JavaScript as an example:

```
<HTML>
<HEAD>
<TITLE>Function Test</TITLE>
<SCRIPT LANGUAGE="JavaScript">
function writeMyName ()  {
   MyName="John Doe"
alert (MyName)
}
</SCRIPT>
</HEAD>
<BODY>
<FORM>
<INPUT TYPE="button" NAME="button1" VALUE="Click Me!"
onClick="writeMyName()"><P>
</FORM>
</BODY>
</HTML>
```

The writeMyName function is defined within <SCRIPT>...</SCRIPT> tags. It is activated (otherwise known as *called*) when the form button is pushed. This calling action is accomplished using the onClick event handler, defined in the <INPUT> tag for the form button.

Note that the syntax for defining functions can vary greatly between Web languages. The syntax shown above is common to JavaScript, Java, and C/C++. The syntax is similar for Perl, except that Perl uses the word *sub* to define a function. And in VBScript, a function is defined using either the Function or Sub keyword and ended with End Function or End Sub. However, the general structure and use of functions remains the same for all languages.

if...else

The *if*—along with its optional *else*—statement is used to build an "if conditional" expression. It is called a *conditional* expression because it tests for a specific condition:

- If the expression is *true*, the script performs the instructions following the *if* statement.

- If the expression is *false*, the script jumps to the instructions that follow the *else* statement. If there is no *else* statement, the script jumps past the *if* statement entirely and continues from there.

The syntax for if, as found in Java, JavaScript, and C/C++, is simply this:

```
if (expression)
```

The result of the *if* expression is always either *true* or *false*. The following syntax is acceptable when there's only one instruction following the *if* and *else* statements.

```
if (ExampleVar == 10)
        Start();
else
        Stop();
```

Should there be more than one instruction that follows the *if* or *else* statement, the { and } characters must be used to define an *if statement block*. With the { and } characters in place, the program knows to execute all of the instructions within the block.

```
if (ExampleVar == 10) {
   Count = 1;
   Start();
} else {
   Count = 0;
   Stop();
}
```

Expressions in *if* statements are not limited to the == equality operator. You can test whether values are not equal to one another, greater than, less than, and more. See "Understanding Expressions," earlier in this chapter, for more information on expressions.

As you might have guessed, the different Web languages approach the syntax of the *if/else* structure a little differently, so be sure to consult the individual chapters on each language for specific syntax details. For example, the VBScript syntax is:

```
If Expression Then
        do this
Else
        do that
End If
```

However, you can see that the basic concept of the *if/else* structure is the same. The only real difference is the use of additional keywords, including a specific End If command. Also note that in VBScript, as in all flavors of Basic, parentheses are not required to enclose the expression.

return

The *return* statement is used to mark the end of a function. When the program encounters the *return* statement, it "returns" to that spot immediately after the call to the function. The *return* statement can be used with and without a *return* value:

- If a value is included with the *return* statement, then the function returns that value.
- If no value is included with the *return* statement, then the function returns a null (nothing).

Here are two examples of return, with and without a value:

```
function myFunc() {
   OutString = "This is a test";
   return (OutString);
}

function myFunc() {
   OutString = "This is a test";
   return;
}
```

while

The *while* statement sets up a repeating loop that causes a program to repeat a given set of instructions. The looping continues as long as the expression in the *while* statement is *true*. When the *while* statement proves false, the loop is broken and the script continues. Any code inside the *while statement block*—typically defined by using the { and } characters in most Web languages—is considered part of the loop and is repeated.

The syntax of the *while* statement is as follows:

```
while (Expression) {
   // stuff to repeat
}
```

In the following example the *while* loop is repeated for a total of 10 times. With each iteration of the loop it prints text to the browser.

```
Count=0;
WHILE (Count <10) {
   print "Iteration: "+Count+"<BR>", "\n";
   Count++;
}
```

Here's how this example works. First, the Count variable is set to 0. This is the initial value that will be compared in the *while* expression, which is Count <10. Count starts at 0. With each iteration of the loop, text is printed to the screen, and the Count variable is increased by 1.

The first 10 times the loop is repeated Count <10 is true, so the loop continues. After the tenth trip, the Count variable contains the number 10, and the *while* expression proves false. The loop is broken, and the program skips to the end of the *while* statement block (that portion after the } character).

Chapter

5

Using Forms with Web Programs

Perhaps the most common application of Web programming and CGI is forms processing. Forms processing involves accepting data from a form in an HTML document, processing it in some way (typically extracting each piece of information, then manipulating that information in some way). The result of this might be to prepare the form data for an e-mail message, to set up a database query, or to add an item to a shopping cart.

The use of forms and CGI involves two separate steps: the form itself, which is contained in the HTML of the Web page, and the Web program that processes the form. In this chapter you'll learn how to prepare forms for later processing. This includes learning how to use all of the common control types, which include text boxes, push buttons, check boxes, radio buttons, and list boxes.

If you are already familiar with Web forms, by all means skip the chapter and move on to the next. Or, use the information contained in this chapter as a refresher course.

> **NOTE** This chapter reviews the most common form elements used in Web pages. HTML is a constantly developing language, and new features for supporting additional form elements are added all the time. This chapter is not meant to cover all of the options available for HTML forms, but rather the ones you are likely to use the vast majority of the time. If you're interested in learning more about HTML forms, consult *HTML Sourcebook, Third Edition,* by Ian Graham (Wiley Computer Publishing, 1997). Also see Chapter 20 of this book for more information on HTML basics.

Creating the Form

A form can be placed anywhere in a Web HTML document. In fact, some HTML documents contain nothing more than a form. Most forms, however, are part of a larger page, which may include text, headings, images, and so forth. The form is specified in HTML using the <FORM> and </FORM> tags. The <FORM> tag specifies the start of the form, and the </FORM> tag specifies the end. It is not uncommon to include other HTML tags within the <FORM> block. They typically include body text, headings, links, anchors, images, and other common elements.

The basic structure of the <FORM> block is:

```
<FORM>
...Additional tags and text go here...
</FORM>
```

where ...Additional tags and text go here... is one or more controls or objects (also sometimes called *widgets*). These objects include the text box, the push button, and the check box.

The <FORM> tag is optionally used with the following attributes, which tell the browser how to submit the form to a server.

- *NAME.* The name of the form
- *METHOD.* The submission method, either POST or GET
- *ACTION.* The URL for submitting the form (the form is sent here)

- *TARGET*. The window or frame name where the form output (from the CGI program) should be placed
- *ENCTYPE*. The encoding format of the form

For example,

```
<FORM NAME="myform" ACTION="http://mydomain.com/cgibin/form.cgi" METHOD=get>
```

The NAME="myform" attribute specifies a form with the name "mnform." While naming a form is not a requirement, it can be helpful if an HTML page contains more than one form.

The ACTION="..." attribute specifies the URL that is to be used for processing the form. In other words, upon sending the form (usually by pressing a button labeled "Submit"), the browser will go to the URL specified in the ACTION attribute, which in this case is

```
ACTION="http://mydomain.com/cgibin/form.cgi"
```

In almost all cases, the URL to which the ACTION attribute points is a CGI program on the Web server. Upon reaching this URL, the browser attempts to send the data from the form to the server. Assuming that the ACTION attribute points to a valid and working CGI program, the program will accept the data and begin to process it.

Finally, the METHOD=get attribute specifies one of two common methods for transferring data from the browser to the server (the other common method is POST). See Chapter 2, "Web Servers and CGI at Work," for more information on the GET and POST methods.

Specifying Form Controls

The whole purpose of a form is to display a form control—like a push button or text box—and this is where the <INPUT> tag comes in. The <INPUT> tag is used to create most of, but not all, the controls used in a form. Controls created using the <INPUT> tag are the following:

- *check box*. Selects or deselects an option
- *button*. Creates a push button with any text on it

- *submit.* Creates a special "Submit" button to submit the form to the server
- *reset.* Creates a special "Reset" button to return the controls to their default values
- *text.* Creates a text entry box to enter a line of text
- *hidden.* Creates a hidden text field that can contain data but does not appear in the browser
- *password.* Creates a text entry box for storing a password; text the user types does not appear in the box
- *image.* Creates an "image button" that when clicked submits the form and passes the X/Y coordinates of the mouse to the server

Except for the reset and submit types, form controls support these optional attributes:

- Check box and radio
  - *NAME.* Name of the control
  - *VALUE.* Unique value for control when form is submitted
  - *CHECKED.* Initial checked state
- Push button
  - *NAME.* Name of the control
  - *VALUE.* Text of the button
- Text, password, hidden
  - *NAME.* Name of the control
  - *VALUE.* Initial text
  - *SIZE.* Width of the text box
  - *MAXLENGTH.* Maximum allowable characters
- Image (not often used)
  - *NAME.* Name of the control
  - *SRC.* Source for image

A Simple Form Example

The following example creates a text box and a Submit button.

```
<FORM NAME="myform" ACTION="http://mydomain.com/cgibin/form.cgi" METHOD=get>
<INPUT TYPE="text" NAME="textbox" VALUE="">
<INPUT TYPE="submit">
</FORM>
```

Figure 5.1 shows how this form appears in a browser such as Netscape Navigator. Pressing the Submit button submits the form, which sends whatever text was typed into the text box to the assigned URL (in this case, a program named form.cgi located in the cgibin directory at http://mydomain.com/).

Note the attributes used with the <INPUT> tags. The first tag defines a text box, using TYPE="text." The text box is given a name, so that it can be identified by the CGI program running on the computer, in case there are other controls in the

Figure 5.1 Little HTML coding is required to make a fairly complex-looking form.

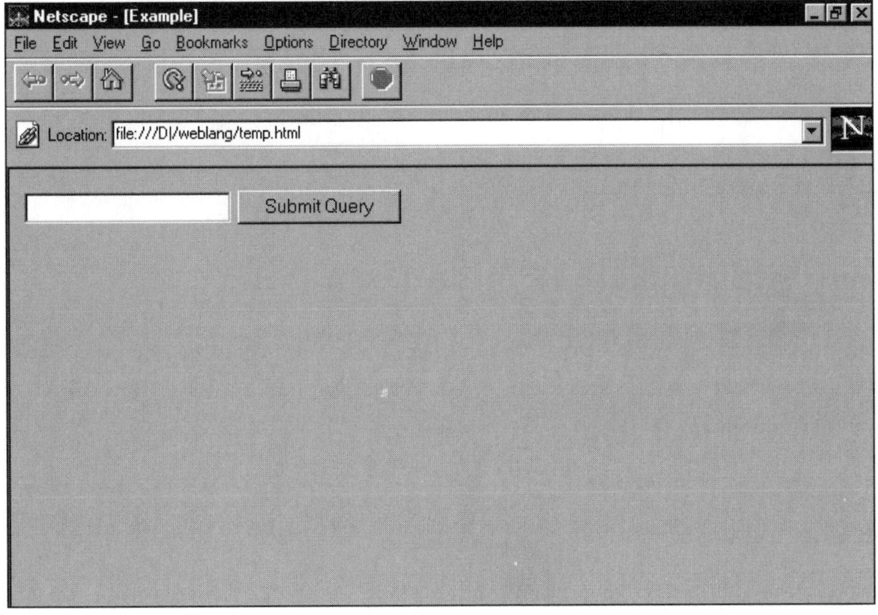

NOTE Most browsers (including Netscape Navigator and Microsoft Internet Explorer) allow you to include just a single text box to create a workable form. When you press the Enter key the browser interprets that as a Submit request.

form. In this case, the name of the lone text box is "textbox." Of course, you are free to use any name, but short names, without special characters or spaces, are preferred.

The VALUE attribute serves a special purpose for the text box. As shown in the example above, the VALUE is specified as "", which means blank. When the form first appears, the text box will be empty. If you want the text box to be initially filled when you display the form, you can specify text for the VALUE attribute, and that text will appear already in the box. For example, if you want the text box to contain the words "Type something here," you'd write the <INPUT> tag as:

```
<INPUT TYPE="text" NAME="textbox" VALUE="Type something here">
```

NOTE When the form is submitted the CGI program reads the VALUE attribute of the text box. If the user doesn't type anything, then the VALUE of the text box will be blank.

Unlike the text box, the submit button does not require any additional attributes (however, if you wish you may use the VALUE= attribute to change the default "Submit" text on the button to something else of your choosing).

Understanding Name/Value Data Pairs

The main purpose of an HTML form is to collect data from the user and pass that data to the server when the form is submitted. Basically, the data takes the following route (see Figure 5.2.):

1. User enters data into form.
2. User clicks Submit button.
3. Browser records data in form and contacts server at the URL listed for ACTION attribute of the form.

Figure 5.2 The route of the data sent from browser to server.

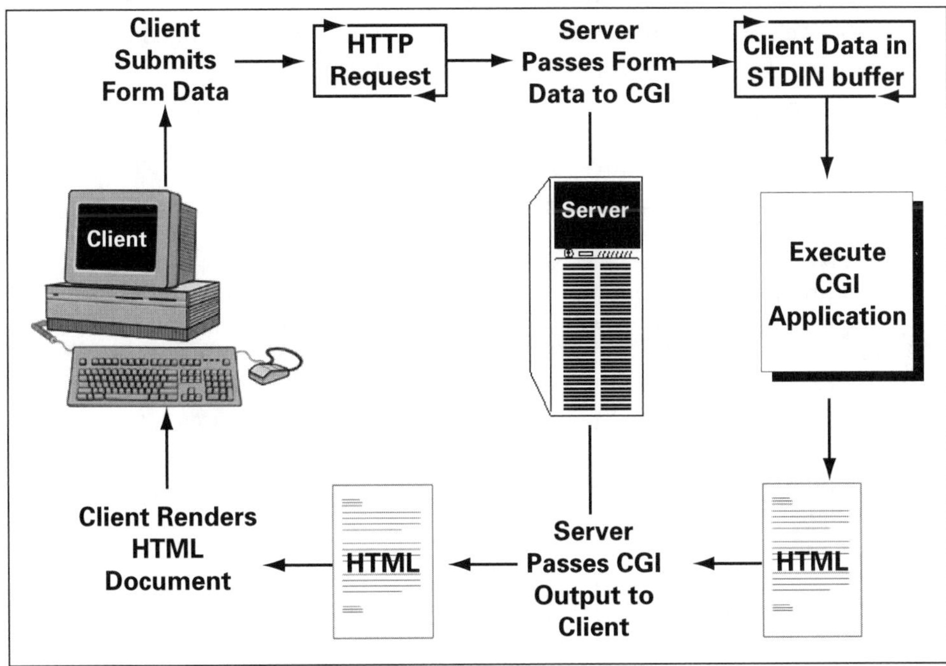

4. Server is contacted; browser passes data to server.
5. Server stores data received by form in environment variables.
6. Server activates CGI program specified in URL for ACTION attribute.
7. CGI program retrieves data in environment variables.
8. CGI program processes form data.

The CGI program receives the data from the form in what's known as data pairs: The first part of the pair is the name of the control on the form. The second part of the pair is the value of the control. For example, suppose you've submitted a form with a single text box to a CGI program. This text box is named "phoneno," as specified by the NAME attribute in the <INPUT> tag. You type "555-1212" in the text box. The CGI program therefore receives the following data pair for the form:

```
phoneno=555-1212
```

It is then up to the CGI program to split the data pair into something meaningful. This is actually pretty easy to do, as you'll see in the upcoming chapters for each of the Web programming languages. You need only write a program that looks for the = (equal) sign. The portion from the start of the string up to the = sign is the name of the control; the portion after the equal sign and to the end of the string is the value of the control.

> **NOTE** Retrieving data from server environment variables and splitting up the name/value pairs is so common in Web programming that you'll find plenty of ready-made routines for just this purpose. You can simply use the routine in your own program whenever you need to process form data. Such routines are provided for the chapters on Perl, UNIX shell scripts, and C/C++. You'll also find plenty of ready-made name/value "parsers" in various script repositories on the Web. See Chapter 19 for more information on finding and using script repositories, and make sure you check out sources.htm on the CD-ROM for the latest URLs.

Using Password and Hidden Text Boxes

The HTML syntax for password and hidden text boxes is identical to that for regular text boxes; however, the uses of these two form controls are completely different.

Password text boxes display a string of asterisks—******—as you type text into them. Though the user's entry is displayed as a string of asterisks in the browser, it is received as standard by the server. The asterisks displayed when typing are supposed to make it harder for anyone to look over your shoulder and watch you enter your secret password. Of course, this only makes a difference when the form is filled out in public—something few people actually do.

Hidden text boxes are not shown on the screen, but instead are meant to store information for the server. A typical use of the hidden text box is in shopping cart applications. As a user adds an item to his or her shopping cart, the server uses the hidden text boxes to store data about those items. When the user reaches the "checkout stand" and is ready to pay for the order, the server reads back the contents of the hidden fields and uses that to display the items ordered and calculate the total.

Using Radio Buttons

Radio buttons allow the user to choose one—and only one—item from a group. A typical use of a group of radio buttons is to ask for an exclusive response, such as the means of payment for an order (credit card, check, and so forth) Because there can only be one payment type specified, the radio buttons ensure that only the selected payment type is shown as selected.

Radio buttons are always used in a group of two or more. There is a practical limit of no more than 8 to 10 radio buttons per group—any more than that and the form becomes too difficult to follow. (If you do need the user to choose from among more than 8 or 10 items, use a select list, as detailed later in this chapter.) An example of how this form looks in the browser is shown in Figure 5.3.

Figure 5.3 Radio buttons allow the user to choose one item, and one item only, from a list.

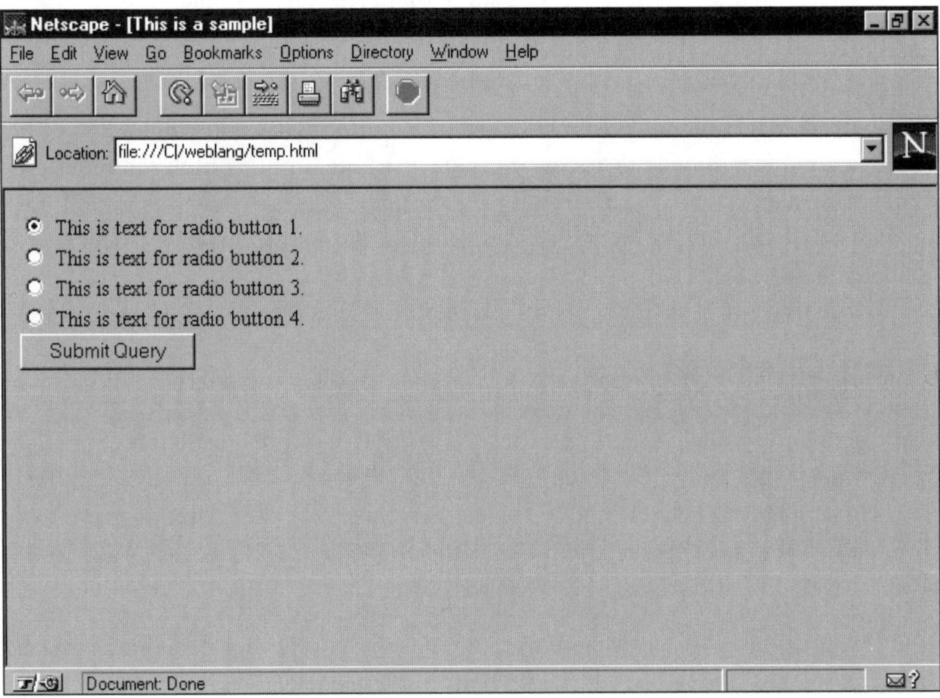

```
<FORM NAME="myform" ACTION="http://mydomain.com/cgibin/form.cgi" METHOD=get>
<INPUT TYPE="radio" NAME="rad" VALUE="1" CHECKED>
This is text for radio button 1.<BR>
<INPUT TYPE="radio" NAME="rad" VALUE="2">
This is text for radio button 2.<BR>
<INPUT TYPE="radio" NAME="rad" VALUE="3">
This is text for radio button 3.<BR>
<INPUT TYPE="radio" NAME="rad" VALUE="4">
This is text for radio button 4.<BR>
<INPUT TYPE="submit">
</FORM>
```

Four radio buttons are defined here, but note that the name for all four is the same. When the form is submitted, only the number of the radio button—from 1 to 4—is of interest to the CGI program. For example, if the third radio button is selected, the CGI program will receive the value rad=3, which means button 3 is selected for the rad radio button group.

There is no rule that says you are limited to only one radio button group per form. You may add as many groups as you wish (keep it reasonable, of course!). Merely provide a different NAME attribute for each group.

In the above example, the optional CHECKED attribute is used for the first radio button. When the form is first loaded, this button will be initially selected. It's usually a good idea to include the CHECKED attribute on one of the radio buttons; it does not need to be the first button in the group. Of course, only one radio button may be selected at any one time, so only one radio button may be given the CHECKED attribute.

Using Check Boxes

Check boxes are similar to radio buttons in that they indicate a selection choice by the user. But unlike radio buttons, the setting of a check box is not designed to be exclusive among other check boxes. You can have just one check box or many in a form, and all the check boxes are independent of one another. You may select and deselect any or all of the check boxes as you wish.

Check boxes use a similar syntax to radio buttons, except that the name for each check box should be unique (with radio buttons the name is the same for all buttons in the group). Here's an example, using four check boxes (shown in Figure 5.4):

```
<FORM NAME="myform" ACTION="http://mydomain.com/cgibin/form.cgi" METHOD=get>
<INPUT TYPE="checkbox" NAME="chk1" CHECKED>Checbox 1.<BR>
<INPUT TYPE="checkbox" NAME="chk2" >Checbox 2.<BR>
<INPUT TYPE="checkbox" NAME="chk3" CHECKED>Checbox 3.<BR>
<INPUT TYPE="checkbox" NAME="chk4" >Checbox 4.<BR>
<INPUT TYPE="submit">
</FORM>
```

In this example, the four check boxes are named chk1 through chk4. The optional CHECKED attribute is used with boxes 1 and 3.

When this form is submitted to the server, the browser will supply setting data about the check boxes by specifying the name of the box, followed by an equal sign, then a 0 or a 1 (0 means the box is not set; 1 means it is). For example, if boxes 1 and 4 are selected when the form is submitted, the server receives the following:

```
chk1=on
chk4=on
```

If the name of a check box is not returned it is assumed to be off.

Figure 5.4 Check boxes allow the user to specify options.

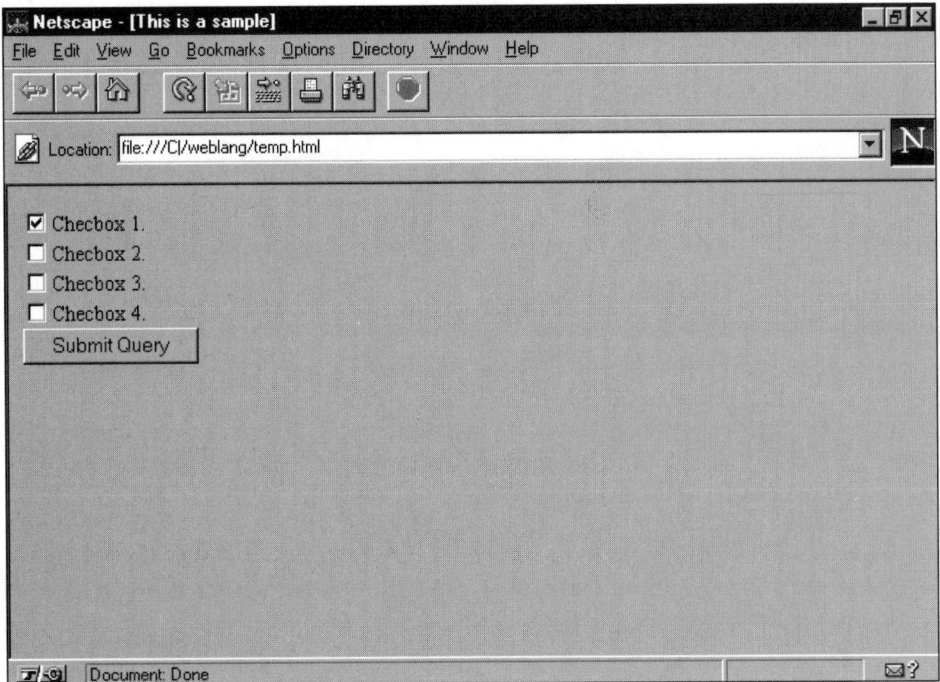

Using Select Lists

A select list presents options in a convenient scrolling list. The options can appear in a "drop-down" list where only one item is shown unless the user clicks on the list with the mouse. Or the options can appear in a list of almost any size. The size can be dictated by the HTML writer. Scroll bars appear on the right of the list if there are more options than can be shown at one time. The list also allows for single selection or multiple selection. The attributes for a select list are as follows:

- *NAME.* Name of list
- *SIZE.* Size of list (number of rows to display)
- *MULTIPLE.* Specifies multiple choice

One or more <OPTION> tags are placed in a selection list. The <OPTION> tags use the following attributes:

- *SELECTED.* Default selection
- *VALUE.* Value of item when form is submitted

The following example displays a selection list with four items (see Figure 5.5 for an example):

```
<SELECT NAME="selectlist" SIZE=4>
<OPTION SELECTED VALUE=1>This is item 1
<OPTION VALUE=2>This is item 2
<OPTION VALUE=3>This is item 3
<OPTION VALUE=4>This is item 4
</SELECT>
```

This list appears with all four items shown because the SIZE of the list is specified as 4.

- Specifying no size or specifying a SIZE of 1 makes the list appear as a drop down box (see Figure 5.6).
- Specifying a SIZE of 2 or 3 makes the list appear with scroll bars because there are more items in the list than can be shown at once.
- Specifying a SIZE of more than 4 displays a list box with extra white space because there aren't enough items to fill the list.

Figure 5.5 With SIZE=4 the list displays four items.

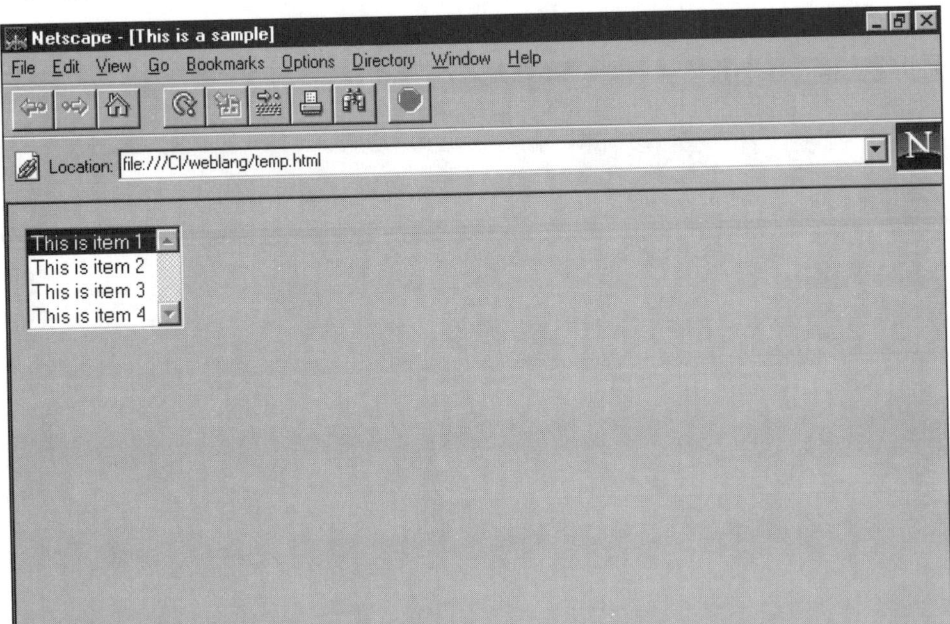

Note the SELECTED attribute used in the example above. This causes the item to be initially selected when the form first loads. If a SELECTED attribute is not provided the list appears without an item already selected. If the list is the drop-down type, no text will appear in the box. This is usually undesirable, so it's a good idea to include the SELECTED attribute.

> **NOTE** It is customary in HTML design to size the select list to accommodate the number of items in the list, when there are no more than five or six items in the list. If there are more items using a drop-down list is customary.

As stated above, <SELECT> lists can be single-selection or multiple-selection. The default is single-selection: Only one item can be selected at a time. When the form is submitted to the Web server, the browser sends the following data for the SELECT list:

```
Name_of_list=value
```

Figure 5.6 With SIZE=1 the list displays one item, and the list appears as a drop-down box.

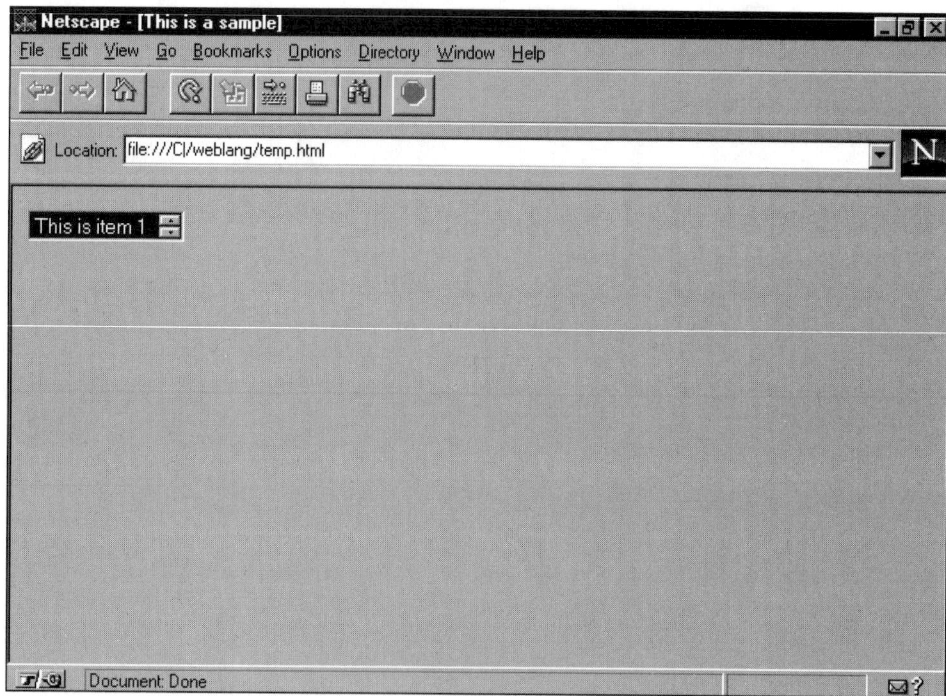

In the above example, the name of the list is selectlist, and the VALUE attributes of the list items are numbered 1 through 4. If the third item is selected, the browser sends the following:

```
selectlist=3
```

There is no reason why you have to use numbers for the VALUE attributes. A common practice is to duplicate the list item text (the text that follows each <OPTION> tag) as the text for the VALUE attribute. If this approach is taken, be sure to enclose the VALUE text in quotes, as follows:

```
<SELECT NAME="selectlist" SIZE=4>
<OPTION SELECTED VALUE="This is item 1">This is item 1
<OPTION VALUE="This is item 2">This is item 2
<OPTION VALUE="This is item 3">This is item 3
```

```
<OPTION VALUE="This is item 4">This is item 4
</SELECT>
```

In this case, the browser sends the following for the selection list when the form is submitted (in this example we'll again assume the third item in the list is selected):

```
selectlist=This is item 3
```

Multiple-selection lists are created simply by adding the MULTIPLE attribute to the <SELECT> tag, as in:

```
<SELECT NAME="selectlist" MULTIPLE SIZE=4>
```

This permits more than one item to be selected at once. The user can select and deselect items by clicking on them with the mouse. When the form is submitted, the browser sends one or more data pairs for each selected item. For example, if the user selects the second and fourth item in the example list, the browser sends these data pairs:

```
selectlist=This is item 2
selectlist=This is item 4
```

Using Text Areas

Text areas are similar to regular text boxes, except in a text area you can enter more than one line. Depending on the attributes you use, the text will automatically wrap as it reaches the right side of the text box. Or, the user can press the Enter key to begin a new line.

The <TEXTAREA> tag creates a multiple-line text box. There are three standard attributes for the textarea control:

- *NAME*. Names the control
- *ROWS*. The height of the control, in lines
- *COLS*. The width of the control, in characters

The <TEXTAREA> tag is always used with its end tag, which is </TEXTAREA>. Text that you wish to appear initially in the text box can be placed between these tags. Formatting, including new lines, is retained. Example (see Figure 5.7):

Figure 5.7 Use a text area to allow the user to enter large amounts of text.

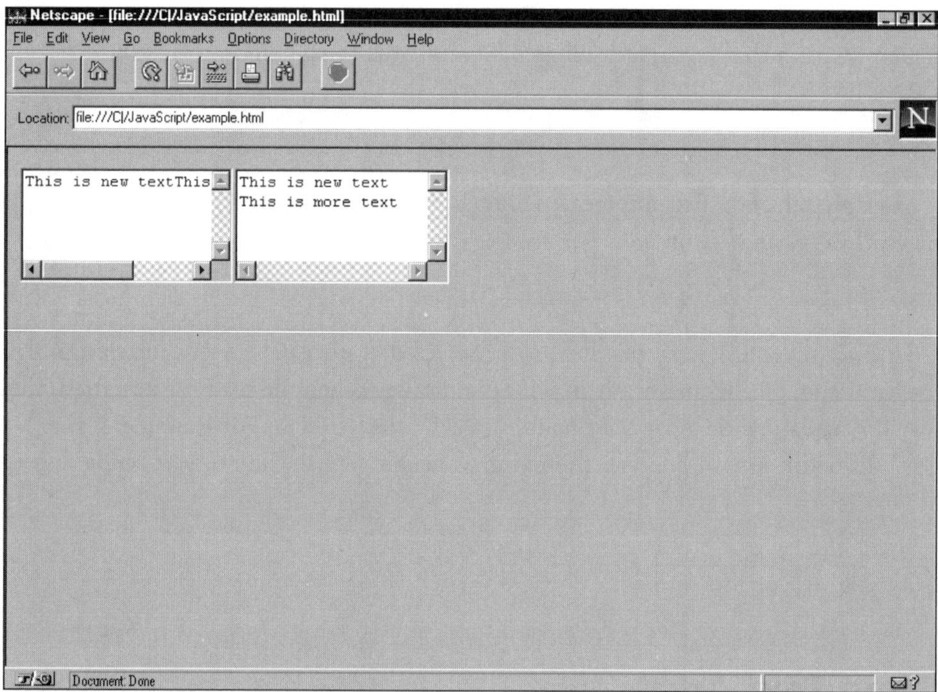


```
<TEXTAREA NAME="textarea" ROWS=6 COLS=40>
This is default text
</TEXTAREA>
```

Be wary of not using the ROWS and COLS attributes because the default size for the text area is too small to be of much use as a multiple-line entry box. For best results, the box should have no fewer than four or five lines and be at least 25 to 30 characters (COLS) wide.

Text areas behave the same as text boxes when data is received by the server. The name associated with the <TEXTAREA> tag is followed by the text entered into the text area box. For example, if the user types, "This is a test," and the <TEXTAREA> control is named "textarea," the data returned to the server is:

```
textarea=This is a test
```

Chapter

6

Choosing a Programming Language

Perhaps the largest obstacle facing a Web programmer is choosing the right language for the job. Not only must the language fit the job, but the language must fit the programmer. Compounding the problem is that, in many cases, a given problem has many possible solutions, and it's not uncommon to combine solutions to arrive at the best possible outcome.

This chapter reviews the major language choices available to Web programmers, including Perl, Java, JavaScript, VBScript, C/C++, and UNIX shell languages. You'll discover the strengths and weaknesses of each language, the jobs they are best suited for, and how to reasonably "share the load" by combining the languages when needed.

NOTE Some programming languages are not covered in this chapter, or in this book, because they either are too specialized or have not yet become commonplace in the Web programming circle. This does not mean these languages are not well suited for Web programming tasks; simply it means that other languages have already become adopted standards. Keep in mind that change on the Internet comes swiftly and that a reasonably obscure language today may be the number one choice of tomorrow.

Programming Choices—An Overview

Most tasks used for Web programming involve CGI. As CGI is just a program running on a computer, it stands to reason that any programming language that runs on the server can be used to support CGI.

On UNIX servers—the most common on the Web as of this writing—it's not unusual to find CGI programs written using a shell language, which is similar to a DOS batch file. Such CGI programs are more accurately called *scripts* or *shell scripts* because they are not self-running programs; rather, they require another program on the computer to operate. One advantage of shell scripts for Web programs is that if you're already familiar with a UNIX shell ("sh" and "bash" are the most common), you know most of what you need to write a Web program. Because the Web was begun on UNIX machines, operated by UNIX aficionados, it's no wonder so many UNIX shell scripts are used for Web programming tasks.

Another popular CGI programming language for UNIX is Perl. Perl is not a simple language, but it isn't a difficult one, either. It is now often favored by CGI programmers because it offers extensive string handling functions. Like a shell script, Perl does not build stand-alone programs. It needs an external *Perl interpreter* program to run.

And, of course, UNIX supports CGI scripts written in the C language. C is favored in some circles because it offers a great deal of speed, power, and flexibility, and it is reasonably portable. A C program written for a UNIX computer has a fair chance of running under DOS or Windows.

While UNIX remains the most common operating system for the Internet and the World Wide Web, it is by no means the only one. Other operating systems include SunOS (from Sun Microsystems), Windows 3.1, Windows 95, Windows NT, MacOS, and even DOS; see Table 6.1. Each of these operating systems offers its own variations for writing CGI programs. SunOS is UNIX-like and so uses a lot of UNIX programs. The Windows platforms can run a variation of the UNIX Perl language, as well as programs written in Visual Basic or C, and the MacOS generally uses AppleScript. DOS can run CGI programs of just about any flavor, including those written with old-fashioned DOS batch files and Basic!

Table 6.1 Platforms and Languages Used for CGI

Platform	Common Languages Used for CGI
UNIX	Perl
	Shell (e.g., *sh* or *bash*)
	C/C++
Windows*	Perl
	C/C++
	WinCGI (includes Visual Basic and Delphi)
DOS	Perl
	C/C++
	Batch files
Macintosh	AppleScript

* Includes Windows 95, Windows 97, and NT

Approaches to Running Server Programs

CGI is merely one method of running client-initiated programs on a server. (For background, a client-initiated program is one that is started at the request of a client; a server-initiated program is one that is run from the server, for the server. An example of a server-initiated program is a "hit statistics" application that collates the requests for each URL at a site and displays a summary.)

There are, in fact, three primary methods of running programs on a Web server, and all go by strange acronyms: CGI, SSI, and API.

CGI (Common Gateway Interface)

CGI is the most common approach to client-initiated programs. It uses a standardized method for passing data from the client to the server. A benefit of CGI is that nearly all Web servers support it, for all three primary server platforms (UNIX, Windows, and Macintosh). Most of the examples in this book revolve around CGI applications.

SSI (Server-Side Includes)

SSI provides a method of inserting data into an HTML document. Though SSI is often classified as a means to run programs, it actually offers greater flexibility than that. In all cases, server-side includes are placed as comments within an HTML document, such as:

```
<!-- #exec - example -->
```

Three of the most commonly used SSI directives are echo, include, and exec.

- *echo*. Display a server environment variable, such as the IP address of the client or the date as set on the server computer
- *include*. Place the entire contents of an HTML document within the main HTML document
- *exec*. Execute (run) a server program

Server-side includes are ideal when you wish to include dynamic elements in your HTML pages, such as a visit counter. A disadvantage to SSI is that not all servers support it. Another disadvantage is that SSI isn't generally as efficient as standard CGI. Some of the examples in this book rely on SSI programming.

API (Application Programmer's Interface)

APIs offer a proprietary means to interact with a server. API programs are designed to run under a given server, such as the Netscape Commerce server or Microsoft's IIS server, and are based on a set of programming commands that can be accessed using a compatible programming language.

API support is predominantly the domain of commercial Web servers (Netscape, Microsoft); the public domain Web servers such as Apache and NCSA rely instead on CGI applications. The API for Netscape server is known as NSAPI; the API for Microsoft servers is known MSAPI. The two APIs are different, so a program for one server will not work on the other, at least not without some revision.

An advantage of developing programs using the API is that the program is generally faster than a CGI-only version (this applies mainly to server-intensive applications, such as databases). The disadvantage is that APIs are not standardized. Change to a different server, and you must rewrite your programs—often from scratch. Because of its highly proprietary nature, this book lacks specific examples of API programming. If you choose to develop using an API you should consult the documentation provided by the Web server software publisher. Table 6.2 lists popular Web servers and the programming alternatives they support.

Table 6.2 Web Servers and Applications They Support

Server	Application	Supported
Apache*	CGI	X
	SSI	X
	API	
NCSA	CGI	X
	SSI	X
	API	
CERN	CGI	X
	SSI	**
	API	
Netscape /UNIX	CGI	X
	SSI	X
	API	X
Netscape/NT	CGI	X
	SSI	X
	API	X
Microsoft IIS	CGI	X
	SSI	
	API	X
WebStar	CGI	X
	SSI	
	API	X

* Applies to the public domain Apache Web server. The commercial Apache-SSL Web server supports additional features.

** SSI is supported under the CERN Web server through the fakessi.exe CGI program.

Programming Concepts You Should Know

New to programming and programming concepts? Before getting too involved with a discussion of the programming choices available to you, be sure to read this short section on programming language principles. Note that programming basics—such as variables, expressions, and statements—are covered separately in Chapter 4.

Procedural versus Object-Oriented

These days programming languages are routinely classified into two camps: procedural versus object-oriented. These categories loosely describe the approach taken to create a program as well as the general structure of the program:

- A procedural program is the more classic of the two, and it is how computer programs have been written for years. The typical procedural program contains one or more lines of instructions (otherwise known as commands); each line is executed in turn by the program.
- An object-oriented program consists of self-contained modules, with each module consisting of one or more lines of instructions. In the typical object-oriented program, each module is activated by a specific "event," such as a mouse click or a key press.

In reality, both kinds of programming languages—procedural and object-oriented—tend to have elements of the other. For example, the individual modules of an object-oriented program usually consist of procedural code—programming instructions that tell the computer to do something, and in a specific order. And, procedural programs can also be written so that they act on external events, like mouse clicks and key presses. In fact, thousands of procedural programs written for the Windows operating system work in this manner.

The methods by which the modules of a program are created, used, and maintained are used to more completely differentiate object-oriented programs from procedural programs. In a true object-oriented programming language, the modules—more accurately called objects—are created under strict accordance with the rules of the language. These objects are designed to accept certain kinds of data and output certain kinds of data, using properties, methods, and events intrinsically related to each object. For example, one object may be designed to accept a value and round it out to the nearest whole number, and other object may be designed to accept text characters and convert them all to uppercase.

Examples of procedural languages used on the Web include Perl, C, and UNIX shell script. Examples of object-oriented languages used on the Web include C++ and Java.

Object-Based Languages: The Inbetweener

Similar to, but not the same as, an object-oriented programming language is the object-based language. An object-based language is part procedural and part object-oriented, using the advantages of each. An object-based language relies on premade objects for the bulk of its work. Whereas the object-oriented language requires the programmer to create and manage objects, much of the preliminary work has already been done with an object-based language.

Examples of object-based languages used on the Web include VBScript and JavaScript.

Interpreted versus Compiled

All programs are originally in a text form readable by humans. But computers can't read the way humans can. Programs must eventually be converted to a form more suitable for computer consumption. The point of this conversion differentiates computer languages into two categories: interpreted and compiled:

- In an interpreted language, the program is processed from the original human-readable version (called the "source") to the computer-readable version when the program is run. If the application contains errors, they are not discovered until the computer attempts to process the program.
- In a compiled language, the program is processed from its source-code version to a computer-readable version ahead of time. This process is called compiling. Major mistakes are identified during this compiling phase. The compiled version of the program is then fed to the computer, and the program is run.

Compiled applications are often preferred by programmers because they tend to be faster. With an interpreted language the computer must do extra processing to convert the program from its human source code to the computer-compatible version. This step is already done with a compiled program, and, therefore, the program executes faster.

On the other hand, compiled programs are generally considered more difficult to write because creating such a program requires more steps. The program is written and initially compiled. Errors, if any, are identified, and the program is rewritten accordingly, after which it is recompiled. This process is repeated until the program is finished. An interpreted program, on the other hand, can be written and tested interactively.

Examples of interpreted languages used on the Web include JavaScript, VBScript, Perl, and all UNIX shell scripts. Examples of compiled languages used on the Web include Java and C.

Strong versus Loose Data Typing

Programming languages deal with different types of data, such as numbers or characters. Data typing is the automatic or manual categorization of data types for use in the program. Some programming languages—namely Java, C, and C++—require the programmer to define the type of data you wish to use. This technique, called *strong data typing*, requires more effort for the programmer but helps improve the performance and reliability of the finished program.

The bulk of the programming languages used on the Web, including JavaScript, VBScript, Perl, and all UNIX shell scripts, automatically detect the type of data being used. This approach, called *loose* (or *weak*) *data typing*, is easier on the programmer but makes the finished program somewhat less efficient. And when used carelessly, loose data typing can cause some programming errors.

String Management

As you saw in Chapter 4, a string is a collection of text characters that follow one after the other—like beads on a string. Because the bulk of what Web programs do is to manipulate strings in one way or another, the string management features of a Web programming language are very important.

In some languages, namely C and C++, strings are treated as extensions to the basic program variable: Each variable contains a separate character of the string. This makes string management much more difficult because it requires extra effort to access all of the characters in the string, and even requires the programming to first set aside enough space in the computer's memory to hold the string. On the plus side, such low-level control of strings allows the programmer more flexibility in working with strings.

Many Web programmers prefer a language with built-in, low-level string management, where such tasks as memory allocation are automatically handled. These languages include Perl, UNIX shell scripts, JavaScript, and most others. Even the Java programming language, though based on C++ syntax, uses built-in string management, to make the language easier to use by programmers and less susceptible to misuse by hackers.

String management features also extend to built-in commands for such tasks as converting all characters to uppercase or lowercase, searching for characters within a string, combining two or more strings into one, and more. Of all the languages used for Web programming, Perl arguably offers the most widely useful set of string manipulation tools.

Graphics versus Text-Based

On the Web, programming languages are always used to produce text output. That's because the graphics portion of a Web page is taken care of by the browser, such as Netscape Navigator or Microsoft Internet Explorer. Many programs used on the Web were originally created to provide graphics output, and some—such as Microsoft Visual Basic and Borland Delphi—were even made to present a graphical user interface, like that used in Windows or the X Window system.

These graphics or visual display capabilities are left unused in Web programming, except for a few esoteric applications. Rather, for use on the Web, all languages are used to create data files (text or special data types, such as images or sounds), which will eventually be combined in a Web browser for display to the user. As you work with languages in the Web you can safely ignore the visual display features offered by the language and concentrate on those capabilities of the language for creating and processing data, most commonly text.

Note that while a wide variety of languages are used on the Web—some more than others—only a few languages are truly well suited for the bulk of Web programming. For example, Microsoft Visual Basic can create Web-based applications, but its forte is in helping you to create Windows-based user interfaces, like dialog boxes, quickly. The Perl language, on the other hand, is a poor choice as a language for speedy Windows application development. But on the upside, Perl is specifically designed to manipulate text and is a perfect contender for Web work. That's one of the reasons Perl is so popular.

Core Language

Literally hundreds of programming languages have been developed over the last several decades, but many of them are based on previous languages that have caught the fancy of the programming community. Two such languages hold the record as being the "grandparents" of languages that followed—Basic and C:

- Basic is a programming language popularized by Microsoft and used in almost all of its consumer-oriented products. Basic is renowned for being easy to learn, but it has the reputation of producing slow programs.
- C is the primary language used by professional programmers. It can be difficult to learn and use, but it is known for producing fast and efficient programs.

The majority of programming languages used on the Web are based on either Basic or C. In the Basic camp are VBScript and Visual Basic (the latter not covered in this book)—not surprisingly, both of these languages were developed by Microsoft. In the C camp are JavaScript, Java, and C/C++. Perl uses its own unique structure, and the UNIX shell scripts (of which there are three in common use) use both usual and unusual programming syntax.

If you have prior experience in a programming language such as Basic or C, you may want to consider a Web programming language that uses the same or a similar language base. For example, if you are already comfortable with C, many of the fundamentals of Java and JavaScript will already be familiar to you.

Learning Curve

Not all programming languages are equally easy to learn. Some, like C++ and Java, can be very difficult to learn, especially if you have little or no prior programming experience. If you're just starting out, it's a good idea to pick one of the easier programming languages, such as Perl or one of the UNIX shell scripts. (Exception: the *csh* shell scripting language borrows a lot from C and is more difficult to master because of it.)

Language Cross-Reference Chart

Refer to Table 6.3 as a cross-reference to the Web's most commonly used programming languages. This table provides the program type, compilation model (interpreted or compiled), the data typing model, the level string of string management tools, and other important aspects of each language. See the sections above for more information on each category of the chart.

Table 6.3 Web Programming Languages

Language	Program Type	Compilation Model	Data Typing	String Management	Primary Application	Core Language	Learning Curve
Perl	Procedural	Interpreted	Loose	Excellent	Text	N/A	Fair
UNIX shell	Procedural	Interpreted	Loose	Fair	Text	N/A	Low
C	Procedural	Compiled	Strong	Poor	Text	C	Very high
C++	Object-oriented	Compiled	Strong	Fair	Text	C	Very high
Java	Object-oriented	Compiled	Strong	Excellent	Text	C	Very high
JavaScript	Object-based	Interpreted	Loose	Good	Text	C	Fair
VBScript	Object-based	Interpreted	Loose	Good	Text	Basic	Fair
Visual Basic	Object-based	Compiled	Loose	Good	Visual	Basic	High
Delphi	Object-based	Compiled	Loose	Good	Visual	Pascal	High

Perl: A Web Programmer's Favorite

The Perl language was originally designed for the UNIX operating system, intended to be an all-around replacement for UNIX shell languages (*sh*, *Korn*, and others). Perl is an interpreted language, so it doesn't need a separate compilation step. The language itself is generally easy to learn, though it does have its arcane and obscure elements. Perl is amazingly flexible and capable once you learn its syntax.

Perl is perhaps the most popular language used on the Web because of its string management capabilities. Perl makes it fairly easy to inspect strings, tear them apart, and put them back together again. Perl's loose data typing relieves the programmer from having to specify (also called "declare") the type of data to be used.

Though Perl was originally developed for the UNIX operating system, it is now available on all major operating systems used by Web servers, including Windows 3.1, Windows 95, and Windows NT, DOS, Macintosh, and even OS/2. A Perl program written for one operating system has a fair chance of running on another, though some difference between Perl versions does exist.

Perhaps the biggest benefit of Perl is the amount of free and nearly free examples available for it. Enter "perl+CGI" as a keyword in an AltaVista or Yahoo! search, for example, and hundreds—if not thousands—of listings appear. (See sources.htm, on the CD-ROM that accompanies this book, for links to Alta Vista, Yahoo!, and other search engines on the Web.)

UNIX Shell Scripts: Easy and Always Available

UNIX uses a command shell to allow user input and provide visual feedback (in MS-DOS, a similar command shell is used to allow for user entry at the command prompt). The UNIX shells—the three primary ones go by the names *sh*, *Korn*, and *csh*—provide for automated control via a script (again, in the MS-DOS world, this is equivalent to a batch file). Unix shell scripts were among the first used by Web programmers for tasks such as CGI because they are relatively easy to implement and always available.

Not all Web servers make all three primary UNIX shells available to users. Typically, only one shell is routinely available. You use the shell that has been installed on your UNIX Web server.

Probably the most common UNIX shell used today on Web servers is a public domain variant of *sh*, called *bash*, for Bourne Again shell. (The original *sh* shell is sometimes known as the Bourne shell, after its developer; the Bourne Again shell is an obvious play on words.) *Bash* offers the same functionality as the original *sh* shell, but it also adds a number of useful features, most of which are user-interface related and aren't used in Web programming work.

The two other UNIX shells (*Korn* and *csh*) are waning in popularity for Web programs. In fact, you rarely see example programs written using *Korn* or *csh*. For this reason, the bulk of Part II of this book is devoted to discussing UNIX shell scripting using the *bash* shell. Short reference sections on *Korn* and *csh* are included for your convenience.

C and C++: For Heavy-Duty Programming

C and its object-oriented cousin, C++, are the primary languages used to create commercial-grade applications, such as word processors and electronic spreadsheet programs. The major advantage of both C and C++ is that the finished program is very fast. The major disadvantage is that programs are fairly difficult to write in either C and C++ (they are more difficult to write in C++ than in C).

Because C and C++ are so popular in the creation of applications programs, it's no surprise the languages are also used to create programs for the Web. Both C and C++ can be used to create efficient Web programs, useful for applications such as database search engines that need to be fast.

Client-Side Programming: Another Way to Skin the Cat

CGI (as well as SSI and API) applications involve writing programs that run on the server. These are so-called server-side programs and require a great deal of access privileges to the server. Not all Web publishers have such access privileges; because of security worries (most of them unfounded) many users are restricted from deploying CGI, SSI, and API applications. To the rescue: client-side programming.

Client-side programming uses applications that run in the client, that is, the browser. As of this writing there are two primary client-side programming languages, JavaScript and VBScript.

JavaScript is the brainchild of Netscape, and it is fully supported in Netscape Navigator 2.0 and later. VBScript is the creation of Microsoft, and it is the main scripting language built into Microsoft's Internet Explorer 3.0 and later. Internet Explorer 3.0 also supports a form of JavaScript (under the generic term "Jscript"), but the support is not complete as of this writing. With JavaScript and

VBScript, the program code is included as part of the HTML document provided by the server.

Client-side programming is valuable on a number of fronts:

- It provides a means to create dynamic HTML pages without requiring programming access to the server.
- No server interaction is required, beyond sending the HTML document to the browser. This reduces the load on the server.
- It's generally easier to write a client-side program because the language is simpler than Perl, C, or other typical programming languages used with server-side programming.

> **NOTE** Both JavaScript and VBScript can also be used for server-side programs, though this use is not nearly as common as client-side programs. Netscape offers server-side JavaScript support in its latest Web server software; Microsoft offers server-side VBScript support in its latest Web server software.
>
> The advantage of using JavaScript or VBScript in a server-side program is familiarity. If you already know client-side JavaScript or VBScript, writing a server-side program in these languages involves learning only a few more commands. However, the same restrictions to server-side programming apply to server-side JavaScript and VBScript. If you are restricted from creating programs that run on your server, you are restricted from writing them in any language, including JavaScript or VBScript.
>
> Conversely, because client-side JavaScript and VBScript applications don't run on a server, you are generally free to include these in your HTML pages.

Java: In a Class of Its Own

Java is another form of client-side programming, but its capabilities and complexities take it beyond JavaScript and VBScript. Whereas JavaScript and VBScript are primarily intended to enhance the HTML content of a page, Java can be used to create and manipulate almost any kind of content imaginable.

Recall that JavaScript and VBScript are interpreted languages, meaning that the browser—Netscape Navigator or Internet Explorer, for example—receives the text of the program in the same form as the author wrote it. From there, the browser "interprets" the program and figures out how to run it.

Conversely, Java is a compiled language, meaning that a special compiler first condenses the program you write, and the condensed version is the one that the browser receives. While compiled programs are more difficult to write (the program must be recompiled for each change, and mistakes take longer to fix), they run faster on the browser.

Java is also designed to be more capable than either JavaScript or VBScript and is that much more complex because of it. Java supports libraries of functions that a programmer can access, and learning about these functions adds to the learning curve of Java. Once mastered, Java provides for a great deal of flexibility and control, allowing you to add features to the browser that didn't exist before.

Windows CGI

Even though Delphi and Visual Basic are not detailed in this book, they are worthy of mention as possible choices for Web programming work. Both Delphi and Visual Basic are designed to be used with the Windows operating system. Though these programming languages are typically used for creating full Windows applications with user interfaces, they can also be applied to the tasks most often associated with CGI Web programming work, such as generating HTML text or creating a counter graphic to show the number of visitors to a site.

The standard destination for the output of a Delphi or Visual Basic program is the Windows display manager, which is a portion of Windows that controls what appears on the monitor. Programming on the Web does not involve displaying an application on the user's screen; rather, it involves sending data to a browser, which in turn has complete control over the presentation of that data.

To use Delphi and Visual Basic for Web work, you must use them with a translation program that captures the normal output (typically text, but also binary data) generated from the program and routes it to the Web server. From the Web server, the data can be transmitted to the user's browser. The generic term for this translation program is WinCGI.

Because WinCGI is an extra layer between the program and the server, it's not unusual for Delphi and Visual Basic to be slower than their C/C++ or even Perl counterparts. Still, if you already know Delphi or Visual Basic, you can save time and effort by using one of these languages to program for the Web.

Suitability to Task

Although there are a number of Web languages to choose from, none is the perfect choice for all applications. Programming languages excel in certain areas, and it's a good idea to match the language with the application whenever possible. You wouldn't, for example, think of driving the kids to school in an 18-wheel tractor trailer. Instead, you'd use the family station wagon, a vehicle better suited for transporting people.

Similarly, you'd be hard pressed to justify learning about and writing a 30-line program in C for a simple dynamic content script that displays "Good morning" or "Good evening," depending on the time of day. It can be done in just a few lines using JavaScript, a much easier language to master and use.

Suitability to task involves weighing all the pros and cons of a language for each common programming job. Table 6.4 lists a dozen common Web programming chores and compares the suitability to task for each of the primary Web languages. The suitability to task ratings take the following into account:

- *Integrated support.* The more a language offers as built-in commands the better, as opposed to using third-party libraries that you must add to provide extra functionality. Example: String management functions like those are required for any task that interacts with forms filled in by the user, making Perl an especially good contender, as it has strong built-in string management functions.

- *Ease of programming.* It's best to match the language to the task, so that you use the more complex languages for the jobs that require that complexity. Example: Dynamic page content displaying custom images (time of day, for instance) requires little complex programming. A user-scripting language such as JavaScript is better suited for this level of programming than C or Java.

- *Speed of execution.* Some tasks benefit from faster programming languages. Example: Large database systems require speed, making compiled C or C++ the better choice over an interpreted language such as Perl.

The scoring in the following table ranges from poor to excellent, using these three items as weighting factors. As you develop Web programs you will undoubtedly devise your own weighting factors, and you will develop customized suitability to task scores for the types of Web programming you do.

Considering Server Resources

Web pages depend on the smooth operation of your Web server. No doubt you've visited other people's pages, only to wait for minutes on end as the page loads. Some slow-loading pages are the result of "over design," where the page author uses files—especially image and sound—that are too large for conventional dial-up Internet access.

But not all slow-loading pages are the result of overzealous design. Often, the page contains limited text and small files. The culprit is the server. The computer is

Table 6.4 Suitability to Task Ratings

Task	Perl	UNIX shell	C/C++	Java	User-script
Dynamic page content:					
Custom greeting	Excellent	Good	Fair	Good	Excellent
Custom images	Excellent	Good	Fair	Good	Excellent
Random/custom links	Excellent	Good	Fair	Good	Excellent
Form processing, mailer	Excellent	Fair	Fair	Fair	Poor
Form processing, shopping cart	Excellent	Poor	Fair	Poor	Fair
Guestbook	Excellent	Fair	Fair	Poor	Poor
Search database (small)	Good	Fair	Good	Fair	Fair
Search database (large)	Fair	Poor	Excellent	Poor	Poor
Visit counter, text	Good	Good	Good	Poor	Poor
Visit counter, graphic	Good	Poor	Excellent	Poor	Poor
Server support software (spiders, indexers, statistics, etc.)	Good	Fair	Excellent	Poor	Poor

overtaxed and is unable to serve all of the pages to all of the users simultaneously connected.

There are three primary reasons why Web servers are overburdened:

- *Too many users.* The site is simply too popular to support all the users connected at once. The popular site doesn't even have to be yours if you share server space with other Web publishers. For example, it's not unusual to rent space on a Web server and be one of several dozen—or even several hundred—other tenants. Even though it may not be your site that is receiving all the hits, the one server must administer to all the sites.
- *High-bandwidth files.* Users alone are not the bane of a Web server. The biggest issue is the size of the files that are served. The larger the file, the more time the server must provide to any given user. Image files tend to be the number one cause of server bottlenecks (large Java applets and sound files come in a close second). A site with many large image files—say, over 10K each—can easily become overburdened as users request those images.
- *Heavy use of programs and scripts.* CGI and other programs can quickly sap the speed of any server. The larger and more complex the program, the more time the server allocates to complete it. Even though most Web server computers use a multitasking operating system (that is, UNIX or Windows NT), the server can do only one thing at a time. A program that hogs the server's CPU will steal time away from serving pages. This effect is most noticeable with server support programs (rather than simple CGI scripts that process forms), such as those that index a site or roam the Web indexing other people's sites.

Server slow-downs from program scripts is the topic of most interest to us. If you notice your Web server is not acting as sprightly as it should and you've already determined that the cause is not from the first two possibilities, you should consider investigating the efficiency of your server programs.

The efficiency of all Web servers diminishes when running CGI and other programs. Even small CGI programs can reduce the speed of a server. Each time a user submits a form to a CGI program, for example, the server must accept the data from the user, process it, start the CGI program, run the program, process the return data, and submit the finished result back to the user. The occasional CGI program does little harm to the average Web server because many Web servers have more idle time than processing time. However, multiply even one relatively simple form processing script by several hundred simultaneous users of a heavily trafficked site, and you get a better idea of the work load of such a server.

For this reason, you should strive for program efficiency whenever possible, especially if your site is heavily accessed. Extra care should be given to programs requiring extensive server interaction—databases primarily. The more efficient you can make such programs, the more easily your server will be able to process them. That makes your server run faster for all users.

When efficiency is paramount you should consider using a compiled language, such as C or C++, as these generally execute faster on any given server. Such languages are more difficult to learn and use, however, so you must balance the needs of your program and server with your programming knowledge.

Combining Programming Languages

Because no one programming language is ideal for all tasks, combining languages to take advantage of the best each has to offer is not unusual. For example, you might write a simple UNIX shell script that returns a value representing the number of people who have visited your site and combine that with a JavaScript client-side program that retrieves that value and displays a series of GIF images; one image for each digit of the count.

Combining programming languages gives you more flexibility because you can choose to exploit those facets of a language in which you're most interested. Perl is particularly handy for processing string input, for example, from a form. But as Perl is an interpreted language, it isn't as well suited for large and complex programs, such as a database engine that searches through hundreds of thousands of records. This is more the job of a program written in C.

There is no stopping you from writing the "front end" of a program in one language and the "back end" or working portion in another. In the previous example, you could use Perl to process the user's request via a form on your page, taking advantage of Perl's enhanced string management features. Once your Perl program has validated the user's response, it can pass the data to a C database program, which does the actual database lookup function.

There are many ways to combine languages. The exact combination will depend on your application, programming experience, and preference. Table 6.5 lists the tasks for which each of the primary Web programming languages are best suited. The list is by no means comprehensive or absolute, but it is a good starting point in determining which language is best suited for specific Web programming chores.

Table 6.5 Web Programming Languages and Their Best Uses

Language	Best Used for
Perl	Forms processing String-intensive applications
UNIX shell scripts	Simple forms processing Basic automation chores
C/C++	Graphic visit counters Database search engines Server support software (robots, etc.)
Java	Moderate-to-complex client-based applications (including graphics, sound, and animation)
User scripting	Quick scripting of moderate-sized client-side applications (less effective than Java for animation)

Chapter

7

Installing Your Web Program on a Server

Writing a Web program is only half the battle. The other half is getting that program onto your server. Problems arise because on many servers access is restricted for most users, and executable programs are not allowed, or they are not allowed except in certain directories of the server. In addition, servers that use the UNIX operating system require you to assign very specific "rights" to program files, which involves a step not necessary when uploading simple HTML-only documents.

We'll tackle the subject of uploading program files to a Web server in this chapter. Because file uploading in general is an extensive subject, we'll assume you already know how to connect to your Web site and upload files, whether you connect to your Web site via your company network or via a dial-up phone connection. Rather, this chapter will concentrate on what to do with the program file once it is on the server.

Where to Put the Web Program

In theory, a Web program can be placed in any location of a Web server. The directory used for holding programs is not really that important. The main issue is that the Web server can access the program. In practice, most Web servers restrict the directories that can contain Web programs. This is both a security issue and an administrative issue:

- On a security level, limiting Web programs to just one or two directories allows for easier protection of those directories. For example, the directories can be locked out so that only certain users can access them (in a typical Web server, access is allowed for a user called "nobody," which effectively means *everybody*!).
- On an administrative level, limiting Web programs to a given directory or two makes it easier to maintain the system. This is especially true if the Web server is shared by many users, which is the case with leased Web server space.

The standard directory for Web programs is cgibin, a name that has stuck from the first Web servers. The *cgi* part comes from the access method used by most Web programs—CGI. The *bin* part comes not from the word *bin* as a holding place, but rather from *binary*. In common parlance, the directory for CGI/Web programs is referred to as "CGI bin." That's how we will refer to the CGI/Web program directory throughout this chapter.

CGI Bins and Multiuser Web Servers

Leased Web space is becoming more and more common. With leased Web space, you lease (or rent) portion of the Web server for your own pages. Other people share space on the Web server with you. Everyone's material is kept separate, however, by using virtual home directories. Visitors to your pages never know you are sharing a Web server with other people.

Web servers that lease space to many users take three general approaches to CGI bins accessible to individual users:

- *Not allowed at all.* This actually is quite common, unfortunately. Many Web site administrators worry about security issues with user-supplied CGI programs, and they don't allow them unless they are inspected—usually for a fee—first.
- *Allowed in central CGI bin.* Some Web servers provide space for users' CGI programs in a common CGI bin, though this usually entails quite a few restrictions. Typically, users are not allowed to install the program in the CGI bin directory; that is left to the site administrators.
- *Allowed in individual user CGI bins.* An increasing number of leased Web servers allow for individual CGI bins. This is the best all-around scenario because it allows you direct access to your own CGI bin, usually without any restrictions about what you can place there and when (of course, you're still responsible for any program you upload that runs amok!).

In the last case, there are multiple CGI directories on one server, but users each have control over their own CGI bin. This means your programs will not interfere with anyone else's, and theirs will not interfere with yours.

Virtual Path versus Actual Path

Depending on how you've uploaded files to your server, you may or may not have encountered the concept of virtual paths versus actual paths. A *virtual path* is one that starts at the home directory for your specific Web site. This is the path users take to visit your Web path. For example, if your Web site is named mysite.com, and the page they want to take to the site is mypage.html, they'd enter the following URL in their browser to get to it: http://mysite.com/mypage.html.

The actual location in the Web server of your site, and the mypage.html document, is completely different from the URL someone specifies to view your page. The root directory of your site is located in your home directory, which is typically buried two, three, four, and even more directories underneath the server's root directory. Therefore, the actual path to mypage.html might be something like this: /web/users/mysite/mypage.html.

Individual CGI bins are almost always located off the user's home directory, not the server's root directory or some other directory. For example, if the CGI bin is named cgibin, then its actual path (assuming the above example) is: /web/users/mysite/cgibin/.

> **NOTE** The name of the CGI bin directory may or may not be cgibin. The name itself doesn't matter, only that the server knows executable programs are located within it.

This is the directory where you will place your CGI programs. To access those programs via the Web, you specify its virtual URL, which is http://mysite.com/cgibin/.

Understanding Acceptable Program Names

Acceptable filenames you give your Web programs depend on the type of server you use. Web servers that use the UNIX operating system usually don't much care what names you give to Web programs. Unlike Windows, the extension of a file is not always used to define its file type. Rather, under UNIX, its file type—whether document or executable—is determined by setting what's known as access rights (we'll get to these later in this chapter).

However, this doesn't mean you can give just any filename extension because most Web server software is set up to recognize only a set of extensions for CGI. This approach helps speed up the server, as it knows by extension what type of file it is dealing with. The typical filename extension used with UNIX servers is .cgi. Some UNIX servers also accept .pl, which is used for Perl scripts. And yet some other UNIX servers accept any extension—including no extension at all—for Web programs.

> **NOTE** Windows allows for filename extension association—an extension is associated with a given application. For example, Windows knows to associate files with the .bat extension as a DOS batch file. If you apply a .bat file as a URL for a Web program (for the ACTION attribute in a form, for example), Windows will know to run the file as a DOS batch file. You can use this feature to add filename extensions to run executable files that don't end with .exe.

Windows servers use traditional DOS/Windows filename extensions; the most common is .exe, which stands for executable. While it is possible to set up additional extensions for executable files, most Web administrators don't do this because of the common use of the .exe extension.

Uploading the Program File

Most of us do not have the benefit of being able to work directly with the Web server that contains our Web site. Most of us must connect to the server through some other means, either via a company or school network or via a dial-up phone connection. For the latter, the Web program must first be uploaded to the Web server before it can be used. This can be accomplished using any of three methods:

- Use an FTP (file transfer protocol) program to transfer the files from your computer to the Web server. FTP programs for the Windows and Macintosh operation systems make file transfer particularly easy with their pull-down menus.
- Use a Telnet program (typically used with UNIX servers only), which allows you to communicate with the server as if you were sitting behind a terminal.
- Use the file upload feature of your browser. Many of the latest browsers, such as Netscape Navigator, allow you to log into your Web site and upload files by choosing them from a file list.

Once the program has been uploaded, you must be sure that file rights are properly set. This is especially true when using a UNIX server.

> **NOTE** Setting file permissions on a Windows Web server depends on the server software being used, as well as the version of Windows and any additional networking software that is used (such as NetWare). For this reason, you need to consult with the system administrator or the Web site documentation guide for more information on setting file rights when using a Windows Web server.

Setting File Rights in UNIX

UNIX was developed to be used by many people at the same time. Access by many individuals requires some sort of rights access system. Allowing just anyone access to the critical files of a computer system only invites trouble. UNIX provides for a way to set up access rights on a file-by-file basis and on a directory basis. The access rights divide users into three distinct categories:

- *User*. Files can be restricted on a user-by-user basis.
- *Group*. Users can be classified into groups, and anyone in a particular group can be given blanket access to a file. In most Web applications the group category is not particularly important, though you must still accommodate it when setting file rights.
- *Other*. Access can be allowed to anyone. Other is an important set of people because it's what makes the Web work. Anyone visiting your page is treated as other (otherwise called "unknown" because the server doesn't ask for identification to access the page).

UNIX supports three types of access: read, write, and executable:

- Read access allows or disallows access to read a file. The typical HTML file on the Web is set so that everyone can read it.
- Write access allows or disallows access to write a file. The typical HTML file on the Web is set so that only authorized users can alter it.
- Executable access allows or disallows a file from being run as a program. Web programs must be given executable access, or they won't work.

UNIX uses the chmod command to set file access. Chmod (which stands for "change mode") is actually pretty easy to use once you understand how it works. You can use alternative syntax with chmod if you prefer to use mnemonics. We'll cover the "traditional" method of using chmod, then detail the alternative mnemonic syntax.

> **NOTE** To use the chmod command you must access your UNIX Web server in terminal mode. If the server is local (you can sit behind a terminal for it), you need only log on and begin typing. If the server is available only via a dial-up connection, you must use Telnet to communicate with it in terminal mode. Telnet applications are available for free on the Web. If you've never used a Telnet program before, you'll want to download one and give it a spin before you try to manipulate files on your Web server.

To use the chmod command, you provide the name of the file you want to alter, along with a specific number that tells chmod how to set access for the three user types (remember: user, group, other). The value you set for each of these groups determines whether to give file access for reading, writing, and/or executing. The numbering system is in octal (digits 0 through 7), and it works like this:

0 = no rights at all

1 = set execute

2 = set write

4 = set read

You may use these numbers alone or add them up if you want to combine access. For example, if you want to set just read access, use the value 4. If you want to set read and execute and write access (common for CGI programs), add 4+2+1, and use the value 7.

You set rights for all three types of users at the same time, simply by specifying the value for user, group, and other, in that order. For example, suppose you want to set the following rights for a file named myfile.txt:

```
user = read and write
group = read
other = read
```

The chmod command to set these rights is

```
chmod 644 myfile.txt
```

You can readily see where the numbers come from. The 6 sets rights for the user, the first 4 sets rights for the group, and the second 4 sets rights for other.

Most CGI programs require that their read, write, and execute bits be set. The execute and read "bits" set for all three types of users. You don't want group and other (user "unknown") to be able to write—and therefore modify—your program, so you disallow write access. Therefore, the values to use are these:

7—sets read, write, and execute

5—sets read and write

Given a CGI program called myprogram.cgi, the chmod command to set proper rights to execute it as a program is

```
chmod 755 myprogram.cgi
```

Remember the value 755—with few exceptions, you will use this number to set access rights for all of your Web programs.

Should you need to set other forms of access rights, you may wish to use the mnemonic method of chmod. Some users find it easier than the octal numbering system described above. To use the mnemonics system, you specify for whom who you are setting rights (user, group, other) and the rights you are providing or denying.

The three categories are identified using a single letter:

u—user

g—group

o—other

Likewise, the rights are identified using a single letter (other permission mnemonics are used, but these are the most common):

r—read

w—write

x—execute

You use + to set a given access right, and – to remove it. You can set multiple rights by separating the settings with commas (don't use spaces).

Here's an example that adds the executable rights to user, using a file named myfile.html:

```
chmod u+x myfile.html
```

Conversely, this example removes executable rights:

```
chmod u-x myfile.html
```

You can specify one or more rights using the = character. This example sets read, write, and execute to both user and group (note that commas separate the user categories):

```
chmod u=xrw,g=xrw myfile.html
```

> **NOTE** Software on some Web servers provides alternative means to setting execution rights. For example, the server may provide special HTML forms where you can choose a file on the server and assign the appropriate rights. If you don't have access to a Telnet application (and you really should), the HTML form is an acceptable, if not slower, alternative.

Troubleshooting

Even the pros upload programs to their Web servers that don't work right off the bat. Don't beat yourself over the head when this happens. Odds are it's one of the simple things that can go wrong, and these are relatively quick and easy to fix.

Nothing Happens When the Program Is Called

The program may be faulty, or the server is not configured properly.

Try these tips:

- Double-check the program for proper execution. For example, if the program is in Perl and it is designed to output text, be sure that you are using the print statement correctly and that the program is generating correct HTML.
- Double-check the operation of the server. Do any CGI programs work?

The Browser Displays the Text of the Program File and Doesn't Run the Program

The server is not aware that the file is an executable. Because of this, the file is rendered as text, rather than executed.

If using UNIX, be sure that these items are handled correctly:

- The file access bits have been properly set with chmod.
- The file is located in cgibin or another directory known by the server for executables.
- The file uses an extension that the server associates for executables (for example, .cgi or .pl).

If using Windows, be sure that these items are handled correctly:

- The file is located in cgibin or another directory known by the server for executables.
- The file uses an extension that the server associates for executables (for example, .exe).

The Server Returns an Error Message

The program caused an internal error, and the server reports an error condition in the browser.

Be sure that these items are handled correctly:

- Double-check the program for proper operating. Typically, the program failed before it could complete, and it returned an error condition.
- Double-check the operation of the server. Some server settings may restrict program execution. Do any CGI programs work?
- The CGI program may be attempting to call another program on the server, and this program is not present, not in the directory specified, or restricted.

Using the UNIX Command Line to Test a Program

If you are running under UNIX and the program outputs some form of text, you can verify that the program is working properly by executing it at the command line. Merely type the name of the program and press Enter. It should echo back the text it is supposed to output to the browser. If the text appears, you know the program is working properly, and the problem may exist in some Web server setting.

Conversely, if the text does not appear, you have a pretty good idea that the program is not working correctly. You will need to review the program carefully to make sure the syntax is correct. Here are some things to check.

If the program is written in Perl or UNIX shell, be sure the first line of the script contains the path to the Perl or shell interpreter. This path begins with #!, followed by the path. For example:

```
#!/usr/local/perl
```

points to the UNIX Perl interpreter located in the /usr/local/ directory. Failure to include the proper path will result in the program's not working. If you're not sure where the Perl (or other) interpreter is, try typing

```
which perl
```

at the command line. Most UNIX systems will echo the full path of the Perl interpreter.

It's not uncommon for a CGI program to rely on another program on the server to complete its task. This is particularly true of UNIX Perl and shell scripts, which work in concert with other UNIX features to process mail, scan through documents, and so forth. UNIX (and to some degree, Windows) is not a universal operating system. There are many different implementations of UNIX, so you can never rely on the "helper" programs, being available or being in the directories in which they are normally placed.

Your CGI program will end with an error if any external program cannot be found, or if its access is restricted for one reason or another. Therefore, if your CGI program uses an external program to complete its tasks, review the program to ensure that the programs are available on the server, are located in the directories specified, and are accessible with normal execution rights.

As an example, suppose your CGI program is designed to interface with the UNIX sendmail application, which sends a message via e-mail. The sendmail application is commonly called on when working with CGI programs that process mail forms. Most all UNIX servers have sendmail installed, but not always in the same place. If the sendmail program on your server is located in a different place than that specified in the program, an error will occur. Double-check the location of the sendmail program (and verify that it's there to begin with!), and modify the program accordingly.

Of course, Windows lacks the sendmail utility; instead it uses one or more proprietary mail servers to shuttle e-mail. To use the form mail program, you will need to determine the name and location of this mail processing program on the server. Once you have determined this you can modify the CGI program accordingly.

Chapter

8

Developing Applications with Server-Side Includes

Most Web programming tasks involve CGI, the common gateway interface. CGI programs are commonly employed to interface an HTML form with an application on the server and allow for truly interactive Web use.

Many Web servers also allow for another form of program, called *server-side includes*, or SSI. SSI is typically used when interactivity between the user and the Web program is not required. You can use SSI to run a program when an HTML page is delivered to the user, such as a "hit counter," a program that counts the number of times your page has been visited.

Server-side includes also provide for additional capabilities, including displaying the current date and time and almost any number of Web server environment variables, such as the domain or IP address of the person accessing the page.

Server-side includes are a standard part of the NCSA and Apache Web servers for UNIX. Other Web servers, such as those from Netscape and Microsoft, also support SSI but usually in a limited way or with the aid of an additional programming layer. For this chapter, we'll talk about SSI as it is found on the NCSA and Apache servers—the most commonly used servers running under UNIX. If you are using a different Web server, you'll want to consult its documentation for additional information on SSI.

Understanding SSI

SSI is a Web program or command that runs without user intervention. SSI uses a "directive," which is placed in a comment tag among the rest of the HTML of your Web page. A typical SSI directive looks like this:

```
<!--#echo var=" HTTP_REFERER"  -->
```

The SSI directive is composed of the following main parts:

- The entire directive is enclosed in an HTML comment. The comment begins with the characters <!-- and ends with -->.
- The #echo is the directive itself. This directive tells the server to "echo" (print) the result of the directive argument that follows.
- The directive argument is var="HTTP_REFERER." This argument specifies what the server is to do with the echo directive.

When the server encounters this SSI directive, it executes the action and replaces the entire comment tag with the result of the action. So, when the user sees the page, all he or she sees is the result of the SSI directive—in this case, it's the "referring page" that got the user to your page (the *referring page* is a page that has a hypertext link to your page).

There are other SSI directives, and not all servers support them all. Among them are #exec and #include. We'll cover these in a bit.

Getting SSI to Work on Your Server

SSI is something of the unwanted stepchild of Web programming techniques. It is often (and usually unfairly) criticized as being a security risk and a waster of server resources, and it is therefore treated as an option in the setup of a Web server. More than likely, if your Web server supports SSI at all, the system administrator has turned it off.

Before you can use SSI, you'll need to make sure it's been enabled. If the system administrator has disabled SSI, there is nothing you can do to turn it on remotely. Only the root user of the Web server can do this. If you are the root user of your server, you'll probably need to check the configuration files of your server to ensure that SSE is enabled (check the conf.srm file as well as the access.conf files of your server). Refer to your server documentation if these files are unfamiliar to you.

Even if SSI is enabled for your server, you will likely be required to add one or more lines to the .htaccess file contained in the directory where you wish to place the HTML page that contains the SSI directive (if this directory doesn't already have a .htaccess file, you can create it using any text editor). Add the following lines to the .htaccess file:

```
Options Indexes FollowSymLinks Includes
AddType text/x-server-parsed-html .shtml
```

This tells the server to "parse" all files that end with the .shtml extension. As the file is parsed, the server looks for SSI directives among the HTML tags and executes those directives when found. Files with other extensions are not parsed.

Alternatively, you may use the standard .html extension, which will parse all files ending with .html:

```
AddType text/x-server-parsed-html .html
```

> **NOTE** Avoid using the .html extension if the directory contains many non-SSI documents that end with the .html extension. The server will parse each of these files every time they are served to visitors. Parsing files unnecessarily adds an extra burden to the server. If the server is a busy one, your users will notice a speed degradation.

As an alternative to adding the AddType line to the .htaccess file, as shown above, many servers support a feature known as XBITHACK. If your server supports this feature, you need only specify the file as executable and the server will understand that it is to perform SSI parsing on it. To specify the file as executable, use the UNIX chmod command as follows:

```
chmod 755 filename.html
```

This sets the file filename.html, and only this file, to executable. Any SSI directives contained with it are parsed and executed.

Adding an SSI Directive to an HTML File

You may place an SSI directive anywhere in a file, though the <BODY> portion is the most common location. The general syntax is

```
<!--#directive argument=" value" >
```

Important note! Be watchful of spaces. You may not have any spaces between the <!-- comment and the hash (#) character that begins the SSI directive. Otherwise, your server will treat the SSI directive as a regular HTML comment. No error is generated in this case because your server simply doesn't know anything is wrong. The following formats are incorrect:

```
<!--  #directive ...>

<! --#directive ...>

<  !--# directrive...>
```

Note that some SSI directives can take multiple arguments and values, as in:

```
<!-- #directive argument1="value1" argument2="value2">
```

You may use the directives for SSI listed in Table 8.1:

Table 8.1 SSI Directives

Command	Argument	What It Does
#config		Sets server configuration options.
	errmsg	Specifies the message to display if an error occurs parsing the document.
	timefmt	Specifies the time format when displaying dates.
	sizefmt	Specifies the size of file format when displaying the size of a file.
#include		Includes a file with the current file

Table 8.1 ***Continued***

Command	Argument	What It Does
	virtual	Specifies the virtual path to the file (the HTTP URL).
	file	Specifies the actual path of the file, relative to the current directory. The ./ and ../ directory shortcuts are not allowed.
#echo	var	Displays an environment variable (see below for more details on the environment variables you can use).
#fsize		Displays the size of a file.
	virtual	Virtual path; see #include for details.
	file	Actual path; see #include for details.
#flashmod		Displays the date of last modification of the file.
	virtual	Virtual path; see #include for details.
	file	Actual path; see #include for details.
#exec		Executes a program on the server.
	cmd	Specifies a UNIX command or shell script.
	cgi	Specifies a CGI program.

NOTE Recall from earlier in this chapter that not all SSI directives are supported on all servers. Of all the directives listed above, the #exec directive is the most often featured by Web site administrators because of the potential for misuse. Because of this fear, the #exec directive is commonly disallowed, even though the other SSI directives are not. If you are having trouble getting your SSI #exec directives to work, contact your site administrator to determine if the #exec has been disabled.

Using Environment Variables with SSI

Perhaps the most common application of SSI is to display one or more server environment variables within the text of an HTML document. These variables include the current time and date, the user's domain name, and even the IP address used by the user.

You may use any of the standard environment variables normally accessible via CGI programming. For example, to display the name and ID of the browser used by the person visiting your page, you use

```
<!--#echo var=" HTTP_USER_AGENT" >
```

The most commonly used environment variables are listed in Table 8.2:

Table 8.2 Environment Variables

Environment Variable	What It's For
AUTH_TYPE	Access authentication type
CONTENT_LENGTH	Length of the data to follow
CONTENT_TYPE	The MIME type of the data to follow
GATEWAY_INTERFACE	CGI version running on the server
HTTP_ACCEPT	Accept list of MIME types
HTTP_USER_AGENT	Name/ID of client browser
PATH_INFO	"Extra path" information
PATH_TRANSLATED	Virtual to physical mapping of file on server
QUERY_STRING	Query portion (part of ? character) of URL
REMOTE_ADDR	IP address of client
REMOTE_HOST	Domain name of client
REMOTE_IDENT	Identify data about client
REMOTE_USER	USER ID of client (now rarely provided)
REQUEST_METHOD	Request method by client (that is, POST or GET)
SCRIPT_NAME	URL path of CGI program
SERVER_NAME	Name of server
SERVER_PORT	Server port where request was received (typically 80)

Table 8.2 *Continued*

Environment Variable	What It's For
SERVER_PROTOCOL	Name and version of request protocol
SERVER_SOFTWARE	Name and version of server software

AUTH_TYPE

The AUTH_TYPE environment variable provides rudimentary server-access restrictions. Example: AUTH_TYPE=Basic.

CONTENT_LENGTH

The CONTENT_LENGTH environment variable indicates the length in bytes of the STDIN virtual file. (Recall that STDIN is used only with the POST method.) Example: If the data in STDIN is 72 bytes, then CONTENT_LENGTH contains 72.

CONTENT_TYPE

The CONTENT_TYPE environment variable indicates the type of data being requested, if that information is important. The data type is specified using a standard MIME description, which takes on form type/subtype. The most common MIME types used with CGI Web programming is CONTENT_TYPE=text/html, which specifies that the data is in text format, and HTML tags. Other MIME types are used for binary graphics, binary application programs, and other data.

GATEWAY_INTERFACE

The GATEWAY_INTERFACE environment variable is used to hold the version number of the CGI protocol in use. Example: CGI/1.1.

HTTP_ACCEPT

The HTTP_ACCEPT environment variable provides a list of MIME types (separated by commas) that the browser accepts. The server and/or CGI program can use this information to determine the type of content the browser should receive in return. For example, HTTP_ACCEPT=image/gif, image/x-bitmap, image/jpeg, */*. Note the final */*, which tells the server/CGI program that any content is acceptable. The MIMI types described earlier are preferred.

HTTP_USER_AGENT

The HTTP_USER_AGENT environment variable contains the name, version, and other descriptor of the browser making the request. The format of the user agent information is variable and depends entirely on the whim of the browser maker. Example: Netscape/3.0 (Win95; I).

PATH_INFO

The PATH_INFO environment variable contains extra information supplied as part of the URL for a CGI program. The CGI program can then use this information as a list of command-line parameters. For example, if the URL is

```
http://myserver.com/cgi-bin/cgiprog.pl/extradir/special
```

it indicates a CGI program named cgiprog.pl contained in the cgi-bin directory of myserver.com. The PATH_INFO environment variable contains the text /extradir/special.

QUERY_STRING

The QUERY_STRING environment variable is, by far, the most commonly used. This variable contains any text following the ? "search" character in the URL. The data following the ? character is in the format of name/data pairs, where information is defined by name, then by value. The name and data are separated by an equal signs. Additional name/data pairs can be appended simply by adding an ampersand character (&) between them.

The most common source of the name/data pairs is an HTML form. If the form is submitted using the GET method, the browser automatically appends the URL specified in the ACTION= statement of the <FORM> tag with the name/data pairs for each control in the form.

For example, if the URL is

```
http://myserver.com/cgi-bin/cgiprog.pl?name=George&birthmonth=May
```

then the QUERY_STRING environment variable contains the string

```
name=George&birthmonth=May
```

It is the job of the CGI program to break this query string apart. The first job is to split apart the two name/data pairs (name=George and birthmonth=May). The next job is to separate the name and data values.

REMOTE_ADDR

The REMOTE_ADDR environment variable contains the IP address of the client browser making the request. The data is in the format xxx.xxx.xxx.xxx, where the xxx's denote numbers for a real IP address.

REMOTE_HOST

The REMOTE_HOST environment variable contains the resolved domain name used by the client browser making the request. This data is not always available, depending on how the client connected with the server. In addition, many Web server administrators disable this environment variable because it causes extra work for the server. Example: mydomain.com refers to a domain named mydomain.com.

REMOTE_IDENT

The REMOTE_IDENT environment variable contains the identification string (usually e-mail name) used by the client browser making the request. Example: me@myself.com. Even though this environment variable exists, it is usually blank, having been squelched by the browser for privacy reasons. And when it's not blank, there is no assurance that the information is accurate because this information can be set by the user.

REMOTE_USER

The REMOTE_USER environment variable contains the user name, as set in the client browser making the request. This environment variable is typically used for user authentication (password) purposes. The server is able to fetch the user name and request just the password, thereby saving the user some time.

REQUEST_METHOD

The REQUEST_METHOD environment variable supplies the information by which a CGI program was invoked, typically GET or POST. This information is useful if the CGI program is designed to work with either GET or POST request (and, quite often, the better-written CGI programs are).

SCRIPT_NAME

The SCRIPT_NAME environment variable contains the name of the CGI program being invoked. Example: /cgi-bin/cgiprog.pl.

SERVER_NAME

The SERVER_NAME environment variable contains the Web server's host name, alias, or IP address. For example, if your server is named www.myserver.com, then that's what is in the SERVER_NAME environment variable. This variable is useful when you want to restrict your CGI program and execute it only from yours or some other server. If the SERVER_NAME variable doesn't match the one(s) in the script, the program doesn't run. For best results, be sure to check for at least domain name and IP address.

SERVER_PORT

The SERVER_PORT environment variable contains the port used to access the Web site. The default port number for Web pages is 80, but it can be set to nearly anything.

SERVER_PROTOCOL

The SERVER_PROTOCOL environment variable is used to contain the name and version of the server protocol. Example: HTTP/1.0.

SERVER_SOFTWARE

The SERVER_SOFTWARE environment variable is used to contain the name and version of the software used for the Web server. Example: Apache/1.1.

Using Time Formats in SSI

You may wish to display the time and/or date of the server for your users. The server uses a default time to format the time string, and this format may be acceptable to you. If it is not, use the SSI #config directive as follows:

```
<!--#config timefmt=" format-string" >
```

where format-string is one of the strings in the table below. Once the configuration has been set, you may display the date/time with the #echo directive, using any of several date-related environment variables listed in Table 8.3.

Tables 8.4 through 8.9 detail the date formats that can be used with the config directive in server-side includes.

Table 8.3 Date-Related Environment Variables

Environment Variable	What It Does
DATE_LOCAL	Displays the date/time local to the server
DATE_GMT	Displays the date/time referenced to Greenwich Mean Time
LAST_MODIFIED	Displays the date/time the current file was last modified

Table 8.4 Preformatted Elements

Format	What It Does
%x	Date without the time, in default format
%X	Time without the date, in default format
%c	Date and time, in default format

Table 8.5 Year Elements

Format	What It Does
%y	The year as a two-digit decimal—e.g., 99 for 1999
%Y	The year as a four-digit decimal—e.g., 1999

Table 8.6 Month Elements

Format	What It Does
%b	Month abbreviated by name (Jan, Feb, etc.)
%B	Month spelled out (January, February, etc.)
%m	Month as a decimal (1 to 12)

Table 8.7 Week Elements

Format	What It Does
%U	The number of week as a decimal value, starting with the first Sunday
%W	The number of week as a decimal value, starting with the first Monday

Table 8.8 Day Elements

Format	What It Does
%a	Abbreviated weekday name (Mon, Tue, etc.)
%A	Full weekday name (Monday, Tuesday, etc.)
%d	Day of month as a decimal (1 to 31)
%j	Day of year as a decimal (001 to 366)
%w	Day of week as decimal (Sunday=0)

Table 8.9 Time Elements

Format	What It Does
%p	Adds “am” or “pm”
%H	Hour as decimal, in 24-hour format
%I	Hour as decimal, in 12-hour format
%M	Minutes as decimal
%S	Seconds as decimal
%Z	Time zone

Including Files in the Main HTML Document

A handy but little used feature of SSI is to include other files within the current file. The server intelligently strips out anything but the body portion of the included document, so that the user receives a single, seamless document. You can use this method to build documents from smaller portions.

The basic syntax for including documents using SSI is

```
<!--#include virtual " /mypath/included_file.html"  -->
```

where /mypath/included_file.html is the URL of the document on your server. When the server encounters this directive, it will replace the comment tag with the entire document that is referenced. Once the document has been included, the remainder of the main document is served.

Running Programs Using SSI

SSI can be used to run programs on your server. Typical programs of this type are logging scripts, which log the visitors to a site. For example, the following CGI script records the URL of the page that linked to your page (this technique uses the HTTP_REFERER environment variable):

```
#!/usr/bin/perl

$dir = " /mydomain/logs/" ;
$logfile = " $dir/refer.log" ;
$user = $ENV{" HTTP_REFERER" };
unless(open(WLOG," >> $logfile" )) {
exit;
}
seek(WLOG, 0, 2);
print (WLOG $user, " \n" );

close(WLOG);
chmod(0666, $logfile);
exit;
```

In use, each visit is appended to the log file, which is named “refer.log” and stored in the directory specified in the $dir variable. The contents of the log file might look like this:

```
www.somedomain.com/links
www.anotherdomain.com/mylinks
mydomain.com/index.html
```

Each of these URLs contains a hypertext link to your page on your server. When a user clicks on that link, he or she is taken to your page. When they arrive, your logging program is run—thanks to SSI—and the address of the referring page is recorded for your review.

> **NOTE** Many Web servers offer specific logs that contain the referring URL for all your pages. The above script is useful if your server does not provide referral logs. If yours does, it's recommended that you use the standard referral log and consider the above as an example only.
>
> Of course, you can replace the HTTP_REFERER environment variable with anything you like, such as the IP address of the visitor or the remote user name (handy if your site uses password protection and you want to see who has visited).

To run the logging program, include the following SSI directive somewhere near the top of the HTML page:

```
<!--#exec cgi=" /cgi-bin/logger.cgi" >
```

For example purposes we've used "logger.cgi" for the name of the logging script and have placed it in the cgi-bin of the site. Of course, remember to change the path and name of the program if you use something different.

When someone visits your page, the server will parse the HTML document looking for server-side includes. When it finds the #exec directive, it will run the CGI script above and log the referring URL of the visitor. The remainder of the page is then furnished to the user. Note that all of this happens without the user's knowledge.

Considerations When Using SSI

While SSI is a great way to add interactivity and control to your Web pages, it does suffer from some drawbacks:

- As we mentioned earlier in this chapter, SSI is not available on all servers. You should verify that SSI is available before you spend any time trying to develop a page or site that uses it.

- And, as we mentioned, even if SSI is available, parts of it may be disallowed for security purposes. Check with the Web site administrator for any restrictions on the use of SSI.
- Running programs slow down a Web server. This includes CGI as well as SSI. SSI imposes a second load to the server, in that the server must parse each document to locate the SSI directives within it. You can reduce the load to the server by making sure that only documents that contain server-side directives are parsed (used a .shtml extension, for example). You can also reduce the load by restricting the size of parsed documents. The larger the document, the more parsing the server must do, and therefore, the more extra work it must perform.
- SSI can interfere with page caching and may cause an unnecessary increase of bandwidth. This is especially true if the user visits your site through a proxy server, which is used by some companies and Internet Service Providers (such as America Online and Prodigy). The proxy server stores pages visited by others; if you want the same page, you're given the copy. When SSI is added to the page, the page is typically considered new each time it is delivered, so it is never cached by the proxy server. Because it is not cached, your server must deliver a separate copy to each and every visitor. Because users from services like America Online and Prodigy can represent a large number of your visitors, the increase in bandwidth can be considerable.

Chapter

9

Web Programming with the UNIX Shell

An operating system needs some way for the human operator to interact with it. In the Windows and Macintosh world, this interaction is accomplished using a fancy graphical interface. In the DOS world, this interaction is accomplished using a text-based "command-line processor."

Like DOS, the UNIX operating system uses a text-based command-line processor. The UNIX command-line processor is more commonly called a *shell.* The shell allows for user input and displays the output from UNIX. For example, type

```
cd mydir
```

at the UNIX shell prompt, and UNIX responds by changing to the "mydir" directory. Internally, UNIX did a multitude of steps to change the current directory, but the user needs to issue only this one command.

All operating systems—DOS, Windows, Macintosh, and UNIX—support exchangeable interfaces. Exchangeable interfaces allow you to use a different interface if the "stock" one doesn't fit. In reality, few users of DOS, Windows, and the Macintosh ever use an alternative interface. Not so in the UNIX community. The UNIX shell is a highly personal—and personalized—issue.

Literally dozens of UNIX shells are in use today, many of them specially written by programmers to perform a unique computing task. Of the many UNIX shells in use, three are found with any regularly; one—called *sh* (for shell)—is among the most popular.

UNIX wouldn't be the operating system for gearheads that it is if the shell weren't programmable. In fact, almost all UNIX shells allow for a great deal of programmability—miniature applications that are a combination of UNIX commands and special shell language statements. Shell programs are very much like batch programs in DOS and recorded or scripted macros in Windows and Macintosh.

The basic idea of a shell program is to automate some UNIX task by replicating UNIX commands. It's also possible to build intelligence into the shell program using if, while, and other programming statements.

In this chapter, UNIX shell programming, especially programming for the bash shell, will be covered Bash is an updated and improved version of the basic sh shell that comes with most versions of UNIX. Though no one has made an official survey so far, I'd estimate that bash is almost universally used on UNIX Web servers (and when it's not used as the shell, it's offered as an alternative and is available for any programming script that calls for it).

If you rent space on a UNIX server, there's a very good chance that the shell used with that server is bash, rather than one of the others (these include the Korn shell and tsh). Because of the commonality of bash, we'll concentrate on it almost exclusively in this chapter. From here on out, unless we say otherwise, when we say "UNIX shell," we really mean bash.

In addition, throughout this chapter we will assume you know how to connect and log on to your UNIX server. If you are not familiar with this topic, read Chapter 7. You may also wish to contact your Web server provider and ask for specific help.

Understanding the bash Shell

At its basic level, the shell is an interactive command-line processor for communicating with UNIX. UNIX carries out the commands as you type them and press Enter. For example, if you type:

```
ls -l
```

and press Enter, this tells UNIX to display a directory list, showing attributes for all nonhidden files.

You really can't effectively program with the bash shell (or any UNIX shell) unless you've used it to command UNIX. If you have little experience with using UNIX, you're best off boning up on using the standard UNIX commands. Most any book on UNIX will provide the necessary information you need to get your way around the operating system. A popular reference is *UNIX in a Nutshell*, by Daniel Gilly, published by O'Reilly and Associates (1996). You will also want to get a book or file on using the basic bash interactive commands. Ask your system administrator if a "man page" (manual page) is available on the server that details or summarizes the bash shell commands.

NOTE If you're not sure which shell your UNIX server uses, you can find out by typing

```
echo $SHELL
```

at the UNIX prompt (if you are connecting to the server via telephone, you will need to establish a Telnet connection first). You will get one of several responses. The most common are:

```
bash—the bash shell
sh—the standard UNIX shell
ksh—the UNIX Korn shell
csh—the UNIX C shell
```

If your server doesn't respond with bash, don't fret. It merely means that bash is not the default shell. It is likely available for use as a program interpreter. You can test this by typing

```
bash
```

at the shell prompt. If you do not get an error message, it means that bash was located and run. If you do get an error message, it means UNIX couldn't find the bash interpreter. You should contact the system administrator for assistance.

The Most Important Shell Commands

When learning about UNIX and basic shell commands, the topics listed in Table 9.1 are the most important (we won't be able to cover them here—they really need their own book to do them justice). See Table 9.1.

In addition, Unix supports a number of data filtering utilities, and these are commonly used with the shell, both interactively—you type commands at the shell prompt—and in Web programs. The most often used data filtering utilities are listed in Table 9.2.

What the Shell Really Is

The shell is an interpreter program that resides in a common directory of the server, typically /bin or /sbin. When you log on to the system, UNIX runs a dedicated

Table 9.1 Basic Shell Commands

Command	What It Does
cd	Changes directory
cp	Copies a file
rm	Removes a file
mkdir	Makes a directory
rmdir	Removes a directory
echo	Prints a line of text or contents of a variable
help	Gets help on a topic

Table 9.2 Data Filtering Utilities

Utility	What It Does
grep	Searches for strings in the input
sort	Sorts lines in the input
cat	Copies input to output
sed	Performs editing operations on input
tr	Translates input characters to something else

instance of the shell program just for you. That way, whatever you type is filtered through the shell. (Similarly, for shell programs run on the Web, UNIX starts a separate instance of the shell each time the program is run. This is one reason why Web programs are sometimes slow to start up, but once they have begun are fairly fast. The slow start is UNIX preparing a separate instance, or "fork," of the shell.)

In the UNIX world, the terms *input* and *output* are used heavily to denote data going in and data coming out. When using a shell interactively, it's pretty easy to understand how the terms are used. Input is most commonly the command line you type in; output is most commonly the printed response that appears on your screen.

Input and Output

However, input and output can also be files. And when used with the Web, input and output can be HTML forms and browser screen. Because the terms input and output are general, it's important never to attach specific functionality to either one.

For instance, you may type a shell command or write a shell program that searches one file (the input) and creates a second file (the output). Or you may write a shell program for the Web that accepts data from an HTML form (the input), compares it with some information in a previously stored file (the filter input), and generates a report on the browser window (the output).

> **NOTE** In reality, everything UNIX does is treated as a file. UNIX makes no real distinction between text you type and text that's stored in a disk file. To UNIX, both are files. UNIX even considers the display screen a file. This simplification of the structure of input and output is both easy and confusing.
>
> It's easy because you don't really have to think in terms of different types of input and output. You can mentally treat everything as a file, no matter what its source or destination. It's confusing because this is not the approach taken by many other operating systems. If you're familiar with another operating system, you may need to unlearn some old habits before you become comfortable with UNIX.

Standard I/O

The UNIX "everything is a file" approach is based on the concept of *standard I/O*. UNIX offers a single way of accepting input called *standard input*, often referred to as *STDIN*. It offers a single way of generating output, called *standard output*, or

STDOUT. In addition, UNIX provides a standard route for error messages, called *standard error* or *standard error output*.

Standard I/O is fairly straightforward for interactive shell use, but it can get confusing when applied to Web programs. When standard I/O is used with the Web, there is no typing at the command line, which would be one form of standard input. Rather, standard input with a shell program used on the Web would be to accept data or instructions from a Web browser. Similarly, standard output would not be to the UNIX console, but back to the Web browser so that the user could see the response from the server.

When you see a reference to standard input (or STDIN) in relation to a Web program, it generally means the "input stream" from the browser, such as data from an HTML form. When you see a reference to standard output (or STDOUT) in relation to a Web program, it generally means the "output stream" back to the browser. For example, a typical standard output in response to a Web CGI program is a simple "Thank you for submitting the form."

> **NOTE** If you're wondering about standard error, most Web servers deal with it as well. For example, the popular Apache and NCSA Web servers send all error messages to a log file, typically named error_log. You can view the log file to see errors that occurred when users visited your site.

What Are Shell Programs Good For?

The bash shell supports all the standard conventions you'd expect to find in a programming language. You can assign variables, manipulate text, compare values, perform loops, and activate programs on the server. You can, in fact, create very large and sophisticated programs using the shell, especially if you "borrow" functionality from built-in UNIX commands and utilities, such as grep and sed.

While bash (or another modern shell) offers all the tools you need to create Web applications, other programming languages—specifically Perl—are often better suited for more demanding tasks. First, the UNIX shell is not known for blinding speed. If the program has any complexity, you may find it runs significantly more slowly than a similar program written in Perl or, especially, C. Second, the syntax requirements of bash and other shells is stricter. For example, many shells disallow the use of "white space" around the equal sign when assigning a variable. The following produces an error or at best a nonfunctioning script:

```
myname = "fred"
```

Bash and other shells expect

```
myname="fred"
```

Third, the Web is slowly moving away from using shell program for Web applications. There are still plenty of example scripts written for the bash shell, but the current trend is toward Perl, Java, JavaScript, and other updated languages. Compared to regular updates of all three of these programming languages, bash and other UNIX shells are seldom updated beyond simple fixes—and often these fixes are related to newly found security issues.

That said, if you need to whip up a quick application for the Web, a shell program is a perfect way to do it. Shell programs can be easy to write and test, and you can even write one interactively—try out the command at the command line; if it works, incorporate it into your program.

An Introduction to Shell Programming

The best way to learn bash shell programming is to create a simple program and run it on the server. The following program is not meant to work with the Web. Rather, it's designed to be run from the UNIX command prompt. The output of the program will appear on the screen.

```
#!/bin/sh

echo The shell is $SHELL
```

Create this program using a suitable text editor (you may use the UNIX vi or emacs editor, or another editor of your choice. Provide a name for the program—we'll call this one first.sh. Note that the "sh" extension is optional. Most UNIX servers do not require a specific filename extension for executable programs (note: this does *not* always apply to CGI programs used for the Web; we'll address this issue later in this chapter).

Note line 1. This line tells UNIX the location and name of the shell interpreter. This line will probably need replacing to conform to the proper location of the sh interpreter on your server, such as

```
#!/sbin/sh
```

Also note that although the program calls for sh (the regular UNIX shell), it is assumed that the standard shell is bash. If this is not the case, replace sh with bash, as in

```
#!/bin/bash
```

As before, modify the location of the bash interpreter as needed for your server.

Before you can run the program, you must change its access mode. By default, UNIX assumes all new files are just that—basic files. To make your program an executable program you must use the chmod command and specify the access mode you wish. The chmod command was described in detail in Chapter 7, but in review, you create an executable program with the following syntax:

```
chmod 755 progname
```

where progname is the name of the program, in this case first.sh.

Test the program by typing its name, first.sh, and pressing Enter. If all is well, the program should print a line like the following:

```
The shell is bash
```

This example program is very straightforward. Line 1 defines the name location of the shell to use. Line 2 is blank. Finally, line 3 returns (echoes) the text "The shell is," along with the actual name of the shell used on the system.

Note the use of $SHELL. This is a built-in UNIX environment variable. As you'll see in the next section, the shell understands that $SHELL is a variable because the name is preceded by a dollar sign.

Using Shell Variables

Probably the most important element of any programming language is variables. Recall from Chapter 4 that variables are temporary repositories for data. Shell variables are very simple creatures, able to hold a simple text or number value. There are two kinds of shell variables: built-in and user-defined:

- Built-in variables are provided by the server. The $SHELL variable is one example. Additionally, when used with the Web, Web-related variables such as USER_AGENT and QUERY_STRING are available for use in a shell program.
- User-defined variables, as the name implies, are those defined by the user. To use a user-defined variable, you must first assign a value to the variable. You may then reference the variable elsewhere in the shell program.

The shell uses a simplified variable assignment syntax; it is merely

```
varname=value
```

Varname is the name of a variable. The name should contain only text. By convention, variables you define yourself are spelled with all lowercase letters. All uppercase variable names are typically used to denote built-in variables, such as $SHELL.

To reference a variable—either a built-in or user-defined variable, you provide its name and precede it with a dollar sign, as in

```
$varname
```

The most common way to check the innards of a variable is to use it with the echo command, which returns the text and displays it in standard output (that is, the UNIX console or a Web browser). For example, the sample program

```
myname=John
echo My name is "$myname"
```

appears as

```
My name is John
```

when the program is run.

Note that unlike most other programming languages, bash doesn't require you to enclose the assigned value, in this case John, of a string in quotation marks.

Quotation marks can be inserted into the echoed output by "escaping" them with a backslash. For example, if you want the text to read

```
My name is "John"
```

> **NOTE** It's worthwhile to discuss positional parameter variables before leaving the subject of shell variables. Just about any book on bash shell programming with talk about special positional parameter variables with the names $0, $1, $2, and so forth. These are built-in variables, and each one contains an optional command-line parameter. Most applications for the Web, especially CGI applications, do not use command-line parameters, so the positional parameter variables are considered.

you can include backslashes and quote marks, like so:

```
echo "My name is \"&myname\"."
```

Special String Operators

The bash shell uses an unusual syntax for several obtuse but nevertheless useful string operators. These include the substation operators and the pattern/pattern-matching operators.

The substitution operators test for the existence of a variable. If the variable exists and is not empty (otherwise known as "null") the shell returns the value of the variable. If the variable doesn't exist or is empty, the shell return a specified value.

Table 9.3 Substitution Operators

Operator	What It Does
${varname:-word}	Returns contents of variable if it exists and isn't null; otherwise returns word
${varname:?message}	Returns contents of variable if it exists and isn't null; otherwise prints message
${varname:+word}	Returns word if variable exists and isn't null; otherwise returns null

There are three substitution operators you may regularly use. In Table 9.3 note the special syntax, including the brace characters.

The first substitution operator is perhaps the most commonly used. Here's an example that sets a counter variable to 0 if it doesn't exist:

```
${counter:=0}
```

The pattern and pattern-matching string operators are unique to bash, and they can help you manipulate strings without the need to write special "string parsing" code. All of these operators (see Table 9.4) can accept the * wild card character.

For example, suppose you want to return just the filename of a URL and leave out the domain name. Because the domain name is always at the start of a URL, you'd use the ## operator. Suppose the $path variable contains the URL http://mydomain.com/path/myfile.html. The expression

```
${path##/*.*}
```

results in myfile.html.

Running a Command from a Shell Program

A common task for almost any shell program performing duty on the Web is to execute a UNIX command. The command might be to delete a file or to use the grep

Table 9.4 Pattern and Pattern-Matching String Operators

Operator	What It Does
${variable#pattern}	If pattern matches start of the value in the variable, deletes the shortest part that matches and returns the rest
${variable%pattern}	If pattern matches the end of the value in the variable, deletes the shortest part that matches and returns the rest
${variable##pattern}	If pattern matches the start of the value in the variable, deletes the longest part that matches and returns the rest
${variable%p&attern}	If pattern matches the end of the value in the variable, deletes the longest part that matches and returns the rest

filter to search through an access log to determine how many times a particular URL was accessed. The bash shell offers a simple means to run UNIX commands and programs. One method is to use command substitution, which has the format:

```
$(UNIX_command)
```

where UNIX_command is the full command line you wish to use.

Another, and somewhat more common, approach (though supposedly archaic, at least in the eyes of some UNIX programmers) is to use "back ticks" to denote a command that is to be run. The syntax is

```
'UNIX_command'
```

where UNIX_command is the full command line you wish to use. For example, suppose you want to see how many times visitors accessed a given URL at your Web site. Assuming that your Web server maintains an access log file (called access_log) in a directory named logs in your site and that the URL you're interested in is named mybigdir/index.html, you'd do something like this:

```
        echo My URL has been accessed this many times: 'grep -c
mybigdir/index.html logs/access_log'
```

The main work-horse here is the grep filter, which wears many hats. grep can be used to read a text file and return any and all lines that contain (or don't contain) given text. When used with the -c option, grep doesn't return the actual lines, but merely shows a count of the lines. The output of the above line would be something like this:

```
My URL has been accessed this many times: 1063
```

The count of 1063 denotes that there are 1063 lines in the access_log file that contain the URL mybigdir/index.html.

Here is an extended example of using grep to retrieve counts on known URLs at your site. This version uses a variable called *logfile* to hold the name and location of the log file you want to process. It's very likely that at least the location of the log file will be different on your server, so change the path accordingly. And, of course, change the name of the log file from access_log to whatever name is used on your system.

You will also want to modify the URLs that you wish to inspect. We show two URLs: maindir/index.html and subdir/index.html. Change these accordingly. You can add as many URLs as you want to display as many counts as you'd like, but remember that if your log file is any size, it will take additional time for your server to count each URL. Using separate grep statements to count individual URL accesses is not particularly efficient, though it is an easy way to tackle the problem.

```
#!/bin/sh
logfile=/disk1/mydomain.com/logs/access_log
echo "Content-type: text/html"
echo
echo "<HTML>"
echo "<PRE>"
echo "maindir/index.html": 'grep -c maindir/index.html $logfile'
echo "subdir/index.html": 'grep -c subdir/subdir.html $logfile'
echo "</PRE>"
echo "</HTML>"
```

The main difference between the example above and this example is that the $logfile variable is referenced as part of the grep statement. UNIX replaces the $log-file variable name with the actual path and name of the log file. The output of the script looks like this:

```
maindir/index.html: 30
subdir/index.htm: 73
```

Understanding bash Shell Statements

The bash shell offers an assortment of programming statements, including if/else, for, case, and while. These statements can be used to make your shell programs more powerful by controlling the flow of execution. For the most part, the implementation of these statements is fairly standard fare—the bash shell is similar to most other programming languages in how these control flow statements are used.

However, the syntax of many of the bash shell statements is a tad unorthodox. For example, bash uses reverse-spelling of statement names to denote the end of the statement block. The end of the if block is denoted by an "fi" statement, for example. This peculiar syntax, albeit unusual, is not difficult to learn. Once you are familiar with the way bash works, its unique syntax will seem second nature to you. It actually makes pretty good sense!

Note that the UNIX Korn and C shells use different syntax for its statements. These are summarized in the quick reference section at the end of the chapter.

if/else

The basic building block of any program is the *if* statement, which allows you to test if an expression is true or false. The basic syntax of the bash if statement is

```
if condition
then
      true statements
fi
```

The *condition* is an expression, such as an equality test to determine if a value in a variable matches a specified value. The true statements are one or more commands to carry out if the condition is true.

In the above basic syntax, there is no separate set of statements to carry out if the condition is false. Separate "do this if false" statements can be included by adding an *else* statement, as in:

```
if condition
then
      true statements
else
      false statements
fi
```

Expressions for use with if are fairly straightforward. String comparisons are perhaps the most common. The bash shell supports several string comparison operators that you can use (see Table 9.5).

As an example of a string comparison in an *if* statement, suppose the variable myname includes the user's name. The following test determines if the contents of myname is "Fred."

Table 9.5 String Comparison Operators

Operator	What It Does
string1 = string2	Returns true if string1 matches string2
string1 != string2	Returns true if string1 does not match string2
-n string	Returns true if string is not null (empty)
-z string	Returns true if string is null

> **NOTE** Notice that there is only one equal (=) sign in string equality tests. This is different from many other languages based on C syntax (C, Java, JavaScript), which use a double equal sign, such as string1 == string2. When programming with the bash shell, be sure to include just one equal sign.

```
if $myname = "Fred" then
     echo "Your name is Fred"
else
     echo "Your name is not Fred"
fi
```

Or suppose you want to determine if the myname variable is empty. You can use the following syntax:

```
if [ -n "$myname" ] then
     echo "Good!  You have a name!!"
else
     echo "Too bad you don't have a name"
fi
```

Another useful application of the if statement is testing for file attributes. The bash shell sets aside special operators for this. Table 9.6 lists several of the more commonly used file attribute operators. In all cases, file is the name (usually with path if it's not in the current directory) of the file to check.

Table 9.6 File Attribute Operators

Operator	What It Does
-d file	Determines if file exists and is a directory
-c file	Determines if file exists
-f file	Determines if file exists and is a regular file (not a directory, etc.)
-s file	File exists and isn't empty
-r file	Determines if current user has read rights for the file
-w file	Determines if current user has write rights for the file
-x file	Determines if current user has execute rights for the file

As an example, suppose the myfile variable contains the name of a file you want to check. You'd use the following syntax to check if the file actually exists:

```
if [ ! -e $myfile ] then
     echo "Sorry, file $myfile doesn't exist"
fi
```

for

The *for* statement allows you to set up a repeating loop and execute statements within that loop a specified number of times. Quite often, the number of times the loop repeats is set programmatically—the value can change depending on external conditions, such as a value entered by the user or a value obtained by the server. The basic syntax for the for statement is as follows:

```
for x := start to stop do
     statements
done
```

X is a placeholder variable that contains the current iteration of the loop. The start and stop values determine the starting value of the counter and the ending value of the counter, respectively. For example, if you want the loop to count from 1 to 10, the *for* statement would read

```
for x := 1 to 10 do
```

Between the do and done go the statements you wish to repeat. One practical example of using the for loop in a Web application is to separate the value pairs from a submitted form. The bash shell offers a convenient special variable, known as IFS, that makes this extraordinarily simple. Here's the script.

```
#!/bin/sh
IFS="&"
qstring=$QUERY_STRING

echo "Content-type: text/html"
echo
echo "<pre>"
for element in $qstring
do
     echo $element
done
echo "</pre>"
```

Line 1 defines the location and name of the shell to use, in this case /bin/sh (be sure to change this to suit the particulars of your server). Line 2 specifies the contents of the IFS variable, which is implicitly used in the for loop (lines 8 through 11). The IFS variable is set to use & as a "parsing character." The & character is used because this is the character that separates the value pairs in an HTML form.

Line assigns our own variable qstring with the contents of the $QUERY_STRING environment variable. Recall from Chapter 5 that this variable contains the name/value pairs submitted from the form, when the form is submitted to a CGI application using the GET method. For example, suppose you have a form with two text boxes, named box1 and box2. You then enter the text "one" and "two" into the boxes, respectively. When submitted to the server, the contents of the $QUERY_STRING environment variable will be

```
box1=one&box2=two
```

To test this script you need a form document in HTML. The following creates a form with four text boxes, named box1 through box4. Fill in each box with sample text. Submit the form to the CGI program (named test1.cgi in this instance), and the output should look something like this:

```
box1=This is box 1
box2=This is box 2
box3=This is box 3
box4=This is box 4
```

```
<HTML>
<FORM ACTION="test1.cgi" METHOD=GET>
<INPUT TYPE=text NAME=box1><BR>
<INPUT TYPE=text NAME=box2><BR>
<INPUT TYPE=text NAME=box3><BR>
<INPUT TYPE=text NAME=box4><BR>
<INPUT TYPE=submit>
</FORM>
</HTML>
```

case

The *case* statement allows you to compare one or more values against a test expression. These values can be numbers or strings, but the most common application is to compare strings. When a match is made, the shell executes the statements associated with that match. The basic syntax for the case statement is as follows:

```
case expression in
     pattern1 )
          statements ;;
     pattern2 )
          statements ;;
     ...
esac
```

Note that some of the unusual syntax is not shared by other programming. First note that the case structure is composed of a case statement, which starts the structure, and an esac (case, spelled backward) statement that ends the structure. Also note the parenthesis that terminates each matching pattern, as well as the double semicolons that terminate the statements for each matching pattern.

As an example, suppose the myname variable contains the name of a user. You want to display a matching greeting for each user.

```
case $myname in
     george )
          echo "Howdy, George."
     phil )
          echo "Phil, your rent payment is overdue!" ;;
     betty )
          echo "Hello, Betty. Long time no see" ;;
     * )
          echo "Hi, human user" ;;
esac
```

Note the additional pattern test after the test for each name. The asterisk (*) is a catch-all that acts as a default if none of the other patterns matches. If the name in myname is "george," then the greeting for George is printed. Same with "phil" or "betty." If the myname variable does not contain any of these three names, the generic greeting is printed instead.

while and until

The bash shell supports two powerful loop statements, *while* and *until*. Both do much of the same thing, except they work with opposite logic:

- The while loop continues as long as the condition is true.
- The until loop continues as long as the condition is false.

Because they are used in the same way, except for the negation of logic, we'll concentrate on the *while* statement here (it's also the more commonly used of the two). The basic syntax for the *while* statement is as follows:

```
while condition do
     statements
done
```

The *condition* is the expression that is evaluated. As long as the expression returns true, the loop continues. Because a while loop is effectively "open-ended"—its termination is dependent on the expression eventually proving false—you need to make sure that the while loop always terminates, sooner or later. Otherwise, your script will continue until it is forcibly stopped, which is decidedly uncool!

"Statements" are one or more statements you want executed as part of the loop. Note that if the while condition is false to start, the statements within the loop are never executed. This is actually a feature of the while loop.

```
#!/bin/sh
IFS="&"
qstring=$QUERY_STRING

echo "Content-type: text/html"
echo
echo "<pre>"
while [ $qstring ]; do
   path=${path#:*}
    echo $path
 done
 echo "</pre>"
```

Using Shell Functions

Functions allow you to create self-contained code that you can reuse. Functions are ideal for code that is repeated two or more times in a program or for code that you find yourself reusing for each new project. Instead of repeating the same code each time you wish to use it, you merely have to place all the code in a function. To activate the code, you call the function.

Functions are composed of two parts: the function body itself and the calling statement. In a shell program the two parts look like this:

```
myfunction
...
myfunction ()
{
statements go here
}
```

The myfunction function is specified by name, followed by parentheses (the parentheses can be empty). All the code you want executed when the function is called is placed between { and } brace characters. The matching pair of brace characters is vitally important. If you forget the closing brace, your program will not function properly.

To call the myfunction function, you need only reference it elsewhere in the program. For example, suppose you have a simple shell program that prints your name. Here's how it might look if you used functions:

```
#!/bin/sh

myname
myname ()
{
echo "John Doe"
}
```

The *myname* statement calls the myname function. You can repeat the *myname* statement any number of times throughout the program, and each time your name will be echoed.

Functions are particularly handy when used in conjunction with Web programming because the vast majority of programming tasks use common pieces of code. We've already looked at one common piece of code: a program that splits up the data pairs submitted by a CGI form. Recall that the nonfunction version of this program looks like this:

```
#!/bin/sh
IFS="&"
qstring=$QUERY_STRING

echo "Content-type: text/html"
echo
echo "<pre>"
for element in $qstring
do
```

```
        echo $element
    done
    echo "</pre>"
```

The *for* statement can be readily enclosed in a function so that you can easily transport this code to whatever program you are working on. You can add whatever other pieces you need to the program. Here's one way of making a function of the for loop that extracts the data pairs and prints them. Note that although this version of the program is slightly longer, it is actually far more versatile. You need only copy and paste the getpairs() function from program to program whenever you need it. Use this program with any HTML form that uses the GET method for transmitting data from browser to server.

```
 1  #!/bin/sh
 2
 3  echo "Content-type: text/html"
 4  echo
 5  echo "<pre>"
 6  getpairs
 7  echo "</pre>"
 8
 9  getpairs ()
10  {
11      for element in $qstring
12      IFS="&"
13      qstring=$QUERY_STRING
14      do
15          echo $element
16     done
17   }
```

- Line 1 is the standard statement for locating the path and name of the shell program to use. Lines 3 through 5 prepare the output of the HTML page that will appear in response to running the CGI program. These lines set the content-type to text/html and send a <pre> tag so that the text is formatted with the line breaks furnished by our program.

- Line 6 is the call to the getpairs function. When the shell encounters this statement, it temporarily branches off to the getpairs () function, which is on lines 9 through 17. Line 9 specifies the name of the function (getpairs in this case), and lines 11 through 16 contain the actual code of the function. Note lines 10 and 17. These contain the required { and } brace characters, which "bound" the start and end of the function.

bash Shell Quick Reference

The following quick reference guide is handy when you are programming with the UNIX bash shell.

Reserved Words

These words are reserved by bash as commands or for future enhancements. Note that many of these commands are not used in Web programming (some are downright dangerous to use on the Web), but they are listed here for the sake of completeness. You should be acquainted with this list of reserved words—these words should not be used for variable names or function names.

(period)	export	pushd	unset
alias	fc	pwd	until
bg	fg	read	wait
bind	for	readonly	while
builtin	function	return	
brak	getopts	select	
case	hash	set	
cd	help	shift	
command	history	suspend	
continue	if	test	
declare	jobs	times	
dirs	kill	trap	
echo	let	type	
enable	local	typeset	
eval	logout	ulimit	
exec	newgrp	umask	
exit	popd	unalias	

Built-in Shell Variables

The bash shell supports several dozen built-in variables, but only a select few of them are suitable for use in Web programming, as listed in Table 9.7. (The others are used for local script programming; that is, a program that is designed to be run by a user on a local UNIX machine.)

FileTest Operators

The filetest operators test the condition of a file. InTable 9.8, file is the name (and path when necessary) of the file to test. The bash shell supports additional file test operators than those shown here, but these are the most common for Web programming applications.

Table 9.7 Built-in Shell Variables

Variable	What It Is
* and @	Positional parameters given to current program or function
#	Number of arguments passed to program or function
?	Exit status of previous command
$	Process ID of shell process
0	Name of shell or shell program
BASH	Full pathname needed to invoke bash shell
BASH_VERSION	Version of bash shell
IFS	Internal field separator
HOME	Home or login directory
HOSTTYPE	Type of server running program
PATH	Search path for commands
PWD	Current working directory
RANDOM	Random number between 0 and 32767
SHELL	Full pathname of shell
UID	User ID of current user

Table 9.8 File Test Operators

Operator	What It Is
-b *file*	*file* exists, is block device file
-c *file*	*file* exists, is character device file
-d *file*	*file* exists, is a directory
-e *file*	*file* exists
-f *file*	*file* exists, is a regular file
-r *file*	*file* exists, is readable
-s *file*	*file* exists, is not empty
-w *file*	*file* exists, is writable
-x *file*	*file* exists, is executable
file1 -nt *file2*	*file1* is newer than *file2*
file1 -ot *file2*	*file1* is older than *file2*

String Test Operators

The string operators test the equality of strings or the content of strings. In Table 9.9, string is the actual string or the name of a string variable. Varname is the name of a string variable.

Table 9.9 String Test Operators

Operator	What It Is
-n *string*	*string* is non-null
string1 = *string2*	*string1* equals *string2*
string1 != *string2*	*string1* does not equal *string2*
${*varname*:-word}	Returns contents of variable if it exists and isn't null; otherwise returns word
${*varname*:?message}	Returns contents of variable if it exists and isn't null; otherwise prints message
${*varname*:+word}	Returns word if variable exists and isn't null; otherwise returns null

Table 9.9 Continued

Operator	What It Is
${*varname*#pattern}	If pattern matches start of the value in the variable, deletes the shortest part that matches and returns the rest
${*varname*%pattern}	If pattern matches the end of the value in the variable, deletes the shortest part that matches and returns the rest
${*varname*##pattern}	If pattern matches the start of the value in the variable, deletes the longest part that matches and return the rest
${*varname*%p&attern}	If pattern matches the end of the value in the variable, deletes the longest part that matches and returns the rest

Logical Test Operators

The logical test operators test the equality of expressions (which can be numbers or real expressions). In Table 9.10, expr is a value, an expression, or a variable.

Table 9.10 Logical Test Operators

Operator	What It Is
expr1 -eq expr2	expr1 equals expr2
expr1 -ne expr2	expr1 does not equal expr2
expr1 -lt expr2	expr1 is less than expr2
expr1 -gt expr2	expr1 is greater than expr2
expr1 -le expr2	expr1 is less than or equal to expr2
expr1 -ge expr2	expr1 is greater than or equal to expr2
expr1 -a expr2	both expr1 and expr2 are true
expr1 -o expr2	expr1 and/or expr2 is tru

Chapter 10

Introduction to Perl

Perl is a powerful yet easy to use interpreted language. Perl was designed to manipulate text, but it is suitable for a variety of common programming tasks.

Perl includes popular features from several other environments like the UNIX shells, the C language, and the AWK and SED utilities. Perl is best suited for tasks that are beyond the capability of utilities like SED and AWK, but that do not require the complexity of C.

Perl is available for most modern operating systems including UNIX, Microsoft Windows, Microsoft DOS, and IBM OS/2.

At the time of this writing, the current version of Perl is 5.003.

Understanding the Pros and Cons of Perl

Perl is the most widely used language for Web applications today. Most of the common tasks in Web programming involve text manipulation of some sort.

Processing input from HTML forms, sending e-mail, and scanning log files are tasks that require a strong aptitude for text processing.

Another reason for Perl's popularity is the variety of Perl programs, or scripts, available for free on the Internet. Programmers from around the world have made their creations freely available for downloading. Because it is an interpreted language, Perl programs are distributed as text in the form of source code. The source code enables you to see exactly what each program does and learn from the efforts of others.

Programming in an interpreted language is simple because no explicit compile and link steps are necessary. Perl interprets and executes the human-readable text of your programs. The Perl interpreter performs nearly identically on all platforms. This means that many scripts developed on UNIX platforms will run with minor modifications on Microsoft Windows or OS/2.

On the downside, large or complex interpreted programs run more slowly than compiled programs. Each time a Perl program is run, the Perl interpreter must scan, decode, and translate the program text before executing the actual instructions of the program. A compiled language like C performs these steps once during compilation, saving the output into a natively executable binary file that requires no further processing to run.

Perl provides a rich assortment of compact but powerful programming features, and it often has alternate ways of accomplishing the same thing. In fact, the Perl motto is "There's more than one way to do it." This approach can be a blessing to experienced programmers, but it can lead to program code that is not easily readable by beginners (or even experts).

Last, you may have to download the Perl source code and compile it yourself to build a Perl interpreter for your system if a binary executable version is not available for your operating system. Fortunately, binaries are available for most of the systems to which Perl has been ported.

Basic Perl

The following is a minimalist Perl program:

```
#!/usr/bin/perl

print "Greetings from Perl!\n";
```

This program simply displays the text "Greetings from Perl!" followed by a newline character (the \n). The first line is necessary on UNIX systems to specify the location of the Perl interpreter. Ask your system administrator for the appropriate path on your system. This line is not necessary and is ignored on Microsoft DOS or Windows systems. The second line uses the *print* statement output text.

To run this program on a Microsoft-based system you would use a command line similar to the following:

```
perl greeting.pl
```

This example assumes that you saved the program in a file named "greeting.pl." It also assumes that your Perl interpreter is named "perl.exe" (or "perl.com" or "perl.bat") and that it resides in a directory included in your PATH environment variable.

On UNIX, you will first need to adjust the file permissions to set the "executable bit" for this file using the chmod utility. This lets UNIX know that the file is an executable program. Assuming that the file name is "greetings," an easy way is this one:

```
chmod +x greetings
```

Consult the system administrator for details on your specific system. If you are uploading your Perl scripts to a computer running UNIX, you must perform this operation after uploading. FTP client software often has a feature that enables you to do this from within the ftp program; consult your documentation for details. Once the executable bit is set, you can run the program by simple entering its name, as in:

```
greetings
```

On UNIX it is not necessary to explicitly invoke the Perl interpreter because the first line of the script specifies its location.

Understanding Perl's Scalar Variables

In Perl, simple variables are called *scalars*. A scalar variable holds a single value. This value may change during execution of your program, but a scalar variable may contain only one value at a time. Scalar variable names are prefixed with a dollar sign $ to identify them as such.

For example, $alpha identifies a scalar variable named "alpha." Do not confuse this prefix character with those used in the BASIC language. The prefix characters in BASIC ($, %, etc.) specify the type of value that a variable may contain (string, number, and so on). The $ prefix in Perl merely identifies a word as the name of a scalar variable.

Perl automatically creates variables when they are first referenced. A variable is empty, or "undefined," until it is assigned a value. It is not an error to refer to a variable that has not yet been defined or used. Undefined variables have the value of an empty string or zero if evaluated in a numeric context. Part of the philosophy of Perl is always to attempt something reasonable instead of generating an error.

You can assign values to variables using the assignment operator = as in most other languages. For example,

```
$count = 3;
```

assigns a value of 3 to the variable named "count." The trailing semicolon is required at the end of every statement in Perl.

Strings and Numbers

Variables may contain either numbers or character strings. Values are automatically converted between numeric and character representation as needed. If a variable containing a string is used where a number is expected, Perl attempts to convert the string to a numeric value. The general rule is to translate digits into the indicated numeric value and ignore nonnumeric characters. For example:

```
$a = "123xyz";
$a = $a + 1;
print "$a\n";
```

The first line assigns a string of characters to the variable a. The addition operator + on the second line sets a numeric context for the a variable. The digits "123" are translated, but the remaining characters are ignored because they are not numeric digits. The third statement prints the new value of a, 124 (123 + 1).

A value of x would be converted to 0 because it contains no numeric digits. Again, Perl quietly deals with the unexpected instead of stopping the program with an error.

Numbers are specified as in most other languages, and they do not need to be enclosed in quotes. 123, 123.45, and 123e2 are examples of numeric values (the last one is in scientific notation, equivalent to 12300). You may use underscores in numeric values in place of commas for readability, as in 1_234_567 (you can't use actual commas within numbers as Perl recognizes them for other purposes).

String Quoting

Character strings are enclosed in either single or double quotes. Double-quoted strings are subject to backslash interpretation and variable substitution; single-quoted strings are not.

Backslashes indicate that the following character (or characters) should be translated to a special character or that it modifies the case of subsequent characters. Backslashes may be used to insert characters that would otherwise be used by Perl (see Table 10.1).

The following string contains the text This is a "test":

```
"This is a \"test\""
```

Table 10.2 lists single-character mnemonics for commonly used special characters.

Table 10.1 Use of Backslashes

Sequence	Result
\"	Double-quote character
\'	Single-quote character
\\	Backslash character

Table 10.2 Single-Character Mnemonics

Sequence	Result
\b	Backspace
\f	Formfeed
\n	Newline
\r	Carriage return
\t	Tab

For example, it is common practice to end an output line with a newline character to separate it from any lines that follow:

```
print "This is a test\n";
```

Backslash sequences may be used to specify any character by its numeric or ASCII equivalent; see Table 10.3. The character immediately following the backslash specifies the format of the sequence.

The previous example could be rewritten as

```
print "This is a test\xA";
```

or

```
print "This is a test\012";
```

or even

```
print "This is a test\cJ";
```

Additionally, some backslash sequences can change the case of subsequent characters in a string (see Table 10.4).

Table 10.3 Backslash Sequences, Character Equivalents

Sequence	Interpretation
\xA	Hexadecimal notation (hex A = decimal 10, the newline character)
\012	Octal notation (octal 12 = decimal 10, newline)
\cJ	Control-J (newline)

Table 10.4 Backslash Sequences, Changing Case

Sequence	Result
\l	Converts only the next character to lowercase
\u	Converts the next character to uppercase
\L	Converts all following characters to lowercase
\U	Converts following characters to uppercase
\E	Ends case conversion specified by earlier \L or \U

The following statement prints THIS is a Test:

```
print "\Uthis\E is a \utest\n";
```

Variable substitution, or "interpolation," is also performed on strings enclosed in double quotes. Variable interpolation means that variable names inside double-quoted strings are replaced by their associated values. For example:

```
$name = 'Stuart';
print "Hello $name!\n";
```

This will print "Hello Stuart!". Single quotes are used in the first line since no backslashes are used and no interpolation is needed. The variable interpolation in the second line requires double quotes.

If a variable name is immediately followed by another alphanumeric character, the variable name must be placed within braces ({}) to separate it from the surrounding characters. For example, the following prints bobcat:

```
$type = 'bob';
print "${type}cat\n";
```

Another way of quoting strings are the q/ and qq/ constructs, which are used for single and double quoting, respectively. This is convenient for strings that contain quotes. Any nonalphanumeric character can be used in place of to specify an alternate quoting character. For example:

```
$single = q/This is a 'test'/;
$where = 'Here';
$double = qq#$where is a "slash" /#;
print "$single\n$double\n";
```

which prints:

```
This is a 'test'
Here is a "slash" /
```

The first line stores a single-quoted string that contains quote characters in the variable single. The third line stores a double-quoted string containing a variable to be interpolated as well as quote characters and a slash to the variable double. The last line uses interpolation and embedded newline characters to print the variables single and double on separate lines.

Yet another way of quoting strings is a line-oriented format. This construct is handy for grouping multiple lines of text into a single value. The opening “quote” consists of a double chevron symbol “<<” followed by an identifier that will terminate the value. All data between the opening and closing identifiers is included in the value. For example:

```
$lines = <<END;
This is line one.

This is another line.
END
```

Here the variable lines is assigned all of the text between the two occurrences of “END”, including newline characters. Note that no space is allowed between the “<<” and the accompanying identifier.

Lists and Arrays

A *list* is a collection of scalar values. Lists are represented in Perl programs as a series of values separated by commas, enclosed in parentheses. The parentheses assemble all of the values into a single entity. The individual values in a list may be strings, numbers, or variables. For example:

```
("apples", "oranges", 1, 2, $x, $y)
```

This list contains a pair of strings, a pair of numbers, and a couple of scalar variables named x and y.

Array variables contain lists. Array variables are referenced by placing an @ symbol in front of the variable name. The @ provides an array “context” for the reference. The context of an expression determines whether the result is a single (scalar) value or a list of values. For example, @stuff refers to the list of elements contained in the array named “stuff.”

A list may be assigned to an array variable using the = assignment operator:

```
@citrus = ('grapefruit', 'oranges', 'lemons');
```

This statement assigns the list of values “grapefruit,” “oranges,” and “lemons” to the array variable named citrus. Any values that were previously stored in the array are discarded. Array variables maintain the original order of the list. In this example, “grapefruit” will be the first element in the citrus array, followed by “oranges,” then “lemons”. Single quotes were used here because none of the strings contains backslashes and no interpolation is needed.

List representations may include array variables in addition to scalar values and variables. The individual elements of the array will be inserted into the list. For example:

```
@fruit = ('apples', 'bananas', @citrus);
```

All elements of the citrus array are inserted into the list. The fruit array will contain “apples,” “bananas,” “grapefruit,” “oranges,” and “lemons.”

Arrays may be assigned to other array variables:

```
@produce = @fruit;
```

Here all elements of the fruit array are assigned to the produce array. The elements of the produce array will be in the same order as the fruit array.

Assignment may also be performed to a list of variables. Each variable in the list on the left-hand side of the assignment operator = receives the next value from the list on the right-hand side:

```
 ($one, $two) = ('grapefruit', 'oranges', 'lemons');
```

or

```
($one, $two) = @citrus;
```

The variable one is assigned the value of the first element (“grapefruit”) from the list on the right side, and the variable two receives the second value (“oranges”). All remaining elements from the list on the right side are ignored.

Arrays are also interpolated within double-quoted strings. For example:

```
@citrus = ('grapefruit', 'oranges', 'lemons');
print "Citrus fruits: @citrus\n";
```

which prints:

```
Citrus fruits: grapefruit oranges lemons
```

Perl automatically adds a space between each element of the list during array interpolation.

Individual array elements are accessed by their position, or index, within the array. Array index values must be numbers. By default, the index of the first element of an array is 0, the index of the second element is 1, and so on. The index of the last element in an array is equal to the number of elements in the array minus. The citrus array used earlier has three elements:

```
@citrus = ('grapefruit', 'oranges', 'lemons');
```

The index of the first element "grapefruit" is 0 and the index of the next element "oranges" is 1. The index of the last element "lemons" is 2: number of elements minus 1. You can change the default behavior to use a different starting index value in your programs, but this is not recommended.

A subset of an array is called a *slice*. A slice is a list containing only the specified elements of the original array. Index values are placed within square brackets following the array name. For example:

```
@tasty = @fruit[0,1,2];
```

or

```
@tasty = @fruit[0..2];
```

Both of these slices return an array containing the first three elements of the fruit array. Using the fruit array from earlier examples, either of these expressions would result in a list containing only "apples," "bananas," and "grapefruit." The first example specifies the index value of each element. The second example uses a "range" of index values to accomplish the same thing ("there's more than one way to do it"). A range is simply a pair of starting and ending values separated by the ".." symbol. A slice does not have to refer to a contiguous set of elements:

```
@tasty = @fruit[0,2,3];
```

This slice returns the elements "apples," "grapefruit," and "oranges". The second element, "bananas" (index value 1), is skipped.

To reference a single element of an array, include only a single index value within the brackets. The array name is prefixed with a dollar sign:

```
$favorite = $fruit[2];
```

Why the $ instead of an @ symbol? Because we are referring to a scalar value even though it is an array element.

Assignment to an array element is performed the same way:

```
$fruit[2] = 'papaya';
```

This statement assigns the value "papaya" to the third element (index value 2) of the fruit array.

Associative Arrays

Associative arrays are another way of grouping values into a collection. Unlike the list-type arrays introduced in the previous section, associative arrays do not keep their elements in any particular order. Associative arrays store an index value, known as a "key" with each element. Keys can be any scalar value and are not restricted to sequential numbers. Associative arrays are optimized for efficient access to any item in the array and are commonly used for small databases.

Key values are placed in braces ({}) when referring to a specific element. As with list-type arrays, a $ prefix is used when referring to a single element of an associative array:

```
$shapes{'sphere'} = 'round';
print "$shapes{'sphere'}\n";
```

This example stores the value "round" and associates it with the key "sphere" in the first line. The second line looks up the value associated with the key "sphere" and prints this value ("round").

Associative arrays may be treated as lists. A list may be assigned to an associative array. The list is interpreted as a series of key/value pairs. Note that associate array variables are prefixed with a percent sign % when referring to the array:

```
%shapes = ('sphere', 'round', 'box', 'square');
```

In Perl version 5, the => symbol can be used in place of commas to increase readability by denoting the key/value relationships:

```
%shapes = ('sphere' => 'round', 'box' => 'square');
```

The associative array shapes now contains two elements: "round," associated with the key "sphere," and "square," associated with the key "box."

Similarly, an associative array may be assigned to a list-type array:

```
@shape_pairs = %shapes;
```

The array shape_pairs now contains a list of key/value pairs. The ordering of these elements is unpredictable.

Perl uses associative arrays to provide system information to your programs. One of these is the %ENV array, which contains an element for each environment variable. For example, CGI input is often found in the CGI environment variable named QUERY_STRING:

```
$somefield = $ENV{'QUERY_STRING'};
```

This statement retrieves input from the QUERY_STRING environment variable and stores it in the somefield variable. The example programs shown in the next chapter use this technique to retrieve input from Web browsers.

Associative arrays are popular in CGI programs for storing input from HTML forms. For example, the following HTML form contains two input fields:

```
<FORM>
<INPUT name="EMAIL"><BR>
<INPUT name="HOMEPAGE"><P>
<INPUT type="SUBMIT"> <INPUT type="RESET"><BR>
</FORM>
```

The value of each field could be stored in an associative array using the HTML field names EMAIL and HOMEPAGE as keys. An example program shown in the next chapter demonstrates this type of usage.

Scalar versus Array Context

Every operation in Perl is performed on scalar or list values, or a combination of both. When a list is expected, a list context is provided. This means that if a scalar value is encountered where a list is expected, it will automatically be promoted to a single-element list.

For example, the assignment operator sets the context of right operand (whatever is on the right-hand side of the equal sign) to match the left operand:

```
@fruit = 'mango';
```

Here, a single value is assigned to an array variable. This sets a list context for the right side, and the scalar value "mango" is automatically converted to a single-element list before assignment. The fruit array now contains a single element, "mango."

Likewise, when Perl expects a single value, a scalar context is provided. The value of a list evaluated in a scalar context is determined by the specific operation. For example, the number of elements in the list is returned during assignment:

```
$count = @citrus;
```

Count is a scalar variable, as evidenced by the $ prefix. This sets a scalar context for whatever is on the right side of the = operator. When a list or array is evaluated in a scalar context during assignment, its value is interpreted as the number of elements in the list. Using the three element citrus array from previous examples, the count variable would now contain a numeric value of 3. Other operations may use the first or last element of a list when encountered in a scalar context. The Perl documentation, or "man pages," describes the specific behavior of each operation. The documentation uses the term LIST wherever a list is expected or a list context is provided.

Namespace

Variables of different types are stored in their own namespace. The names of scalar, array, and associative array variables are each stored separately. This means that the names $alpha, @alpha, and %alpha each refer to a separate variable. Although it is possible to reuse variable names this way, it is not recommended as it leads to programs that are difficult to understand.

Variable names in Perl are case-sensitive. This means that a name must be capitalized exactly the same way everywhere it is used in order for it to refer to the same variable. Names using the same spelling that differ only in capitalization do not refer to the same variable. For example, the variable names $alpha, $Alpha, and $ALPHA refer to three different variables.

Chapter

11

Using Perl

The last chapter introduced the basic concepts of Perl. This chapter details Perl and discusses its expressions, operators, statements, and functions. This chapter also includes several useful Perl examples for Web programming applications.

Expressions and Operators

Perl provides a large number of operators. Operators and values combine to form expressions. A Perl expression results in a list, a character string, a number, or a logical value. The type of result is determined by the operators involved in the expression.

Arithmetic Operators

During arithmetic operations, values are automatically converted to numbers. For example, adding two numbers together with the addition operator + results in a number:

```
$total = $count + 2;
```

The variable total will contain a numeric value. The variable count will be evaluated in a numeric context, meaning that its value will be converted to a number before the addition is performed.

In addition to the four basic arithmetic operators found in most other languages (+, –, *, and /), Perl provides modulus and exponentiation operators. The modulus operator % returns the remainder of the division of two numbers:

```
print 7 % 3;
```

This statement prints 1, the value left over after dividing 7 by 3.

The exponentiation operator ** returns the value of a number raised to the power of another number:

```
print 2 ** 3;
```

This statement prints 8, the value of 2 raised to a power of 3 (2 * 2 * 2).

The autoincrement ++ and autodecrement—operators increment or decrement a scalar variable by 1:

```
$a = 3;
print ++$a;
```

This statement prints 4, the value of **a** incremented by 1. Placing the operator before a variable is known as the prefix form of the operator. In the prefix form, the variable is first updated with the modified value before it is used. In the previous example, the variable **a** is updated with the incremented value before it is printed.

When the operator follows a variable, it is considered to be postfix form. In postfix form, the variable is not changed until after its current value is used in the expression:

```
$a = 3;
print $a--;
```

This example prints 3. The variable **a** is not decremented until after its current value is printed. Its value is 2 after the print statement.

String Operators

The increment operator also works with character strings consisting of alphanumeric characters. The last character is incremented to the next value in the set of alphanumeric characters, carrying over to the character on the left as necessary:

```
$id = "abc";
print ++$id;
```

This statement prints "abd".

```
$id = "xyz";
print ++$id;
```

This statement prints "xza". Because the last character "z" is the highest character in the range "a" to "z", it is reset to "a"; the increment operation carries over to the next character position. Only the increment operator behaves this way; the decrement operator does not provide this feature for character strings.

The concatenation operator . joins strings together:

```
$what = 'world';
print 'Hello ' . $what . "!\n";
```

This statement prints "Hello world!". In many cases it is simpler to use interpolation as in:

```
print "Hello $what!\n";
```

The replication operator x repeats a string:

```
print 'abc' x 3;
```

This example prints "abcabcabc", the string "abc" repeated three times.

Assignment Operators

Any of these operators may be combined with the assignment operator = to modify a variable's value. For example:

```
$a = 3;
$a += 2;
```

Here, 2 is added to the current value of a (3), and this modified value (5) is stored in a. This is a simpler way of expressing $a = $a + 2.

Logical Operators

Perl provides the usual assortment of relational operators for comparing values. Different versions are used depending on whether you wish to compare two numbers or two strings. Numbers are compared based on their numeric values. For example, 3 is less than 21 in a numeric comparison. Character strings, however, are compared character by character, so that 3 would be greater than 21 in a string comparison. Table 11.1 lists the operators used to compare two numbers or two strings.

Each of these operators returns either a 1 to indicate that the comparison is true, or ‘’ (empty string) to indicate that the relationship is not true. In general, an empty string or a zero is considered false in a logical expression, and any other value is interpreted as true. For example, the following statement prints only if the value of hand is less than 17:

```
print "Hit me\n" if $hand < 17;
```

An additional three-way comparison operator is provided to test if a value is less than, equal to, or greater than another value. The numeric version is <=> and the string version is cmp. These operators return negative 1 (–1) if the first value is less than the second value; 0 if the values are equal; and positive 1 (1) if the first value is greater than the second value.

Table 11.1 Operators Used to Compare Numbers and Strings

Numbers	Strings	Description
<	lt	Value on the left side is less than value on the right side
>	gt	Left value is greater than the right value
<=	le	Left value is less than or equal to the right value
>=	ge	Left value is greater than or equal to the right value
==	eq	Values are equal
!=	ne	Values are not equal

As in other languages, logical operators are provided for constructing compound logical expressions. The "and" operator && returns true if both the left and right expressions are true, while the "or" operator || returns true if either the left or the right expression is true. Remember that any nonempty value that is not 0 is considered to be true. For example, (1 < 2) && (3 < 4) is true because both conditions are true. The expression (1 > 2) || (3 < 4) is also true because the or operator (||) requires only one of the two conditions to be true.

Perl uses the "short circuit" method of evaluating logical expressions. This means that the entire expression may not be evaluated. As soon as the result of the expression can be predicted, any conditions remaining to be evaluated are skipped. An "and" operation will be terminated prematurely with a false result if the first condition is false. Because "and" requires both conditions to be true, the expression cannot possibly result in a true value if the first condition evaluated to false. Similarly, an "or" operation will be terminated with a true result if the first condition evaluates to true. Because "or" requires that only one condition evaluate to true, there is no need to evaluate any remaining conditions.

The "not" operator! negates the logical value of an expression. This operator evaluates a single expression and returns true if this expression is false and vice versa.

In Perl 5, the words *and*, *or*, and *not* may be used in place of the symbols && and ||.

Input/Output

Perl provides three standard files to every program: STDIN, STDOUT, and STDERR. STDIN is associated with the keyboard, unless the program has been run in a way that redirects STDIN to another file. STDOUT is associated with the display, unless it has been redirected to another file. STDERR is also associated with the display, but it is normally used only to report error messages. These names are known as *file handles.*

File handles are used to access files, either the standard files opened implicitly by Perl or any other files that you explicitly open. File handles are like variables and have their own namespace. Unlike other variable types, however, file handles do not have a prefix character to distinguish them from other elements of the Perl language. Therefore, it is recommended that you use uppercase names for file handles to avoid collisions with reserved words and other symbols.

The easiest way to read from a file is to enclose the file handle in angle brackets (<>). This operator returns the next line of text from a file:

```
$txt = <STDIN>;
```

This statement assigns the next line of text from STDIN to the variable named txt. The file handle is enclosed in angle brackets. Lines of text are separated by newline characters. The newline character is included in the value returned by this form of input. This input operation will return an empty string (false) after the last line of input has been read.

The chop function removes the last character from a line of text:

```
$txt = <STDIN>;
chop($txt);
```

The second statement strips the newline character from the end of the line read in the first statement. Perl 5 provides a similar function named chomp that strips off the last character if it is a newline.

Assigning the result to a scalar variable provides a scalar context for the input operation. Assigning the input to an array provides an array context. The array form of input reads all available input and assigns each line to a separate array element:

```
@lines = <STDIN>;
chop(@lines);
```

Here each line of input is assigned to an element of the lines array. The maximum amount of data that can be read this way is limited only by available memory. Be careful not to read large files this way, though, as this can excessively consume memory and affect performance of your Web server. Note that chop, as with many Perl functions, also works with arrays. Chop strips the last character from each element of the array.

The <FILEHANDLE> operator is useful for reading lines of text, but sometimes you may need to read a specific amount of input regardless of whether the input contains newline characters. The read function reads the specified number of characters from a file:

```
read(STDIN, $input, 16);
```

This statement reads 16 characters of input from STDIN and assigns this input to the variable input.

This form of input is used in CGI programs to retrieve form data submitted via the HTTP POST method. When this method is used, the encoded form data is read from STDIN. The number of characters submitted is specified by the CGI environment variable =CONTENT_LENGTH:

```
read(STDIN, $buffer, $ENV{'CONTENT_LENGTH'});
```

This statement reads the specified number of characters from STDIN to a variable named buffer. This technique is explained further in the example programs shown later in this chapter.

The most common output method is the print function. When a file handle is not specified, output is sent to STDOUT. The following statements have the same effect:

```
print "abc\n";
print STDOUT "abc\n";
```

Perl automatically opens the predefined STDIN, STDOUT, and STDERR file handles. To read or write to any other file, you must explicitly open it. The open function associates a file handle with a file and opens it for access:

```
open (MYFILE, "test.txt");
```

This statement opens the file named "test.txt" for access and associates the file handle MYFILE with this file.

By default, files are opened for read-only access. You cannot write to a file opened for reading. To open a file for writing, prefix the filename with a > symbol:

```
open (MYFILE, ">test.txt");
```

This statement opens the file for write-only access. An existing file having this name will be overwritten. If the file does not exist, a new one will be created. The < prefix is an alternate way of specifying read-only access.

Another form of write access is append. *Append access* is specified with a >> prefix. This mode also allows writing but does not overwrite existing contents. When a file is opened with append access, new data is added to the end of the file. This mode is useful when adding information to an existing file. Adding a + symbol to the > or >> symbol enables reading in addition to write access.

When attempting to open a file, possible problems that may be encountered include not finding the file when opening for read access or insufficient permission when opening for write access. The open function returns true if successful; otherwise, it returns false.

When opening a file you should test this value to ensure that the file was opened successfully. If the file could not be opened, an appropriate error message should be generated to inform you of what went wrong. A common method of opening a file is as follows:

```
open (MYFILE, "test.txt") || die "open: $!";
```

Recall that the or operator (||) evaluates the condition on the right side only if the left side results in a value of false. If the open function returns false to indicate failure, then (and only then) the die function is called. The die function displays the specified error message then terminates the program.

The string passed to die includes the related error message in the special variable $!. This variable is one of many special variables that provide information or allow control over certain aspects of Perl. The $! variable contains the error message of the last system error that was encountered. If evaluated in a numeric context, $! contains the error number of the last error. Unless followed by a newline (\n), $! includes the filename and line number of the program that caused the error.

Once a file has been opened, it can be read using the input operator introduced earlier:

```
open (MYFILE, "<test.txt") || die "open: $!";
while ($txt = <MYFILE>) {
  print $txt;
}
close MYFILE || die "close: $!";
```

The first line opens a file for read access or dies with an appropriate error message. The second statement begins a loop that will iterate for each line of input encountered. This statement takes advantage of the fact that the assignment operator returns the value that was assigned. The input operator will return false after the last line has been read, which terminates the loop. The third statement prints the input line. No newline character is needed on output as the input line still contains a trailing newline. The last statement closes the file. This operation rarely fails, but it is good practice to check for errors anyway.

Another (perhaps the most) commonly used special variable is $_. This is the default space used for input and output when no other variable is explicitly used. The loop in the previous example could be simplified as follows:

```
while (<MYFILE>) {
  print;
}
```

Input from the file handle MYFILE is placed in the special variable $_. This variable is also used by the print function because no other variable is specified.

Statements and Syntax

A *program* statement consists of one or more expressions that combine to form a specific operation. Perl is a free-form language, meaning that statements are not confined to single lines. For example:

```
@citrus =
  ('grapefruit',
  'oranges',
  'lemons');
```

This assignment statement is split over several lines.

A semicolon is required at the end of each *program* statement. This enables Perl to easily recognize the end of each statement.

The hash mark # symbol causes any remaining text on a line to be ignored by Perl. A common practice is to place short comments throughout to document the intent of a program:

```
# check to see if we need another card
print "Hit me\n" if $hand < 17;  # stand on 17
```

The first line is ignored entirely because it begins with a #. The second line is evaluated, but the comment at the end of the line is ignored. The effect of this symbol extends only to the end of the current line, not necessarily the end of the current statement, which may span multiple lines.

Statement Modifiers

Perl provides "statement modifiers" to execute a single statement conditionally or repeatedly. The if modifier causes a statement to execute conditionally:

```
die "open: $!" if ! open (MYFILE, "test.txt");
```

If the open function is not successful, the program is terminated by die. The not operator ! reverses the logical value returned from open.

The *unless* modifier is similar, but it reverses the meaning of if. Unless is handy when you wish to execute a statement only if a condition is false. The previous example could be rewritten in a slightly more efficient form:

```
die "open: $!" unless open (MYFILE, "test.txt");
```

The *while* modifier repeatedly executes a statement while a particular condition is true. The repeated execution of a statement, or group of statements, is known as a loop. The following statement is an example of a loop:

```
print "$_" while <MYFILE>;
```

This statement prints each line from the file referenced by the MYFILE file handle. While a line of input can be read into the default space $_, that line is printed.

The *until* modifier reverses the meaning of while:

```
print "$i\n" until ++$i > 10;
```

This statement repeatedly prints the value of i until it is incremented past 10. The conditional expression ++$i > 10 is executed first. The prefix form of the autoincrement operator ++ modifies the value of i before comparing it is compared with the value 10.

Control Statements

The statement modifiers are useful for controlling the execution of a single statement, but often you will need to control a group of statements. Statements may be grouped into a block by enclosing them within braces. The Perl documentation uses the term BLOCK when referring to statements grouped this way.

If Statement

The *if* statement conditionally executes a statement block:

```
if ($hand < 17) {
  print "Hit me\n";
  $hand += $nextcard;
}
```

Note that this form of if requires that the conditional expression $hand < 17 is parenthesized. The two statements between the braces constitute a statement block that is executed only if the conditional expression is false. The += operator adds the value of nextcard to the current value of hand.

The optional else clause executes an alternate block if the expression is false:

```
if ($hand < 17) {
  print "Hit me\n";
  $hand += $nextcard;
} else {
  print "Stand\n";
}
```

The program now prints stand if the value of hand is not less than 17. Even though a single statement is associated with the else, it must still be enclosed within braces because Perl expects a block statement here.

Also optional is the elsif clause which provides alternate conditional expressions in the event that the first condition evaluates false:

```
if ($hand < 17) {
  print "Hit me\n";
  $hand += $nextcard;
} elsif (21 == $hand) {
  print "Twenty-one!\n";
} else {
  print "Stand\n";
}
```

The program now prints Twenty-one if the value of hand is 21. Notice the order of comparison in the elsif clause. A common error in Perl (and C) programs is to accidentally substitute the assignment operator = for the equality test operator ==. Because the result of the assignment operator is the value that was assigned, any nonzero value causes a conditional expression to evaluate true without any error. When testing for equality, the order of the operands is insignificant. Placing the constant value on the left side, however, will cause a program error if you inadvertently use the assignment operator. This is a defensive programming practice that can spare you from spending considerable time trying to figure out why a program does not perform as expected.

Multiple elsifs may be used within an *if* statement:

```
if ($hand < 17) {
  print "Hit me\n";
  $hand += $nextcard;
} elsif (21 == $hand) {
  print "Twenty-one!\n";
} elsif ($hand > 21) {
  print "Bust\n";
} else {
  print "Stand\n";
}
```

As with the statement modifier of the same name, the *unless* statement inverts the interpretation of the test condition:

```
unless ($hand > 21) {
  print "Won $paid\n";
  $winnings + $paid;
}
```

While/Until Loops

The *while* and *until* statements repeatedly execute a block while or until the specified condition is true:

```
while(<STDIN>) {
  chop;
  $lines++ if $_;
}
print "Number of lines: $lines\n";
```

This example counts the number of nonempty lines read from STDIN. The conditional expression evaluated by this *while* loop is the input operation, which returns true as long as input can be read. The input is placed into the default space $_. The chop function also defaults to operating on $_ as no variable is specified. The third statement increments the lines variable if $_ is not empty (or does not contain only 0). The statement block accompanying a loop is known as the body of the loop.

For and Foreach Loops

The *for* loop executes the statement block that follows for a specific number of times and is usually controlled by a loop counter. This counter is a normal variable whose value determines whether the loop should continue to iterate. The *for* statement comprises three optional sections separated by semicolons. Any section may be empty or may contain one or more expressions. Typically, each section contains one expression:

```
for (initializing expr; conditional expr; control expr)
```

The following example prints the numbers 1 through 10:

```
for ($i = 1; $i <= 10; $i++) {
  print "$i\n";
}
```

The first section, the initializing expression(s), is evaluated only once before the loop begins iterating. This section is typically used to initialize the variable that will be used as a counter. This example initializes the variable i to a value of 1. The middle section contains the condition(s) that must be true for the loop to continue iterating. In this case, the loop will execute for as long as the value of i is less than or equal to 10. The expression(s) in last section is evaluated after each iteration of the loop body. The loop counter i is incremented after each iteration in this example.

The *foreach* loop iterates over a list, providing a single element value through a loop variable on each iteration:

```
@citrus = ('grapefruit', 'oranges', 'lemons');
foreach $fruit (@citrus) {
  print "\U$fruit\n";
}
```

This example prints each element of the citrus array in uppercase (\U). Each iteration of this loop assigns the next element of the citrus array to the variable fruit. If a variable is not specified, the default $_ is used. The previous example could be simplified to:

```
@citrus = ('grapefruit', 'oranges', 'lemons');
foreach (@citrus) {
```

```
  print "\U$_\n";
}
```

Three loop control statements are provided to further control the execution of any loop. The *next*, *redo*, or *last* statements may be used anywhere in the body of a loop. The *next* statement advances to the next iteration of the loop, skipping any remaining statements in the loop body. The *redo* statement repeats execution of the loop body without advancing to the next iteration. The *last* statement terminates execution of the loop, skipping any remaining statements in the body.

Pattern Matching and Regular Expressions

Perl provides a powerful set of string matching and replacement features through regular expressions. *Regular expressions* consist of literal and wildcard characters combined to form a pattern. This pattern can be used to search for a series of characters that match the pattern. For example, the pattern er matches the second and third characters in the string Perl. This pattern does not require that the entire string match the pattern, only that the letters "er" are found somewhere within the string.

The pattern matching operator /pattern/ searches $_ for pattern and returns 1 if there is a match or false if not. The following example searches for the pattern /er/ in $_:

```
$_ = 'Perl';
print "matched\n" if /er/;
```

The =~ operator binds the pattern to any variable:

```
$line = <STDIN>;
print "matched\n" if $line =~ /er/;
```

This example reads a line of input to the variable line. This variable is then searched for the pattern /er/. The =~ operator applies this pattern to the line variable instead of the default $_. The message is printed only if the letters "er" are found in line.

The !~ operator also binds a pattern to an expression, but returns true if the pattern does not match. The following statement prints a message if no match is found:

```
print "no match\n" if $line !~ /er/;
```

The pattern er contains only the literal characters “e” and “r”. The . metacharacter matches any character. The pattern /e./ matches an “e” followed by any character. “Perl” and “here” would be matched by the /e./ pattern, but “e” and “hare” would not (the “e” must be followed by another character).

A set of characters enclosed in square brackets ([]) matches only if one of these characters is found. This is more restrictive than ., which matches any character. The pattern /e[aeiouy]/ matches an “e” followed by any lowercase vowel or a “y”. “Pear” and “barley” match this pattern, but “Perl” and “eA” do not.

Placing a ^ as the first character in a set changes the meaning to match any character except those enclosed in the square brackets. The pattern /e[^aeiouy]/ matches “perl” and “wrench,” but not “pear.”

Ranges may be specified with a dash. The pattern /[A-Za-z]/ includes all alphabetic characters, both uppercase and lowercase. Individual characters and ranges may be intermixed. Perl provides backslash sequences for commonly used character classes, as shown in Table 11.2.

For example, the pattern /\s\d\d/ specifies a whitespace character followed by two numeric digits. The normal backslash sequences used in double-quoted strings are valid in regular expressions as well.

A repeat specifier, or quantifier, may be used to specify how many occurrences of a pattern or subpattern must appear, as shown in Table 11.3.

Table 11.2 Backslash Sequences

Sequence	Description	Equivalent Class
\d	Numeric digits	[0-9]
\D	Nondigits	[^0-9]
\w	Alphanumeric word characters plus underscore	[0-9a-zA-Z_]
\W	Nonword characters	[^0-9a-zA-Z_]
\s	Whitespace characters	[\t\n\r\f]
\S	Nonwhitespace characters	[^ \t\n\r\f]

Table 11.3 Repeat Specifiers

Quantifier	Meaning
*	Zero or more times; a match may occur with or without this part of the pattern.
+	Pattern must occur at least once.
?	Zero or one occurrences; subsequent occurrences are not matched.
{n}	Pattern must occur exactly n times.
{n,}	Pattern must occur at least n times.
{n, m}	Pattern must occur at least n, but no more than m times.

Examples are shown in Table 11.4.

Characters that are normally used as metacharacters in a regular expression may be matched by preceding them with a backslash. For example, the pattern /\.\./ searches for a pair of dots (periods) only; the dots are not interpreted as wildcard characters.

An alternate form of quoting is available when the pattern contains the slashes that would normally surround the pattern. The m// operator has the same effect as //, but it enables you to use nonalphanumeric characters in place of slashes. The pattern m#//# uses the # symbol to quote the pattern and matches a pair of slashes (//). This is easier to read than the equivalent /\/\//.

The ^ (when appearing outside [] brackets) and $ characters "anchor" a pattern to the beginning or end of a string. The pattern /^\d/ means that a string must begin

Table 11.4 Examples of Repeat Specifiers

Pattern	Description	Matches	But Not
/\d+:/	One or more digits followed by a colon	123: or x3:	x: or :
/[a-z]+\d*:/	One or more lowercase letters followed by zero or more digits, then a semicolon	x3: or xyz:	x or :
/\w{3}/	Three word characters in a row	xyz	xx

with a numeric digit for it to match. A value of "3xyz" matches, but "x3" or "3" (leading space) do not match. The pattern /\d$/ specifies that the string must end with a digit to match.

Alternate subexpressions may be specified by separating them with the | symbol. Subexpressions are often placed within parentheses to separate them from surrounding characters. For example, the pattern /f(ea|ou|u)r/ matches "fear," "four," or "fur."

Using Match Results

The parentheses serve another purpose as well. Characters matched by parenthesized subexpressions are remembered for use later on in the pattern. The characters matched by the first subexpression are available in \1, the result of the next subexpression is in \2, and so on. For example, the pattern /f(.)\1/ matches an "f" followed by any pair of matching characters. The . in the parentheses matches any single character. The \1 that follows is called a back-reference and evaluates to whatever character was matched by the first subexpression (the dot).

These same results are available outside the pattern through the special read-only variables $1, $2, etc. The following example extracts lowercase letters, then numbers from a string:

```
$_ = "abc123xyz";
print "$1: $2\n" if /([a-z]*)(\d*)/;
```

This example prints "abc:123". Lowercase letters are matched first with the pattern [a-z]* and placed in $1. Following that, any numeric digits are matched by the pattern \d* and placed in $2. Any remaining input is ignored. If the pattern matches (and it will in this case because the input is specified in the preceding statement) the matched portions are printed.

When evaluated in a scalar context, the pattern-matching operator returns a true or false value to indicate whether the pattern could be matched. When evaluated in a list context, however, the result is a list containing all matched subexpressions:

```
$_ = "abc123xyz";
($letters, $numbers) = /([a-z]*)(\d*)/;
print "$letters:$numbers\n";
```

Here the variables letters and numbers receive any characters matched by the first and second subexpressions of the pattern.

Replacement with Patterns

The substitution operator s/// replaces text matched by a pattern with alternate text. The search pattern is placed between the first two slashes, and the replacement text is specified between the last pair of slashes. For example:

```
$a = 'x12y34z';
$a =~ s/\d+/!/;
print "$a\n";
```

The =~ in the second statement binds the substitution operation to the variable just as it would for the pattern-matching operation. The first series of one or more numeric digits will be replaced with a single !. This example prints "x!y34z".

Adding a g after the substitution operator causes all occurrences of the pattern to be replaced. This version of the previous example prints "x!y!z":

```
$a = 'x12y34z';
$a =~ s/\d+/!/g;
print "$a\n";
```

As with m//, alternate quote characters may be used with s///:

```
print "$_\n" if s#/(\w*)/#{$1}#g;
```

This statement replaces slashes that enclose words with braces enclosing the same words and prints the result if any replacements are made. The # symbol is used in place of / to delimit the patterns so that the slashes can be used in the pattern without preceding them with backslashes.

Character Translation

The translation operator tr/// replaces all characters in the first list, the search list, with the corresponding character from the second list, the replacement list. For example, tr/a-z/A-Z/ translates any lowercase characters in $_ to uppercase. The =~ operator binds the translation operator to a specific variable:

```
$a =~ tr/a-z/A-Z/;
```

Alternate quote characters may be specified:

```
$a =~ tr|/|\\|;
```

This statement replaces / characters with \ characters using | to delimit the search and replacement expressions. A second \ character is required in the replacement list to specify a literal backslash.

Functions

Perl provides a large number of functions that perform a variety of tasks. This section introduces a few of the more popular functions. For more detailed information on these and other functions, see the Perl man pages or documentation for your installation.

warn, exit, and die

The exit function terminates the program without an error. This is similar to the die function introduced earlier, but die terminates the program with an error and prints an error message. The warn function prints an error message without terminating the program.

```
warn "zero" unless $count;  # prints error message and continues
exit;                       # terminates program without error
die "zero" unless $count;   # prints error message then terminates
localtime and gmtime
```

The localtime function returns a list containing the components of the specified date and time. If no parameter is specified, localtime uses the current date and time. The list returned includes elements for seconds, minutes, hours, day, month, year, weekday, day of year, and daylight savings time. The following program prints the current date and time:

```
@months = ('Jan', 'Feb', 'Mar', 'Apr', 'May', 'Jun',
           'Jul', 'Aug', 'Sep', 'Oct', 'Nov', 'Dec');
@days = ('Sun', 'Mon', 'Tue', 'Wed', 'Thu', 'Fri', 'Sat');
($sc, $mn, $hr, $dy, $mo, $yr, $wd, $yd, $ds) = localtime;
print "Today is $days[$wd], $months[$mo] $dy, $yr, day #$yd\n";
print "The time is $hr:$mn:$sc\n";
print "(daylight savings time)\n" if $ds;
```

This code prints the date and time formatted as follows:

```
Today is Mon, Dec 9, 96, day #343
The time is 12:29:26
```

This program first initializes two arrays containing the names of the months and weekdays. The list returned by localtime is assigned to a list of variables. Each variable in this list receives the corresponding element from the list returned by localtime. The first print statement uses the arrays defined earlier to display the day and month names.

Under Perl 5, localtime returns a string containing the formatted date and time when evaluated in a scalar context. The following example demonstrates a much easier way to format the current date and time in version 5:

```
$now = localtime;
print "$now\n";
```

Here the return value from localtime is assigned to a single variable instead of a list of variables, which sets a scalar context. This method prints the current time formatted as "Mon Dec 9 12:29:26 1996."

The gmtime function works the same way, except that the values returned represent the corresponding time in the Greenwich time zone.

The sleep function pauses the program for the specified number of seconds. The return value is the number of seconds:

```
print "Sleeping...";
$slept = sleep 5;
print "Slept for $slept seconds\n";
```

This routine can be useful when you need to pause between attempts at retrying a failed operation.

system

The system function executes a system command or program:

```
system 'ls';
print "\n** DONE **\n";
```

This example prints a listing of files in the current directory using the ls command. Substitute the dir command on Microsoft DOS or Windows systems.

The command may contain shell characters:

```
system 'ls | grep "e"';
```

This statement lists only those filenames containing an "e." Substitute the following command on Microsoft systems:

```
system "dir /b | find \"E\"";
```

The command uses the shell character | to pipe the output from ls to the grep or find program. grep and find print only the lines containing an "e" in this example.

Another method of executing system commands is the "backtick quoting" mechanism. The command is placed within back-quote characters as in 'ls'. An advantage of this construct is that it returns the output of the command in a list. The following example fills an array with filenames that have an "e" in them:

```
@files = 'ls | grep "e"';
chop(@files);
```

This example comes from a Microsoft system:

```
@files = 'dir /b | find \"E\"';
chop(@files);
```

eval

The eval function executes a string as if it were a subroutine. This "program" has access to all variables in the current program:

```
$who = 'you';
$prog = 'print "Hey $who!\n"';
print "$prog\n";
eval $prog;
```

This code generates the following output:

```
print "Hey $who!\n"
Hey you!
```

This example sets the prog variable to a string representing a *print* statement. Single quotes are used to avoid interpolation at this point. The next line prints this string to demonstrate that no interpolation has taken place yet. The last statement calls eval to evaluate this statement, which results in the interpolation of the who variable and execution of the *print* statement.

A more common use of eval is to catch errors that would otherwise terminate the program. The special variable $@ contains an error message if an error is encountered:

```
$n = 2;
eval {$r = 4 / $n};
warn "ERROR: $@" if $@;
print "Result: $r\n";
```

Here eval is used to catch an error that would normally be fatal, dividing by 0. This example prints the result of the division. However, if the first line is changed to:

```
$n = 0;
```

The program will now encounter a division by 0 error. The statement being evaluated is terminated prematurely, and the variable r does not receive a value. The program continues to execute, however, and the resulting error message is printed.

int

This function returns the integer portion of a real number. int does not round, it truncates. The following statement sets variable i to 3:

```
$i = int (3.9);
```

hex

The hex function converts a string of hexadecimal digits to their decimal numeric value. Hexadecimal is a base-16 numbering system that uses the digits 0–9 and characters A–F to represent values between 10 and 15. For example, the "hex" number 20 is equivalent to the decimal number 32. This statement converts the hex digits 2B into their decimal equivalent, 43:

```
print hex('2B');
```

index and rindex

The index function searches for a substring within another string, but it does not use pattern matching. This function returns the position of the first occurrence of the substring, starting from position 0:

```
$pos = index('Perl', 'er');
```

The substring "er" is found within the string "Perl," starting at the second character. This statement sets the variable pos to 1, the position of the second character (0 is the position of the first character).

An optional starting position may be specified:

```
$pos = index('Perl', 'er', 2);
```

This statement begins searching from the third character (position 2). The substring "er" cannot be found from this position on, so the index function returns –1 to indicate failure.

The rindex function performs the same task but begins searching from the end, the right side, of a string, for the last occurrence of a substring.

Unlike most other functions, a return value of 0 from index or rindex does not indicate failure, but rather that the substring was found starting at the first character of the string.

substr

This function extracts a portion of a string:

```
print substr('Perl', 1, 2);
```

This statement prints "er", the portion of the string "Perl" that starts with the second character (position 1) and extends for a length of two characters.

length

The length function returns the length of a string. This statement prints "3":

```
print length('abc');
```

If no string is specified, length operates on $_.

pack

This function converts a list of values into their internal binary representation according the specified template. A common use for this function in CGI programs is decoding nonalphanumeric characters embedded in form data. Most of these characters are encoded by the Web browser into the form %xx, where xx is a pair of hexadecimal digits. The C template converts a number into the corresponding ASCII character:

```
$ch = pack ('C', hex('2B'));
```

This statement first converts the hexadecimal digits 2B (decimal 43) into numeric form using the hex function, then converts this number into the corresponding character + using the pack function.

The pack function recognizes many other formats; see your Perl documentation for details.

push and pop

The push function adds, or "pushes," values onto the end of an array:

```
@citrus = ('grapefruit', 'oranges');
push (@citrus, 'limes', 'lemons');
```

This example adds the elements "lemons" and "limes" to the end of the citrus array. The array now contains the values "grapefruit," "oranges," "limes," and "lemons."

The pop function removes the last item from a list and returns its value:

```
$last = pop (@citrus);
```

This statement removes the last element of the citrus array, "lemons," and assigns it to the variable named last.

shift and unshift

These functions provide the same functionality as pop and push, but they operate on the start of an array rather than the end.

shift removes the first element of an array:

```
$first = shift (@citrus);
```

The first element of the citrus array, "grapefruit," is removed and assigned to the variable first.

unshift inserts elements at the start of an array. The citrus array contains the elements "limes," "lemons," "grapefruit," and "oranges" after the following:

```
@citrus = ('grapefruit', 'oranges');
unshift (@citrus, 'limes', 'lemons');
```

sort

The sort function returns a list sorted in ascending order:

```
@citrus = ('grapefruit', 'oranges', 'limes', 'lemons');
@sorted = sort (@citrus);
```

The sorted array is assigned the elements of the citrus array in the order "grapefruit," "lemons," "limes," and "oranges."

Reverse

```
This function reverses the order of all elements in a list:
@citrus = ('grapefruit', 'oranges', 'limes', 'lemons');
```

```
@backwards = reverse (@citrus);
```

The elements of the array backward are in the opposite order of citrus—"lemons," "limes," "oranges," and "grapefruit."

split

This function splits a string into an array of strings and returns this array. With no parameters specified, this function splits the contents of $_ into separate words:

```
$_ = 'This is a test';
@words = split;
```

The array words now contains the elements "This," "is, "a," and "test."

A pattern may be specified to split a string using a different delimiter than white-space between words:

```
$inventory = 'grapefruit,oranges;limes,lemons';
@citrus = split (/[,;]/, $inventory);
```

This example splits a string into the items array. A character class is used as the pattern to split on either commas or semicolons. The citrus array now contains the elements "grapefruit," "oranges," "limes," and "lemons."

A string other than $_ may be specified after the pattern:

```
@fields = split (/&/, $ENV{'QUERY_STRING'});
$" = "\n";
```

This example splits form data submitted from an HTML form. If the form data consisted of "name=Bob&email=bob@mjhb.com", the elements of fields would be "name=Bob" and "email=bob@mjhb.com".

join

The join function assembles the elements of a list into a single string. The first parameter is a string to be used as a separator between each element:

```
@citrus = ('grapefruit', 'oranges', 'limes', 'lemons');
$list = join (':', @citrus);
```

The list variable now contains the string "grapefruit:oranges:limes:lemons".

keys

The keys function returns a list containing all of the keys from an associative array:

```
%shapes = ('sphere', 'round', 'box', 'square');
@shape_keys = keys (%shapes);
```

The first line assigns two items to the shapes associative array: the value "round" with the key "sphere" and "square" with the key "box." The shape_keys list-type array now contains two elements, "sphere" and "box," but not necessarily in that order. Due to the way data is stored in associative arrays, the keys will be returned in an unpredictable order

Values

This function is similar to the keys function except that it extracts values instead of keys from an associative array:

```
@shape_values = values (%shapes);
```

This statement assigns the elements "round" and "square" to the shape_values array. As with the keys, the values will be returned in a somewhat random order.

Delete

The delete function removes a key and its associated value:

```
delete $shapes{'sphere'};
```

The associative array shapes no longer contains the key "sphere" or its associated value "round."

Subroutines

In addition to the functions provided by Perl, you can write your own functions, known as subroutines. The *sub* statement begins definition of a subroutine:

```
sub PrintRule {
  print "<HR width=400 noshade>";
}
```

This function outputs the HTML for a stylized horizontal rule. This function would be useful in a CGI program that outputs this type of rule several times. If you later decide on different attributes for the horizontal rules, you would need to change them only in this one subroutine.

A subroutine is invoked, or called, by prefixing its name with an ampersand &:

```
&PrintRule;
```

This statement calls the PrintRule subroutine, which prints the HTML for a horizontal rule.

By default all variables in Perl are global. This means that variables used elsewhere in a program are accessible by subroutines as well:

```
sub PrintRule {
  print "<HR width=$hr_width noshade>";
}
```

The width of the rule is now specified by the variable hr_width. This variable should be assigned a proper value before this subroutine is called. It is not an error if hr_width is undefined, but its value will be an empty string, which would cause this routine to print bad HTML <HR width= noshade>.

Parameters to Subroutines

Parameters may be included in a subroutine call to enable the subroutine to customize its behavior. Within a subroutine, the @_ array contains any values passed as parameters:

```
sub PrintRule {
  print "<HR width=$_[0] noshade>";
}
```

The rule width is now specified by the first parameter passed to the subroutine, array index 0. When calling this subroutine, the parameter is passed in the same way that parameters are passed to functions:

```
&PrintRule (500);
```

Often it is convenient to create variables that are local to the subroutine. Local variables exist only during execution of the subroutine and will not conflict with any global variables having the same names. When the subroutine exits, returning control to its caller, any local variables are discarded. The local function creates this kind of variables:

```
sub PrintRule {
  local($width, $height) = @_;
  print "<HR width=$width size=$height>";
}
```

The local function returns a list containing the newly created variables. These variables are destroyed after the last statement of this subroutine, the *print* statement. This example assigns the list of parameters from the @_ array to the list of local variables, width and height. The width variable now contains the value passed as the first parameter, and height contains any value passed as the second parameter. Any additional parameters that were passed to this subroutine are ignored. This subroutine would now be called like this:

```
&PrintRule (500, 10);
```

This call specifies a value of 500 for the width parameter and 10 for height.

Return Value from Subroutines

The return value of a subroutine is whatever value is produced by the last statement in the subroutine. The last statement in our PrintRule example is a *print* statement. The *print* statement returns a value of 1 if successful or 0 if not, and this is the value returned by PrintRule. This enables the following usage:

```
if (&PrintRule (500, 10)) {
  print "<CENTER>Hello</CENTER>";
}
```

Example Scripts

Following are several example Perl programs that demonstrate Web applications. Each example includes the code, plus a description of how the code works.

Test Script

The first script, first.pl, is a simple test to get up and running. This script generates a simple HTML page:

```
#!/usr/bin/perl

$title = 'Test Perl Script';

# print "HTTP/1.0 200 OK\n";   # required by PerlIIS only
```

```
 6 print "Content-type: text/html\n\n";
 7
 8 print "<HTML>\n<HEAD><TITLE>$title</TITLE></HEAD>\n<BODY>\n";
 9 print "<H1>$title</H1><HR>\n";
10 print "Greetings from the first example script.\n";
11 print "</BODY>\n</HTML>";
```

The code can be explained as follows:

- Line 1 is required for Perl scripts that will run on UNIX systems. This line specifies the location of the Perl interpreter. Ask your system or Web administrator for the path that is appropriate on your system.

- Line 3 initializes a variable that will be used later. CGI scripts often initialize several variables near the beginning of the script. This is a common practice that makes it easy to customize the script for each installation.

- Line 5 is a *print* statement that is "commented out." If you have problems running this script on the Microsoft Internet Information Server (MS IIS), you may need to activate this line by removing the leading #. When activated, this statement prints a status response. Normally the http server generates this for you, but certain implementations of Perl running on MS IIS do not.

- Line 6 is the mime header required of all CGI scripts that generate output. This header specifies the type of output that follows. The Web browser uses this information to format the output correctly. The text/html type specifies text that contains HTML. This line ends with two newline characters. A blank line must separate the headers from the document body (the actual HTML). One of the most common errors in CGI programs is to omit the second newline, which prevents the blank line from appearing.

- Line 8 begins the actual HTML. This statement generates the head section and the opening body tag. The title variable from line 3 is used to display the page title. The embedded newline characters are not actually necessary here, nor anywhere further. They are added to make the HTML easier to read when viewing the document source from a Web browser (which you will do frequently while writing your own scripts).

- Lines 9 and 10 print the body of the page. The title variable is used again in the body. The newline characters after each line are not necessary, but they make the HTML easier to read when viewing the document source from a Web browser.

- The last line, 11, prints counterparts for tags generated earlier.

Copy this script into an executable directory on your Web server. Next, you must set the file permissions, as discussed at the beginning of this chapter. At this point you should be able to run the script from a URL like http://www.mydomain.com/cgi-bin/first.pl.

Replace the server name (www.mydomain.com) and directory name (cgi-bin) with whatever is appropriate for your Web server.

This program currently generates output, but it does accept any input. The second version of this script, second.pl, generates a pair of links that send input back to the script. The script looks for this input and prints a message including it if found.

```
1   #!/usr/bin/perl
2
3   $title = 'Test Perl Script';
4   $script_url = "http://$ENV{'SERVER_NAME'}$ENV{'SCRIPT_NAME'}";
5
6   # print "HTTP/1.0 200 OK\n";  # required by PerlIIS only
7   print "Content-type: text/html\n\n";
8
9   print "<HTML>\n<HEAD><TITLE>$title</TITLE></HEAD>\n<BODY>\n";
10  print "<H1>$title</H1><HR>\n";
11
12  if (length($ENV{'QUERY_STRING'})) {
13    print "You clicked the $ENV{'QUERY_STRING'} link!<P>\n";
14  } else {
15    print "No input was found.<P>\n";
16  }
17
18  print qq|<A href="$script_url?first">First Link</A><P>\n|;
19  print qq|<A href="$script_url?second">Second Link</A><P>\n|;
20
21  print "</BODY>\n</HTML>";
```

This code can be explained as follows:

- Lines 1 and 3 are unchanged from the previous version.
- Line 4 creates a variable that contains the URL of the script. The URL is constructed by interpolating a pair of CGI environment variables, SERVER_NAME

and SCRIPT_NAME, into a string. The server name will be something like "www.mydomain.com" (with your server name instead), and the script name should be "/cgi-bin/second.pl" (with your directory name instead). The %ENV associative array contains all environment variables available to the script. Using CGI environment variables avoids the need to maintain the URL inside the script. The script now automatically knows where to "find itself." This URL will be used for the links later on.

- Lines 6 through 10 are unchanged from the previous version.
- Line 12 checks the length of the CGI environment variable QUERY_STRING to see if it contains any text. If so, the statement on line 13 is executed; otherwise, line 15 is executed instead.
- The statement on line 13 prints a message that includes the CGI input. Line 15 prints an alternate message if no input was found.
- Lines 18 and 19 generate a pair of links to the script using the previously defined script_url variable. These links include information in the URL that will appear as input to the script. Anything appearing after the ? in a URL will be interpreted as input and is placed into the QUERY_STRING environment variable before the CGI program is run. The qq/ alternate quoting mechanism is used due to the embedded double quotes. This construct allows the use of a different delimiting character; in this case | is used. Of course, the double quotes could have been prefaced with backslashes in a normal double-quoted string instead.
- Line 21 is unchanged from the previous version.

Install and run this script as before. When you click one of the links, the script is executed again displaying the name of that link. This script is not terribly useful, but it demonstrates a commonly used method for sending and retrieving information through CGI. This mechanism of submitting data from the browser to a CGI program via URL arguments is known as the GET method.

Add-a-Link

This script, links.pl, maintains a list of URLs and titles. A form is displayed at the bottom of the page for submitting new entries. This script demonstrates another popular method of submitting data, the POST method. This script uses several subroutines to isolate the separate tasks that are performed. This makes the script easier to read and understand.

```
#!/usr/bin/perl

$title = 'Links to other pages';
$links = '/usr/web/htdocs/misc/links';
$script_url="http://$ENV{'SERVER_NAME'}$ENV{'SCRIPT_NAME'}";

# print "HTTP/1.0 200 OK\n";  # required by PerlIIS only
print "Content-type: text/html\n\n";

print "<HTML>\n<HEAD><TITLE>$title</TITLE></HEAD>\n<BODY>\n";
print "<H1>$title</H1><HR>\n";

&add_link if $ENV{'REQUEST_METHOD'} eq 'POST';
&show_links;
&show_form;

print "</BODY>\n</HTML>";

sub add_link {
  &parse_form;

  open (LINKS, ">>$links") || die "Can't open file $links: $!"
  flock (LINKS, 2) || die "Can't flock $links: $!";
  seek (LINKS, 0, 2) || die "Can't seek $links: $!";

  print LINKS "$FORM{'URL'} $FORM{'DESC'}\n" ||
    die "Can't print to $links: $!";

  flock (LINKS, 8) || die "Can't un-flock $links: $!";
  close (LINKS) || die "Can't close $links: $!";
}

sub show_links {
  open (LINKS, "$links") || die "Can't open file $links: $!";

  print "<UL>\n";
  while (<LINKS>) {
    ($url, $desc) = split (/\s/, $_, 2);
    print qq|<LI><A href="$url">$desc</A><BR>\n|;
  }
  print "</UL>\n";

  close (LINKS) || die "Can't close file $links: $!";
}

sub show_form {
   print qq/<P><HR><FORM action="$script_url"
```

```
      method="POST">\n/;
48    print qq|<PRE>        <B>Add-A-Link</B>\n\n|;
49
50    print qq/  URL: <INPUT name="URL" size=60 maxlength=60>\n/;
51    print qq/Title: <INPUT name="DESC" size=60
        maxlength=60>\n\n/;
52
53    print qq/         <INPUT type="SUBMIT" value="Add Link"> /;
54    print qq/<INPUT type="RESET">\n/;
55    print "</PRE></FORM>\n";
56  }
57
58  sub parse_form
59  {
60    local($buffer, $name, $value);
61
62    read(STDIN, $buffer, $ENV{'CONTENT_LENGTH'});
63
64    foreach (split(/&/, $buffer)) {
65      ($name, $value) = split(/=/);
66
67      $name =~ tr/+/ /;
68      $name =~ s/%([a-fA-F0-9][a-fA-F0-9])/pack
       ("C", hex($1))/eg;
69
70      $value =~ tr/+/ /;
71      $value =~ s/%([a-fA-F0-9][a-fA-F0-9])/pack
       ("C", hex($1))/eg;
72
73      $FORM{$name} = $value;
74    }
75  }
```

The code can be explained as follows:

- Lines 1 through 11 should look familiar by now, with the exception of line 4. This line specifies the location of the file containing the links. This location is specified not with a URL, but rather by the full path to the file on the local system. This location would look something like c:\\inetpub\wwwroot\\misc\\links on a Microsoft system (extra backslashes are necessary to include literal backslashes).
- Line 13 calls the add_link subroutine, which is defined later, to append a new link to the file if one has been "posted" from the browser. The environment

variable REQUEST_METHOD contains the name of the method that was used to submit the data. The most commonly used method names are GET and POST.

- Line 14 calls the show_links subroutine to display the links, including a new one added by the previous statement. Line 15 calls the show_form subroutine to display the form.
- Line 17 is the last line of the main program.
- Lines 19 through 31 define the add_link subroutine. This routine retrieves and processes the data posted from the form, then appends this data to the links file.
- Line 20 calls a subroutine named parse_form, defined later, to retrieve the field values. parse_form places each field name and value into an associative array named %FORM. This keys of this array correspond to the HTML input field names, and the values are whatever the user entered into the corresponding fields.
- Line 22 attempts to open the file named by the previously defined links variable. The >> symbol opens the file for append access. Data written to a file opened for append access is added to the end of the file without disturbing the existing contents.
- Line 23 introduces a new function, flock. This call attempts to "lock" a file so that no other process, like another Web browser, will update the file at the same time. The parameter 2 instructs flock to wait for the file to become "unlocked" if it is currently locked (see your Perl documentation for detailed information on this function). The file is not actually rendered inaccessible. flock succeeds only in preventing other processes from locking the file at the same time. As such, it is simply a "protocol" for coordinating access to a file. If every program that accesses this file attempts to "lock" it first, only one program will be allowed to write to it at a time. If two or more processes attempt to write to the same file at the same time, the file may be destroyed.
- Line 24 calls another unfamiliar function, seek. This function moves the current position within the file associated with the specified handle. The current position is the location at which the next read or write operation will take place. When a file is first opened, its current position is usually at the start of the file so that the first read operation will return the first line of data. The file handle LINKS was opened for append access, however, which moves the current posi-

tion to the end of the file. The statement on line 24 explicitly moves to the end of the file again. This guards against the possibility that another process added a link to the end of the file after this program opened it.

- Lines 26 writes the new link information to the file via the familiar print function. This statement directs print to send its output to the links file instead of STDOUT. Line 27 dies if print was unsuccessful. It is always a good idea to check for errors after any file operation.
- Line 29 calls flock again, this time with an 8 to remove the lock requested on line 23 (see your Perl documentation for more on flock). Line 30 closes the file.
- Lines 33 through 44 define the show_links subroutine. This subroutine displays the individual links stored in the file.
- Line 34 opens the file, this time for read-only access. Line 36 prints an opening UL HTML tag to begin a bulleted list.
- Lines 37 through 40 constitute a while loop that iterates as long as a line of input can be read from the file. Because no variable is present on line 37, the line of input is placed in the $_ variable.
- Line 38 splits this line into two pieces, a URL and description. The third parameter to the split function specifies the maximum number of items to split. This statement uses the whitespace pattern to separate the first word (the URL) from the rest of the line (the page title).
- Line 39 prints the HTML for a bulleted link using the URL and title obtained in the previous statement.
- Line 41 prints a closing tag to match the one generated by line 36. Line 43 closes the file.
- Lines 46 through 56 define the function show_form. This function consists entirely of print statements that generate HTML for the form used to submit new links.
- Line 47 directs the form to submit its contents to this script and to use the POST method for transmission.
- Lines 58 through 75 define a general-purpose subroutine to retrieve the contents of a form submitted via the POST method. When form contents are sub-

mitted using this method, the encoded data is fed to the CGI program through STDIN. The CONTENT_LENGTH environment variable specifies how much data is waiting to be read. This subroutine decodes the form fields and places them into an associative array named %FORM.

- Line 60 defines a few local variables that are usable only within this subroutine.
- Line 62 reads the encoded form data from STDIN into the local buffer variable. The number of character transferred from STDIN to buffer is specified by the environment variable CONTENT_LENGTH.
- Line 64 splits the form data in buffer into a list of "name=value" pairs. Each of these pairs contains an input field name and its associated value. A foreach loop then iterates over the list returned by split, setting $_ to the next "name=value" pair on each iteration.
- Line 65 performs a split on each of these pairs to separate the name and value. No expression is passed for split to operate on, so it uses $_ by default. $_ contains the current "name=value" pair from the foreach loop in the previous statement.
- Line 67 translates any + symbols in the name to spaces. Plus signs represent spaces in the encoded data.
- Line 68 shows off Perl's powerful pattern matching and substitution abilities. The goal of this statement is to replace %xx hexadecimal sequences with the indicated character. The search pattern looks for a % followed by exactly two hex digits. The parentheses cause any matched digits to be made available in $1. The replacement string is actually an expression that invokes two functions. The hex function converts the hexadecimal digits to their numeric decimal value. This value is then passed to the pack function, which converts the number to the corresponding character. This character then replaces the % and the pair of hex digits. The e suffix to the s// operator specifies that the replacement string is more than a double-quoted string and must be reevaluated before each replacement. The g suffix specifies that all occurrences of the search pattern are to be replaced, not just the first one.
- Lines 70 and 71 repeat this process for the input value.
- Line 73 adds the name and value to the %FORM associative array. The value of any input field from the form may now be referenced by the input field's name, for example, $FORM{'URL'}.

Install this script as before. You will need to create a file with at least one link in it. Each link is formatted as http://www.mjhb.com Title goes here. All that is required is whitespace between the link and its title. The title may consist of multiple words.

Mail Merge

This program formats the contents of a form and sends the results via e-mail. The formatting information is stored in a template file. The template contains text interspersed with markers for form fields. The program reads each line from the template file and replaces field markers with the corresponding value submitted by the form. Each updated line is then sent to the mailer program as part of an e-mail message.

The template filename is submitted to the script along with the form data. This enables a single copy of the script to process different template files. An example template, sample.txt, appears as follows:

```
1  To: sales@fictitious.com
2  Subject: ~SUBJECT
3
4  On ~NOW, ~NAME (~EMAIL)
5  submitted the following comments:
6
7  ~COMMENTS
```

This code can be explained as follows:

- Lines 1 and 2 are header lines that specify the recipient and subject of the message. This template specifies that the message will be sent to sales@fictitious.com; replace this with your e-mail address before using this file. A blank line must separate the header lines from the rest of the message. This is the format used by the UNIX sendmail program. If your system does not use sendmail, you will have to modify the template as well as the program to work with your particular mailer program.
- The subject header on line 2 includes the value of an input field named SUBJECT. Input field names are prefaced with a ~ for the script to recognize them.
- Lines 4 through 7 constitute the body of the message. NOW is a special variable provided by the script that contains the date and time that the form was submitted. The remaining variables are must be provided by the HTML form.

The following, sample.html, is an example feedback form for use with the template shown above:

```
1  <HTML>
2  <HEAD><TITLE>Feedback Form</TITLE></HEAD>
3  <BODY>
4
5  <H1>Feedback Form</H1><HR>
6
7  <FORM method="POST"
8   action="http://www.fictitious.com/cgi-bin/mailmerge.pl">
9
10 <INPUT type="HIDDEN" name="TEMPLATE" value="sample.txt">
11 <INPUT type="HIDDEN" name="RESPONSEURL"
12  value="http://www.fictitious.com/response.html">
13
14 Your name : <INPUT name="NAME"><BR>
15 Email address: <INPUT name="EMAIL"><BR>
16 Subject : <INPUT name="SUBJECT"><BR>
17 Comments: <TEXTAREA name="COMMENTS" rows=3 cols=50>
18 </TEXTAREA><P>
19
20 <INPUT type="SUBMIT"> <INPUT type="RESET">
21 </FORM>
22 </BODY>
```

The script location on line 8 must be modified to identify the script installed on your system.

The code can be explained as follows:

- Line 10 specifies the template name in a hidden field. The location of this file is specified inside the script itself. Line 11 specifies the URL of a page to display after the form has been submitted. Modify this line to identify any page on your system.

- Lines 14 through 18 define input fields that will be submitted to the script. The field names used here define the names available to the template.

The script is located in the file mailmerge.pl:

```
#!/usr/bin/perl

$template_path = '/usr/web/htdocs/misc/templates/';
$mail_program = '/usr/lib/sendmail -t';

```

```
&parse_form;
$FORM{'NOW'} = localtime;

$template_file = $FORM{'TEMPLATE'}
  || &eject('Missing template specification');
$template_file =~ s/\.\.//g;

&process_template($template_path . $template_file);

# print "HTTP/1.0 302 FOUND\n";  # required by PerlIIS only
print "Location: $FORM{'RESPONSEURL'}\n\n";

sub parse_form {
  local($buffer, $name, $value);

  read(STDIN, $buffer, $ENV{'CONTENT_LENGTH'});

  foreach (split(/&/, $buffer)) {
    ($name, $value) = split(/=/);

    $name =~ tr/+/ /;
    $name =~ s/%([a-fA-F0-9][a-fA-F0-9])/
          pack("C", hex($1))/eg;

    $value =~ tr/+/ /;
    $value =~ s/%([a-fA-F0-9][a-fA-F0-9])/
   pack("C", hex($1))/eg;

    $FORM{$name} = $value;
  }
}

sub process_template {
  local($template) = @_;

  open TEMPLATE, "$template"
    || &eject("Cannot open template $template", $!);

  open MAIL, "|$mail_program"
    || &eject("Cannot open mail program $mail_program", $!);

  while ($line = <TEMPLATE>) {
    $line =~ s/~(\w+)/$FORM{$1}/ig;
    print MAIL "$line" || &eject ("print failed", $!);
  }

  close MAIL || &eject("Cannot close mail program", $!);
```

```
51      close TEMPLATE || &eject("Cannot close $filename", $!);
52    }
53
54    sub eject {
55    # print "HTTP/1.0 200 OK\n";  # required by PerlIIS only
56      print "Content-type: text/html\n\n";
57
58      print "<PRE><B>Error</B>:\n";
59
60      print join("\n", @_);
61      print "\n\nPlease go back and try again\n";
62
63      exit 1;
64    }
```

The code can be explained as follows:

- Line 3 specifies the directory that contains all template files. The TEMPLATE field submitted by the form contains only the filename with no path information. This is a precaution that prevents arbitrary files from being mailed by this script. Modify this line to something appropriate for your system.
- Line 4 specifies the command that will invoke the sendmail program. This program handles the details of forwarding a mail message to another computer.
- Line 6 calls the parse_form routine to decode the form data into the %FORM associative array. Line 7 adds the current date and time to this array with the name NOW. This value will then be available as if it had been submitted by the form.
- The statement spanning lines 9 and 10 ensures that the form data includes the template filename. The &eject subroutine simply prints an HTML-formatted error message before terminating the script.
- Line 11 strips the characters ".." from the filename in case someone tries to access a file outside the template directory. Backslashes are used in the search pattern to prevent the . characters from being interpreted as wildcards. The empty replacement string has the effect of removing occurrences of the search pattern. The g suffix ensures that all occurrences are replaced.
- Line 13 calls the &process_template subroutine to merge the form data with the template. A fully qualified filename is constructed by concatenating the template path and filename with the . operator.

- Line 16 is the last line of the main program. This statement prints a header that redirects the Web browser to the specified "response" page. This page should normally inform the user that the input has been processed. Line 15 prints an http response header that may be needed when using the Microsoft Web server. If necessary, remove the # from the beginning of the line to activate this statement.
- Lines 18 through 34 define the parse_form subroutine introduced in the Add-A-Link script.
- Lines 36 through 52 define the process_template subroutine. This routine merges the form data with the template file and mails the results. Line 37 stores the first parameter into the local variable template. This is the full filename passed from line 13.
- Lines 39 and 40 open the template file and call the eject subroutine if an error occurs.
- Line 42 attempts to open a "pipe" to the mail program, and line 43 calls eject if this fails. A pipe is a mechanism for feeding input to another program or reading its output. When data is written using the MAIL file handle, this data will be seen as input by the mailer program.
- Lines 45 through 48 constitute a while loop that iterates for each line of input retrieved form the template file. Line 46 replaces any variable names in the current line with the associated value from the %FORM array. The search pattern looks for a ~ followed by one or more word characters. Any characters matched are used in the replacement string as a key into the %FORM array. The i suffix to the s/// operator enables case-insensitive searches. This means that it is not necessary for variable names to be uppercase in the template; they will be found either way.
- Line 47 writes this modified line as input to the mailer program.
- Line 50 closes the pipe to the mailer program, and line 51 closes the template file.
- Lines 54 through 64 define the eject subroutine, which prints an error message and terminates the program. This program does not normally display any output. If all goes well, a redirection header is generated to display another page. No content-type header has been generated that would enable this script to dis-

play any output. The eject subroutine takes care of this by outputting a content-type header on line 56 before displaying the error message. As usual, uncomment line 55 if you encounter difficulties on the MS IIS web server.

- Lines 58 through 61 format and print the list of messages passed to this subroutine. The join function on line 60 concatenates the elements of the parameter array @_ with intervening newline characters. Line 63 uses the exit function to terminate the program.

Modify lines 1, 3, and 4 for your system, and copy the sample template file to the directory specified on line 3. The sample HTML file may be located anywhere, but be sure to modify lines 8 and 12 before using.

At this point you should be able to read and understand many of the free Perl scripts available on the Internet.

Chapter

12

Introduction to Java

As most any Web-watcher knows these days, Java is not a coffee or an island near a famous volcano. Rather, *Java* refers to a loosely related set of technologies developed by Sun Microsystems, which are now actively promoted through Sun's *JavaSoft* business unit. These technologies include an object-oriented programming language, a platform-independent bytecode specification, a virtual machine specification, and a forthcoming JavaOS operating system and JavaChip chipset.

What Is Java?

According to the creators of the language, Java is meant to provide a "network-centric computing platform that had, among other characteristics, the ability to allow programmers to write applications once and run them on virtually any hardware or software architecture." Recognizing that this goal would require an unprecedented level of cooperation between companies that were cutthroat competitors, Sun released detailed internal specifications of the Java technologies.

The specifications are sufficient to allow other companies to develop compatible "clean room" implementations of the technologies, which don't require royalty payments to, or approvals from, Sun. This has helped create the competitive environment that has moved Java forward so quickly while allaying developer fears of single-vendor systems. Given that nearly every major operating system vendor has committed to including the virtual machine within their operating system and that every major development tool vendor, including Borland, IBM, Microsoft, and Symantec, have released development tools for Java programming, it is reasonable to assume that the Java-related technologies are here to stay.

By leveraging its ownership of Java, Sun has been reasonably successful in maintaining the cross-platform compatibility of both Java *applets* and *applications*. Java *applets* are usually small programs, embedded in Web pages, that are downloaded to and run within the browser on a client machine. To prevent malicious applets from damaging files or surreptitiously gathering the potentially sensitive information stored on the client machine, the browser severely limits the access applets are given to the client machine's file system. In contrast, Java *applications* are full-fledged programs, not related to Web pages, that are installed locally on a machine and have full access to the file system.

Our primary focus will be on how to use the Java programming language, which I'll refer to interchangeably as Java from here on, to develop applets for the Web. However, it is important to recognize that Java is an industrial-strength, general-purpose programming language that can be used to build everything from small applets to full-fledged applications like word processors and spreadsheets. In fact, the principle tenets of Java, and of object-oriented programming languages in general, are intended to provide the capabilities required to manage the complexity of developing very large software systems.

Java is often referred to as a "cross-platform" or "portable" programming language. This simply means that a Java program will run successfully, without being changed or recompiled, on different types of computers and operating systems. So, in theory, any Java applets or applications you write should run equally well on Unix, Macintosh, Windows, and other systems. Sun cleverly designed Java to take advantage of the graphical user interface (GUI) components built into the underlying operating systems. Consequently, the same Java application that looks and operates like a native Macintosh application when running on a Macintosh will look and operate like a native Windows application when running on a Windows machine. This approach suffers somewhat from the "least common denominator" restrictions required to ensure equivalent functionality is available on all of the supported platforms, but it works remarkably well given the formidable technical challenges of any cross-platform solution.

Ironically, Java's cross-platform capabilities are actually provided by the bytecode and the Java Virtual Machine technologies mentioned earlier, which do not depend on the Java programming language at all. In fact, several companies are working on or have released compilers for other languages that compile those languages to the same bytecode format required by the Java Virtual Machine. Consequently, you may soon be able write platform-independent applications in other languages as easily as you can in Java. Because the terms *bytecode* and *virtual machine* may not be familiar, we'll take a moment to examine the critical role of these technologies prior to delving into the fundamentals of the Java programming language.

The Java Virtual Machine and Bytecodes

The Java Virtual Machine (VM) is the key component of Java's cross-platform capabilities. It is functionally equivalent to another type of computer, just like a Macintosh or Windows machine. It is called a "virtual" machine because, unlike real computers that require hardware and an operating system, the virtual machine is usually implemented as a platform-dependent software program. Written primarily in ANSI C, the VM has been ported to nearly all of the predominant computing platforms in use today. Like a "real" computer, the VM understands how to perform only a limited number of primitive functions, such as storing and retrieving values and performing mathematical calculations. The VM processes *bytecodes*, a platform-independent instruction set specifically designed to execute efficiently in the software-based virtual machine.

Because the VM is just a software program, each bytecode it processes is translated, on the fly, into one or more platform-specific *machine code* instructions that are, in turn, executed by the host machine. The overhead of interpreting the bytecodes tends to make Java programs run more slowly than programs compiled to the machine code of a specific platform. However, because the bytecodes were specifically designed for efficient translation to machine code, Java programs tend to be significantly faster than other interpreted languages. In addition, several companies have introduced "just-in-time" compilers that work with the VM to compile the bytecodes to platform-specific machine code while executing the program. This has resulted in very significant performance gains that have allowed Java applications to approach, and in some cases surpass, the speed of other natively compiled programs.

The JavaOS operating system and JavaChip chipset are alternative implementations of the virtual machine intended to eliminate Java's dependence on host operating systems and to allow Java programs to be run in small electronic devices.

Java—An Object-Oriented Language

In a nutshell, the Java programming language is a statically typed, object-oriented language that is syntactically similar to C++. It provides language-level support for encapsulation, inheritance, polymorphism, exception handling, and multithreaded programming. In addition, it handles memory allocation and provides automatic garbage collection. It also includes an extensive class library that provides support for, among other things, i/o, strings, data structures, images, sound, networking, and graphical user interfaces. As of the time of this writing, several additional libraries were being developed, including ones to add support for database access, platform-independent components, and electronic commerce.

Java is not a trivial language. It is both more complex and more capable than scripting languages. Although it is similar in name to JavaScript, the two bear little resemblance to each other beyond some common syntax. While Java may be commonly thought of as a tool for spicing up Web pages, it is, in fact, a full-featured language that is appropriate for a wide range of programming tasks. Its most compelling feature, besides the ease with which it can be used to develop cross-platform, network-aware programs, is its full support of the object-oriented programming paradigm.

Object-Oriented Programming Concepts

It is unfortunate that the obscure and inconsistent terminology related to object-oriented programming (OOP) has made concepts that are relatively straightforward hopelessly confusing to the average OOP newcomer. With new paradigms comes new terminology. However, the terminology associated with object-oriented programming can be particularly maddening because marketing departments have widely perverted the commonly accepted definition of an "object-oriented programming language" and introduced the nearly meaningless terms "object-based" and "object-aware." In addition, nearly all of the most popular true OOP languages use different terms for their respective language constructs that are, for most intents and purposes, identical. We will stick to the terminology commonly used with Java.

Object programmers experienced in other OOP languages will likely find these terms familiar. If this is your first exposure to OOP and you find the amount of new terminology daunting, concentrate on the concepts. The concepts apply equally well to any true OOP language. You'll likely find the terminology tends to come more easily as you begin to work with and understand the language.

The Evolution of Programming Languages

To understand the popularity of OOP languages, it is helpful to review the evolution of programming languages in general. Early computers were programmed by setting toggle switches, attached to the computer, which represented the individual bits of a binary instruction. The introduction of assembly language allowed programmers to ignore the lower-level bit sequences and concentrate on the sequence of instructions required for the task at hand.

Eventually, higher-level languages were created that allowed numerous machine-level instructions to be represented by a single command. Programs were no longer constrained to a particular computer architecture because different sets of machine-level instructions could be substituted for the higher-level commands. This allowed programmers to concentrate on the question of "how" to perform the task at hand, rather than on the architecture of the underlying computer.

As software systems became more complex, new language facilities such as procedures, functions, and data structures were introduced that provided several important benefits. The programs could be partitioned into small, reusable units that performed well-defined tasks. The unit's parameter lists and return values provided a well-defined method of communication between the units. As long as the parameter list and return values of a unit were preserved, the internal steps a unit performed to accomplish its task could be changed at will. Finally, data structures continued the trend of allowing programmers to organize and work with information in a manner that represented the problem at hand rather than the way the information was stored or processed by the computer.

Throughout all of these advances, programs continued to be organized as a series of steps that concentrated on "how" a particular outcome could be achieved. It was very typical for a procedural program to provide a limited number of options and then sit in a loop until a valid choice was made. This enabled the program to control the order in which options were presented to the user as well as the state of the environment in which the program was running. These luxuries disappeared as graphical user interfaces gained popularity and programs were required both to share resources and to respond to the arbitrary requests of the users who were now in control.

Object-oriented programming, which originates from languages designed for the development of simulations, proved to be a particularly effective way to manage this newfound complexity. It represents a significant shift in the design of software, in that it encourages the programmer to focus on "what" objects are in the system and the ways they interact, rather than immediately focusing on "how" a task is to be accomplished. Thus, object-oriented programming continues the evolution that has enabled programmers to develop software systems that model the real-world problems they are intended to solve.

Objects and Classes

As the name object-oriented programming implies, the fundamental concept of any object-oriented programming language is the *object*. If someone were to call you on the phone and ask you to describe the objects in the room with you, you'd have no problem doing so. You might, for instance, list, among other things, a book, a phone, a table, and a computer. If pressed for details, you might further describe the book by indicating things like its size, the number of pages it contains, the author, the title, and its publisher. In fact, you could describe any other books you have in the room by providing values for these same five characteristics: size, number of pages, author, title, and publisher.

In object-oriented terms, each book is a "Book" object. The five characteristics, which fully describe the specific pieces of information we're interested in maintaining about each book, are called a *class*. More specifically, we could name it the "Book" *class*.

A *class* is simply a named definition that fully describes the characteristics and behaviors of a particular kind of object. The process of identifying and creating *class* definitions is one of the most important and time-consuming activities in object-oriented programming. *Classes* can be thought of as the structural blueprints from which *objects* are constructed.

This analogy can be useful because it accurately implies that objects have a lifetime. They are created; they exist for a period of time and then they are destroyed. In programming terms, an object is created when a chunk of memory is allocated to hold its information. The object is destroyed when, after performing its function, it is no longer needed and the memory is freed for another use.

Returning to our example, each book is said to be an *object* or *instance of* the "Book" *class*. (The terms *instance* and *object* have identical meaning and are used interchangeably.) If you have six books in the room with you, then you have six *instances* of the book *class*. Each "Book" instance/object will contain a value for each of the characteristics defined in the "Book" class. Formally, the "characteristics" are referred to as *instance variables*.

Instance Variables

Instance variables are the storage locations that contain the data of an object. Each instance variable contains a specific type of information that may be anything from a simple value, like a single character, to another object. The set of values contained in all of the *instance variables* of a particular object is referred to as the object's *state*.

An object's instance variables are not usually made accessible to anything outside of the object itself. Instead, the object contains specialized functions, called *methods*, that provide strict control over the circumstances and manner in which the value, contained in an instance variable, can be changed.

Methods

Methods are the means by which an *object's* behaviors are defined and implemented. If we wanted to write a program that allowed a simulated book to be shown on a computer screen, the book "object" would have several behaviors. These would likely include the following: display cover, open book, load page, display page, turn page, and close book. These behaviors would be implemented as methods.

Methods are similar to the procedures and functions of traditional programming languages. They consist of the step-by-step instructions required to perform a specific process. Methods can optionally accept parameters and can return values. Often, a method's parameters and return values are objects. A method's name, along with the list of parameters it accepts, is referred to as the method's *signature*.

Methods can access any of the instance variables of the object to which they belong. Methods that exist primarily to return the current value contained in an instance variable are commonly referred to as "access" or "accessor" methods. Conversely, methods that primarily control the process of setting the value of an instance variable are commonly referred to as "assignment" or "mutator" methods.

Messages

Unlike traditional languages, in which procedures and functions directly call other procedures and functions, objects communicate by passing *messages*. A message consists of the name of a method implemented by the target object and any required parameters.

Messages are sent from one object to another to request that the receiving object perform some operation and possibly return a value. This process is similar in concept to ordering products through the mail. A company, through advertising, publishes a list of products that are available for sale. You (the sending object) initiate a transaction by filling out and sending in an order form (the message). The order form contains the specific information (method signature) necessary to let the company (the receiving object) know what action to perform in response to your request. The company processes your request and sends you the requested product (the return value).

Interfaces

Just as a company advertises the products and services it has available for sale, objects advertise the behaviors that other objects can request of them. In Java, this is accomplished by marking specific methods as "public" within the class definition. In object-oriented terms, the set of all of the "public" methods in an object is commonly referred to as the object's *interface*. As this term implies, there are two sides to each object: the public side, that is, the "face" it presents to the rest of the world (in this case, the other objects in the system), and the "private" side, the hidden way that it acts internally.

An object's *interface* serves the same function for software programs that the pedals and steering wheel of a car provide for drivers. It is a form of "contract" that defines the respective responsibilities of the provider and recipient of a service. The driver of a car utilizes the car's *interface* to request services. When he pushes the gas pedal, he is requesting that the car go faster. When she pushes the brake pedal, she is requesting that the car go slower. The driver needn't know anything about "how" the car operates internally. In fact, the way the car operates internally can be completely changed without affecting the driver's ability to operate the car. The engine can be replaced with a surplus jet engine and the brakes with a parachute. As long as the car's *interface* doesn't change, the driver will still be able to operate the car. (Admittedly, it may make for a more interesting ride to the supermarket.)

Encapsulation

As mentioned earlier, Java, like all true object-oriented programming languages, provides language-level support for encapsulation, inheritance, and polymorphism.

The concept of *encapsulation*, as it relates to object-oriented programming languages, refers to the ability to bundle related data (instance variables) and behaviors (methods) into a cohesive software unit whose implementation is hidden from outside view. That bundled software unit is an object. Because the internal representation and implementation of an object is hidden, it can be changed at any time without affecting any other parts of the system.

Encapsulation also facilitates *abstraction*. Through abstraction, the details of highly complex processes can be hidden behind interfaces that are relatively simple. Consider the complexity of the equipment that has to operate successfully to complete a cross-country phone call. Fortunately, those complexities are hidden behind the reasonably simple interface of most phones.

Inheritance

Inheritance is a means of relating similar classes to facilitate the reuse of common characteristics and behaviors without reprogramming. All Java classes are arranged in a hierarchy that descends from the class Object. The Object class implements the common behaviors required of every class to function successfully as part of a Java program. Rather than requiring sections of programming code to be copied and included within each new class that is developed, through inheritance, new classes can automatically gain the instance variables and methods of the class they extend. Thus, every Java class automatically "inherits" the instance variables defined within, and the behaviors implemented by, the Object class.

In object-oriented terms, a class that inherits functionality from another is said to be a *subclass* of the class from which its functionality is inherited. A class from which functionality is inherited is said to be a *superclass* of all of the classes that ultimately inherit the functionality it provides. Subclasses can be thought of as children, grandchildren, and so on. Similarly, superclasses can be thought of as parents, grandparents, and so on. In a Java program, the Object class is a superclass of every other class in the program (think of it as Adam or Eve). Likewise, every class is a subclass of the Object class.

Inheritance defines a relationship between classes that can be described with the words "is-a." For instance, presume you have a "Food" class. Among its many subclasses, you might have a "Vegetable" class and a "Fruit" class. Further, you might have an "Apple" class and an "Orange" class that are subclasses of the "Fruit" class. You can use the words "is-a" to describe the relationship between any subclass and its superclass:

An "Orange" is-a "Fruit"

An "Apple" is-a "Fruit"

An "Orange" is-a (type of) "Food"

An "Apple" is-a (type of) "Food"

Notice that the "Orange" and "Apple" classes are not subclasses of the "Vegetable" class. They do, however, share the common superclass "Food."

Subclasses can optionally override or change any of the instance variables or methods they inherit from their superclasses. They can also add functionality in the form of new instance variables and methods. Subclasses do not usually remove substantial functionality provided by their superclasses. Such a requirement is usually a strong warning of a poor class hierarchy.

Polymorphism

Polymorphism further extends the benefits provided by encapsulation and inheritance. It suggests that because subclasses have all of the functionality of their superclasses, they can be used in any circumstance where the superclass is used. This does not mean that a subclass has to act in the same way that its superclass would, just that the subclass knows how to respond to all of the messages that the superclass can receive. For instance, objects of each class in the "Food" hierarchy might respond to the message "Display" differently. A generic "Food" object might display a collage of meats, vegetables, fruits, and breads. A "Fruit" object would display only fruits. And an "Apple" object would only display apples. Likewise, other objects not related to the "Food" object could also know how to respond to the message "Display." A "Computer" object could display a picture of a computer. A

"Plane" object could display a picture of a plane. In every case, *how* an object produces the image it displays is encapsulated within the object itself. The object that is sending the message "Display" doesn't even need to know the kind of object to which it is sending the message.

Summary of Object-Oriented Terms

Table 12.1 presents a summary of object-oriented terms.

Table 12.1 Object-Oriented Terms

Term	Also Known As	
Object	Instance	Has state and behavior Implements behavior implemented via methods Has a lifetime (constructed, exists, destroyed) "Contracts" to provide specific behavior defined via public method signatures Communicates with other objects via messages Can contain other objects Is associated with a class
Class		Is a way of classifying objects that share common characteristics and behaviors Is a detailed specification that fully describes a set of instance variables and methods Is a user-defined type Acts as a kind of "factory" from which objects are created Maintains class variables (global data accessible to all objects of the class) "Extends" a superclass from which it inherits instance variables and methods Can implement interfaces
Instance Variable	Variable Member Variable Property	A named data item of a specific type (i.e., int, String, Object, etc.) Has a defined visibility (private, protected, public) Is either a primitive type or reference type: *Primitive type*—Holds an actual value (byte, short, int, long, float, double, char)

Continued

Table 12.1 Continued

Term	Also Known As	
		Reference type—Points to an object that is of the same type or is a subclass of the type of the instance variable, or is null (class types, interface types, array types)
Method	Member Function	Is defined within a class Consists of the step-by-step instructions that implement the behaviors of the objects of its class Has access to the instance variables of the object that invoked it Has a defined visibility (private, protected, public) Has a signature (method name + parameters) Can be synchronized to support multithreaded programming Can be declared "final" to prevent subclasses from overriding it
Class Variable	Static Variable	Is a named data item shared by all of the objects of a class Is declared with the keyword "static" Has a defined visibility (private, protected, public) Is either a primitive type or a reference type (see instance variable)
Class Method		A method that belongs to a class and can be invoked without creating an instance of the class Is defined within a class Consists of the step-by-step instructions that implement behaviors of the class in which it is defined Has access to the class variables of the class in which it is defined Has a defined visibility (private, protected, public) Has a signature (method name + parameters) Can be synchronized to support multithreaded programming Can be declared "final" to prevent subclasses from overriding it
Message		Is the sole means of communication between objects Consists of a method name and, optionally, parameters

Getting Started with Java

To create your own Java programs, you'll need a Java compiler. Sun has made available a free suite of programs that can be used for Java program development, which it calls "The Java Developer's Kit" (JDK). The JDK includes, among other things, a Java virtual machine, a compiler, a debugger, an Applet Viewer, and a disassembler. The JDK is available from Sun for Windows, Macintosh, and Sun machines. Several other companies have ported the JDK so that is now available for several flavors of UNIX and other machines as well.

In addition to the JDK available from Sun, nearly every major development tool vender now sells an integrated development environment that includes an editor, compiler, and debugger for Java. These integrated tools are much more comprehensive and easier to use than the command-line tools available in the JDK. Programmers interested in developing anything other than trivial Java programs will find an investment in these more capable tools well worth their time and money.

The examples in this book were developed and tested on machines running Windows 95 and Windows NT. The programs do not employ any vendor-specific extensions so they should run equally well on any platform to which the Java virtual machine has been ported.

While our instructions are geared toward programmers using the JDK, any properly installed integrated development environment can be used instead. Programmers that routinely have access to more capable tools may still find exposure to the JDK helpful. Sun regularly releases beta versions of features scheduled to be added to the language, along with updated versions of the JDK, well before other implementations are available.

System Requirements

Java requires a system that supports long filenames. PC users running Windows 95 or Windows NT will want a fast 486 or Pentium system that has a minimum of 16MB of memory and 50MB of free hard disk space.

Downloading the JDK

You can download the latest version of the JDK from Sun's Web site at http://java.sun.com/products/JDK/CurrentRelease/.

Detailed, platform-specific installation instructions are available there as well. In general, you'll be downloading a self-extracting executable file that contains all of the required files. The download file is nearly 4MB and Sun's site is nearly always busy. Be prepared for a fairly long wait while the file downloads.

After the file finishes downloading, move it to the directory above the one where you want the JDK files installed. When you execute the downloaded file it will automatically create a directory named "java" beneath the directory where it resides. It will then create several subdirectories beneath "java" into which it will expand all of the files it contains. Table 12.2 lists the files that are included.

The file src.zip contains the source code for many of the library classes included as part of the Java language. To view the source code, this file must be unzipped with an unzip program that supports long filenames. (The commonly available DOS program pkzip.exe does not.) Several shareware unzip programs that support long filenames are available and can be located through any of the primary Internet search engines.

You may also notice a file named classes.zip under the /lib directory. *Do not* unzip this file! The compiler and interpreter require this file to locate the library classes that are supplied as part of the language.

Table 12.2 The JDK Files

File	Description
java.exe	Java virtual machine/runtime interpreter
javac.exe	Compiler
appletviewer.exe	Applet Viewer
jdb.exe	Debugger
javap.exe	Class file disassembler
javah.exe	Header and stub file generator
javadoc.exe	Documentation generator
/demo	Demo applications/applets
src.zip	Java Libraries Source Code

Setting Up the Java Programming Environment

The executable files included with the JDK (on Windows 95 and NT platforms) are DOS programs. The easiest way to work with them is to add the \java\bin directory to the default PATH so the programs are always available whenever you launch a DOS shell. In Windows 95, this can be done by directly editing the AUTOEXEC.BAT file. In Windows NT, this can be done by right-clicking on the "My Computer" icon, selecting the "Environment" tab, and then clicking on and modifying the PATH variable.

An environment variable called CLASSPATH must also be created that indicates the paths of the directories that contain the library and user class files. If the JDK was installed off the root directory of drive C: the CLASSPATH would be set up as follows:

```
SET CLASSPATH = c:\java\lib; c:\userDir
```

In this path, c:\userDir represents a directory where you'd like to store the class files you create. You may need to restart your machine after making your changes so that the new settings will take effect.

Running the JDK Samples

Now that you have Java installed, you can explore the demos provided with the JDK to see some of the ways in which it can be used. Launch an MS-DOS shell window by clicking on START, highlighting PROGRAMS, and then clicking on MS-DOS PROMPT (COMMAND PROMPT in Windows NT). Navigate to \java\demo, type DIR, and press ENTER to list the contents of the directory. Each directory in the list contains a demo program that illustrates some of Java's capabilities.

Change directories to the Animator subdirectory. If you list the contents of the Animator directory, you'll see files that end in .html, .java, and .class. The demo program's source code, as for all Java programs, is contained in the files with the *.java* extension. The *.class* files are compiled Java classes. The *.html* files, as you probably know, are Web pages that contain the codes required to activate the example Java applets.

To view the Animator applet from within the \java\demo\Animator directory type, enter this code:

```
appletviewer example1.html
```

Then press ENTER to launch a window containing the applet. When you are finished viewing the applet, close the window by clicking on the "X" in the upper-right corner of the window or by selecting "applet" and "close" from the menu. You can view other applets in the same way. Just substitute the name of the example *.html* file in the command line above.

If you get a message that begins with "I/O Error…" then the Applet Viewer wasn't able to find the .html file you indicated. Java is case-sensitive, so check your spelling. Also, if you're using Windows 95, make sure you type the long filenames that show up to the right of the date and time information in the directory listing.

Creating Your Own Java Programs

Now that you've seen some Java programs in action, let's examine what is involved in creating your own.

Your First Java Application

Creating Java programs is similar to creating programs in any other compiled programming language. The first step is to create a text file containing the program instructions. In Java, a separate file is usually used for each *class*. The filename should consist of the name of the class followed by the extension ".java." Filenames and extensions are case-sensitive.

Use your favorite text editor to enter the program in the listing below (do not include the line numbers). When you are finished, save the program as the file HelloApp.java. Programmers using Windows 95 or NT, which do not have another editor, can use the Notepad program or the MS-DOS Edit program that come with the operating system. Both of these programs have been updated to work with long filenames.

```
public class HelloApp
{
   public static void main( String xArgs[] )
   {
```

```
5           System.out.println( "Howdy, Hi, Hello!" );
6       }
7   }
```

Compile the program with the command:

```
javac HelloApp.java
```

If everything was typed correctly, the program should compile quietly and the DOS prompt will return. There should now be a HelloApp.class file in the directory. This program is a Java *application*, not an *applet* like the examples that came with the JDK, so it is executed using the Java runtime interpreter (java.exe) instead of the Applet Viewer. Type the following command line and press Enter.

```
java HelloApp
```

If the words "Howdy, Hi, Hello!" showed up on the screen, then congratulations, you've just compiled and executed your first Java application.

Let's take a closer look at the program you just created:

- Line 1 tells the compiler that you are defining a class named HelloApp. In Java, everything must be inside a class. In lines 2 and 7 the braces enclose all the instructions that are part of the class.
- Line 3 defines the class method main. In Java applications, program execution begins with the first line of the main method of the class specified on the command line to the interpreter. In lines 4 and 6, the braces enclose all of the instructions that are part of the main method. Finally, line 5 causes the words to be displayed on the screen.

Everything in Java is part of a class. In this very simple application, we define the class HelloApp and the single method, named main, that it contains. The body of the main method consists of the single executable statement (line 5), which prints a message to the screen. After the message is printed, the closing brace that signifies the end of the method is encountered, and the application ends. Now, let's build a Java *applet* that does essentially the same thing.

Your First Java Applet

Using your text editor, enter the program in the following listing (do not include the line numbers). When you are finished, save the program as the file HelloApplet.java.

```java
import java.applet.Applet;
import java.awt.Graphics;

public class HelloApplet extends Applet
{
  public void paint( Graphics xGC )
  {
    xGC.drawString( "Howdy, Hi, Hello!", 50, 25 );
  }
}
```

Recall that Java *applets* differ from Java *applications* in that applets are not stand-alone programs that can function independently. Applets rely on another program, typically a Web browser (or the Applet Viewer included with the JDK), to establish the program environment in which the applet will run and to cue the applet when events pertinent to its execution occur. These programs load and execute applets when they encounter the APPLET tag in an HTML file. Consequently, we need to create an HTML file so that we can test our applet. Enter the following HTML file using your text editor (as always, don't enter the line numbers). When you are finished, save the file as HelloApplet.html.

```html
1     <HTML>
2
3    <HEAD>
4       <TITLE> HelloApplet </TITLE>
5     </HEAD>
6
7     <BODY>
8       <APPLET
9         code   = HelloApplet
10        width  = 200
11        height = 200>
12      </APPLET>
13    </BODY>
14
15    </HTML>
```

This file describes a simple, but complete, HTML page. As you may know, HTML attributes are generally enclosed within matching tags that mark a section of the HTML document. Our primary interest is in the APPLET tag, defined in lines 8 through 11.

The APPLET tag in line 8 provides information about an applet that should be included as part of the Web page. In line 9 the "code" attribute specifies the name of the .class file that contains the applet. In line 10, the "width" attribute specifies the width of the applet window (in pixels) to request from the browser. In line 11, the "height" attribute specifies the height of the applet window (in pixels) to request from the browser.

Finally, you can view the applet in the same manner that you viewed the examples included with the JDK. Type the following command and then press Enter.

```
appletviewer HelloApplet.html
```

The words "Howdy, Hi, Hello!" should be displayed within the appletviewer window. You can also view the applet using any other Java-compatible Web browser that you have installed. To view the applet using Netscape Navigator, start the browser, choose File -> Open Location, and specify the file HelloApplet.html. The equivalent command in Internet Explorer is File -> Open.

So, you've now seen several Java applets and built a couple of simple Java programs. Before continuing with some more comprehensive applets, we'll delve into the elements that make up the Java programming language.

An Inside Look at Java

The following sections break down the Java programming language in detail.

Unicode

Java programs are text files consisting of words containing sequences of Unicode characters separated by white space. Unicode is a 16-bit character-coding system that provides a standardized way to represent characters from languages throughout the world. The first 128 characters of the Unicode encoding system are identical to the 8-bit ASCII characters, which include numbers and the letters of the English alphabet.

Any Unicode character can be represented in the source code of a Java program by preceding the four-digit hexadecimal representation of the character with the Unicode escape sequence "\u." For instance, the hexadecimal value of the Unicode letter "A" is "0041." Therefore, you could include the letter "A" in the source code of a Java program by specifying the Unicode escape sequence "\u0041." Because this is significantly more work than just typing the letter "A," I'd recommend that you reserve this method of character entry for characters that are not readily available through the keys on your keyboard.

White Space

The term "white space" refers to the blank spaces left between words. White space consists of the space, tab, form-feed, and end-of-line characters. Programmers used to working with interpreted languages that read and parse a program's source code at runtime may be used to minimizing the amount of white space in their programs so that the programs will run faster. This is not necessary with Java because it is a compiled language and the white space is removed during compilation.

Comments

Java supports three forms of comments: block comments, documentation comments, and single-line comments.

- Block comments begin with the character sequence "/*" and end with "*/." All of the text that appears between the beginning and ending comment marks will be ignored.
- Documentation comments are a special form of block comment that begins with the character sequence "/**" and ends with "*/."Documentation comments can be automatically extracted by the *javadoc* utility program included with the JDK to produce documentation.
- Single-line comments begin with "//" and end at the end of the line.

Like white space, comments are removed during compilation so they have no impact on the speed or operation of the program. Comments cannot be nested. Consequently, many programmers prefer to use the single-line ("//") comment format for normal comments so that block comments can be used to "comment out" large sections of code, as necessary, during development.

```
/*  This is a block comment.  All of the lines of text between
 *  the opening and closing marks will be ignored.
 */

/** This is a "documentation" comment.  Notice the second
    asterisk in the opening mark.  Like a block comment, all
    of the text between the opening and closing marks will be
    ignored.  This form of comment can be automatically
    extracted by the javadoc utility program to create
    documentation.
 */
```

```
// This is a single-line comment
public class CommentForms   // Also a single-line comment
{
}
```

Tokens

The words in a program, other than white space and comments, are referred to as *tokens*. There are several kinds of tokens including identifiers, keywords, literals, separators, and operators.

Reserved Words

Reserved words are words defined as part of the Java language that have special meaning to the compiler. The majority of these words constitute the keywords that typically define the data types and flow control structures of the language. The remaining words are literal values. None of these words can be used to identify user-defined information in a program. (See Table 12.3.)

Identifiers

Identifiers are the user-defined, single-word names given to classes, interfaces, methods, and variables. They must begin with a letter, which can be followed by any

Table 12.3 Java's Reserved Words

abstract	do	implements	protected	transient
boolean	double	import	public	true
break	else	instanceof	return	try
byte	extends	int	short	void
case	false	interface	static	volatile
catch	final	long	super	while
char	finally	native	switch	
class	float	new	synchronized	
const	for	null	this	
continue	goto	package	throw	
default	if	private	throws	

combination of letters, digits, underscore characters ("_"), and/or dollar signs ("$"). Identifiers in Java are case-sensitive, so sumTotal and SumTotal are different identifiers. By convention, Java class names begin with an uppercase letter. Variable and method names begin with a lowercase letter. If an identifier is best expressed as a combination of multiple words, the first letter of each successive word is usually capitalized; as in makeMyDay. Identifiers can be any length. The benefits of longer, descriptive names for variables, classes, and methods will far outweigh the hassle of extra typing for all but the worst "hunt and peck" typists.

Literals

Sequences of characters or numbers in the source code of a program that represent unchanging values are called *literals*. For instance, the number 123 is an *integer literal*. The letter 'A', enclosed in single quotes, is a *character literal*. And a sequence of characters such as "Java Program", enclosed in double quotes, is a *string literal*. Java also recognizes *floating-point literals*, *boolean literals*, and the *null literal*.

Java is a *strongly typed* language. The integer, character, string, and other *types* mentioned above are some of the kinds, or *types*, of information that are predefined as part of the Java language. In fact, each *literal type* has a corresponding Java *data type*. Although we'll put off a detailed discussion of *data types* until later, they'll be mentioned throughout our discussion of literals.

Integer Literals

Integer literals represent whole numbers. They can entered in decimal (base 10), hexadecimal (base 16), or octal (base 8) notation. Hexadecimal numbers are indicated by preceding the number with 0x or 0X. The letters A through F (ignoring case) are used to represent the hexadecimal digits with values of 10 through 15, respectively. Octal numbers are indicated by preceding the number with a leading 0. Therefore, the decimal value 15 can be entered as the integer literal 15 in decimal notation, 0xF or 0XF in hexadecimal notation, and 017 in octal notation.

By default, an integer literal is stored by the compiler as a 32-bit value that corresponds to the Java data type *int* (integer). Integer numbers that exceed the maximum or minimum values that can be held in a 32-bit number (approximately 2 billion) can be entered by appending the letter "L" (ignoring case) to the end of the number. This indicates to the compiler that the value represents a *long* integer value that is stored as a 64-bit number.

Floating-Point Literals

Floating-point literals represent numbers that have a fractional part. They are entered by including a decimal point or exponent within the number. Exponents are indicated by including the letter "E" (ignoring case) between the number and the exponent; for example 123e10.

By default, floating-point literals are stored as 64-bit values that correspond to the Java data type *double*. The letter "D" (ignoring case) can be optionally appended to the end of a number to document its type. The following are examples of *double* floating-point literals:

123. 0.0 .12 1e10 14D 123.4e-23

The letter "F" can be appended to the end of a number to indicate that it should be treated as a 32-bit floating-point value that corresponds to the Java data type *float*. This is necessary only on the rare occasions when the slightly faster processing or the reduced memory requirements of 32-bit values are significant. The following are examples of *float* literals:

123f 0.0f .12F 3.14F 123.4e-10f

Boolean Literals

Boolean literals represent logical truth values with the words *true* and *false*. The words are case-sensitive. Unlike in other languages, there is no numeric equivalent to these values.

Character Literals

Character literals represent a single Unicode character. They are entered by enclosing the character or the equivalent Unicode escape sequence within single quotes. Unicode escape sequences are indicated by preceding the hexadecimal value of a character with \u. Because the hexadecimal value of the letter "A" is 41, the character literal A can be entered as "A" or "\u0041."

Java also recognizes the special escape sequences listed in Table 12.4.

String Literals

String literals represent a sequence of zero or more Unicode characters. They are entered by enclosing characters and/or escape sequences within double quotes.

Table 12.4 Java's Escape Sequences

Escape Sequence	Character Value	Unicode Value
\b	Backspace	\u0008
\t	Horizontal tab	\u0009
\n	Linefeed / newline	\u000a
\f	Form feed	\u000c
\r	Carriage return	\u000d
\"	Double quote	\u0022
\'	Single quote	\u0027
\\	Backslash	\u005c
\xxx	Octal escape sequence	\u0000 to \u00ff

String literals cannot span source code lines. However, long strings can be created by joining multiple string literals using the string concatenation operator +. The following are examples of *string literals*:

""	Empty String
"A String"	// String containing 8 characters
"Another String\n"	// String containing 15 characters (14 + newline)
"First line of a" + "two-line string"	// Concatenation of two string literals

String literals are unique in that they are actually implemented as instances of the String class included in the Java libraries. Thus, any of the String methods can be applied to string literals. For instance, the expression "Here's A String".length() would return the integer value 15 (the length of the string)

Null Literal

The *null literal* is the word *null*. It is used to indicate that a variable of a *reference type* (array, class, interface) does not point to a value.

Separators

Separators are characters used to delineate, group, and order the various parts of a Java program. They are:

( ) { } [ ] ; , .

Operators

Operators are the symbols used to denote a type of action to be performed on one or two program elements, referred to as operands. Operators that act on a single operand are referred to as *unary* operators. Operators that act on two operands are referred to as *binary* operators.

Mathematical Operators

Table 12.5 provides a description and examples of Java's mathematical operators.

Table 12.5 Java's Mathematical Operators

Operator	Description	Example	Equivalent To:	Result
		x=2, y=10		
++	Increment	x++	x = x + 1	x = 3
--	Decrement	x--	x = x – 1	x = 1
+	Addition	z = x + y	z = 2 + 10	z = 12
–	Subtraction	z = x – y	z = 2 – 10	z = –8
*	Multiplication	z = x * y	z = 2 * 10	z = 20
/	Division	z = y / x	z = 10 / 2	z = 5
%	Modulus (remainder)	z = y % x	Remainder of 10 / 2	z = 0
=	Assignment	z = x		z = 2
+=	Additive assignment	x += y	x = x + y	x = 12
–=	Subtractive assignment	x –= y	x = x – y	x = –8
*=	Multiplicative assignment	x *= y	x = x * y	x = 20
/=	Divisional assignment	y /= x	y = y / x	y = 5
%=	Modulus assignment	y %= x	y = y % x	y = 0

Relational Operators

Table 12.6 provides a description and examples of Java's relational operators.

Boolean Operators

Table 12.7 provides a description and examples of Java's Boolean operators.

Bitwise Operators

The logical bitwise operators compare the corresponding bits of integers a and b and set the corresponding bit in c according to the rules in the truth table (see Table 12.8).

The right and left shift operators shift the bits in a the number of positions indicated in b. The bolded bits in c correspond to the new bits shifted in. Bits that are shifted out are discarded (see Table 12.9).

Data Types

Java is a strongly typed language. This means that a variable in Java is limited to holding a specific type of information that must be declared to the compiler before the variable can be used. This allows the compiler to generate more efficient code.

Java has two kinds of *types*: primitive types and reference types. The primitive types (byte, short, int, long, char, float, double, and boolean) represent simple values

Table 12.6 Java's Relational Operators

Operator	Description	Example	Equivalent To:	Result
		x=2, y=10		
>	Greater than	x > y	2 > 10	False
>=	Greater than or equal to	y >= x	10 >= 2	True
<	Less than	x < y	2 < 10	True
<=	Less than or equal to	y <= x	10 <= 2	False
==	Comparison	x == y	2 equivalent to 10	False
!=	Not equal	x != y	2 not equivalent to 10	True

Table 12.7 Java's Boolean Operators

<table>
<tr><th>Operator</th><th>Description</th><th>Example</th><th>Equivalent To:</th><th>Result</th></tr>
<tr><td></td><td></td><td>x=2, y=10, z=true</td><td></td><td></td></tr>
<tr><td>!</td><td>Logical complement</td><td>! (x > y)</td><td>Not (false)</td><td>True</td></tr>
<tr><td>&&</td><td>Logical AND</td><td>(false) && ((y++) > 0)</td><td>(false) AND (not evaluated)</td><td>False
y = 10</td></tr>
<tr><td>&</td><td>Evaluation AND</td><td>(false) & ((y++) > 0)</td><td>(false) AND (true)</td><td>False
y = 11</td></tr>
<tr><td>&=</td><td>Assignment AND</td><td>z &= false</td><td>z = (true AND false)</td><td>z = false</td></tr>
<tr><td>||</td><td>Logical OR</td><td>(true) || ((y++) > 20)</td><td>(true) OR (not evaluated)</td><td>True
y = 10</td></tr>
<tr><td>|</td><td>Evaluation OR</td><td>(true) | ((y++) > 20)</td><td>(true) OR (false)</td><td>True
y = 11</td></tr>
<tr><td>|=</td><td>Assignment OR</td><td>z |= false</td><td>z = (true OR false)</td><td>z = true</td></tr>
<tr><td>^</td><td>Logical XOR</td><td>true ^ false</td><td>true when different</td><td>True</td></tr>
<tr><td>^=</td><td>Assignment XOR</td><td>z = true ^ true</td><td>false when same</td><td>False</td></tr>
<tr><td>?:</td><td>conditional</td><td>x = ((y>20) ? 10 : 30)</td><td>if (y > 20)
x = 10
else
x = 30</td><td>x = 30</td></tr>
</table>

that can be efficiently stored in a limited amount of memory. The reference types (object, interface, array) represent pointers to more complex structures. These pointers, or references, are managed internally by Java and cannot be directly accessed or manipulated by the programmer.

Primitive Data Types

The primitive data types represent integer and real numbers, single Unicode characters, and boolean values. The size and range of each type are specified as part of the Java language. This plays an important part in ensuring that identical results will be obtained regardless of the kind of computer on which a Java program is run.

Table 12.8 Java's Bitwise Operators

Operator	Description	Example	a (bit)	b (bit)	Result bit (c)
&	Bitwise AND	a & b	0	0	0
			0	1	0
			1	0	0
			1	1	1
|	Bitwise OR	a | b	0	0	0
			0	1	1
			1	0	1
			1	1	1
^	Bitwise XOR	a ^ b	0	0	0
			0	1	1
			1	0	1
			1	1	0
~	Ones Complement	~a	0		1
			1		0

Integral Data Types

With the exception of *char*, the integral data types represent signed integer values. Integral data types "wrap" when operations are performed that cause them to exceed their minimum or maximum values. For instance, adding 1 to a variable of type *short* that contains the value 32767 will result in a value of –32768 (see Table 12.10).

Table 12.9 Right and Left Shift Operators

Operator	Description	Example	a (32-bits)	b (int)	Result (c)
>>	Right shift with	c = a >> b	11110000	4	11111111
>>=	sign extension		00000000		00000000
			11111111		00001111
			00001111		11110000
>>>	Right shift with	c = a >>> b	11110000	4	00001111
>>>=	zero extension		00000000		00000000
			11111111		00001111
			00001111		11110000
<<	Left shift	c = a << b	11110000	4	00000000
<<=			00000000		00001111
			11111111		00001111
			00001111		11110000

Table 12.10 Java's Integral Data Types

Data Type	Size	Minimum Value	Maximum Value
byte	1 byte = 8 bits	–128	127
short	2 bytes = 16 bits	–32,768	32,767
int	4 bytes = 32 bits	–2,147,483,648	2,147,483,647
long	8 bytes = 64 bits	–9,223,372, 036,854,775,808	9,223,372,036, 854,775,807
char	2 bytes = 16 bits	0 or '\u0000'	65,535 or '\uFFFF'

Floating-Point Data Types

Java *floating-point data types* represent signed real numbers according to the rules specified in the IEEE 754-1985 Standard for Binary Floating-Point Arithmetic (see Table 12.11).

Boolean Data Type

The boolean data type represents a logical value. The only two values that it can contain are the boolean literal values *true* and *false*. These values do not have a numerical equivalent.

Reference Data Types

There are three kinds of reference data types: class types, interface types, and array types. Variables of a reference type are simply pointers that can point only to the type of data specified in the variable's declaration. Most often, reference type variables point to an object.

It is important to understand that a variable and the object it points to are two distinct structures. This is especially important when testing reference variables for equality using the equality operators == and !=. These operators test for "reference equality," that is, whether the two variables being compared point to the same

Table 12.11 Java's Floating-Point Data Types

Data Type	Size	Range
float	4 bytes = 32 bits	approx. +– 3.40282347E+38 (7 significant digits)
double	8 bytes = 64 bits	approx. +– 1.79769313486231570E+308 (15 significant digits)

object. They do not test if the contents of the objects being pointed to by the variables are the same. Thus, if you have two String objects, each of which contains the string "So shines a good deed in a weary world," the test obj1 == obj2 will return false. To test for "content equality," you usually use the equals method of an object as in obj1.equals(obj2). There is no limit to the number of variables that can point to a single object.

Converting Between Data Types

Java will automatically convert numeric data types to the largest floating-point or integral data type involved in an operation. A variable can be directly assigned to any other variable whose type appears to the right of the assigning variable's type in the list below:

```
byte -> short -> int -> long -> float -> double
```

Assigning a variable to another variable whose type appears to the left of the assigning variable's type may result in a loss of data. In such cases, the programmer must explicitly state the type of conversion intended by *casting* the variable to the desired type. Casting from one type to another is performed by enclosing the target type within parentheses. For example:

```
double doubleVar   = 8.765;
int         intVar = (int) doubleVar;
```

In this case, the variable intVar would be assigned the value 8 because the fractional part of a floating-point number is discarded when it is cast to an integral type.

Casting can also be performed on variables of a reference type, although the effect is quite different. It is again important to distinguish between the variable and the object to which it points. Objects have *class.* The class that an object is an *instance of* never changes. Variables have *type.* The *type* of a variable determines how the object it points to appears.

For example, a reference variable of type Object can point to any object of any class. However, the instance variables and methods accessible through such a variable are limited to those defined in the Object class. To "regain" the additional functionality of an object that is pointed to by a variable of type Object, the object needs to be *cast* back to a variable of its original type. The following example demonstrates one of the most common uses for *casting* between variables of reference type:

```
1   import java.util.Vector;
2
3   public class Test
4   {
5      public static void main( String xArgs[] )
6      {
7              Vector vectorVar = new Vector();
8          String stringVar = new String("I'll be back");
9          Object objectVar;
10         String string2;
11
12         vectorVar.addElement( stringVar );
13
14         objectVar = vectorVar.elementAt( 0 );
15         System.out.println( objectVar.getClass().getName() );
16
17         string2 = (String) vectorVar.elementAt( 0 );
18         System.out.println( string2.getClass().getName() );
19     }
20  }
```

A Vector is essentially a dynamic array that can grow as elements are added to it. Vectors work with elements of type Object. Because the Object class is the root of all Java classes, any object can be stored in a Vector.

- In Line 7 the variable vectorVar is declared and initialized to a new Vector object. In line 8 the variable stringVar is declared and initialized to a new String object containing the value "I'll be back."
- Lines 9 and 10 declare the variables objectVar and string2. In line 12 the String object pointed to by the variable stringVar is added to the Vector.
- Line 14 causes the variable objectVar to point to the object at position 0 in the Vector. Line 15 demonstrates that the class of the object has not changed even though it is pointed to by a variable of type Object. Line 17 demonstrates the use of a cast to change the type of the Object pointer (reference) retrieved from the Vector to type String so it can be stored in a variable of type String.

Notice the expressions used to retrieve the class names in lines 15 and 18. These expressions are evaluated by first invoking the getClass method of objectVar and string2, respectively. The getClass method, which is defined in the Object class, returns a reference to an instance of the Class class. The getName method, which is defined in the Class class, is then invoked to return a String object containing the name of the class.

This sort of example is usually sufficient to convince programmers new to object-oriented programming that they want nothing more to do with it. We've all been there. If you understand that a variable and the object it points to are two distinct things, then you know all you need to know for now. You'll be amazed at how quickly examples like the one above begin to make complete sense.

Java Variables

Variables are identifiers that represent a storage location that can hold information of a specified type. In Java, every variable must be declared before it can be used. A variable is referred to as a class variable, instance variable, or local variable depending on where its declaration appears.

Declaring Variables

Variables are declared by specifying a data type followed by the variable's name:

```
dataType    varName;
```

Multiple variables of the same type can be declared on a single line by separating the variable names with commas:

```
int  x, y, z;
```

Additionally, an initial value can be specified for a variable by including the assignment operator = and a value after the declaration.

```
float aFloatVar = 100.0f;
int x = 10, y = 11, z = 12;
boolean ok = false;
String whoSaid = "Never tell me the odds";
```

Variable Arrays

An array is a collection of elements of the same type. Array variables are declared by including the symbol [] after the data type in the variable declaration.

```
int[] arrayOfInts;
```

Array variables are references. That means that they are essentially pointers that point to another area in memory where the values of the elements in the array are stored. Declaring an array variable creates only the reference, not the array. The int[] part of the declaration above indicates that the variable can only refer (point) to an array of integers. Because the declaration does not actually create an array, the variable initially contains the value null.

The array itself is created by using the keyword "new," followed by a data type and a quantity enclosed within brackets [ ]. The quantity indicates the number of elements that can be stored in the array so the compiler knows how much room to allocate for it. Arrays, like objects, have to have at least one variable pointing to them to prevent Java from automatically reclaiming the space they occupy. Consequently, the array is created and assigned to an array variable in a single step:

```
arrayOfInts = new int[25];
```

This statement causes an array to be created that has sufficient room to store 25 integers. The array variable arrayOfInts is then set to point to the newly created array. As for other variables, this step can be combined with the declaration of the variable:

```
int[]  arrayOfInts = new int[25];
```

Once the array is created, values can be assigned to and retrieved from its elements by indicating an element number (referred to as an "index"), within brackets, after the name of an array variable that points to it. Arrays, in Java, are zero-based. This means that the elements of arrayOfInts are accessed using index values 0 through 24.

```
arrayOfInts[ 0] = 123;               // Assign the value 123 to the element at
                                     index 0
    arrayOfInts[24] = 123;           // Assign the value 123 to the 25th element
                                     in the array
    int anIntVar = arrayOfInts[12];  // Assign the value of the 13th element in
                                     the array to the
                                     // integer anIntVar.
```

A variable containing a numeric value can also be used to indicate which element of the array to access. The following code segment sets the value of all the elements in the array pointed to by arrayOfInts to 123.

```
for (int element = 0; element < arrayOfInts.length; element++)
{    arrayOfInts[ element] = 123;
}
```

The for loop causes the statement arrayOfInts[element] = 123; to be executed 25 times, once for each element of the array. Notice that the length of the array is retrieved by the expression arrayOfInts.length. As we'll discuss in the section on objects, this is the standard notation used to access the instance variables of objects. Arrays in Java are, in fact, a special kind of object. A reference variable of type Object (the root class of the Java class hierarchy) can point to an array. Also, any of the methods defined in the Object class can be invoked by an array. The primary difference between arrays and normal objects is that the bracket symbol is used to access its elements.

Finally, arrays can also be initialized using a static initializer. A *static initializer* is a series of literal values and/or static variables, separated by commas and enclosed within braces.

```
String[] bondArray = { "Octopussy", "Goldfinger",
   "Thunderbal",  "License To Kill" };
```

This statement creates a five-element array, pointed to by the variable bondArray, that contains the string value "Octopussy" in its first element, "Goldfinger" in its second element, and so on.

Multidimensional Arrays

Java supports arrays of arrays. This is a kind of multidimensional array that is often referred to as a "nested" or "ragged" array because the number of elements in each dimension of the array beyond the first can vary. Multidimensional arrays of fixed dimensions are declared in a manner similar to single-dimension arrays:

```
int[][] multiDimArray = new int[5][10];
```

Nested static initializers can also be used to initialize the values of a multidimensional array:

```
String[][] movieArray = { {  "Revenge Of",
        "Return Of", "Trail Of", "Curse Of" },
     { "Raiders", "Temple", "Crusade" } }
```

This creates a two-dimensional array that has an array of four elements in its first element and an array of three elements in its second element.

Finally, only the first dimension of a multidimensional array needs to be specified in the variable declaration. The declaration:

```
int[][][] lotsOfInts = new [10][][];
```

is perfectly acceptable in Java. It allocates an array with room for 10 elements, each of which must be of the array type int[][].

Object Variables

Object variables, like array variables, are references. The data type of an object variable is the name of a class. Object variables are declared by specifying a class name followed by the name of the variable:

```
Class objectVar;
```

Declaring an object variable creates only the reference (a type of pointer), not an object. An object variable can point to any object whose class is the same as, or is a subclass of, the class specified in the variable's declaration. For instance, because all of the classes in Java are arranged in a hierarchy that descends from the root class "Object," a variable declared with the data type Object can point to any object. A variable declared with the data type Number (an abstract subclass of Object) can point only to objects whose data type is a subclass of Number. Because the declaration of a variable does not actually create an object, the variable initially contains the value null.

Java Objects

Objects are the physical manifestations of the structures described in class definitions. An object is created by allocating memory to hold its instance variables. It lives as long as at least one variable refers to it.

Instantiating Objects

Objects are created by using the keyword "new" followed by the name of a class. The class name is then followed by any required parameters enclosed within parentheses ( ). The process of creating an object is formally referred to as *instantiating* an object. An object is instantiated by invoking a special kind of method, defined within each class, referred to as a *constructor*.

Constructor methods have the same name as the class in which they are defined. A class can have an unlimited number of constructor methods that have different method signatures. Recall that a method's *signature* consists of the method's name as well as the number and type of parameters it accepts. For instance, the Rectangle class, included in the Java libraries, defines six constructor methods:

```
Rectangle()
Rectangle( int width, int height )
Rectangle( int x, int y, int width, int height )
Rectangle( Point point )
Rectangle( Dimension dimension )
Rectangle( Point point, Dimension dimension )
```

A Rectangle object can be instantiated using any one of these six constructors. The Rectangle() constructor that doesn't have any parameters creates a Rectangle object that is initialized to a height and width of zero. The other Rectangle constructors accept parameters that allow the newly instantiated Rectangle object to be initialized to a user-specified height, width, and/or position.

Like arrays, objects must have at least one variable pointing to them to prevent Java from automatically reclaiming the space they occupy. Consequently, an object is created and assigned to an object variable in a single step. Let's presume that the variable rectangleVar was declared:

```
Rectangle rectangleVar;
```

A newly instantiated Rectangle object could be created and assigned to the variable in the following manner:

```
rectangleVar = new Rectangle( 200, 400 );
```

As with other variables, the declaration and initialization can be combined in a single statement:

```
Rectangle rectangleVar = new Rectangle( 200, 400 );
```

Working with an Object's Instance Variables

Recall that *instance variables* are the internal variables, maintained by objects, that hold the object's state. Java class designers can optionally allow direct access to an object's instance variables when they determine that the benefits of doing so (primarily speed) outweigh the costs (reduced encapsulation, greater dependencies between objects). The Java class library designers made four instance variables of the Rectangle class publicly accessible: height, width, x, and y. Presuming the variable rectangleVar references a properly instantiated Rectangle object, the instance variables of the Rectangle object can be set and accessed by appending a period and the instance variable's name to the name of the object variable. For example:

```
rectangleVar.height = 200;      // Set the height instance variable to 200
int rectWidth = rectangleVar.width;
          // Access the value in the width instance variable
        // and assign it to rectWidth
```

Object purists tend to cringe at the thought of allowing direct access to an object's instance variables because it violates one of the primary features of an object-oriented language, namely encapsulation. Any object that directly accesses or changes the instance variables of another, rather than requesting the object return or set a value as the result of a method call, by definition, knows some of the implementation details of the object with which it is interacting. Consequently, both objects will have to be modified whenever a change is required.

The decision to allow or prevent direct access to an object's instance variables needs to be evaluated on a case-by-case basis. Essentially, the decision is one of execution speed versus ease of maintainability. The compromise many class designers settle on is to generally limit the direct access of an object's instance variables to subclasses only. Rare exceptions are then granted for other classes with demanding execution speed requirements.

Invoking an Object's Methods

We mentioned previously that objects communicate by sending messages. A message is simply the name and required parameters of a method implemented by the class of the object to which the message is directed. A method is invoked by specifying the name of an object variable followed by a period; then the name of a method; and finally the parameters required for the method enclosed within parentheses. For instance, the Rectangle class defines a resize() method that allows a Rectangle object's size to be dynamically changed by specifying a new width and height. The resize method of the object referenced by rectangleVar would be invoked in the following way:

```
rectangleVar.resize( 600, 300 );
```

This is a good example of how the method of an object can modify the object's instance variables. As part of its behavior, the resize() method sets the width and height instance variables of the Rectangle object.

Similarly, the Rectangle class defines an inside() method that returns the boolean value true if the point located at the x and y coordinates passed as message parameters falls within the rectangle:

```
Boolean isInside = rectangleVar.inside( 325, 150 );
```

Object Destruction

The space occupied by an object is automatically reclaimed by the "garbage collector" in the Java virtual machine when the object is no longer referenced (pointed to) by any variables. Before destroying an object, the garbage collector will invoke the object's "finalize" method if such a method exists. Even though this might seem useful for last-minute clean-up operations like releasing file handles or gracefully closing communication ports, in current virtual machine implementations, there is no guarantee that an object's finalize method will ever be run. The "garbage collector" decides when, and if, it needs to perform garbage collection to free additional resources.

Java Control Flow

Like most programming languages, Java supports several statements that allow the flow of a program to continue differently based on the result of some runtime expression. Conditional statements such as if-else and switch allow the expression to determine if sections of code should be skipped or executed. Looping statements such as for, while, and do-while allow one or more statements to be executed repeatedly until the expression results in a value that indicates processing should continue.

In this section, we'll examine the form and particularities of these control flow statements. Examples of how these statements are used can be found throughout the programs developed in the next chapter.

if-else statement

The simplest form of the *if* statement is:

```
if (expression)
{
   statement;
   . . .
}
```

If "expression" evaluates to *true*, then the statements enclosed within the braces will be executed. Otherwise, they will be skipped and program execution will continue with the statement immediately following the closing brace. As the ellipses indicate, any number of statements can be included within the braces. Technically, the braces are required only if more than one statement is to be executed in the block of code that follows the expression. However, we have opted always to include the braces because doing so enhances the readability of the code.

An optional *else* clause can be added to specify statements that should only be executed in the event that the expression evaluates to *false*:

```
if (expression)
{
   statement;
   . . .
}
else
{
   statement;
   ...
}
```

switch statement

The *switch* statement allows the result of an expression to be compared against multiple values to determine how processing should continue. The *switch* statement has the form:

```
switch (expression)
{
   case value1:
     statement;
     . . .
     break;
   case value2:
     statement;
     . . .
     break;
   . . .
   default:
     statement;
}
```

The result of the expression will be successively compared against the values given after the "case" keywords until a match is found or the "default" case is reached. The values must be literal values or static variables of the same data type as the expression. If a match is found, the statements following the matching case will be executed. Then, when a "break" statement is encountered, program execution branches to the first statement following the closing brace that marks the end of the *switch* statement. If a "break" statement is omitted, program execution "falls through" any additional case statements that are encountered, executing each statement until a break statement or the end of the *switch* statement is reached. If no matching case is found, and the optional "default" case has been specified, the statements following the default case will be executed.

for loop

The *for* statement is used to execute one or more statements a specific number of times. The *for* statement has the following form:

```
for ( initialization expressions; continuation test; increment expressions
)
{
   statement;
   . . .
}
```

It is usually used in the following manner:

```
for ( int x = 0; x < 10; x++ )
{
   System.out.prinln( x );
}
```

When a for loop is executed, the "initialization expressions" are evaluated. In this case, the variable **x** is declared and initialized to 0. Then the "continuation test" is evaluated and if the result is *true*, all of the statements within the braces are executed. Then the "increment expressions" are executed and the "continuation test" is re-checked. Processing continues within the loop until the "continuation test" evaluates to *false*.

In this case, the value of x is incremented by 1 (x++) after each iteration through the loop until the value of x is no longer less than 10 (x < 10). Consequently, the statement System.out.println(x) is executed 10 times and the values 0 through 9 are printed to the screen.

Although it is rarely done, multiple expressions, separated by commas, can be included in the initialization and increment sections of the for loop.

while statement

The *while* statement facilitates executing one or more statements for as long as a condition remains *true*. The *while* statement has the form:

```
while (expression)
{
   statement;
   . . .
}
```

The expression, which must evaluate to a boolean value, is evaluated when the *while* statement is first encountered. If the expression evaluates to *false*, the statements within the braces are skipped. Otherwise, the statements within the braces are executed and then the expression is reevaluated. The programmer is responsible for ensuring that some modification is made within the loop that will eventually cause the expression to evaluate to *false*. Otherwise, the statements within the loop will execute continuously, in an "infinite loop," until the program is manually interrupted or the computer is shut off.

do-while statement

The *do-while* statement is an alternative version of the *while* statement that is especially useful when it is necessary to ensure that the statements enclosed within the braces of the loop will be executed at least one time. The *do-while* statement has the following form:

```
do
{
   statement;
   . . .
}
while (expression);
```

The statements within the braces are executed prior to the continuation expression being evaluated. Like the *while* statement, the statements within the braces will be executed repeatedly until the expression evaluates to *false*.

try-catch-finally

Java provides built-in exception handling with the *try-catch-finally* clause. Exceptions are unusual error conditions that abruptly interrupt program processing. Typical exceptions include things like not being able to find a file, reaching the end of an input file, and running out of memory. Every exception is a Java class. Each method of a Java class can declare the potential exceptions that are likely to occur given the type of processing performed within the method. If an exceptional condition occurs during processing, the method then "throws" an exception by creating an instance of an exception class. Any class that uses the services of a method that has declared such exceptions must provide code to deal with the exceptions or explicitly indicate that it too will "throw" the exception so higher-level classes can determine how to respond.

The *try-catch-finally* statement has the form:

```
try
{
   statement;
   . . .
}
catch( ExceptionType exceptionVar )
{
   statement;
   . . .
}
catch( ExceptionType2 exceptionVar2 )
{
   statement;
   . . .
}
. . .
finally
{
   statement;
   . . .
}
```

The *try* clause contains the statements that invoke methods that might result in an exceptional condition. The catch clauses allow specific types of exceptions to be "caught" and dealt with appropriately or ignored. The finally clause contains "clean-up" code that must be executed regardless of whether the code within the try clause completed successfully or if an exception was raised.

labeled break and continue statements

Java provides a *continue* statement that is usually used within loops to short-circuit the processing of the loop. The *continue* statement is equivalent to jumping to the closing brace that encloses the statements that are executed as part of the loop. The increment and/or continuation expressions are then evaluated and the loop continues processing normally.

Java allows *break* and *continue* statements to also be used with labels. A *label* is an identifier, followed by a colon, that immediately precedes a statement. A *break* or *continue* statement that is immediately followed by a label causes program execution to branch to the label. Labeled breaks are typically used to simplify the process of "breaking out" of deeply nested code. There are no examples of labeled breaks in the Java programs in this book. The statements are mentioned here for completeness only.

The Structure of Java Programs

To create a Java program, you create one or more text files, each of which contains the definition of a Java class or interface. Each text file is given the name of the class or interface it contains, followed by the extension .java. Each .java source file, after it has been compiled, will correspond to an identically named .class file that contains the platform-independent bytecode expected by the Java virtual machine. In this section, we begin the exploration of the structure and format of .java source files.

Class Structure

Every Java class begins with a declaration that specifies the name of the class followed by nested blocks of code delineated by matching curly braces { }. The outermost block of code defines the entire class. Within the class, there will exist one or more independent blocks of code that define the methods of the class. In turn, each method can contain additional blocks of code that relate to the programming structures used as part of the method's implementation. Variables can be declared, as needed, within any of these blocks of code. The block of code in which a variable's declaration appears determines the kind and scope of the variable.

Variable Scope

Scope refers to the lifetime of a variable. It defines the point in a program where space is initially allocated to hold the contents of a variable, and the point in the program where that space is freed for other uses. There are several kinds of variables, including: class variables, instance variables, local variables, and method parameters.

Class Variables *Class variables* are variables that are shared by all of the objects of a class. They are created when the first object of a class is instantiated. In current virtual machine implementations, class variables exist until the program ends.

Instance Variables You were introduced to instance variables earlier. A copy of each of the instance variables defined in a class is created for each object of the class that is instantiated (created). Instance variables are part of an object. Therefore, they exist as long as the object exists. The scope of an instance variable is the lifetime of the object to which it belongs.

Method Parameters *Method parameters* are variables that contain values passed to a method as part of the message that caused the method to be invoked. Method parameters exist throughout the block that defines the body of the method to which they were passed.

Local Variables *Local variables* are variables declared within a method that are part of the method's implementation. A local variable generally exists from the point in a program where its declaration appears until the first closing brace is encountered that does not correspond to an opening brace encountered after its declaration. The primary exceptions to this rule are variables that are declared within a statement that defines a loop structure. The scope of these variables is limited to the block of code that defines the statements that can be executed as part of the loop. (We'll examine loops in more detail in the section "Control Flow Statements".)

An Example of Scope

The following program illustrates the basic structure of a Java application and the scope of various kinds of variables. This program defines the class named ScopeDemo, whose objects will contain the instance variables ivInt and ivString. It also defines a method named aMethod and a class method named main.

```
public class ScopeDemo
{
    int ivInt = 123;

    public void aMethod( String xMsg )
    {
```

```
 7          int localVar = 456;
 8
 9          for ( int loopVar = 1; loopVar <= 2; loopVar++ )
10          {
11             System.out.println( "Loop Pass #" + loopVar );
12             System.out.println( "Loop   : " + ivInt );
13             System.out.println( "Loop   : " + ivString );
14             System.out.println( "Loop   : " + xMsg );
15             System.out.println( "Loop   : " + localVar );
16         System.out.println();
17          }  // loopVar destroyed here
18
19          System.out.println( "Method: " + ivInt );
20          System.out.println( "Method: " + ivString );
21          System.out.println( "Method: " + xMsg );
22          System.out.println( "Method: " + localVar );
23       }  // xMsg & localVar destroyed here
24
25       public static void main( String xArgs[] )
26       {
27          ScopeDemo demo = new ScopeDemo();
28
29          System.out.println( "Main   : " + demo.ivInt );
30          System.out.println( "Main   : " + demo.ivString );
31          System.out.println();
32          demo.aMethod( "You can't handle the truth!" );
33       }
34
35    String ivString = new String( "It's been, fun!" );
36     }  // ivInt, ivString & xArgs destroyed here
```

The code can be explained as follows:

- In line 1, the keyword "class informs the compiler that you are defining a user-defined data type (class) called ScopeDemo. The word *public* indicates that this class can be accessed by any other class in the system.
- In line 2, this opening brace marks the beginning of the block of code that constitutes the Java class that was declared in line 1. It corresponds with the closing brace in line 36 that marks the end of the class.
- In line 3, the scope of the instance variables ivInt (declared and initialized in line) and ivString (declared and initialized in line 35) is the entire body of the class. They are created as part of each object instantiated from the ScopeDemo class and remain in existence until the object is destroyed. This example illus-

trates that instance variables can be declared and initialized anywhere within the class that is outside of any methods. In practice, you'd usually group all of the instance variables together at the beginning or end of the class definition.

- Line 5 declares a method named aMethod. The keyword "public" indicates that this method can be called from any object in the system. The keyword "void" indicates that this method does not return a value. The words "String xMsg" define the type and name of the parameter required for this method. Specifically, it indicates that a reference to a String object must accompany any message that requests that this method be invoked. A copy of the String reference will be stored in the parameter variable named xMsg, which will be accessible throughout (has a scope of) the body of the method. The body of the method is delineated by the opening and closing braces in lines 6 and 23.
- In line 7, the local integer variable localVar is declared and initialized to the value 456. localVar is called a "local" variable to indicate that the variable exists only within the method in which it was defined. As soon as the program execution reaches the end of the method in line 23, localVar is destroyed.
- The for loop in line 9 causes the statements between the opening and closing braces in lines 10 and 17 to be executed two times. Within the parentheses that follow the keyword "for" are three statements separated by semicolons. We'll examine these statements more thoroughly in the section on flow control, but for now, notice that the first statement declares and initializes to 0 the variable loopVar. The scope of loopVar is the for loop. As soon as the for loop is exited, loopVar will cease to exist.
- Line 25 declares a special method named main. Java begins the execution of an application with the main method of a class. The keyword "public" indicates that this method can be called from anywhere in the system. The keyword "static" indicates that this is a class method (class methods are discussed in the section on classes). The keyword "void" indicates that this method does not return a value. The words "String xArgs[]" indicate that this method expects an array of String objects as a parameter. Java passes any command-line arguments that were entered when the application was started, to main via the String array parameter.
- The opening brace on line 26 marks the beginning of the body of the main method. It corresponds with the closing brace in line 33 that marks the end of the method.

- In line 27 the variable demo is declared to be of type ScopeDemo. A new ScopeDemo object is then instantiated and assigned to demo (that is, demo now points to an object of class ScopeDemo). Recall that an instantiated object causes space to be allocated to hold the object's instance variables.
- In line 29, the value of the instance variable ivInt, of the object referred to (pointed to) by the variable demo, is retrieved and printed.
- In line 30, as in line 29, the instance variable (ivString) of the object demo is retrieved and printed. (Although it is not entirely accurate, the distinction between an object and a variable that refers to it is often blurred, as I've done here. It's harmless as long as you recognize that the object and the variable are, in fact, two distinct structures.)
- The method aMethod of the object demo is invoked in line 32. The String literal "You can't handle the truth!" is passed as a parameter.
- In line 33, When this closing brace, which marks the end of the class method main, is reached, the program ends.

Java Packages

A *package* is a named collection of Java classes that is roughly analogous to a "library" in other languages. Packages can contain other packages in a hierarchical fashion. For instance, the class libraries included with Java are supplied as a package named java. Within the java package are several other packages including applet, awt, io, lang, net, and util. Additionally, the awt package contains two additional packages named image and peer. Fully qualified package and class names include all of the higher-level package names separated by periods. Thus, the fully qualified name of the image package is:

```
java.awt.image
```

The fully qualified name of the DirectColorModel class that is contained within the image package is:

```
java.awt.image.DirectColorModel
```

Java classes can always be referred to by their fully qualified names. To reduce typing and improve readability, classes can also be referred to by their "simple" names (for example, DirectColorModel) if they are explicitly imported at the beginning of a class file using an *import* statement. The import statement is covered in more detail in the section on classes.

Packages correspond to the directories in the file system that specify the location of the compiled *.class* files that the package contains. The compiler uses the CLASSPATH environment variable to find the root directory from which to search to find compiled classes. Sun recommends using Internet domain names in reverse order, as the higher-level names of packages, to eliminate the potential of conflicting names. Thus, any package created by the Widgets company would be:

```
com.Widgets.packageName
```

Java Classes

Everything in a Java program happens within a class. Recall that a class is a detailed specification that defines the set of data (instance variables) and behaviors (methods) that objects, created from the class definition, will have. The source code of each Java class is usually stored in a separate text file that is given the same name as the class it contains followed by the extension *.java*. In this section, we'll take a detailed look at the parts and organization of the class definitions stored in *.java* files.

Package Declaration

Classes can explicitly state the name of the package to which they belong by including a package declaration statement as the first line (other than comments or whitespace) of the class definition. A package declaration statement has the following form:

```
package <packageName>;
```

where <packageName> corresponds to the name and path of the class file specified from a directory included in the CLASSPATH environment variable. Classes that do not explicitly state the name of the package to which they belong are grouped by the compiler into one more unnamed "default" packages.

Import Statements

Most Java programs have one or more import statements that tell the compiler where to locate any other classes that are used within the one being defined. Import statements can specify a single class or all of the classes contained within a package.

The following import statement tells the compiler that you will be using the DirectColorModel class that is in the java.awt.image package.

```
import java.awt.image.DirectColorModel;
```

All of the classes in a package can be imported in a single statement using the "wildcard" operator *:

```
import java.awt.image.*;
```

Note that this only imports the classes from a single package. It does not automatically import the classes from subpackages contained within the specified package.

Class Declaration

The class declaration statement informs the compiler of the name of the class that is being defined. A class declaration has the form:

```
[ public ] [ final | abstract ] class <ClassName>
        [ extends <SuperClassName> ]
        [ implements <Interface1> [, <Interface2> ,…] ]
```

Everything within brackets [ ] is optional. Only one of the options separated by | can appear within the declaration of a class. The items within <> represent programmer-supplied identifiers.

Class Accessibility Modifiers

The modifiers that can be specified as part of the class declaration are public, abstract, and final.

By default, classes are accessible only by other classes in the same package. The "public" modifier makes this class accessible to classes outside of the package that contains this class.

The "abstract" modifier declares that this class is an "abstract" class. *Abstract classes* are classes that are, by design, not fully implemented. They are useful for "abstracting" the common behaviors of similar classes into a superclass so the implementation of the common behaviors can be shared.

The "final" modifier prevents this class from being subclassed. It is intended to allow class developers to protect the integrity of certain classes by ensuring that others do not extend and modify critical behaviors. This modifier should be used very sparingly.

Extends Clause (Superclass) The "extends" clause declares that this class is a subclass of the indicated superclass. All of the nonprivate instance variables and methods of the specified superclass, and all of its superclasses, are then inherited by the class being defined. If the extends clause is not provided, the class is automatically made a subclass of the class java.lang.Object.

Implements Clause (Interfaces) The implements clause specifies the interfaces that are implemented by this class. Multiple interfaces can be listed separated by commas. An interface can extend a superinterface in the same manner that a subclass extends its superclass. A class is automatically considered to implement any superinterfaces of interfaces declared in its "implements" clause.

Class Body

The body of a class is the code that exists between the opening brace that immediately follows the class declaration and the matching closing brace. All of the elements that constitute a class are defined and implemented within the class body. This includes class variables, class methods, instance variables, and instance methods.

Accessibility Modifiers Variable and method declarations can be prefixed by an accessibility modifier that determines whether the variable or method can be accessed from outside the class in which it was declared. The keywords and rules that affect the accessibility of variables and methods are detailed in Table 12.12.

Variable Declarations Variables that are declared within the body of a class, but outside of any methods, are instance variables or class variables.

Instance Variables *Instance variables*, as you may recall, are the variables that hold the values that represent the state of an object. A separate copy of each instance variable is allocated for each object of the class that is instantiated. If five objects of the class exist, then five separate copies of each of the instance variables also exist.

Instance variables can be declared anywhere within the body of a class that is not within a method. Instance variable declarations have the form:

```
    [ public | protected | private ] [ final ] [ transient ]
[ volatile ]  <DataType> <varName>;
```

Everything within brackets [ ] is optional. Only one of the options separated by | can appear within the declaration of a variable. The items within <> represent programmer supplied identifiers.

Table 12.12 Accessibility Modifiers

Keyword	Accessibility Type	Accessible From
<none>	Default	Class in which it was declared Any class in the same package (including subclasses)
Public	Public	Everywhere
Protected	Protected	Class in which it was declared Any class in the same package (including subclasses) Subclasses outside of the package
Private	Private	Class in which it was declared

Instance variable declarations can be explained as follows.

- The keywords "public," "protected," and "private" determine the accessibility of the variable as explained in the section "Accessibility Modifiers."
- The keyword "final" indicates that this variable contains a constant value as explained in the section "Constants."
- The keyword "transient" indicates that this variable should not be saved as part of an object's persistent state. Future versions of Java will likely provide language-level support for saving and retrieving objects to a hard disk or other persistent storage device. Transient variables contain information that does not need to be saved or retrieved.
- The keyword "volatile" will be supported in future versions of the language. Java is a multithreaded programming language, which means that multiple tasks can be performed simultaneously. For efficiency, each thread in a program can keep a private copy of a shared variable. The "volatile" keyword ensures that a thread reconciles the private copy of a variable with the "master" copy every time it accesses the variable.
- <DataType> represents the data type of the variable. The data type of a variable can be any of the data types defined by the language or a programmer-defined data type such as a Class or an Interface.
- <varName> is the name of the variable.

Class Variables *Class variables* are variables that are shared among all of the objects of a class. Only one copy of a class variable is ever created. It is created when the class is first initialized and exists until the program ends or the class is unloaded.

Class variables are declared in the same manner as instance variables except that class variable declarations include the additional keyword "static." The following are examples of class variable declarations:

```
static int anInt;
public static String myString;
private final static double income;
```

Constants To simulate constant values, Java allows you to precede the declaration and initialization of a variable with the keyword "final." The declaration and initialization of the variable must occur in a single statement. The keyword "final" tells Java to ensure that no other assignments are made to the variable. Thus, the value of the variable will not change during its lifetime. Both class variables and instance variables can be declared "final."

As we've repeated often, a variable of a reference type and the object it points to are two distinct structures. Declaring a variable of reference type "final" means the reference cannot change. In other words, the variable will always point to the same object. However, the values contained in the instance variables of the object that the varialbe points to can still be changed at will. This can lead programmers who do not understand this distinction to believe that Java constants do not work correctly.

Here are some examples of Java constants:

```
final static  int MAX = 100;      // class variable constant
final         int MIN = 15;           // instance variable constant
final         String[] MOVIE = { "Raiders Of The Lost Ark",
                         "Temple Of Doom","The Final Crusade" }
```

Methods

Methods are structures, similar to functions in other languages, that consist of the step-by-step instructions required to accomplish a task. They can accept parameters and optionally return a value. In Java, a method is uniquely identified by its *signature*. A method's *signature* consists of the name of the method and the quantity and data types of its parameters. It is not at all uncommon for several methods within a class to share the same name and differ only in the number and data types of their parameters.

Additionally, a subclass can override the implementation of a method declared in one of its superclasses by declaring and implementing a method of same name with the same parameters. Messages, directed to an object of the subclass, with the appropriate method signature, will then automatically invoke the method of the subclass. If necessary, a subclass can invoke the overridden method by using the keyword "super" followed by the method name and parameters:

```
super.method( param1, param2 );
```

Like classes, methods have both a declaration and a body. A method declaration can appear anywhere within a class that is not inside another method. The body or implementation of a method immediately follows the method declaration and is enclosed within braces { }. There are several kinds of methods including instance methods, class methods, native methods. and abstract methods. The kind of method is determined by the keyword modifiers that precede its declaration.

Instance Methods A method declaration provides, among other things, the name of the method, determines whether the method can be invoked from outside the class in which it is defined, and declares the data types and names of any parameters required by the method. Method declarations have the form:

```
[ public | protected | private ] [ final ] [ synchronized ] [ native ]
<ReturnType> <methodName> ( [ <ParamType> <paramName> [, ...] ] )
[ throws <Exception1> [ , <Exception2>, ... ] ]
```

Everything within brackets [ ] is optional. Only one of the options separated by | can appear within the declaration of a method. The items within <> represent programmer supplied identifiers. Following is an explanation of the keywords and data types used with instance method declarations.

- The keywords "public," "protected," and "private" determine the accessibility of the method. This works in exactly the same manner as it does for variables. Please see the section "Accessibility Modifiers"for detailed information.
- The keyword "final" indicates that this method cannot be overridden by a subclass.
- The keyword "synchronized" tells Java to ensure that only one thread modifies the object (if it is an instance method) or the class (if it is a class method) at a

time. It is used to prevent a sequence of uncoordinated modifications from putting the object in an invalid state.

- The keyword "native" informs the compiler that this method is implemented using platform-dependent code written in another language, such as C or C++. Because native methods are implemented elsewhere, native method declarations do not have an associated method body enclosed within braces. Instead, the declaration is followed by a semicolon.
- <ReturnType> represents the data type of the value returned from this method. The return type can be any of the data types defined by the language or a programmer-defined data type such as a Class or an Interface. Methods that do not return a value must specify the keyword "void" in place of a data type.
- <methodName> is the name of the method.
- <ParamType> and <paramName> represent the data type and name of a parameter, respectively. Multiple parameters can be declared by separating <ParamType> <paramName> declarations by commas.
- The throws clause informs the compiler of the types of errors that objects that invoke this method must make provisions to handle. The <Exception?> identifiers represent the names of classes that represent error conditions and exceptions. These classes are all subclasses of the Throwable class in the java.lang package.

Class Methods *Class methods* are methods that do not require an object to be invoked. They are invoked in the same manner as instance methods except that the name of the class is substituted for the reference variable that identifies the target object in an instance method call. The Math class that is part of the Java libraries is implemented using class methods. To calculate the square root of the number 1941, you'd call the class method sqrt in the following manner:

```
double result = Math.sqrt( 1941 );
```

Notice that no objects are allocated. Class methods are the closest thing that Java provides to the normal function calls of other languages.

Class methods are declared in the same manner as instance methods except that class methods, like class variables, include the keyword "static" in their declaration.

Abstract Methods *Abstract methods* are methods that are declared, but not implemented, within the class definition. They exist to allow a superclass to define behaviors that subclasses are required to implement. Like native methods, abstract methods consist only of a declaration followed by a semicolon. A class that contains one or more abstract methods is referred to as an *abstract class*. Objects cannot be instantiated from an abstract class because the implementation of the class is incomplete.

The declaration of an abstract class has the form:

```
[ public | protected ] abstract
<ReturnType> <methodName> ([ <ParamType> <paramName> [, ...]])
[ throws <Exception1> [ , <Exception2>, ... ] ]
```

Following is an explanation of the keywords and data types used with abstract method declarations.

- The keywords "public" and "protected" determine the accessibility of the method. This works in exactly the same manner as it does for variables. Please see the section "Accessibility Modifiers" for detailed information.
- <ReturnType> represents the data type of the value returned from this method. The return type can be any of the data types defined by the language or a programmer-defined data type such as a Class or an Interface. Methods that do not return a value must specify the keyword "void" in place of a data type.
- <methodName> is the name of the method.
- <ParamType> and <paramName> represent the data type and name of a parameter, respectively. Multiple parameters can be declared by separating <ParamType> <paramName> declarations by commas.
- The throws clause informs the compiler of the types of errors that objects that invoke this method must make provisions to handle. The <Exception?> identifiers represent the names of classes that represent error conditions and exceptions. These classes are all subclasses of the Throwable class in the java.lang package.

Constructors A *constructor* is a special kind of method, named the same as the class in which it is declared, that is invoked when an object of the class is instantiated (created). Like other methods, a class can declare several constructors that differ in the number and type of their parameters. Constructors are typically used to initialize the instance variables of an object to appropriate values. Constructor declarations have the form:

```
[ public | protected | private ] <ClassName>
( [ <ParamType> <paramName> [, …]  ] )
[ throws <Exception1> [ , <Exception2>, … ] ]
```

Following is an explanation of the keywords and data types used with constructor declarations.

- The keywords "public," "protected," and "private" determine the accessibility of the constructor. This works in exactly the same manner as it does for variables. Please see the section "Accessibility Modifiers" for detailed information.
- <ClassName> is the name of the class and of the constructor.
- <ParamType> and <paramName> represent the data type and name of a parameter, respectively. Multiple parameters can be declared by separating <ParamType> <paramName> declarations by commas.
- The throws clause informs the compiler of the types of errors that objects that invoke this method must make provisions to handle. The <Exception?> identifiers represent the names of classes that represent error conditions and exceptions. These classes are all subclasses of the Throwable class in the java.lang package.

It is often useful for subclasses to invoke a constructor of their superclass. In fact, Java automatically invokes the default constructor of an object's superclass (the one without any parameters) unless the programmer explicitly indicates another action to take. To explicitly invoke a superclass constructor, specify the keyword "super," followed by any required parameters within parentheses, as the first statement within the constructor of the subclass:

```
super( param1, param2 );
```

Interfaces

A Java *interface* represents a named set of behaviors. It consists of a declaration followed by an interface body, enclosed within braces, that contains a list of method declarations and constant values. Any class can *implement* an interface by including the name of the interface in the *implements* clause of the class declaration and by declaring and implementing all of the methods listed in the body of the interface.

Like a class, an interface is a user-defined data type. This means that reference variables can be declared with the name of an interface as their data type. Variables declared with an interface data type can reference (point to) any object that is of a class that implements the interface.

Recall that polymorphism refers to the ability of an object, typically a subclass, to respond to all of the messages to which its superclass can respond. Thus, a subclass object can be used within the system, anywhere that its superclass can, without having to modify the objects that send the messages. Interfaces allow objects of classes that are not related through inheritance to act in a similar polymorphic manner.

An interface declaration has the form:

```
[ public ] interface <InterfaceName>
[ extends <SuperInterface1> [, <SuperInterface2>, …] ]
```

Following is an explanation of the keywords and data types used with interface declarations.

- The keyword "public" determines the accessibility of the interface. This works in exactly the same manner as it does for class declarations.
- The required keyword "interface" indicates that this is an interface declaration.
- <InterfaceName> is the programmer-supplied identifier that names the interface.
- The extends clause indicates that the interface being declared extends each of the named superinterfaces. Thus, in addition to implementing all the methods listed in the body of the interface being declared, any class that implements the interface must also implement all of the methods declared in the listed superinterfaces.

Chapter

13

Programming with Java

In this chapter, we will take a closer look at applets. We'll begin by briefly examining the security restrictions that most Web browsers currently impose on applets. Then, we'll examine the type of interaction that occurs between Java applets and the Web browser in which they run.

Afterward, we'll proceed to build several applets that demonstrate many of the language constructs discussed in the last chapter while simultaneously introducing several of the key Java library classes that you'll be using in almost every Java program you write. Finally, we'll conclude with a comprehensive list of the core classes included in the Java libraries and a brief look at where Java is headed.

Applet Overview

We mentioned, in the last chapter, that applets are typically small programs that are embedded within Web pages. When a Web page that contains an applet is retrieved by a Java-enabled browser, the browser automatically downloads and executes the applet. Java-enabled browsers have a Java virtual machine built into them. Because applets are automatically downloaded and executed by the browser, it would be very easy for an unscrupulous programmer to write a malicious applet that deleted files or surreptitiously gathered information from the hard disk of any user who viewed a particular Web page. To limit incidents of this nature, most browsers impose several restrictions on the applets they run.

Security Restrictions

Ordinarily, applets are prevented from reading or writing files that reside on the host machine on which the browser is running. Additionally, applets cannot load libraries, define native methods, access certain system properties, or execute other programs installed on the host machine. To ensure that applets cannot successfully mimic native password entry or other confidential screens, applet-controlled windows contain obvious, browser-supplied warning messages. Finally, an applet is limited to making network connections with the machine from which it was initially downloaded.

It is important to note that the restrictions imposed on applets are imposed by the Web browser and its embedded virtual machine. There is nothing inherently less capable about Java applets than any other Java program. In fact, work proceeds on several fronts to remove many of the current security restrictions from "trusted" applets. Trusted applets are applets that can be verified as having come from a reputable source designated by the user.

The <APPLET> Tag

A Web page consists of text and HTML (HyperText Markup Language) codes that specify, for a browser, the general layout and appearance of the page. As you saw in Chapter 12, an <APPLET> HTML tag can be embedded within a Web page to indicate the name and location of an applet that should be automatically downloaded and executed as part of the page. The <APPLET> tag has the form:

```
< APPLET
          [ CODEBASE = <url> ]
          CODE = <ClassName>
          [ ALT = <JavaChallengedBrowserText> ]
          [ NAME = <AppletID> ]
          WIDTH = <AppletWidthInPixels>
          HEIGHT = <AppletHeightInPixels>
[ ALIGN = [ LEFT | RIGHT | BOTTOM | TOP | TEXTTOP |
          MIDDLE | ABSMIDDLE | BASELINE | ABSBOTTOM ] ]
[ VSPACE = <VerticleSpace> ]
[ HSPACE = <HorizontalSpace> ]
```

```
>

[  < PARAM = <Parameter1>   VALUE = <value1> > ]
[  < PARAM = <Parameter2>   VALUE = <value2> > ]
. . .

[ <AppletChallengedBrowserText> ]

</APPLET>
```

Everything within brackets [ ] is optional. Only one of the options separated by | can appear after the ALIGN attribute. The items within <> represent programmer-supplied identifiers. The <> characters that surround the <APPLET>, </APPLET>, and <PARAM> tags are required. Keep the following in mind when using the <APPLET> tag:

- The <APPLET> tag contains the attributes that specify the name and location of the applet and control the size and appearance of the applet on the page. It may optionally be followed by one or more <PARAM> tags, which must precede the required </APPLET> tag that marks the end of the applet specification.
- The optional CODEBASE attribute allows a URL to be specified that provides the name of the directory that contains the *.class* file for the applet.
- The required CODE attribute provides the name of the applet's *.class* file.
- The optional ALT attribute specifies text that should be displayed by browsers that understand the <APPLET> tag but cannot execute Java applets.
- The optional NAME attribute provides an identifying name that other applets in the same page can use to find and communicate with this applet.
- The required WIDTH and HEIGHT attributes provide the width and height (in pixels) of the applet's display area.
- The optional ALIGN attribute specifies the position of the applet in relation to the margins of the page (LEFT, RIGHT) or to the text that surrounds the applet.
- The VSPACE and HSPACE attributes specify the amount of space (in pixels) above and below, and to the left and right, respectively, to reserve around the display area of the applet.

- The optional <PARAM> tags allow parameter names and values to be specified within the page that will be available to the applet when it is executed. Applets can read the values of these parameters by calling the getParameter method of the Applet class with the name of the parameter to retrieve.

- Text (<AppletChallengedBrowserText>) and HTML codes can optionally be included between the <APPLET> and </APPLET> tags that will be displayed only by browsers that do not understand the <APPLET> tag.

What Is an Applet?

An applet is a programmer-developed subclass of the Java library class java.applet.Applet. The Applet class, in turn, is a subclass of java.awt.Panel, which is a subclass of java.awt.Container, which is a subclass of java.awt.Component, which is a subclass of the root Java class java.lang.Object. As you may recall, subclasses "inherit" the nonprivate methods and instance variables of their superclasses. Consequently, the programmer-developed subclasses of java.applet.Applet automatically gain the capabilities implemented in the nearly 100 methods defined in the Applet class and its superclasses, just by including the clause "extends Applet" in the class declaration. This is an excellent example of the power of object-oriented programming and, in particular, of inheritance.

Recall that a subclass is related to its superclasses in a manner that can be described with the words "is-a." In other words, we can say that the programmer-developed class "is-a" Applet, "is-a" Panel, "is-a" Container, and "is-a" Component. To fully understand what this means for applets, it is helpful to examine what Components, Containers, and Panels are.

The Component class is the abstract superclass of all of the nonmenu user interface objects provided in the Java class libraries. The graphical user interface (GUI) classes provided in the Java libraries are collectively referred to as the Abstract Windowing Toolkit or AWT. Hence, the name of the package that contains the GUI class files: java.awt. The Component class defines and implements in excess of 50 methods that relate to the size, appearance, and location of Java GUI components. In addition, the Component class provides methods that implement the component's part of controlling the program's input focus (where keystrokes are directed) and handling events (mouse clicks, keystrokes, and so on). In essence, a Component is a user-interface object of arbitrary complexity.

The Container class is an abstract class that implements the behaviors required for a component to "contain" other components. The items that a user of a GUI program interacts with, to control the operation of a program, are objects. Each button, scrollbar, text field, and check box displayed on the screen is an object. The Container class allows a higher-level object to be created that contains, organizes, and controls the interaction between, these lower-level objects. With respect to applets, this means that applets can contain buttons, text fields, scrollbars, and any of the other user-interface objects normally used within a GUI program.

Recall that abstract classes cannot be instantiated. Therefore, you cannot create an object of either the Component class or the Container class. That's where the Panel class comes in. Because the Panel class is not abstract, objects of the Panel class can be instantiated. Because a Panel object "is-a" Container, it can contain other objects. Because a Panel object "is-a" Component, it can be inserted into an object that can contain components. Therefore, a Panel object can be inserted into another Panel object. This "nesting" of components is the primary mechanism that allows complex user interfaces to be developed using the AWT. There is essentially no limit to the number of Panels that can be contained within another Panel. Likewise, there is essentially no limit to how deeply Panels can be nested within each other. Because an applet "is-a" Panel and it can therefore contain other Panels, the applet's user interface can be as sophisticated as desired.

The Applet Class

The Applet class is a specialized kind of Panel that is designed to be embedded within a specialized container called an *applet context*. Web browsers and the *appletviewer* program you used earlier are examples of applet contexts. Among other things, an applet context provides the environment in which one or more applets are executed. Several of the methods, declared and implemented within the Applet class, allow an applet to retrieve information from the applet context in which it is running. Several other methods simplify, for Applets, the process of retrieving image and audio files given the URL where they are located, playing audio files, and displaying messages on the status line of the applet context. The complete list of public methods declared and implemented by the Applet class is shown in Table 13.1.

Table 13.1 Public Methods of the Applet Class

Method	Return Type	Description
destroy()	void	Called by the applet context when the applet is about to be destroyed.
getAppletContext()	AppletContext	Returns a reference to the applet context in which the applet is running.
getAppletInfo()	String	Allows an applet to provide miscellaneous information such as the name of its author, copyright details, and contact phone numbers or e-mail addresses.
getAudioClip (URL u) getAudioClip (URL u, String name)	AudioClip	Retrieves an audio clip from the specified URL. If a "name" is specified, it is appended to the URL indicated in "u."
getCodeBase()	URL	Returns the base URL from which the applet was loaded. The returned URL does not include the name of the applet's *.class* file. The code-base URL is usually used to locate other files, such as default image or audio files, that can be used by the applet.
getDocumentBase()	URL	Returns the base URL of the HTML page in which the applet is embedded. The document base URL is usually used to retrieve image or audio files, which can be used by the applet, that relate to the document in which the applet is embedded. Often, the names of the files are embedded in the HTML page and are retrieved by the applet using the getParameter() method.
getImage(URL u) getImage(URL u, String name)	Image	Retrieves an image from the specified URL. If a "name" is specified, it is appended to the URL indicated in "u."
getParameter (String s)	String	Returns the value given for the parameter "s." Recall that applet parameters are specified in optional

Table 13.1 *Continued*

Method	Return Type	Description
		<PARAM> tags within the <APPLET> tag of the HTML page in which the applet is embedded.
getParameterInfo()	String[][]	Allows an applet to provide information about the parameters it accepts. If implemented by a subclass of Applet, this method returns an array of string arrays, each of which contains the name of a parameter, a String containing the para meter type, and a description of the parameter.
init()	void	This method is called by the applet context shortly before the applet is made active for the first time.
isActive()	boolean	Applets are always in an active or inactive state. They are made active when the start() method is called and made inactive when the stop() method is called. This method allows the back ground threads of an applet to check the applet's state.
play(URL u) play(URL u, String name)	void	Retrieves and plays an audio clip from the specified URL. If a "name" is specified, it is appended to the URL indicated in "u."
resize(Dimension d) resize(int width, int height)	void	Changes the size of the area on the page occupied by the applet. Browser support for this method is currently unreliable.
setStub()	void	This is a final method that is used internally by the Applet class.
showStatus (String s)	void	Passes the message "s" to the applet context. The applet context can optionally display the message in its status bar.
start()	void	This method is called by the applet context to inform the applet that it is now active. Upon receiving this message, applets usually proceed to "do their thing."

Continued

Table 13.1 *Continued*

Method	Return Type	Description
stop()	void	This method is called by the applet context to inform the applet that it is no longer active. This method is often called when the Web browser is minimized or the user moves to another page. Well-behaved applets typically pause when this message is received.

Applet Contexts and Applets

The relationship of an applet context to the applets it contains is similar to that of a conductor to the orchestra. A conductor tells the members of the orchestra when to show up and be ready to play, and when to pack up and go home. He or she cues the musicians to indicate when they should start playing and when they should stop. Additionally, he or she provides information related to how the musicians should play their music; the tempo, the volume, and so on.

An applet context gives the applets it has loaded the opportunity to "wet their reeds" (get ready to play), by invoking the applet's init method. Within the init method, an applet can load images, prepare data structures, or perform any other functions that are necessary to ensure that the applet will be ready to play when cued. Configurable applets, those that can alter the way they operate based on user-supplied information, will often, within the init method, read the parameters supplied in the HTML page that specify how the applet should operate.

To inform an applet that it should begin playing, the applet context invokes the applet's start method. Within the start method, most applets will display information to the screen, accept input, and/or interact with the user according to the way they were designed.

To inform an applet that it should stop playing, the applet context invokes the applet's stop method. Applets that perform continuous activities, such as animations, will usually pause the threads that perform those activities within the stop method. This method is usually invoked when the user moves on to another Web page or another action was performed that will ultimately result in the applet being destroyed and unloaded. Like an overly ambitious musician, the applet does not have to stop when cued. However, the applet context calls the applet's stop method only as a courtesy; how the applet responds does not affect the applet context's ability to shut down and unload the applet.

To convey the message "Thanks for coming, now go home!" to an applet, the applet context invokes the applet's destroy method. Rather than just pausing threads, applets respond to this message by performing any final clean-up operations.

The first example applet in this chapter illustrates the activities that cause each of these methods to be invoked. Some of the more popular Web browsers operate in slightly inconsistent ways. Thus, the circumstances that cause the init, start, stop, and destroy methods to be invoked may vary slightly from browser to browser.

Example Java Applets

The following example applets are intended to get you used to the "look and feel" of the source code of a Java program. They provide working examples that illustrate many of the concepts and programming structures covered in the last chapter. They also introduce several of the Java library classes that you will work with in the majority of the Java programs you develop.

By scanning the names of the classes listed in the Java Library Class Hierarchy section later in this chapter, you'll be able to get a feel for the breadth of functionality provided in the libraries. However, to develop your own Java programs, you'll need documentation that lists the public methods and instance variables of each of the supplied classes. This application program interface (API) documentation can be obtained in several ways. The latest version of the API can be downloaded from Sun's Web site: http://java.sun.com/products/JDK.

Sun has also released a 1660-page book entitled *The Java Class Libraries—An Annotated Reference* that has become the de facto reference for the library classes.

DisplayMessage Applet

The DisplayMessage applet is a simple applet that retrieves and displays a message provided by the HTML page in which the applet is embedded. The font used to display the message, along with the size and style of the text, can also be specified in the HTML page. The applet illustrates the type of interaction that takes place between a Web browser (or other applet context) and an applet. It demonstrates how applet parameters, which are embedded within an HTML page, are retrieved and processed by the applet. Additionally, it provides examples of many of the flow control structures mentioned in the last chapter and introduces the Graphics and Font library classes.

The default behavior of the DisplayMessage applet, if no message is specified in the HTML page, is to create a message consisting of the current font name, style, and size. Each of these attributes can be individually set by including the appropriate "applet parameter" in the HTML page. We'll begin by examining one of the demonstration HTML pages included on the CD-ROM.

```
1    <HTML>
2    <HEAD>
3        <TITLE> DisplayMessage Applet
4        </TITLE>
5    </HEAD>
6    <BODY>
7        <APPLET CODE=DisplayMessage.class
8                WIDTH="600" HEIGHT="300">
9            <PARAM NAME=message    VALUE="">
10           <PARAM NAME=fontName   VALUE="Times Roman">
11           <PARAM NAME=fontSize   VALUE="24">
12           <PARAM NAME=fontStyle VALUE="BOLD/ITALIC">
13       </APPLET>
14   </BODY>
15   </HTML>
```

As before, our interest is limited to the information contained within the <APPLET> tag. The <APPLET> tag that spans lines 7 and 8 specifies the name of the Java class file that contains the applet and the width and height of the region of the screen in which the applet is to be displayed. In lines 9 through 12, the name and value of four applet parameters are given. The "message" parameter allows a text message to be entered that will be displayed instead of default information about the current font. The "fontName," "fontSize," and "fontStyle" parameters allow you to manipulate the individual characteristics of the font used to display the message so as to affect its appearance.

To view the applet, use the appletviewer program or a Web browser in the same manner as you did for the examples in the previous chapter. In case you've forgotten, as long as you're in the directory containing the applet's *.class* file (DisplayMessage.class), you should be able to view the applet using the appletviewer program by typing the command:

```
appletviewer DisplayMessage.html
```

and pressing Enter. Substitute the names of the other .html files in the same directory for other examples. You can also use a text editor to modify the values of the parameters in the .html files and observe the effect.

We've overridden the applet's init, start, stop, paint, and destroy methods so that a short status message is printed to the console whenever they are invoked. The paint method is invoked by the applet context when the applet needs to display its user-interface. When you run the applet within the appletviewer program, these messages will be printed to the DOS "console" window where you started the program. You may need to move the appletviewer window so that you can see the messages. If you are running a Netscape browser, you'll need to turn on the option "Show Java Console." Microsoft's Internet Explorer browser sends console output to a file called "javalog.txt" so you won't be able to view the output while the applet is running.

By selecting the menu options or buttons to reload and close the applet, you'll be able to see the order and circumstances in which the applet context invokes the applet's methods. Additionally, if you position another window so that it partially occludes the applet's window and then click on the applet window to bring it to the front, you'll see one of the circumstances in which the applet's paint method is invoked.

If you're viewing the applet with a browser, select the option to "disable" Java support while the applet is running. Then re-enable the support and observe the corresponding status messages. Finally, within a browser, load the HTML page containing the DisplayMessage applet. Then load another HTML page (perhaps one of the ones containing a sample applet included with the JDK). Notice how the DisplayMessage applet's stop method is called when the second page is loaded. When you return to the page containing the DisplayMessage applet, its start method will be called. This allows a well-behaved applet to discontinue resource-consuming activities, such as displaying an animation, when the page it is embedded within is not being viewed.

Now let's take a look at the source code of the DisplayMessage applet:

```
// ___Imported Classes
    import java.applet.Applet;
    import java.awt.Font;
    import java.awt.Graphics;
```

```

// ___Class Definition
public class DisplayMessage extends Applet
{

// ___INSTANCE VARIABLES
   protected Font    font;
   protected boolean fontChanged = true;
   protected String  fontName    = "TimesRoman";
   protected int     fontStyle   = Font.BOLD;
   protected int     fontSize    = 24;
   protected String  msgText;

// ===================================================

// ___METHOD: destroy
   public void destroy()
   {  System.out.println( "Applet Destroyed!" );
   }

// ___METHOD: getAppletInfo
   public String getAppletInfo()
   {  return new String( " DisplayText Applet \n " +
                         " by Cyberian Foundations " );
   }

// ___METHOD: getParameters
   protected void getParameters()
   {
      String param;

//    ___Read The Font Name Parameter
      param = getParameter( "fontName" );

      if ( param.equalsIgnoreCase( "Helvetica" )   ||
           param.equalsIgnoreCase( "TimesRoman" )  ||
           param.equalsIgnoreCase( "Courier" )     ||
           param.equalsIgnoreCase( "Dialog" )      ||
           param.equalsIgnoreCase( "DialogInput" )   )
      {
         fontName = param;
      }

//    ___Read The Font Style Parameter
      param = getParameter( "fontStyle" );

      if ( param.equalsIgnoreCase( "BOLD/ITALIC" ) )
```

```
        {  fontStyle = Font.BOLD|Font.ITALIC;
        }
        else if ( param.equalsIgnoreCase( "ITALIC" ) )
        {  fontStyle = Font.ITALIC;
        }
        else if ( param.equalsIgnoreCase( "PLAIN" ) )
        {  fontStyle = Font.PLAIN;
        }
        else
        {  fontStyle = Font.BOLD;
        }

//      ___Read The Font Size Parameter
        param = getParameter( "fontSize" );

        try
        {
           if ( param != null )
           {
              int size = Integer.parseInt( param );
              setFontSize( size );
           }
        }
        catch( NumberFormatException badNumber )
        {  setFontSize();  // Set To Default Font Size
        }

//      ___Read The Message Text
        param = getParameter( "message" );
        if ( param != null && param.length() > 0 )
        {  msgText = param;
        }
//      ___No message passed:
//      ___    Display font name, style, and size
        else
        {
           String style;
           switch ( fontStyle )
           {  case Font.BOLD:
                 style = "BOLD";
                 break;
              case Font.ITALIC:
                 style = "ITALIC";
                 break;
              case Font.PLAIN:
                 style = "PLAIN";
                 break;
```

```
                default:
                   style = "BOLD/ITALIC";
                   break;
            }

            msgText = "Font: "  + fontName + ", " +
                      "Style: " + style    + ", " +
                      "Size: "  + fontSize;
         }
      }

//    ___METHOD: init
      public void init()
      {
         resize( 600, 300 );
         getParameters();
      }

//    ___METHOD: paint
      public void paint( Graphics xGC )
      {
         if ( fontChanged )
         {
            font = new Font( fontName,
                             fontStyle,
                             fontSize  );
            fontChanged = false;
         }

         xGC.setFont( font );
         xGC.drawString( msgText, 10, 150 );
         System.out.println( "- Paint Called -" );
      }

//    ___ACCESS/ASSIGN: fontSize
      public int getFontSize()
      {  return fontSize;
      }

      public void setFontSize()
      {  setFontSize( 24 );
      }

      public void setFontSize( int xSize )
      {
//       ___Limit valid sizes to between 5 & 50
         if ( xSize > 4 && xSize < 51 )
```

```
146             {  fontSize = xSize;
147                fontChanged = true;
148             }
149         }
150
151     //  ___METHOD: start
152         public void start()
153         {  System.out.println( "Applet Started!" );
154         }
155
156     //  ___METHOD: stop
157         public void stop()
158         {  System.out.println( "Applet Stopped!" );
159         }
160     }
```

The example program can be explained as follows:

- *Lines 2–4*. These lines import the Applet class, which this class extends, and the AWT Font and Graphics classes, which are necessary to produce output to the GUI screen.
- *Line 7*. This line declares the DisplayMessage class. Note the "extends Applet" clause.
- *Lines 11–16*. These lines declare and initialize instance variables that will hold information regarding the selected font and message text to be displayed.
- *Lines 21–23*. These lines declare and implement the destroy method. As you may recall, an applet's destroy method gives an applet a last chance to perform clean-up operations before the applet is unloaded and disposed of. In line 22, we just print a message to the console indicating that the destroy method had been called.
- *Lines 26–29*. These lines declare and implement the getAppletInfo method. This is the method called by the applet context when the user requests information about the applet. Note the *return* statement that begins on line 27 and continues on line 28. The "new String(...)" expression creates a new String object that is returned to the calling routine. The two String literals, enclosed within double quotes, are concatenated to create the value of the new String object. Also, note the "newline" escape operator \n included within the first String literal.
- *Line 31*. This line declares the method getParameters. The getParameters method (not to be confused with the Applet class getParameter method) is an

instance method that retrieves the parameter values specified in the <APPLET> tag of the HTML document in which the applet is embedded. The parameter values are then validated and corresponding instance variables are set based on the values provided. Because the getParameters method performs an internal function of the DisplayMessage class that should not normally be invoked by other classes, the "protected" accessibility modifier is used.

- *Line 34*. This line declares the local String variable param. This variable will be used to temporarily refer to each parameter value retrieved from the HTML document. Because this is a local variable, it is destroyed when the closing brace that marks the end of the getParameters method (line 108) is reached.
- *Line 37*. This line invokes the getParameter method of the Applet class to retrieve the value of the "fontName" parameter from the HTML document. A reference to the String value returned from the getParameter method is stored in the variable param. Note that "fontName" refers to the name of the parameter specified in the "<PARAM NAME=..." tag in the HTML file, not the fontName instance variable. The fact that the applet parameters and the DisplayMessage class's instance variables are identically named is a matter of convenience. There is no requirement that they match.
- *Lines 39–46*. This *if* statement compares the value specified in the applet's "fontName" parameter to the names of the fonts that we'll accept. The expression param.equalsIgnoreCase(...) causes the equalsIgnoreCase method of the String object referred to by param to be invoked. If the value of the String object is equal (ignoring case) to the string literal value passed to the method, the boolean value true will be returned. The equalsIgnoreCase method is invoked up to five times as each successive font name is compared. The "logical OR" operator || is a "short-circuited" operator, which means that it exits as soon as a *true* value is returned so no unnecessary comparisons will be made. As long as the specified font name is valid, it is stored to the instance variable fontName in line 45. Otherwise, the passed value is ignored and the value that the instance variable was initialized to in line 13 will be used instead.
- *Lines 49–62*. In this section of code, the applet parameter "fontStyle" is read from the HTML document and compared with the valid font styles. Lines 51 through 62 demonstrate how *if* statements can be nested. If the conditional expression in line 51, 54, or 57 evaluates to *true*, the block of code, enclosed

within braces, that immediately follows the expression will be executed and processing will continue at line 65. Otherwise, the *else* condition following line 60 will cause the fontStyle instance variable to be set to the default value Font.BOLD. Font.BOLD, Font.ITALIC, and Font.PLAIN are constant (final) int values defined in the Font class. Note the "bitwise OR" operation used in line 52 to determine if both the bold and italic values are set.

- *Lines 65–77.* The applet parameter "fontSize" is read and validated in this section of code. Because there are several noteworthy structures in these few lines of code, the detailed instructions will be broken out into several additional bullets.
- *Line 67.* This line recalls that the braces immediately following a "try" clause enclose a section of code that invokes one or more methods that have declared "exceptions" that might occur during the processing performed by the method. An exception means that a failure occurred and the method did not complete its operation successfully. The "try" clause is associated with a "catch" clause (lines 75–77) that indicates what to do when an exception occurs.
- *Line 69.* In a production program, this simple check should also have been included after the previous applet parameter values were read. The reference variable param will contain the null value if the getParameter method does not find the requested parameter in the HTML document. The *if* statement, in this line, ensures that a value was returned from the getParameter method before any validations are performed on the value.
- *Line 71.* In this line, the variable size is declared to be of type int. It is then assigned the value returned from the expression Integer.parseInt(param). "parseInt" is a class method of the Integer class. Recall that class methods are invoked using the name of the class instead of the name of a variable that refers to an instance of the class. The "parseInt" method accepts a String containing numeric characters as a parameter and returns the int value represented by those characters. If the String is not properly formatted, that is, it contains letters instead of numbers, the parseInt method "throws" a NumberFormatException. That is the reason that this section of code is enclosed with a "try" block.
- *Line 72.* This line invokes the method setFontSize() and passes the int value extracted in the previous line as a parameter. Note that there are two

setFontSize methods declared in this class (lines 138 and 142). Recall that a method's signature consists of both the method's name and the number and types of its parameters. Because, in this case, we are passing an int value as a parameter, the method declared in line 142 would be invoked.

- *Lines 75–77*. If the String value referred to by param was not properly formatted, then the parseInt method in line 71 would throw an exception. When an exception occurs, within a "try" block, the execution of the program is interrupted and it branches to the "catch" clause. All of the *program* statements, within the "try" block, that follow the statement where the exception occurred, are skipped. Exceptions are objects. The parameter to the "catch" clause defines the type of exception that the block of code that follows the "catch" clause can deal with. In this case, the parameter variable badNumber would contain a reference to the exception object that was created when the failure occurred. We ignore the exception object and, in line 76, call the setFontSize method that has no parameters (line 138), which causes the font size to be set to the default value of 24. Note that lines 75–77 are executed only if an exception occurs within the "try" block. Otherwise, when the closing brace of the "try" clause is encountered in line 74, execution skips past the "catch" clause and continues with the next executable statement in line 80.

- *Lines 80–83*. Here the "message" applet parameter is read and validated. In line 81, the same check used previously first ensures that a value (not null) was returned from the getParameter method. If so, the other side of the "logical AND" operator && is evaluated. In this case, the length() method of the object referred to by param is invoked, which returns an int value representing the length of the string. If the String isn't empty, the length of the string will be greater than 0 and the instance variable msgText will set to the passed message text in line 82.

- *Line 86*. This line begins the "else" clause of the *if* statement in line 81. The "else" clause is evaluated if the applet "message" parameter is missing or empty. In that case, we create a message that consists of information about the current font name, style, and size.

- *Line 88*. This line declares a local String variable named style.

- *Lines 89–102*. These lines demonstrate the use of a *switch* statement to assign a description of the font style represented by the int value contained in the instance variable fontStyle to the String variable style.

- *Lines 104–106.* These lines are a single statement that creates the message to be displayed. Note the use of the concatenation operator + to join the various values into a single String. In particular, note the automatic conversion of the fontSize instance variable from type int to type String.
- *Lines 111–115.* Declares and implements the init method. The init method is called one time, by the applet context, after the applet has been loaded but before it is made active. We have included a precautionary call to the resize method of the Applet class in line 113. The instance method getParameters is then invoked to read the applet parameter values specified in the HTML document and make any required adjustments.
- *Lines 118–131.* These lines declare and implement the paint method. Applet contexts call the paint method to inform the applet that it needs to draw, or redraw, its user interface to the screen.
- *Line 120.* In this line, the boolean instance variable fontChanged is checked to see if the font has been changed since the last time the screen was painted. If so, a new Font object is created in lines 122–124 and then the fontChanged variable is updated to indicate that a new Font object will not need to be created the next time the screen is painted.
- *Lines 122–124.* The appearance of text, displayed in a GUI environment, depends on the font in use when it is drawn. In Java, information about a font is represented by a Font object. A Font object is created in lines 122–124 by specifying the name of the font, the style of the font (bold, italic, plain, and so on), and the size of the font in points. A point is approximately one seventy-second of an inch. Because not all font sizes and styles are available on all platforms, platforms "map" the requested fonts to ones that are available. Thus, the appearance of text can vary from platform to platform.
- *Line 128.* In most GUI environments, programs are allocated a portion of the screen in which they can display their user interface. Java hides the operating system specific details of how to access the allotted portion of the screen by passing a Graphics object to the applet routines that normally handle drawing the applet's user interface. Among other things, the Graphics object contains information about background and foreground colors, the current font, and regions of the screen that need to be updated. A Graphics object is interchangeably referred to as a *graphics context.* The Graphics class defines several methods that provide ways to draw and fill shapes, lines, images, and text. All

drawing is done using these methods. In this line, the setFont method of the Graphics object referred to by the method parameter xGC is invoked. The setFont method sets the font of the graphics context to the Font object passed as a parameter. In this case, we are setting the font to the Font object we created based on the applet parameter values retrieved from the HTML file.

- *Line 129*. This line invokes the Graphics object's drawString method, which causes the String referred to by msgText to be displayed at a location that is 10 pixels to right of and 150 pixels down from the upper-left corner of the display area of the applet.
- *Lines 134–149*. The three methods declared and implemented in this section of code are typical access and assign methods. Access and assign methods are no different from normal instance methods. However, they are often referred to as access and assign methods because their sole function is to provide a "safe" way for other objects to manipulate the value contained in one of the object's instance variables. A common pattern is often used for naming access and assign methods. Access methods consist of the prefix "get" followed by the name of the instance variable. Assign methods consist of the prefix "set" followed by the name of the instance variable.
- *Line 135*. This line represents the entire implementation of the method getFontSize (which gives other objects "access" to the value of the instance variable fontSize). It simply returns the current value of fontSize.
- *Lines 138–140*. These lines declare and implement the method setFontSize. This method allows a default font size to be specified by providing a setFontSize method that does not take any parameters. It simply calls the setFontSize method declared in line 142 with the default font size value of 24.
- *Lines 142–149*. In this section of code, the setFontSize method that accepts an int parameter specifying a font size is declared and implemented. In line 145, the requested font size is checked to ensure that it is between 5 and 50 points. In line 146, the fontSize instance variable is updated with the new value. In line 147, boolean fontChanged flag is set to ensure that a new Font object is created before the screen is drawn again.
- *Lines 152–154*. The start method declared and implemented in these lines is automatically called by the applet context to make the applet active. In this

case, we simply display a message to the console indicating that the start method had been called.

- *Lines 157–159*. The stop method declared and implemented in these lines is automatically called by the applet context to make the applet inactive. In this case, we simply display a message to the console indicating that the stop method had been called.

Image Viewer Applet

The ImageViewer applet facilitates downloading and viewing a set of images within a Web page. We saw, in the DisplayMessage applet, how applet parameters that are specified in an HTML page can be retrieved and used by an applet. The ImageViewer applet reads the names of the images that it is to download and display in the same way that the DisplayMessage applet read its parameters. However, to enable the image viewer to work with an arbitrary number of images, the image filenames, separated by commas, are specified in a single parameter that is read and processed by the ImageViewer applet.

The process of extracting the individual filenames from the list specified in the parameter is referred to as *parsing*. Rather than writing code that is specific to this applet, which we would likely have to repeat in many of the other applets that we write, we'll write a reusable Parser class that will extract the filenames for us and return them as an array of String values.

Unlike most of the classes that we've seen, which define internal data that is manipulated by the methods of the class, the Parser class just accepts data as a parameter, manipulates that data, and then returns it in another form. This may seem more similar to the normal functions of other programming languages, which you may be familiar with, than the classes and objects we've been droning on about here, and in fact, it is. This is our chance to escape back to what may be more familiar territory.

The four methods implemented in the Parser class are class methods. Recall that you don't need an object to invoke a class method. You just specify the name of the class, a period, and the method name and provide the required parameters. In many ways, invoking class methods is like using an obscure syntax to call functions.

The Parser class also demonstrates one of the ways that can be used to simulate "optional arguments" in Java. Programmers accustomed to Visual Basic or other languages that allow function parameters to be optionally omitted may dislike the rigidness of Java method calls. As you'll see, the Parser class includes versions of the extractTokens and extractTokensToVector methods, which accept only a single String parameter. Both of these methods provide default values for other parameters and then call an identically named method, which accepts the additional parameters, to actually perform the task. The objective is to provide a high level of default capability, that can be invoked using a simple syntax, while preserving the ability to provide specific values for each parameter when circumstances warrant.

The Parser class utilizes, in addition to the String class, two other Java library classes. It uses the StringTokenizer class to extract the tokens (in our case image filenames) from the String value passed as a parameter. It also uses the Vector class, which was briefly reviewed in the last chapter, to store the tokens that have been extracted. The extractTokensToVector methods return the Vector in which the extracted tokens were stored. The extractTokens methods, which utilize the extractTokensToVector method to actually extract the tokens, convert the resulting Vector into the array of String values that they then return. Here's the Parser class source code:

```
// ___Imported Classes
   import java.util.StringTokenizer;
   import java.util.Vector;

// ___Class Declaration
public class Parser
{

// ___INSTANCE VARIABLES
   protected static final String
         COMMA_DELIMITER = ",";
   protected static final boolean
         TRIM_SPACES     = true;

// ==================================================

// ___METHODS: extractTokens
   public static final String[] extractTokens
         ( String xString )
```

```
    {
       return ( extractTokens(
                    xString,
                    COMMA_DELIMITER,
                    TRIM_SPACES ) );
    }


    public static final String[] extractTokens
          ( String  xString,
            String  xDelimiters,
            boolean xTrimSpaces )
    {

//     ___Use extractTokensToVector to extract tokens
       Vector vector = extractTokensToVector(
                         xString,
                         xDelimiters,
                         xTrimSpaces );

//     ___Convert the Vector to an array of Strings
       String[] tokens = new String[ vector.size() ];

       for ( int x = 0; x < vector.size(); x++ )
       {
          tokens[x] = (String) vector.elementAt( x );
       }

       return tokens;
    }
// -------------------------

// ___METHODS: extractTokensToVector
    public static final Vector extractTokensToVector
          ( String xString )
    {
       return extractTokensToVector(
                   xString,
                   COMMA_DELIMITER,
                   TRIM_SPACES );
    }


    public static final Vector extractTokensToVector
          ( String  xString,
```

```
65                 String  xDelimiters,
66                 boolean xTrimSpaces )
67         {
68             Vector tokens = new Vector();
69             StringTokenizer tokenizer =
70                 new StringTokenizer(xString, xDelimiters);
71
72     //      ___For every token in the list
73             while ( tokenizer.hasMoreTokens() )
74             {
75     //          ___Read the token
76                 String token = tokenizer.nextToken();
77
78     //          ___If asked to trim spaces, do so
79                 if ( xTrimSpaces )
80                 {
81                     token = token.trim();
82                 }
83
84     //          ___Add the token to the Vector
85                 tokens.addElement( token );
86             }
87
88             return tokens;
89         }
90     // -------------------------
91     }
```

The example program can be explained as follows:

- *Lines 10–13*. These lines declare and initialize two Java "constants." Recall that the keyword "static" means that these are class variables (as opposed to instance variables) and that the keyword "final" means that their values cannot be changed. Also, recall that Java statements can span multiple lines and end in a semicolon. Consequently, lines 10–11 represent a single statement that declares the constant variable named COMMA_DELIMITER.
- *Lines 18–19*. These lines declare the class method extractTokens, which accepts a single String parameter "xString."
- *Lines 21–24*. This compound statement invokes the extractTokens method declared in lines 28–31 passing the COMMA_DELIMITED and TRIM_SPACES constants as default values. In line 48, a copy of the reference

to the resulting array of String values is returned to this method. Through the "return" statement that begins on line 21 and ends on line 24, this method, in turn, returns the reference to the routine that originally invoked it.

- *Lines 28–31.* This is the declaration of the multiple parameter version of the extractTokens method.
- *Lines 35–38.* This statement declares the variable vector, which is then initialized to refer to the Vector that is returned from the call to extractTokensToVector. The returned Vector contains all of the extracted tokens.
- *Line 41.* This line declares the variable tokens that can refer to an array of String objects. The variable is then initialized to refer to the array created by the expression "new String[vector.size()]." The size() method of the Vector class returns the number of elements (in this case tokens) that are stored in the Vector. That value is used to determine how much room needs to be allocated in the String array. In essence, we're just making the String array big enough to hold the tokens that are in the Vector.
- *Lines 43–46.* This loop extracts each of the elements from the Vector and stores them into the corresponding position of the String array. Notice the (String) cast that is required in line 45. Recall that every Java class is a subclass of the Object class. Vectors see every object as being of "type" Object. The (String) cast checks to make sure that the object that we're going to assign to a variable of "type" String is, in fact, a String object.
- *Lines 52–60.* The method declared and implemented in these lines is essentially equivalent, excepting the name of the method it calls, to the extractTokens method declared and implemented in lines 18–25.
- *Lines 63–66.* This is the declaration of the method that does most of the work.
- *Line 68.* This line declares the variable tokens, of type Vector, and initializes it to an empty Vector object.
- *Lines 69–70.* These lines declare the variable tokenizer, of type StringTokenizer, and initialize it to the StringTokenizer object created in line 70. The String xString that is passed as a parameter to the StringTokenizer constructor contains all of the comma-separated image filenames. The xDelimiters parameter con-

tains all of the characters that the StringTokenizer should look for to determine that indicate the beginning of a new token. In our case, the only character we're using for a delimiter is the comma. Using character escape sequences, you could also indicate special characters such as tabs and newlines. See the section "Character Literals" for the list of special escape sequences.

- *Lines 73–86.* This while loop continues until all of the tokens in the list have been extracted. The hasMoreTokens method of the StringTokenizer class returns true as long as there are more tokens in the list.
- *Line 76.* The nextToken method of the StringTokenizer class retrieves the next token in the list and returns it as a String value.
- *Line 81.* Here, we conditionally invoke the trim method of the String class to remove any leading and trailing spaces from the String value returned by nextToken. The trim method creates a new String object that we assign right back to the token variable that formerly referred to the String on which the trim operation was performed. This is another good example of the difference between a variable and the object to which it refers. Java String objects are immutable. That is, once they have been created, they cannot be changed. However, a reference variable of type String can refer to (point to) any String object. In this case, we're making the token variable point to the new String object that is created as a result of invoking the trim method of another String object. The original String object, whose trim method was invoked, no longer has a variable pointing to it. Consequently, the internal Java garbage collector will eventually come along and make the space it occupies available for another use.
- *Line 85.* In this line, the String object, referred to by the variable token, is added to the Vector object tokens by invoking the Vector method addElement.

Now that we've seen the Parser class, let's take a look at how it is used. This is one of the HTML documents in which we've embedded the ImageViewer applet. The value of the "images" applet parameter is the list of the 10 .gif image files that are separated by commas. This applet does not have any particular constraints as to how many images it will work with. The Parser we just developed will just keep extracting filenames until the end of the list is reached. The ImageViewer applet does presume that the images are located at the same URL from which the *.class* file was loaded.

```
<HTML>
<HEAD>
   <TITLE> ImageViewer Applet
   </TITLE>
</HEAD>
<BODY>
   <APPLET CODE=ImageViewer.class
         WIDTH="200" HEIGHT="200">
      <PARAM NAME=images VALUE="sun.gif,
                                mercury1.gif,
                                venus2.gif,
                                earth3.gif,
                                mars4.gif,
                                jupiter5.gif,
                                saturn.gif,
                                uranus7.gif,
                                neptune8.gif,
                                pluto9.gif">
   </APPLET>
</BODY>
</HTML>
```

If you haven't done so already, now would be a good time to run the ImageViewer applet. The ImageViewer can be run the same way that the other applets have been. To run it using the appletviewer program, switch to the appropriate directory and type the command:

```
appletviewer ImageViewer.html
```

Pressing any key while the applet is active will cause the next picture to be displayed. Clicking a mouse button within the image area of the applet will cause the previous picture to be displayed. A couple of the images are rather large, so be patient if the applet does not immediately display an image.

The example images that come with the ImageViewer applet were downloaded from NASA's Web site at: http://www.nasa.gov.

Although most of the images have been compressed to be suitable for downloading with Web pages, the images of the sun and of Saturn are not. The ImageViewer applet will automatically resize the images to fit the size of the applet's display area. The image quality of compressed images will deteriorate quickly as the display area is enlarged. The images of the sun, and in particular, of Saturn, will scale well to the full size of the screen. Neither of these images would be particularly appropriate for most Web pages, without copious warning messages, because the download times would likely be unbearable.

If you have some .gif or .jpeg images available, you can view them by including them in the list of files specified in the HTML file. For now, the .gif and .jpeg file formats are the only image formats that Java natively supports.

Now we're ready to look at the source code.

```
// ___Imported Classes
   import java.applet.Applet;
   import java.awt.Color;
   import java.awt.Event;
   import java.awt.Graphics;
   import java.awt.Image;
   import java.awt.MediaTracker;

// ___Class Declaration
public class ImageViewer extends Applet
{

// ___INSTANCE VARIABLES
   protected MediaTracker imageLoader;
   protected int          imagePointer = 0;
   protected Image[]      images;

// ===================================================


// ___METHOD: getAppletInfo
   public String getAppletInfo()
   {  return new String( "  ImageViewer Applet  \n" +
                         "by Cyberian Foundations \n" +
                         "    Photos by NASA       ");
   }


// ___METHOD: getParameters
   protected void getParameters()
   {
//    ___Read the list of images
      String param = getParameter( "images" );
      if ( param != null )
      {
         String[] names =
            Parser.extractTokens( param );
         loadImages( names );
```

```
        }
        else
        {
            System.out.println( "No Image List" );
            System.exit( 1 );
        }
    }


//  ___METHOD: handleEvent
    public boolean handleEvent( Event xEvent )
    {
//      ___Keypress -> Advance To Next Image
        boolean eventHandled = false;
        if ( xEvent.id == Event.KEY_PRESS )
        {
            imagePointer = (imagePointer + 1)
                            % images.length;
            paint();
            eventHandled = true;
        }

//      ___Mouse Click -> Go To Previous Image
        else if ( xEvent.id == Event.MOUSE_DOWN )
        {
            imagePointer =
                (imagePointer - 1 + images.length ) %
                images.length;
                paint();
            eventHandled = true;
        }
        return eventHandled;
    }


//  ___METHOD: init
    public void init()
    {
        getParameters();
        resize( 200, 200 );
        show();
    }


//  ___METHOD: loadImages
    protected void loadImages( String[] xImageNames )
    {
```

```
         images = new Image[ xImageNames.length ];
         imageLoader = new MediaTracker( this );

         Image image;

         for (int x = 0; x < xImageNames.length; x++)
         {
            image = getImage( getCodeBase(),
                               xImageNames[x] );
            if ( image != null )
            {
               images[x] = image;
               imageLoader.addImage( image, x );
            }
         }

         try
         {
            imageLoader.waitForAll();
         }
         catch( InterruptedException xIgnore )
         {
            System.out.println( " Error Loading!!!" );
            System.exit(1);
         }
      }


//  ___METHOD: paint
      public void paint( Graphics xGC )
      {
//       ___Retrieve the current image
         Image image = images[ imagePointer ];

//       ___Get the image width and height
         int imageWidth  = image.getWidth( this );
         int imageHeight = image.getHeight( this );

//       ___Blacken The Entire Background
         xGC.setColor( Color.black );
         xGC.fillRect( 0, 0,
                       size().width, size().height );

//       ___Calculate Scaling Amount
         double pctChg;        // % To Scale Image
         double pctHeightChg;
         double pctWidthChg;
```

```
133
134          pctWidthChg  = ( (double) size().width  /
135                           (double) imageWidth );
136          pctHeightChg = ( (double) size().height /
137                           (double) imageHeight);
138
139          pctChg = Math.min( pctWidthChg, pctHeightChg );
140
141    //    ___Draw The Image
142          xGC.drawImage( image,
143                         0,
144                         0,
145                         (int) (imageWidth * pctChg),
146                         (int) (imageHeight * pctChg),
147                         this );
148       }
149
150
151    // ___METHOD: update
152       public void update( Graphics xGC )
153       {  paint( xGC );
154       }
155    }
```

The example program can be explained as follows:

- *Lines 2–7.* These lines import the classes used in this class. Alternatively, "import java.awt.*;" could have been used to import all of the java.awt classes instead of importing the individual classes in lines 3–7. Also, we would normally explicitly import the Parser class rather than counting on it being in the same directory as this class.

- *Line 10.* This line declares a typical applet subclass.

- *Line 14.* This line declares the variable imageLoader to be of type MediaTracker. MediaTracker objects can be used to manage the process of downloading image files. Because downloading files can be a time-consuming process, many Java imaging routines are designed to immediately return control so the program can continue while the requested image is asynchronously downloaded in the background. MediaTracker objects can be used to monitor the status of the images being downloaded and to optionally delay the program until the downloading is complete.

- *Lines 22–26.* These lines declare and implement the getAppletInfo method. You've seen the getAppletInfo method before. It is called by the applet context to get information about the applet. In the appletviewer program, the String returned by this method will be displayed when the "Info" menu option is selected.

- *Lines 30–45*. These lines declare and implement an instance method named getParameters. We've retained the name "getParameters" to be consistent with the previous example. However, because the name does not reflect the other responsibilities of this method, namely to process the parameter that is returned and to invoke the routine to load the images, the name probably ought to have been changed to something like "setup."
- *Lines 36–37*. This is the statement that invokes the extractTokens class method of the Parser class we built previously. The local variable param, which is passed to extractTokens, contains the String list of image names that was retrieved in line 33. The array of Strings, returned from extractTokens, is assigned to the String[] variable names.
- *Line 38*. This line invokes the instance method loadImages, declared in line 84, that is responsible for actually loading the images indicated in the list.
- *Lines 49–71*. These lines override the handleEvent method defined in the Component class. The handleEvent method is invoked when something has happened (the "event") to which the Java program may need to respond. Usually, events represent user activities such as clicking a mouse or pressing a key. The Event object, which is passed to the handleEvent method, contains sufficient information to allow the program to determine the type of event that occurred and to respond appropriately.
- *Line 53*. In this line, we check the "id" instance variable of the Event object to determine if a key was pressed. "Event.KEY_PRESS" is a constant (static final variable) that is defined in the Event class.
- *Lines 55–56*. The variable imagePointer contains an int value that represents the position in the images array of the image that is currently displayed. This line increments imagePointer to the next image in the array. The modulus operator % is used to wrap the image pointer back to the first image in the array after the end of the array is reached.
- *Line 57*. In this line, we invoke the paint method to cause the image that is now pointed to by imagePointer to be displayed.

- *Line 58*. In this line, we set the value of the boolean variable eventHandled to "true" to indicate that the event was processed by this component. If an event that is directed to this component is not handled, the components that contain this component will be given the opportunity to handle it.
- *Lines 62–68*. In this section of code, we determine if a mouse button was clicked, and if so, decrement imagePointer so that it points to the previous image in the array. The expression in lines 65–66 causes the imagePointer to wrap to the last image in the array from the first image in the array.
- *Lines 75–80*. Recall that an applet's init method is called to allow the applet make any preparations that are required so the applet will be ready to run when its start method is invoked. Line 77 causes the images specified in the <APPLET> tag to be loaded. Lines 78–79 set the size of the applet window and cause it to be displayed.
- *Line 84*. This line declares the method loadImages, which, as its name implies, handles the loading of the images. The array of image names, returned by the Parser class we developed, is passed to this method in the parameter xImageNames.
- *Line 86*. The array instance variable images, which was declared in line 16, is initialized to hold as many Image objects as there are image names.
- *Line 87*. In this line, we create a new MediaTracker object and assign it to the instance variable imageLoader. The keyword "this" creates a reference to our ImageViewer object. It is used to allow the MediaTracker object to communicate with the component that created it. Specifically, the MediaTracker object will call the prepareImage method of the component that created it to start the process of loading the image pixels.
- *Lines 91–100*. This loop iterates through each of the image filenames, creates a corresponding Image object for each (line 93), and registers each of the Image objects with the MediaTracker (line 98). Recall that the getImage method (declared in the Applet class) does not wait for the image to actually load. As long as the image file exists, an Image object is created and returned. If the image file is not found, the "null" value is returned. The call to the getCodeBase method (line 93) returns the base URL, from which the ImageViewer *.class* file was loaded. If you'd prefer to load the images from the URL where the *.html* document is located, change "getCodeBase()" to "getDocumentBase()."

- *Lines 102–110.* After all of the images have been registered with the MediaTracker, we invoke the MediaTracker's waitForAll method to suspend further execution of the Applet until all of the images have been loaded. The "try" block, which encloses the call to the waitForAll method, enables us to respond if the process of loading the images is unexpectedly interrupted. If the loading process is interrupted, we catch the error in line 106, print an error message to the console (line 108), and cause the applet to terminate (line 109).

- *Lines 115–148.* The paint method is responsible for actually displaying the current image to the screen.

- *Line 118.* Here, we store a reference to the Image object, which is stored in the images array at the location indicated by imagePointer, into the local variable image. This is done just to simplify the syntax required to work with the image.

- *Lines 121–122.* In these lines, we retrieve the width and the height of the image from the image object and store them to local variables.

- *Lines 125–127.* Before displaying the image, we use the setColor and fillRect methods of the graphics context to blacken the background of the applet's display area because the scaled image may not cover the entire area. The size() method (declared in the Component class), which is called twice in line 127, returns a Dimension object that indicates the size of the applet's display area. The dot operator is used to access the "width" and "height" instance variables of the returned Dimension object.

- *Lines 130–139.* These lines calculate how to scale the image to fit the display area without changing the image's proportions. This is done by calculating the ratio of the display area width to the image width and the ratio of the display area height to the image height. The lessor of these ratios is the correct amount to scale the image. The lessor ratio is determined using the class method min of the Math class in line 139. Note the (double) casts that are performed in the calculations in lines 134–137. Because the operands are int values, if we failed to include the casts, an int result would be returned and the decimal portion of the result would have been lost.

- *Lines 142–147.* The image is actually displayed by passing the Image object, the x and y positions (in pixels) of the northwest corner of the image, the scaled width and height of the image, and a reference to the ImageViewer applet to the drawImage method of the graphics context. Because the drawImage method requires int values for the width and height, we cast the results of our calculations in lines 145 and 146 to int values.

- *Lines 151–154.* The default implementation of the update method causes the background to be erased prior to displaying the image. Because, in the paint method, we are always blackening the background before displaying the image, we override the update method here to avoid having the background unnecessarily cleared.

Java Library Class Hierarchy

The simple example applets that we've developed just barely scratch the surface of the functionality provided in the Java library classes. The Java library classes are organized into packages, as listed in Table 13.2.

Table 13.2 Java Library Classes

java.applet	Applets
java.awt	Abstract Window Toolkit
java.awt.image	Image manipulation
java.awt.peer	Platform-specific component management
java.io	Input/output streams
java.lang	Language elements
java.net	Networking
java.util	Data structures/utilities

java.awt

The java.awt package contains the classes that are collectively referred to as the Abstract Window Toolkit. This package includes several classes that represent GUI interface objects such as the Button, Checkbox, Label, Menu, Scrollbar, and TextArea classes. It also includes classes that relate to the size and shape of two-dimensional objects (Dimension, Point, Polygon, Rectangle). In addition, the java.awt package includes classes that represent regions of the screen (Canvas, Window, Panel, Dialog, Frame) and classes that control how the components contained within those regions are laid out within the region's display area (BorderLayout, CardLayout, FlowLayout, GridBagLayout). There are also classes that deal with the appearance of text (Font, FontMetrics, Color), the class that actually draws all of this stuff on the screen (Graphics), and the class that lets the program know of actions taken by the user (Event). Finally, there are the image and peer subpackages that respectively handle the manipulation of images and coordinate the actions of the underlying operating-system-specific implementations of these GUI objects.

java.io

The java.io package contains classes that handle working with data streams. A *data stream* is simply series of bytes. Streams read in by the program are referred to as *input streams*. Streams output by the program are referred to as *output streams*. The most common form of input and output streams are files. The java.io package includes classes that allow input and output streams to be created, buffered, filtered, and updated. It also includes some classes that allow StringBuffers (essentially an array of characters) and arrays of bytes to be treated as streams.

java.lang

The java.lang package includes the classes that supplement the Java language. Classes that correspond to the primitive types (Boolean, Character, Double, Float, Integer, Long) are included that simplify working with those types as objects (Byte and Short classes will be added in Java 1.1). The String and Stringbuffer classes are part of this package, as are several system classes that deal with the operation of the virtual machine. In addition, the java.lang package includes a number of classes that represent errors and exceptional conditions that can occur while a Java program is running.

java.net

The java.net package provides classes that deal with network applications. The INetAddress class represents the host and IP address of an object on the Internet. The URL, URLConnection, URLEncoder, and URLStreamHandler classes provide the means to identify and communicate with network resources. Communication via sockets is facilitated by the Socket, ServerSocket, DatagramPacket, and DatagramSocket classes.

java.util

The java.util package contains basic data structure classes such as Dictionary, Hashtable, Vector, and Stack. It also includes the StringTokenizer class used in the example Parser class, a Date class, and a class (Random) that produces a sequence of random numbers.

Class Hierarchies

Table 13.3 lists all of the classes provided in the core Java libraries. Subclasses are indented beneath their immediate superclass. Recall that all Java classes are subclasses of the root Java class java.lang.Object.

Table 13.3 Java Class Hierarchies

CLASS HIERARCHY	A	1	2	3	4	5	6	7	8
BitSet									X
Boolean							X		
BorderLayout			X						
CardLayout			X						
Character							X		
CheckBoxGroup			X						
Class							X		
ClassLoader	A						X		
Color				X					
ColorModel	A			X					
DirectColorModel				X					
IndexColorModel				X					
Compiler							X		
Component		A		X					
Button			X						
Canvas			X						
Checkbox			X						
Choice			X						
Container	A		X						
Panel			X						
Applet	X								
Window			X						
Dialog			X						

Continued

Table 13.3 ***Continued***

CLASS HIERARCHY	A	1	2	3	4	5	6	7	8
FileDialog			X						
Frame			X						
Label			X						
List			X						
Scrollbar			X						
TextComponent			X						
TextArea			X						
TextField			X						
ContentHandler	A							X	
DatagramPacket								X	
DatagramSocket								X	
Date									X
Dictionary	A								X
HashTable									X
Properties									X
Dimension		X							
Event		X							
File						X			
FileDescriptor						X			
FilteredImageSource				X					
FlowLayout			X						
Font			X						
FontMetrics	A		X						
Graphics		A		X					
GridBagConstraints			X						
GridBagLayout			X						

Table 13.3 *Continued*

CLASS HIERARCHY	A	1	2	3	4	5	6	7	8
Image		A		X					
ImageFilter				X					
CropImageFilter				X					
RGBImageFilter	A			X					
InetAddress									X
InputStream	A					X			
ByteArrayInputStream						X			
FileInputStream						X			
FilterInputStream						X			
BufferedInputStream						X			
DataInputStream						X			
LineNumberInputStream						X			
PushbackInputStream						X			
PipedInputStream						X			
SequenceInputStream						X			
StringBufferInputStream						X			
Insets			X						
Math							X		
MediaTracker			X						
MemoryImageSource				X					
MenuComponent	A		X						
MenuBar			X						
MenuItem			X						
CheckboxMenuItem			X						
Menu			X						
Number	A						X		

Continued

Table 13.3 *Continued*

CLASS HIERARCHY	A	1	2	3	4	5	6	7	8
Double						X			
Float					X				
Integer							X		
Long							X		
Observable									X
OutputStream	A					X			
ByteArrayOutputStream						X			
FileOutputStream						X			
FilterOutputStream						X			
BufferedOutputStream						X			
DataOutputStream						X			
PrintStream						X			
PipedOutputStream						X			
Point			X						
Polygon			X						
PixelGrabber				X					
Process	A						X		
Random									X
RandomAccessFile						X			
Rectangle			X						
Runtime								X	
SecurityManager	A						X		
ServerSocket								X	
Socket								X	
SocketImp	A							X	
StreamTokenizer						X			

Table 13.3 ***Continued***

CLASS HIERARCHY	A	1	2	3	4	5	6	7	8
String								X	
StringBuffer							X		
StringTokenizer									X
System							X		
Toolkit	A		X						
Thread							X		
ThreadGroup							X		
Throwable							X		
Error							X		
AWTError			X						
LinkageError							X		
ClassCircularityError							X		
ClassFormatError							X		
IncompatibleClass ChangeError						X			
AbstractMethod Error							X		
IllegalAccessError							X		
InstantiationError							X		
NoSuchFieldError							X		
NoSuchMethod Error							X		
NoClassDefFound Error							X		
UnsatisfiedLinkError							X		
VerifyError							X		
ThreadDeath							X		

Continued

Table 13.3 *Continued*

CLASS HIERARCHY	A	1	2	3	4	5	6	7	8
VirtualMachineError		A					X		
InternalError							X		
OutOfMemoryError							X		
StackOverflowError							X		
UnknownError							X		
Exception							X		
AWTException			X						
ClassNotFoundException							X		
CloneNotSupported Exception							X		
IllegalAccessException							X		
InstantiationException							X		
InterruptedException							X		
IOException						X			
EOFException						X			
FileNotFound Exception						X			
InterruptedIO Exception						X			
MalformedURL Exception								X	
ProtocolException								X	
SocketException								X	
UnknownHost Exception								X	
UnknownService Exception								X	
UTFDataFormat Exception						X			
NoSuchMethodException							X		

Table 13.3 *Continued*

CLASS HIERARCHY	A	1	2	3	4	5	6	7	8
RuntimeException							X		
ArithmeticException							X		
ArrayStoreException							X		
ClassCastException							X		
EmptyStackException									X
IllegalArgumentException							X		
IllegalThreadState Exception							X		
NumberFormat Exception							X		
IllegalMonitorState Exception							X		
IndexOutOfBounds Exception							X		
ArrayIndexOutOf BoundsException							X		
StringIndexOutOf BoundsException							X		
NegativeArraySize Exception							X		
NoSuchElementException									X
NullPointerException							X		
SecurityException							X		
URL								X	
URLConnection	A							X	
URLEncoder								X	
URLStreamHandler	A							X	
Vector									X
Stack									X

Continued

Table 13.3 *Continued*

CLASS HIERARCHY	A	1	2	3	4	5	6	7	8

Column A:
A = Abstract Class
Column Package
1 java.applet.
2 java.awt.
3 java.awt.image.
4 java.awt.peer.
5 java.io.
6 java.lang.
7 java.net.
8 java.util.

Table 13.4 Java Interface Hierarchies

INTERFACE HIERARCHY	A	1	2	3	4	5	6	7	8
Cloneable	I						X		
ComponentPeer	I				X				
ButtonPeer	I				X				
CanvasPeer	I				X				
CheckboxPeer	I				X				
ChoicePeer	I				X				
ContainerPeer	I				X				
PanelPeer	I				X				
WindowPeer	I				X				
DialogPeer	I				X				
FileDialogPeer	I				X				
FramePeer	I				X				
LabelPeer	I				X				
ListPeer	I				X				
ScrollBarPeer	I				X				
TextComponentPeer	I				X				
TextAreaPeer	I				X				

Table 13.4 *Continued*

INTERFACE HIERARCHY	A	1	2	3	4	5	6	7	8
TextFieldPeer	I				X				
ContentHandlerFactory	I							X	
DataInput	I					X			
DataOutput	I					X			
Enumeration	I								X
FileNameFilter	I					X			
ImageConsumer	I			X					
ImageObserver	I			X					
ImageProducer	I			X					
LayoutManager	I		X						
MenuComponentPeer	I				X				
MenuBarPeer	I				X				
MenuItemPeer	I				X				
CheckboxMenuItemPeer	I				X				
MenuPeer	I				X				
MenuContainer	I		X						
Observer	I								X
Runnable	I						X		
SocketImplFactory	I							X	
URLStreamHandlerFactory	I							X	

Column Package
1 java.applet.
2 java.awt.
3 java.awt.image.
4 java.awt.peer.
5 java.io.
6 java.lang.
7 java.net.
8 java.util.

Interface Hierarchies

Table 13.4 lists all of the interfaces provided in the core Java libraries. Subinterfaces are indented beneath their immediate superinterfaces.

The Future of Java

The best place to get current information on the extensions and modifications planned for Java is Sun's Web site. While this book was being written, portions of the design specifications for version 1.1 of the Java Development Kit were made publicly available. The enhancements planned for version 1.1 include the following:

1. *Internationalization.* Increased support for the display of Unicode characters and for handling locale specific information such as date and time formats.
2. *Security API.* Allows classes to be "signed" so that the source of the class can be verified. This will likely play a significant role in allowing "trusted" applets to run with relaxed security restrictions.
3. *AWT enhancements.* Printing, popup menus, clipboard support, and a revamped event model are just a few of the additions and improvements to be made to the AWT.
4. *JAR files.* JAR (Java Archive) files allow multiple files to bundled into a single file in a manner similar to ZIP files. Because they will support compression and can be downloaded in a single session,. JAR files should significantly reduce download times.
5. *Networking enhancements.* Include support for BSD-style socket options and make the Socket and SocketServer classes nonfinal so that they can be extended.
6. *Remote Method Invocation (RMI).* Supports distributed Java programs by allowing an object's methods to be invoked by Java code running in another virtual machine, even one that is running on another computer.
7. *Object serialization.* Allows objects to be read from input streams and written to output streams. This capability supports persistence (ability to store and then later retrieve the object) and RMI.
8. *Reflection.* Enables information about the instance variables, methods, and constructors of a class to be discovered at runtime. This capability is particu-

larly useful to enable visual development tools to determine and present to the developer the configurable options of prewritten Java components (Java Beans).

9. *JDBC (Java Database Connectivity).* This specification, which is similar to ODBC, provides a standard interface that Java programs can use to access relational databases.
10. *Java IDL (Interface Definition Language).* An industry standard way of specifying the interface between an object on a server and a client on a different platform in a language-neutral manner.
11. *Inner classes.* Essentially allow a class to be defined within another. This approach simplifies creating classes that support an interface but delegate the processing to one or more enclosed classes.
12. *Standardized Native Method Interface.* Ensures binary compatibility across all of the Java virtual machine implementations on a given platform.

In addition to the enhancements slated for the JDK, several additional APIs are being developed that will expand the usefulness of Java in several areas:

1. *Java Server API.* Supports the development of Java programs specifically designed to be run on a server.
2. *Java Beans API.* Supports the development of software "components" that can be composed together into applications by end users. Java Beans are intended to be platform-neutral components that are similar to, and in many cases provide compatibility with, other component models such as Microsoft's OLE/COM, CI Lab's OpenDoc, and Netscape's LiveConnect.
3. *Java Commerce API.* Facilitates credit card, debit card, and electronic cash purchases and other secure financial transactions.
4. *Java Management API.* Supports building Java-based network management programs.
5. *Java Media API.* Adds support for 2D and 3D images, playing audio, video and MIDI, animation, telephony, and creating multiple user sharing applications such as a shared white board.

Chapter

14

JavaScript

The HTML language used to create pages for the World Wide Web was originally designed to produce plain and static documents. When the Web first started the only browsing software available for it was text-based, so "plain and static" was acceptable.

The Web took a major step with the release of Mosaic, the first graphical Web browser. Suddenly, it was obvious to most everyone that "plain and static" wasn't enough. Users cried out for more creative control over the pages they published on the Web, which ushered in such features as in-line images, tables, and frames.

JavaScript was the first major technology that brought power to ordinary Web publishers. JavaScript is a scripting language for HTML, and it is supported by Netscape Navigator, Internet Explorer, and other Web software. JavaScript "scripts" are small programs that interact with the browser and the HTML content of a page. You can create a JavaScript program to add sound or simple animation, prevalidate a form before the user's response is sent to your company's server, search through a small database, set options based on user preferences, and much more.

The Birth of JavaScript

JavaScript started life as "LiveScript." The concept of LiveScript began at Netscape, as it planned the features of Netscape Navigator 2.0. LiveScript was designed as a simple way to augment HTML pages, and Netscape planners saw it as a tool for the average Web page designer. At first, interest in LiveScript was mild, due mostly to the frenzy surrounding a more robust Internet programming language released a few months earlier, one named Java.

When Netscape announced its intention to support Java in Netscape 2.0, it also announced a collaboration with Sun to redevelop LiveScript. It called the "new" language JavaScript, and suddenly everyone was interested in it! Whereas Java requires in-depth programming knowledge and a software development kit, JavaScript programs can be written by most any HTML page designer. No software development kit is needed.

JavaScript is used in Netscape 2.0 and above, as well as Microsoft Internet Explorer 3.0 and later. As the co-developers of JavaScript, Netscape has wanted to make JavaScript an "open standard," meaning that other companies can use and implement JavaScript in their own Internet products. When JavaScript was first announced in December of 1995, over two dozen companies jumped on the bandwagon promising to support it for future products. Those products—from companies such as America Online, Borland, IBM, Symantec, and many others—are just now coming out or will be released shortly.

The Importance of JavaScript

JavaScript is poised to do for Web publishing what Visual Basic did for Windows programming. Consider the following points:

- JavaScript offers a scripting language accessible to "mere mortals," allowing most anyone to use it in Web pages. JavaScript closely follows the Web principle of bringing electronic publishing to the masses. You don't need lots of money or technology to publish on the Web; likewise with JavaScript, you don't need a programming degree to take advantage of the language.
- Because of its name recognition, and the support of Netscape, both Java and JavaScript are already becoming de facto standards for Web page program-

ming. As a developer, this means you can be reasonably assured that the technology you invest in today will not disappear tomorrow.

- All major online services, including CompuServe and America Online, are now offering Web document space to their customers. This means a lot of people are just now getting the taste of Web publishing, and they are looking for ways to improve their work. Many are turning to JavaScript to add value and spice.

Of course, there are many other reasons to use JavaScript. If you are running a commercial Web site, you can use JavaScript as a quick and simple means to enhance your page. For example, a common use of JavaScript is to display a warning or alert message when entering a page or before performing some action, like submitting a script. You might display an alert message—which appears in a dialog box to which readers must respond—to your customers to remind them of an important sale, for example.

If you're running a personal site (on CompuServe, AOL, or Prodigy, for instance), you likely don't have access to the CGI functions of the Web server, and you cannot run server-side programs. You can use JavaScript as a client-side program to do some of the things for which you might have used the server. As an example, with JavaScript you can create simple dynamic pages, such as displaying one image background in the daylight hours and another background in the nighttime hours.

Uses for JavaScript

If you've spent much time on the Web you've probably encountered a few JavaScript examples. Probably the most popular use of JavaScript is as a calculator—you know, the kind you can buy at WalMart for $3.97. This application by no means indicates the full breadth and scope of JavaScript! Rather, JavaScript calculators spread because they are relatively easy to write. And Netscape's first JavaScript examples were calculators, so this is what pioneer JavaScripters emulated.

Feel free to write as many JavaScript calculators as you like, but don't limit JavaScript to just that. Like many things new, it can be hard to imagine practical uses for this new technology called JavaScript. Here are some ideas that can get you started in thinking about what JavaScript can do for you.

Tailor Pages for the User

Imagine a Web page with JavaScript that responds to the user's choice of preferences, such as asking if the reader wants to view simple low-resolution thumbnail images for an entire page or wait a little while longer for larger, high-resolution images. Offering these and other custom interface choices helps you tailor your pages to the user's needs and preferences. Readers no longer all get the same page.

Make Interactive Pages

You can use JavaScript's built-in commands to add interactively to your Web pages. For instance, a JavaScript page can determine what time it is on the user's computer and display the current time on the screen (see Figure 14.1). It can even select one of several images to display an appropriate graphic or background for the time of day—a sunrise for morning, full sun for the day, a sunset for late afternoon, and the moon for evening.

Another great use of JavaScript for interactivity is conditionally displaying text and hypertext links, depending on the user's response to a query. Suppose, for example, your page contains descriptions of products for your company. Your company makes lots of diverse products in various product lines. Rather than display text and hypertext links for products the user may not be interested in—or worse, that may confuse the reader—you can use JavaScript to display only text and links that relate to the user's field of interest. This streamlines the content of Web pages.

JavaScript for Computer-Aided Instruction

You can easily use JavaScript for computer-aided instruction. A JavaScript page can be "smart"—it can determine if the reader provides proper answers to questions,

Figure 14.1 Interactivity is easy using JavaScript. A few simple lines of code can "personalize" your pages for users.

and it can tally up the score. It can even keep track of how long it takes for a reader to answer questions. If your test has a time limit, you can use JavaScript to automatically end the test when the limit is up.

The JavaScript Form Connection

JavaScript is also ideal for use with form-processing programs located on an Internet server. (For the uninitiated, a *form* is a collection of text boxes and buttons that provide for user feedback, much like a Windows or Macintosh dialog box provides for user feedback.) The traditional way to use forms on a Web page is to send all the user's entries to a "script" or program running on the computer, typically using a technique called *common gateway interface*, or CGI. The bulk of most any CGI program is verifying that the user entered valid data. Entry validation, like that shown in Figure 14.2, is something JavaScript can do, and it can do it very easily, thus making CGI programs much easier to write and implement.

Figure 14.2 Form validation is a favorite application for JavaScript. The form can be prevalidating before it is sent to a server for processing.

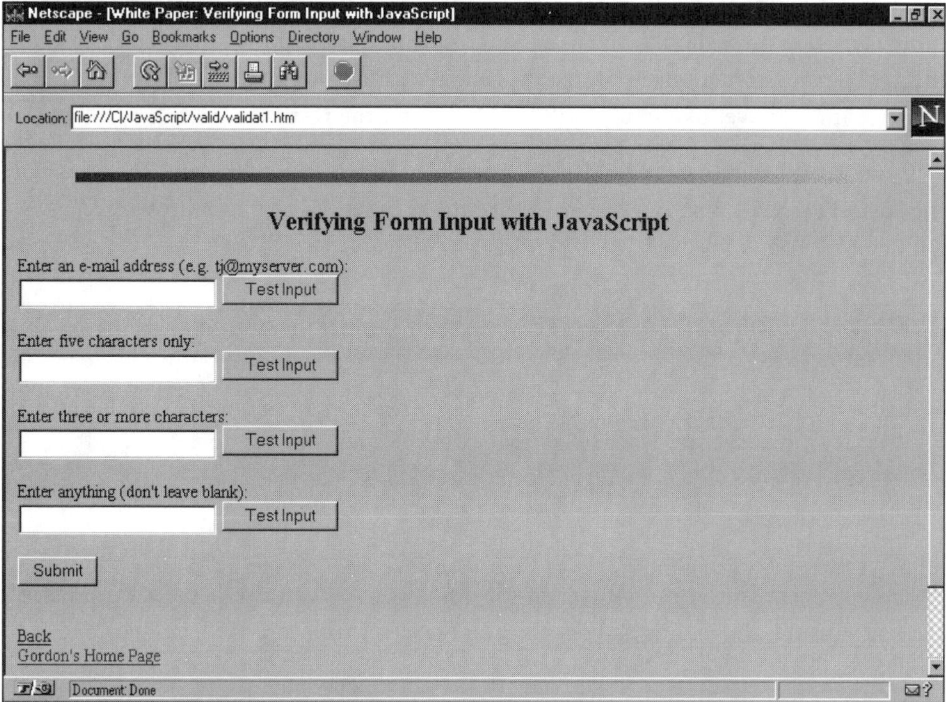

Oh, Yes—and Special Effects, Too!

An oft-cited use of JavaScript is for special effects. With JavaScript you can easily add sound to your page—even background or repeating sound. Click a button, and a voice might ring out. Plus, there's lots you can do with animation, color effects, even "fading" a page slowly from black to white, like a movie.

JavaScript gives you greater control over the graphical elements of your page. For instance, you can use JavaScript to intelligently resize an image. This is useful if you have a solid-color GIF. You can use JavaScript to expand or contract the size of the GIF, as it appears in Netscape. Possible uses: bar charts, colored divider lines (no more plain <HR> horizontal rules!), and more.

Using JavaScript in an HTML Document

A JavaScript program consists of one or more *instructions* (also referred to as *code* or *commands*) included with the *HTML markup tags* that form your Web documents. When Netscape encounters a JavaScript instruction, it stops to process it. For example, the instruction might tell Netscape to format and display text and graphics on the page. Unlike a program written in Java, JavaScript programs are not in separate files (though this is an option using Netscape 3.0 and later). Instead, the JavaScript instructions are mixed together with the familiar HTML markup tags you've come to love, like <H1>, <P>, <IMG>, and the rest.

Consider the very basic HTML document. It renders a heading and some text on the page. Figure 14.3 shows how the page looks when viewed in a browser.

```
<HTML>
<HEAD>
<TITLE>This Is a Basic Document</TITLE>
</HEAD>
<BODY>
<H1>This Is a Basic Document</H1>
<P>This is a pretty basic document. It doesn't have much of anything in it.
Just a heading, and this text.</P>
</BODY>
</HTML>
```

Though there is no rational reason for doing so, you can use JavaScript to insert the text you see above. Here's how to use JavaScript to insert the heading.

Figure 14.3 A basic HTML document, as rendered in Netscape Navigator.

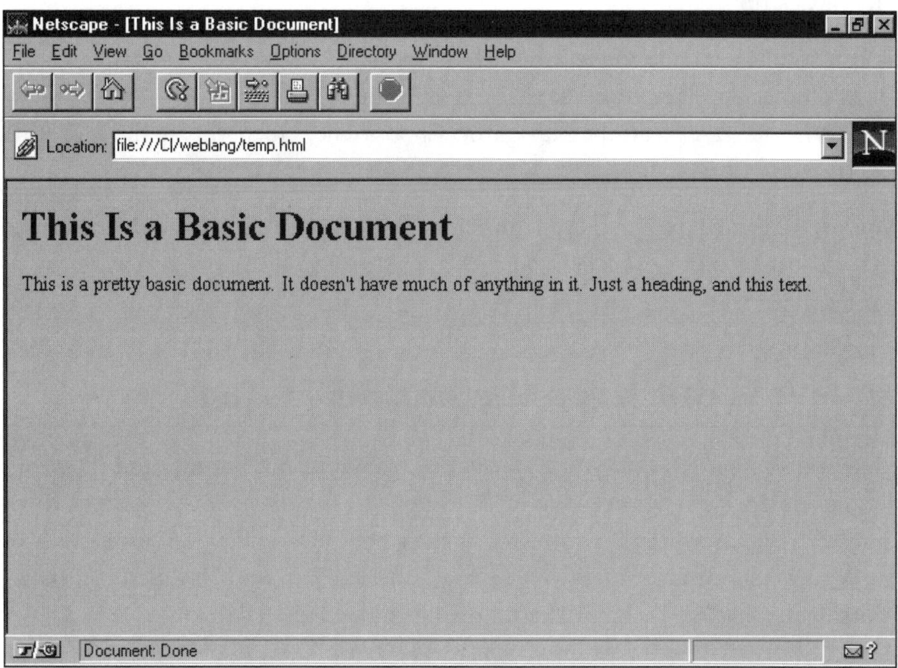


```
<HTML>
<HEAD>
<TITLE>This Is a Basic Document</TITLE>
</HEAD>
<BODY>
<SCRIPT>
document.write ("<H1>This Is a Basic Document</H1>");
</SCRIPT>
<P>This is a pretty basic document. It doesn't have much of anything in it.
Just a heading, this text, and a graphic of some line.</P>
</BODY>
</HTML>
```

Using JavaScript in Your Own Pages

Because JavaScript is embedded in the HTML document, you can use almost any text editor or Web page editor to write your JavaScript programs. The only requirement is that the editor must allow direct input. Web page programs that let you insert only a given set of HTML markup tags cannot be used because they don't allow you to insert the JavaScript code.

You can try the example to see how JavaScript works. Retype the example exactly as you see it. When done, save the document as *sample.htm*. Close the file (if necessary), and start Netscape Navigator. Choose File, Open, locate the file, and choose Open.

If you get an error box like the one in Figure 14.4, it means you didn't properly type the text between the <SCRIPT> and </SCRIPT> tags. Carefully review your work and try again.

How JavaScript Uses the <SCRIPT> Tag

Netscape needs to be told that you're giving it JavaScript instructions, and these instructions are enclosed between <SCRIPT> tags. Within the script tag you can have only valid JavaScript instructions. You can't put HTML tags for Netscape Navigator to render inside the <SCRIPT> tags, and you can't put JavaScript instructions outside the <SCRIPT> tags. The following is allowed:

```
<HTML>
<BODY>
<H1>Here's JavaScript-generated text!</H1>
<SCRIPT>
document.write ("Hello there!");
```

Figure 14.4 JavaScript displays an error message if it detects a problem in the code.

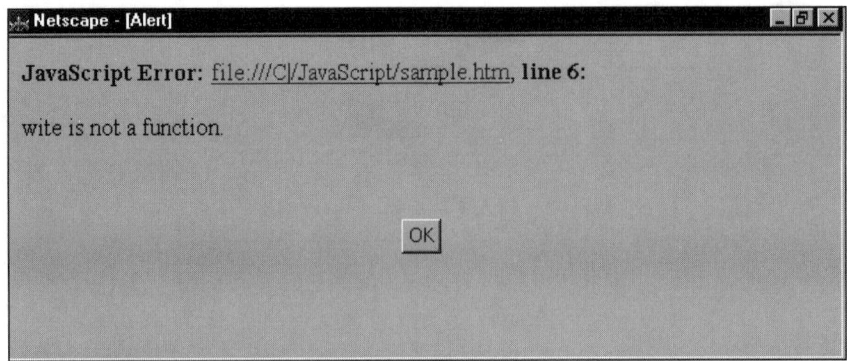

```
</SCRIPT>
</BODY>
</HTML>
```

But these are not allowed:

```
<!--No script tags around the JavaScript instruction-->
<HTML>
<BODY>
<H1>Here's JavaScript-generated text!</H1>
document.write ("Hello there!");
</BODY>
</HTML>

<!--HTML markup tags inside the script tags -->
<HTML>
<BODY>
<H1>Here's JavaScript-generated text!</H1>
<SCRIPT>
<H1>Here's JavaScript-generated text!</H1>
document.write ("Hello there!");
<P>
</SCRIPT>
</BODY>
</HTML>
```

NOTE There may be other HTML scripting languages in the future, and the <SCRIPT> tag is designed to allow for differentiation in the language used. So, from here on in this book, the first instance of the <SCRIPT> tag in complete JavaScript programs in a document will also include the LANGUAGE="JavaScript" attribute. Example:

```
<SCRIPT LANGUAGE="JavaScript">
```

Strictly speaking, this attribute is optional, but we'll include it for the sake of completeness.

A Real-World Use of JavaScript

Obviously, you don't use JavaScript to insert the text that HTML can otherwise do all by itself. We used the example above because it's simple and demonstrates the basic JavaScript concept of embedded scripts in an HTML page.

JavaScript is ideal for making your Web pages "smart." Here's an example. Suppose you want to change the graphic depending on whether it's day or night. JavaScript has a rich selection of date-oriented functions, one of which returns the current hour, as set by the user's computer. Here's how that basic document uses JavaScript instructions to programmatically select the right GIF for the time of day:

```
<HTML>
<HEAD>
<TITLE>This Is a Basic Document</TITLE>
</HEAD>
<BODY>
<H1>This Is a Basic Document</H1>
<P>This is a pretty basic document.  It doesn't have much of
anything in it. Just a heading, this text, and a graphic of
some line.</P>
<SCRIPT>
now = new Date();
if ((now.getHours() > 5) && (now.getHours()<18))
     document.write ("<IMG SRC='http://mydoamin.com/day.gif'>");
else
     document.write ("<IMG SRC='http://mydomain.com/night.gif'>");
</SCRIPT>
</BODY>
</HTML>
```

This example uses a JavaScript *if* statement to determine the time of day. The *if* statement does one thing if the *expression* is true, or it does another if the expression is false. If the hour is greater than 5 A.M. but less than 6 P.M., it's daylight. So, JavaScript inserts an image (<IMG>) tag using the DAY.GIF image. If the current time is not between these hours, it is nighttime, so JavaScript inserts the NIGHT.GIF image.

HTML alone lacks any decision making, so this example is a perfect job for JavaScript. The page contains the basic HTML tags to render the document and JavaScript for any tasks that require "thinking."

Understanding the Use of JavaScript Objects

You've probably heard of *object-oriented programming*. It's a style of programming where software is created using self-contained modules. Each module is designed to take a certain type of data and do something with it. The term *object-oriented* comes from how the data is viewed: as an object. Although object oriented programming is more difficult than the traditional "precedural" programming (like BASIC and C), the end result is usually easier to maintain and fix. Almost all major software products released today are written using object-oriented techniques.

JavaScript uses *objects*, but it is not an object-oriented programming language. It's strictly procedural, which means you don't have to learn anything about object-oriented programming (if you did this book would be over twice its current size). Objects are used in JavaScript to represent "things." The document as viewed in the Netscape Navigator browser is a "thing." The fill-in form that you see on the browser page is a "thing." The hypertext link you click on to go to another URL is a "thing."

Objects are best viewed as a total entity to make programming easier. Objects are composed of *properties*, which is stuff that belongs to that object. As in real life, not all objects have the same properties. A good example of a JavaScript object is the document that you view in the Netscape Navigator window. The document has many properties, including the background color, the text color, and the title. When you work with JavaScript, you uniquely identify the properties you want as belonging to a certain object. You don't just say "change the color of the background to green"; JavaScript won't have the slightest idea what you're talking about. *What* background? Rather, to change the background of the document, you must specify the document object.

JavaScript uses a special syntax for the object-property relationship. You use the object name (in this case document), a period, and the property name, which is bgColor. Put 'em together and you have:

```
document.bgColor
```

This is enough to tell JavaScript what object you want to work with and what property of that object you want to change or test. For example, want to change the background of the document? That's easy. The following instruction changes the background color to black:

```
document.bgColor = "black";
```

Test this for yourself. Here's a short script that sets the background according to the time of day. It uses document.bgColor to set the background color and fgColor to set the foreground (text) color. The page is rendered black-on-white for the daytime, and white-on-black for the nighttime. We'll use the color names for this example, rather than the #nnnnnn color triplet values you may be used to. Both are valid with Netscape Navigator.

```
<HTML>
<HEAD>
<TITLE>This Is a Basic Document</TITLE>
<SCRIPT LANGUAGE="JavaScript">
now = new Date();
if ((now.getHours() > 5) && (now.getHours()<18)) {
      document.bgColor = "white";
      document.fgColor = "black";
} else {
      document.bgColor = "black";
      document.fgColor = "white";
}
</SCRIPT>
</HEAD>
<BODY>
<H1>This Is a Basic Document</H1>
<P>This is a pretty basic document.  It doesn't have much of anything in it.
Just a heading, this text, and a graphic of some line.</P>
</BODY>
</HTML>
```

When you retype this, be sure to check all of your work. Don't forget the { and } brace characters for the *if* statement. Netscape Navigator will display an error message if these are missing. (For the curious, the braces are needed in this example because more than one line of code follows the *if* statement.)

> **NOTE** Placement of the <SCRIPT> tags can make a difference. You can change the background property of the document at any time, even after the page has been rendered in the browser (this applies to the Windows platforms only when using Netscape 2.0; bugs in the Macintosh and X-Windows platforms cause the text to be obliterated when the background changes).
>
> However, the same doesn't apply to the foreground (text) property. You can change the property, but only before the text is rendered in the browser. Therefore, putting the <SCRIPT> tag after the text will not yield proper results. Keep this in mind when writing your JavaScript programs.

JavaScript supports the objects shown in Figure 14.5. These objects are depicted in hierarchical order, so you can get a sense of how they interact. Notice that it is entirely possible for one object to belong to another object.

This object-to-object hierarchy is very important in JavaScript, and it can make JavaScript a bit bewildering at first. The reason: an object can be both an object and a property of an object up the hierarchical ladder. For example, as you can see from the illustration, *document* belongs to the window object (it is said to be a "property of the window object"), and *document* is an object in its own right.

Table 14.1 lists JavaScript's main objects, briefly described, in alphabetical order. These objects are supported by both Netscape Navigator 2.0 and later and Microsoft Internet Explorer 3.0 and later. More recent versions of Netscape Navigator support additional JavaScript objects.

Understanding JavaScript Properties

Properties are behaviors of objects. There are actually two kinds of properties, shown graphically in Figure 14.6.

Figure 14.5 JavaScript supports numerous objects.

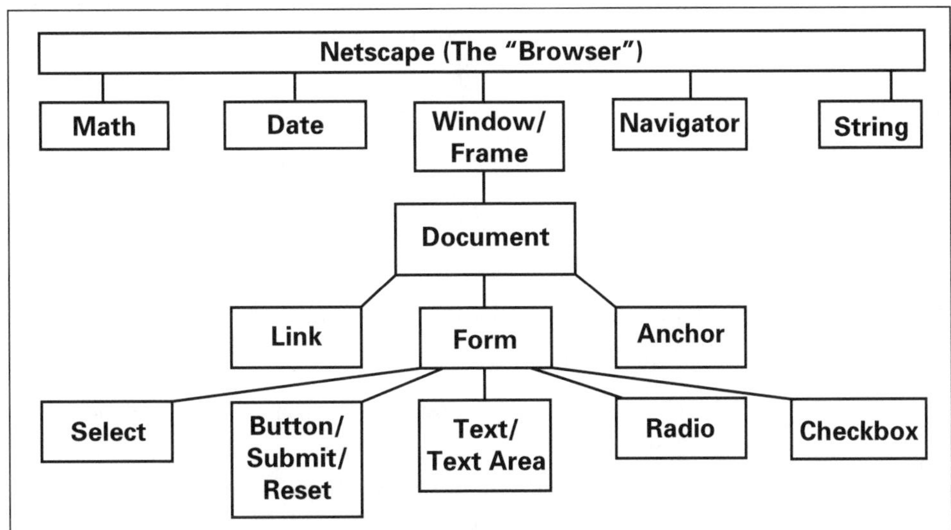

Table 14.1 JavaScript's Main Objects

Object	Description
anchor	A target (that is, destination) for a hypertext link. Anchors always belong to the document object.
anchors[]	An array (list of variables sharing a common function) of the anchors in a document.
button	A push button in a form. Buttons always belong to the form object.
checkbox	A check box in a form. Check boxes always belong to the form object.
date	Gets or sets the date or time. Date is a top-level object.
document	The document as viewed in a browser window or in a specific frame when the window is separated into frames. Documents can belong to a window object or a frame object.
elements[]	An array of all the items in a form. Elements always belong to the form object.
form	A form in a document. The form can contain buttons, text boxes, and list boxes. Forms always belong to a document object.
forms[]	An array of forms in a document.
frame	A window that is divided into many panes called frames. Each frame can contain a different document. Frames belong to a "parent" window object.
frames[]	An array of frames in a "parent" window.
hidden	A hidden (nonvisible) text box in a form. Hidden boxes always belong to the form object.
history	A list of pages the browser has visited. History always belongs to the document object.
link	A hypertext link. Links always belong to the document object.
links[]	An array of links in a page.
location	The URL of the current document. Location always belongs to the document object.
math	Performs math with numbers. Math is a top-level object.
navigator	Information about the browser, including its name and version. Navigator is a top-level object.

Table 14.1 *Continued*

Object	Description
options[]	An array of all the items in a selection list (see select).
password	A password text box in a form. Password boxes always belong to the form object.
radio	A radio button in a form. Radio buttons always belong to the form object.
reset	A reset button in a form. Reset buttons always belong to the form object.
select	A selection list in a form. Select lists always belong to the form object.
string	A series of text. Strings belong to the document that created them.
submit	A submit button in a form. Submit buttons always belong to the form object.
text	A text box in a form. Text boxes always belong to the form object.
textarea	A textarea (multiple line) box in a form. Text areas always belong to a form object.
window	A browser window. Window is a top-level object.

- *Other properties are themselves objects.* These are properties of a parent object, but they also act as an object to their own child properties. For example, form is a property of the document object. Form is also an object.
- *Some properties are "single-ended," containing a specific value.* Single-ended properties do not themselves support objects of their own. For example, the bgColor property represents the background color of the document object.

Here are JavaScript's properties, listed by group. Many properties can be both retrieved and set using JavaScript; that is, you can use the property to determine the current state of an object, and you can change the value of the property to make the object change. But other properties are read-only, meaning that you can read the value contained in them, but you can't directly change them.

Figure 14.6. Properties can contain values (strings, numbers, and so on) or other objects.

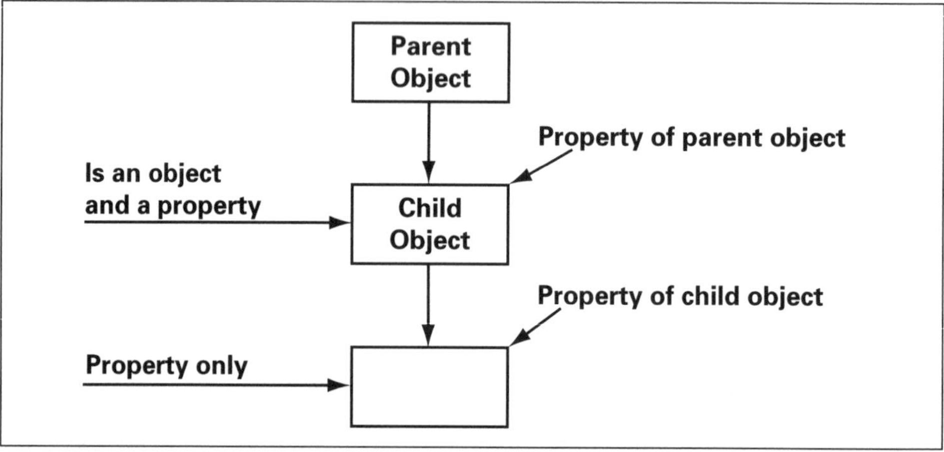

Browser Info Properties

The browser info properties return settings in the navigator object; see Table 14.2.

Document Info and Appearance Properties

The properties for document appearance return and change the look of the document. Additional properties for document info return current information about the document; see Table 14.3.

Forms Properties

The forms properties return (and some change) form elements, including the form itself, and all controls (also called "widgets") in the form; see Table 14.4.

Table 14.2 Browser Info Properties

Property	What It Does
appCodeName	"Code name" for the current browser
appName	Application name for the current browser
appVersion	Version number of the current browser
userAgent	The user agent string sent from the browser to the server

Table 14.3 Document Info and Appearance Properties

Property	What It Does
alinkColor	The color for active links in the document
anchors[]	List of all anchors in the document
bgColor	Background color of the document
cookie	Semipermanent storage of textual information
defaultStatus	Default text of status bar
fgColor	Text color of the document
forms[]	List of forms in the document
lastModified	The date the document was last modified
linkColor	The color of unvisited links in the document
links[]	A list of links in the document
location	The complete URL of the document
referrer	The URL of the referring (linked from) document
status	The current text of the status bar
title	The title of the document
vlinkColor	The color of visited links in a document

Table 14.4 Forms Properties

Property	What It Does
action	Destination URL for a form
defaultChecked	Default selection state of a check box or radio button
defaultSelected	Default selection of an option list
defaultValue	Default value of text box or text area
checked	State of a check box or radio button in form
elements[]	List of form elements in the document
encoding	MIME encoding format for a form
form	Parent form object
index	A specific option in a selection list within a form

Continued

Table 14.4 *Continued*

Property	What It Does
length	The number of items in the list
method	Posting method for a form (get or post)
name	The name of a form object
options[]	A list of options in a selection list within a form
selected	Current state of a check box or radio button
selectedIndex	The selected option in a selection list within a form
target	The name of the targeted form
text	The text of an option in a selection list within a form
value	The text of a text box or text area

Link and Anchor Properties

The links and anchors properties return and change aspects of links (<A HREF=...>) and anchors (<NAME=...>); see Table 14.5.

Math Properties

The properties listed in Table 14.6 provide standard values used in math equations.

Table 14.5 Link and Anchor Properties

Property	What It Does
hash	Text following the hash (#) symbol in a URL
host	The hostname:port portion of a URL
hostname	The host and domain (or IP address) of a URL
href	An entire URL
length	The number of anchors or links
pathname	The path portion of a URL
port	The port portion of a URL
protocol	The protocol portion of a URL
search	The search portion of a URL
target	The name of the targeted link

Table 14.6 Math Properties

Property	What It Does
E	Euler's constant.
LN2	The natural logarithm of 2
LN10	The natural logarithm of 10
LOG2E	The base 2 logarithm of e
LOG10E	The base 10 logarithm of e
PI	The numeric equivalent of PI: 3.14 etc.
SQRT1_2	The square root of one-half
SQRT2	The square root of 2

Strings

As Table 14.7 shows, the string object has one property, which is length (the content of the string is not a true property).

Window URL Properties

The URL property returns or changes the current document URL; see Table 14.8.

Window and Frame Properties

The window and frame properties turn and change aspects of the browser windows, and the frames within the windows. All window and frame properties, listed in Table 14.9, are typically used as read-only.

Understanding JavaScript Methods and Functions

Closely related to objects are *methods*. A method is something you can do with an object. Like properties, methods are contextually tied with the object to which they belong, and not all objects have the same methods. Think of a method as an action

Table 14.7 String Property

Property	What It Does
length	The length of a string

Table 14.8 Window URL Properties

Property	What It Does
hash	Text following the hash (#) symbol in a URL
host	The hostname:port portion of a URL
hostname	The host and domain (or IP address) of a URL
href	An entire URL
pathname	The path portion of a URL
port	The port portion of a URL
protocol	The protocol portion of a URL
referrer	The URL of the referring (linked from) document
search	The search portion of a URL

that causes the object to change or respond in some way. Consider that window and desk lamp again. A valid method for the window might be to open and close it. A valid method for the lamp might be to turn it off and on.

> **NOTE** As a point of interest, JavaScript also supports functions, which are similar to methods, except that they are not related to any single object. Rather, JavaScript supports functions generically for all objects. Typical JavaScript functions deal with numbers, such as converting a string to an integer value.

Table 14.9 Window and Frame Properties

Property	What It Does
frames[]	Array (list) of frames in the window
length	The number of frames in a window
name	The name of a window object
parent	The parent window or frame
self	The current window or frame
top	The top browser window
window	Current window or frame

You've already seen a JavaScript method at work: document.write. Write is a method of the document object. It causes JavaScript to send HTML output to the document. Whenever you want to insert text or tags in the document, use *document.write*. Similarly, there are methods for the document property to open a new document, to close a document, and much more.

In many ways, methods can be considered JavaScript "commands," as they cause something to happen to an object. There are dozens of methods, each one contextually related to the object it serves. Adding to this canopy of choices are a very small sprinkling of JavaScript *functions*. Unlike methods, however, functions are not intrinsically tied to an object. For example, a commonly used JavaScript function is parseInt, used in converting number formats.

Here is a list of JavaScript methods and functions separated by category. Unless specifically indicated, everything in the tables below is a method.

Date Methods

The date methods, listed in Table 14.10, are used with the built-in Date object. The majority get or set different parts of the time or date.

Table 14.10 Date Methods

Method/Function	What It Does
getDate	Returns the day of month of a specified date
getDay	Returns the day of week of a specified date
getHours	Returns the hour of a specified date
getMinutes	Returns the minutes of a specified date
getMonth	Returns the month of a specified date
getSeconds	Returns the seconds of a specified date
getTime	Returns the number of seconds between January 1, 1970, and a specified date
getTimeZoneoffset	Returns the time zone offset in minutes for the current locale
getYear	Returns the year of specified date
parse	Returns the number of milliseconds in a data since January 1, 1970, 00:00:00

Continued

Table 14.10 *Continued*

Method/Function	What It Does
setDate	Sets the date
setDay	Sets the day of a specified date
setHours	Sets the hours of a specified date
setMinutes	Sets the minutes of a specified date
setMonth	Sets the month of a specified date
setSeconds	Sets the seconds of a specified date
setTime	Sets the time of a specified date
setYear	Sets the year of a specified date
toGMTString	Converts a date to a string using GMT conventions
toLocaleString	Converts a date to a string using locale conventions
toString	Converts the value of a Date object or current location object to a string
UTC	Converts a comma-delimited date to the number of seconds since January 1, 1970

Document Methods

The document write methods listed in Table 14.11 let you open, close, and write to a document window.

Table 14.11 Document Methods

Method/Function	What It Does
clear	Clears the window
close	For a document, closes the output stream; for a window closes the window
open	Opens a document or a window
write	Writes text to a document or window
writeln	Writes text to a document or window with new line character appended

Table 14.12 Form Methods

Method/Function	What It Does
blur	Removes focus from a text, textarea, and password form control
click	Simulates click on a form button (push button, radio button, checkbox)
focus	Sets focus to a text, textarea, and password form control
select	Selects the text inside a text, textarea, and password form control
submit	Submits a form to a server

Form Methods

Form methods, listed in Table 14.12, allow you to interact with form objects. These objects include text boxes, radio buttons, and check boxes. (In Netscape 2.0 many of these methods are broken, depending on the platform.)

History Methods

The history methods, listed in Table 14.13, let you change the URL of a window or frame using previously visited URLs.

JavaScript Functions

JavaScript functions are built into the core language and do not "belong" to any given object. Therefore, they are considered functions rather than methods. See Table 14.14.

Math Methods

The math functions, listed in Table 14.15, apply to the built-in Math object and give you extra arithmetic and computational capabilities, such as square roots and

Table 14.13 History Methods

Method/Function	What It Does
back	Loads to the previous URL from the history list
forward	Loads the next URL from the history list
go	Loads a URL from the history list

Table 14.14 JavaScript Functions

Method/Function	What It Does
escape	Returns the encoded ASCII value (%xx) of a character in the ISO Latin-1 character set
eval	Evaluates an expression
isNAN	Tests a number to determine if it's "not a number"
parseFloat	Converts a number string to a floating point value
parseInt	Converts a number string to an integer value
toString	Converts an object to a string
unescape	Returns the ASCII character for a specified value

rounding. A number of trig functions, like acos and tan, are thrown in for good measure.

String Methods

String methods, listed in Table 14.16, are used with text strings. The write and writeln methods listed here really belong to the document object, but they are

Table 14.15 Math Methods

Method/Function	What It Does
abs	Returns the absolute value of a number
acos	Returns the arc cosine of a number
asin	Returns the arc sine of a number
atan	Returns the arc tangent of a number
ceil	Returns the least integer greater than or equal to a number
cos	Returns the cosine of a number
eval	Evaluates the contents of a string expression (for example, "2 + 2"); Eval is a function
exp	Returns e (Euler's constant) to the power of a number
floor	Returns the greatest integer less than or equal to its argument
isNAN	Determines if a value is a number (or "not a number")
log	Returns the natural logarithm (base e) of a number

Table 14.15 *Continued*

Method/Function	What It Does
max	Returns the greater of two values
min	Returns the lesser of two values
pow	Returns the value of a number times a specified power
random	Returns a random number (X-platforms only)
round	Returns a number rounded to the nearest whole value
sin	Returns the sine of a number
sqrt	Returns the square root of a number
tan	Returns the tangent of a number

always used to print a string of characters to the document, so they are included in this category, too.

User Interface Methods

User interface methods, listed in Table 14.17, let you interact with the user with a variety of message boxes (additional user interface methods are available under the Form category).

Table 14.16 String Methods

Method/Function	What It Does
anchor	Creates a named anchor (hypertext target)
big	Sets text to big
blink	Sets text to blinking
bold	Sets text to bold
charAt	Returns the character at a specified position
fixed	Sets text in fixed-pitch font
fontcolor	Sets the font color
fontsize	Sets font size
indexOf	Returns the first occurrence of character x starting from position y

Continued

Table 14.16 *Continued*

Method/Function	What It Does
italics	Sets text to italics
lastIndexOf	Returns the last occurrence of character x starting from position y
link	Creates a hyperlink
small	Sets text to small
strike	Sets text to strikeout
sub	Sets text to subscript
substring	Returns a portion of a string
sup	Sets text to superscript
toLowerString	Converts a string to lowercase
toUpperString	Converts a string to uppercase
write	Writes text to a document or window
writeln	Writes text to a document or window with new line character appended

Window Methods

Use the window control methods, listed in Table 14.18, when you need to interact with the browser window—typically to change the URL of the current window or to move back and forth in the history list.

Understanding JavaScript Statements

Statements are programming commands. You've already been introduced to the *if* statement. There are others, including return, var, while, and for. Statements are used to construct the thinking and doing portion of your JavaScript programs.

Table 14.17 User Interface Methods

Method/Function	What It Does
alert	Displays a message box with OK button
confirm	Displays message box with Yes and No buttons
prompt	Displays a message box prompting the user for text entry

Table 14.18 Window Methods

Method/Function	What It Does
clear	Clears the window
clearTimeout	Clears a previous set timer (using setTimeout)
close	For a document, closes the output stream; for a window closes the window
open	Opens a document or a window
setTimeout	Sets a timer

JavaScript currently supports few statements—about a dozen—but more will come as the language matures. With new statements come additional capabilities. This doesn't mean JavaScript is anemic when it comes to programming prowess. On the contrary, with a bit of ingenuity and imagination you can construct very complex programs, even with the limited selection of statements JavaScript offers.

There are relatively few JavaScript programs; they are listed in Table 14.19 in alphabetical order.

Table 14.19 JavaScript Programs

Statement	What It Does
break	Breaks out of a while or for loop
comment (//)	Inserts a comment that is not interpreted by JavaScript as a command
continue	Starts a new pass in a for or while loop, skipping any commands following
for	Repeats a series of instructions one or more times
for...in	Iterates through the properties of an object (one pass through the loop for each property of the object)
function	Defines a user-created function or object
if...else	Tests if an expression is true or false
return	Returns execution from a function
var	Declares a variable
while	Repeats a series of instructions until an expression proves false
with	Associates an object with properties and methods

Understanding JavaScript Event Handlers

JavaScript also supports something called an *event handler*. An *event* is a condition generated by the browser when some action takes place—usually the result of something the user did. For example, when the user clicks a button in a form, it generates a "click event." JavaScript picks up this event and will tell you about it, if you wish.

You can always tell an event handler its name: all start with the word *on*. There are relatively few event handlers, and even fewer still are used to any degree. The most common are onClick, onLoad, and onMouseOver. The majority of the event handlers are used in conjunction with forms.

Note that several of the event handlers, as listed in Table 14.20, deal with "focus." Focus occurs when the flashing insertion point is placed in a form control, such as a text box, text area, or selection list.

Authoring Programs in JavaScript

Like all computer programming languages, JavaScript insists you format things in a specific way. Otherwise, JavaScript cannot interpret what you want to do, and it will display an error as it gives up in despair. Here are some basic programming fundamentals you'll want to keep in mind as you learn and use JavaScript.

Table 14.20 Event Handlers

Event Handler	What It Does
onBlur	Trigger when focus leaves a text box, textarea, or selection list
onChange	Trigger when text changes in a text box, textarea, or selection list, and focus leaves the control
onClick	Trigger when a form button or hypertext link is clicked
onFocus	Trigger when focus is set in a text box, textarea, or selection list
onLoad	Trigger when a document has been completely loaded
onMouseOver	Trigger when the mouse passes over a hypertext link
onSelect	Trigger when text is selected in a text box or textarea
onSubmit	Trigger when a form has been submitted to a server
onUnload	Trigger when a document is about to be unloaded

Saving in Text Format

JavaScript is contained in the same document as the HTML used to define a Web page. As such, all JavaScript programs are in text-only format. You can use most any word processor, text editing, or HTML editing program to write JavaScript programs, as long as the program saves in text-only format.

Always Put JavaScript Code Between <SCRIPT> Tags

As you read earlier in this chapter, the JavaScript interpreter built into the browser is designed to ignore any text unless it is placed within <SCRIPT> tags. Material within the <SCRIPT> tags is considered for JavaScript's use only. You don't put any HTML markup tags in there.

To start the tag you insert:

```
<SCRIPT LANGUAGE="JavaScript">
```

The LANGUAGE attribute is optional, but it's a good idea to include it for future compatibility. To end the tag you insert:

```
</SCRIPT>
```

Example:

```
<SCRIPT LANGUAGE="JavaScript">
alert ("Welcome to JavaScript!!");
</SCRIPT>
```

This short script is executed as the browser loads the page.

Use Quotation Marks

Quotes are always used to define strings of text. Without the quotes JavaScript will mistake the text for something else, like the name of a variable or object. JavaScript understands two kinds of quotes—the single quote character, or ‘, and the double quote character, or “. You can use either quote type, but you must remember to use the same one to start and stop the string; see Table 14.21.

You can also use the two types of quotes to “embed quotes” in a string. Suppose you want to display the word *don't*. As you can see the word has an apostrophe in it—*apostrophe* is another word for a single quote. Ordinarily this would result in an error because JavaScript always insists on using quotes in pairs. But JavaScript allows you to use both quote types so you can “embed” one in the other.

Table 14.21 Use of Quotation Marks

Allowed	Not allowed	Why It's Not Allowed
"Hello"	Hello	No quotes at all
"Hello"	"Hello	No ending quote
'Hello'	"Hello'	Mismatched quotes

In addition, JavaScript lets you include quote characters by "escaping" them with the \ backslash character. The escape method lets you sneak in a quote when JavaScript might otherwise throw a fit. Examples include these (the results are shown in Figure 14.7):

```
"Don't do that."
'"Do not do that," she said.'
'"Don\'t wear that again around me!," she yelled"'
```

Insert a Comment in a JavaScript Program

Comments are notes designed for human readers. JavaScript ignores the comment because it knows it doesn't contain anything worthwhile for it. You might use a comment to help remind you of what you did to make that great new feature work or to document a procedure for someone else trying to use your script.

Two types of comments are used within JavaScript: the single-line comment and the multiple-line comment.

- The single-line comment is created using the // characters. All text up to the next hard return is treated as a comment.
- The multiple-line comment is created using the /* and */ characters. All text between these characters is treated as a comment.

Here are some examples:

```
// This is a comment
alert ("Welcome to JavaScript!") // This is a comment
/*This is the start
of a multiple-line comment*/
```

Hide JavaScript Code from Non-JavaScript Browsers

Not all Web browsers understand JavaScript. This can be a problem if you need your Web documents to be viewable with non-JavaScript browsers. The natural ten-

Figure 14.7 The ' and " quote characters can be inserted into text using the \ "escape" character.

dency of browsers is to ignore an HTML tag it doesn't understand. Any text outside the tag is rendered, and is visible, in the browser screen.

To prevent non-JavaScript browsers from printing your JavaScript code enclose it in HTML comments. The HTML comment tag begins with <!-- and ends with --> (although many browsers, especially non-Netscape browsers, consider just the > character as the end of the comment).

```
<SCRIPT>
<!-- Hide this code from "old" browsers
<H1>Here's JavaScript-generated text!</H1>
document.write ("Hello there!")
// stop hiding-->
</SCRIPT>
```

Notice the double slash (//) characters on the line with the end comment tag. JavaScript treats double slashes as its own comment and ignores anything on that line. If you forget the // characters, JavaScript will try to interpret the —> characters, and that will result in the error you see in Figure 14.8.

JavaScript Syntax: A Lot Like C

The syntax of JavaScript was intentionally modeled after Java, which was itself modeled after the C++ language. And, the basic syntax of C++ was modeled after C. So it can be rightfully said that the syntax of JavaScript is a lot like C.

If you're familiar with C, then you'll be instantly familiar with JavaScript. They both use similar syntax and structure, and they share many of the same statements. In fact, some C code can actually be plugged into a JavaScript with little or no

Figure 14.8 The syntax error message complains when you forget to add the // comment characters to force JavaScript to ignore the --> end tag of an HTML comment.

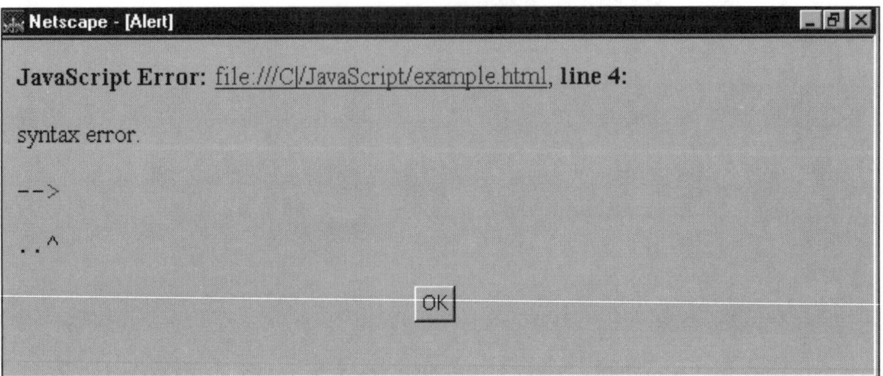

change. If you're not familiar with C—perhaps you've worked with BASIC or Cobol or Pascal—the syntax will look odd and perhaps a bit like Sanskrit. Unlike BASIC and especially Pascal, C is not known for being a "readable" language; that is, you can't easily read over a C program and instantly get a grasp of the whole process. The C language was designed this way for speed in writing and compiling. They made the syntax of the language rather threadbare, thus making it easier for the compiler to turn the code into a form the computer could understand. In the process they made the C language harder to learn and use—a classic example of a trade-off.

C is a "dot every 'i'" kind of language, where a special character misplaced here or there will cause the whole program to stop in its tracks. That said, JavaScript is generally very lenient in what it expects of its programs. Keep the following few points in mind and you'll do well:

- JavaScript uses semicolons at the end of command lines. This is a C tradition. But unlike C, the use of semicolons in JavaScript is optional. I use it for consistency; if you don't want to use it, no one will shoot you.
- JavaScript is a *case-sensitive* language. Names of objects, methods, properties, and other elements must use the proper capitalization, or the program will not work.

- JavaScript uses the { and } brace character to form what's known as "statement blocks." There are rules (covered in later chapters) about the proper use of these characters. Forget one, and your script will fail.
- Like C, JavaScript is a minimalist language. A lot is inferred because of context. For example, unlike languages such as BASIC and Pascal, there are no End If commands to mark the end of an *if* statement. Instead, the "End If" is inferred or is marked using the { and } statement block characters.
- When defining text, enclose it in ' (single) or " (double) quotes. This tells JavaScript that the text should be treated as an assemblage of characters and not as a command name or some other element.
- To test for equality in an expression (like that used in an *if* statement), use two equal signs, as in ==.

What Are the Main Differences Between Java and JavaScript?

This question comes up a lot. Java is a sophisticated and advanced programming language designed to create self-contained programs as well as "applets" for use with software such as a World Wide Web browser. Java is based on the C++ programming language, and it deeply embraces object-oriented programming precepts. Java programs must be compiled to an a binary form before a browser such as Netscape Navigator 2.0 can use them. This compiling requires a software development kit, which is available free from Sun Microsystems, Java's creators, as well as from several third-party language development companies, such as Borland and Symantec.

JavaScript is a user-level scripting language. The JavaScript "program" is included as part of the HTML document retrieved by the browser program and need not be compiled before use. JavaScript programs don't need to be developed using a software developers' kit, and there's no need to compile JavaScript code before you can use it in a browser.

The JavaScript language was intentionally kept simple so that Web authors with limited programming experience can adequately harness its power. Because of this, JavaScript does not have the same power and capabilities as Java. Java allows for specific control of screen objects, files, and data. With it you can program complete computer applications, including a World Wide Web browser (such a browser is HotJava, published by Sun).

Conversely, JavaScript limits access to the computer, prohibiting programmers from manipulating the screen or from opening or saving data files. Many of these limitations in JavaScript also help to make it a "safer" programming language for the Internet. Lacking the ability to read, write, or erase files on your disk drive makes JavaScript an unlikely candidate for a damaging computer virus.

JavaScript Example

JavaScript is a favorite for Web page creators because it can create dynamic page content with little or no programming fuss. A good example of using JavaScript for dynamic page content is the clock.html script, shown on pages 373–374. This script displays the current time using a set of GIF numbers: 0 through 9, the colon separator, and an A.M. or P.M. indicator. The GIFs to use are selected by JavaScript according to the time. An example of the clock.html script is shown in Figure 14.9.

Figure 14.9 An example of the JavaScript clock.

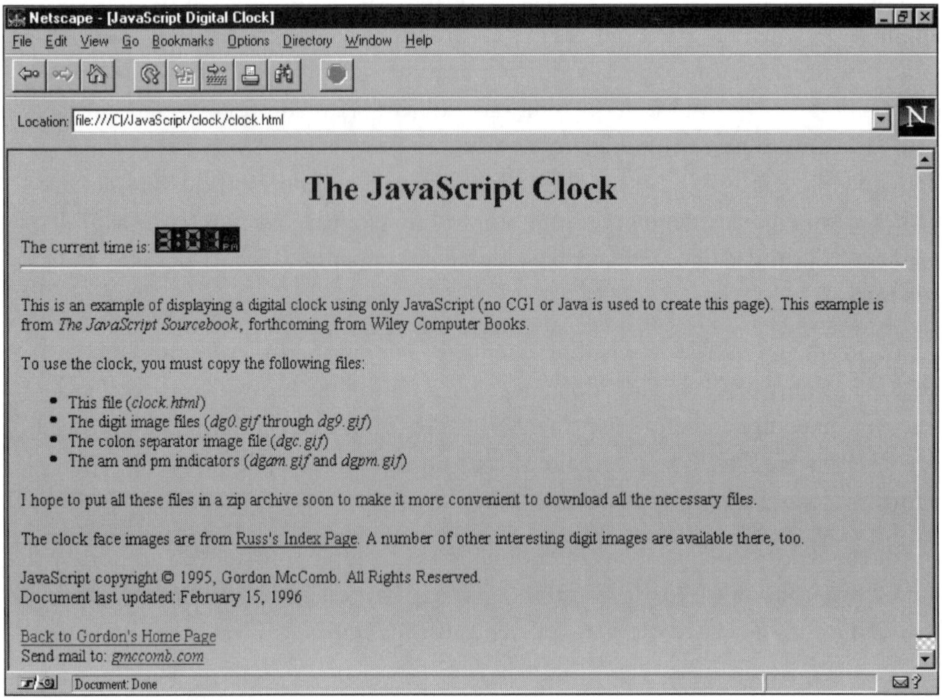

```
<HTML>
<HEAD>
<TITLE>JavaScript Digital Clock</TITLE>
<SCRIPT LANGUAGE="JavaScript">
<!--
/* Copyright 1996, by Gordon McComb. All Rights Reserved.
You may use this JavaScript example as you see fit, as long as
the copyright notice above is included in your script.

This example is from Web Languages Sourcebook, from Wiley
Computer Books. */

var Temp;
setClock();

function setClock() {
    var OpenImg = '<IMG SRC="'+pathOnly(location.href)+'dg'
    var CloseImg='.gif" HEIGHT=21 WIDTH=16>'
    Temp = ""
    now = new Date();
    var CurHour = now.getHours();
    var CurMinute = now.getMinutes();
    now = null;
    if (CurHour >= 12) {
         CurHour = CurHour - 12;
         Ampm = "pm";
    } else
         Ampm = "am";
    if (CurHour == 0)
         CurHour = "12"
    if (CurMinute < 10)
         CurMinute = "0" + CurMinute
    else
         CurMinute = "" + CurMinute

    CurHour = "" + CurHour;

    for (Count = 0; Count < CurHour.length; Count++) {
         Temp += OpenImg + CurHour.substring (Count, Count+1)
              + CloseImg
    }
    Temp += OpenImg + "c" + '.gif" HEIGHT=21 WIDTH=9>'
    for (Count = 0; Count < CurMinute.length; Count++) {
         Temp += OpenImg + CurMinute.substring (Count, Count+1)
              + CloseImg
    }
```

```
47          Temp += OpenImg + Ampm + CloseImg
48      }
49
50      function pathOnly (InString)  {
51          LastSlash=InString.lastIndexOf ('/', InString.length-1)
52          OutString=InString.substring  (0, LastSlash+1)
53          return (OutString);
54      }
55
56      //-->
57      </SCRIPT>
58      <BODY>
59      <H1 ALIGN=CENTER>The JavaScript Clock</H1>
60      The current time is:
61      <SCRIPT>document.write(Temp);</SCRIPT>
62      </BODY>
63      </HTML>
```

The example program can be explained as follows:

- Line 4 uses the <SCRIPT> tag to define JavaScript as an in-line scripting language to use, and Line 5 begins a browser comment, using the <!-- characters, to prevent the script text from appearing on browsers that do not support JavaScript or understand the <SCRIPT> tag.
- Lines 6 through 10 are a multiline JavaScript comment, defining the copyright and source of the script.
- Line 13 defines a variable named Temp, which is used at various times throughout the script.
- Line 14 is a "call" to the setClock function, which gets the current time—as set by the clock in the user's computer—and formats a string of <IMG> tags to display the current time using image GIFs.
- Lines 16 through 48 define the setClock function. Notice that the function begins with a { brace character and ends with a } brace character. All of the commands within these characters are construed as being a part of the function.
- Lines 17 and 18 define the text to use for the beginning and ending of the string for formatting the <IMG> tags. Each <IMG> tag requires the source of the image, a full path (because of a JavaScript bug), and the requisite < and > characters.

- Lines 20 through 22 obtain the current time from the user's computer. The CurHour and CurMinute variables contain the current hour and current minutes, respectively.
- Lines 24 through 28 determine if it's A.M. or P.M. JavaScript returns the hour in 24-hour format, but the clock uses 12-hour format. If the hour is between 0 and 11, it's A.M.; if it's 12 to 23, it's P.M.
- Lines 31 through 34 "pad" a zero to the minutes, if the current minute is 0 through 9.
- Lines 38 through 41 constitute a for loop, which determines which GIF image to use for each digit of the hour. Note that the for loop is defined within { and } characters. The <IMG> tag for each GIF is added—otherwise known as "concatenated"—to the Temp string to build one long string of <IMG> tags.
- Line 42 adds the <IMG> tag for the semicolon to the Temp string.
- Lines 43 through 46 constitute a for loop, which determines which GIF image to use for each digit of the minute.
- Line 47 adds the <IMG> tag for the A.M. or P.M. indicator to the Temp string.
- Lines 50 through 54 are a self-contained function, used to return just the path of the current location of the clock.html script. This path is assumed to also contain the GIFs for the images, which are named dg1.gif, dg2.gif, and so on.
- Lines 56 and 57 end the JavaScript script section.
- Lines 58 through 63 constitute the HTML portion of the document, which displays a heading and some basic text. Also included is an additional <SCRIPT> tag container, which is used to output (using the document.write method) the content of the Temp variable.

The Temp variable is the key to the clock.html script. It is used to hold the <IMG> tags that display the full time. Not including the path of the images or other attributes except for the image source, the content of the Temp variable may look like the following, after being processed by the setClock function:

```
<IMG SRC="dg1.gif"><IMG SRC="c.gif"><IMG SRC="dg3.gif">
<IMG SRC="dg2.gif"><IMG SRC="am.gif">
```

The time displayed in this case is 1:32 A.M.

Chapter

15

VBScript

JavaScript and VBScript are strikingly similar, which is not surprising as VBScript was designed as a direct competitor to JavaScript. If you already know JavaScript, you'll be pleasantly surprised by its many similarities to VBScript; you'll be writing your first VBScript programs in a matter of minutes. For example, the Internet Explorer "object model" in VBScript is virtually identical to that found in Netscape and JavaScript. There are so many similarities we could have combined both languages in one chapter. Instead, we separated the two languages to avoid confusion, which can occur because JavaScript is based largely on C syntax, and VBScript is based largely on the syntax of Visual Basic. Because of similarities between the languages, this chapter is fairly repetitious of Chapter 14, " JavaScript," but has been modified to directly reflect the nuances and capabilities of VBScript.

If you're familiar with Visual Basic, you'll be right at home with Microsoft's VBScript, a scripting language built into Microsoft Internet Explorer 3.0 and later. VBScript is to Internet Explorer what JavaScript is to Netscape Navigator, though Internet Explorer also supports JavaScript.

It's important to note that while VBScript "borrows" the Visual Basic name, or at least its initials, it is not Visual Basic. VBScript, as found in Internet Explorer, lacks many of Visual Basic's powerful features, including all of Visual Basic's commands for manipulating files. VBScript is solely a client-side scripting language, meaning that it is designed to be run on the user's browser. As such, there are specific restrictions as to what you can and can't do in a VBScript program. It would be considered a breach of security if a VBScript program could read or write files directly on someone's computer.

You should also note that VBScript is a generic scripting language provided by Microsoft. A version of VBScript is included with Internet Explorer 3.0 and later. Other products—some by Microsoft, some by others—may also include VBScript support, but the exact language parameters and capabilities may differ. What follows in this chapter is a discussion of VBScript as found in Internet Explorer 3.0 and later.

Why VBScript Is Important

VBScript is an enabling technology. It offers to do for Web publishing what Visual Basic did for Windows programming. Like JavaScript, VBScript offers these benefits:

- VBScript offers a scripting language accessible to "mere mortals," allowing most anyone to use it in his or her Web pages. VBScript closely follows the Web principle of bringing electronic publishing to the masses. You don't need lots of money or technology to publish on the Web; as with VBScript, you don't need a programming degree to take advantage of the language.

- Because of its name recognition and the support of Microsoft, the world's largest maker of software for personal computers, VBScript is on the fast track to becoming a de facto standard for Web page programming. For a developer, this means you can be reasonably assured that the technology you invest in today will not disappear tomorrow.

- All major online services, including CompuServe and America Online, now offer Web document space to their customers. This means a lot of people are just now getting the taste of Web publishing, and they are looking for ways to improve their work. Because these services offer Internet Explorer as part of their basic package, many users are taking advantage of the power of VBScript to augment their Web pages.

If you are running a commercial Web site, you can use VBScript as a quick and simple means to enhance your page. For example, a common use of VBScript is to display a warning or alert message when a user enters a page or before a user performs some action, such as submitting a script. You might display an alert message—which appears in a dialog box to which users must respond—to remind your customers of an important sale, for example.

If you're running a personal site (on CompuServe, AOL, or Prodigy, for instance), you likely don't have access to the CGI functions of the Web server and cannot run server-side programs. You can use VBScript, as a client-side program, to do some of the things for which you might have used the server. As an example, with VBScript you can create simple dynamic pages, such as displaying one image background in the daylight hours and another background in the nighttime hours.

Exploring the Uses for VBScript

If you've spent much time on the Web you've probably encountered a few applications of VBScript. Here are some of the more popular applications VBScript can help you develop.

Tailor Pages for the User

Imagine a Web page with VBScript that responds to the user's choice of preferences, such as asking if the reader wants to view simple, low-resolution, thumbnail images for an entire page or wait a little while longer for larger, high-resolution images. Offering these and other custom interface choices helps you tailor your pages to the user's needs and preferences. All readers no longer get the same page.

Make Interactive Pages

You can use VBScript's built-in commands to add interactivity to your Web pages. For instance, a VBScript page can determine what time it is on the user's computer and display the current time on the screen. It can even select one of several images to display an appropriate graphic or background for the time of day—a sunrise for morning, full sun for the day, a sunset for late afternoon, and the moon for evening.

Another use of VBScript for interactivity is conditionally displaying text and hypertext links, depending on the user's response to a query. Suppose, for example, your page contains descriptions of products for your company. Your company makes lots of diverse products in various product lines. Rather than display text and hypertext links for products in which the user may not be interested—or worse, that may confuse the reader—you can use VBScript to display only text and links that relate to the user's field of interest. This approach streamlines the content of Web pages.

Enhance Computer-Aided Instruction

You can easily use VBScript for computer-aided instruction. A VBScript page can be "smart"—it can determine if the reader provides proper answers to questions and can tally up the score. It can even keep track of how long it takes for a reader to answer questions. If your test has a time limit, you can use VBScript to end the test automatically when the limit is up.

Use VBScript with Forms

VBScript is also ideal for use with form-processing programs located on an Internet server. (For the uninitiated, a form is a collection of text boxes and buttons that provide for user feedback, much as a Windows or Macintosh dialog box provides for user feedback.) The traditional way to use forms on a Web page is to send all the user's entries to a "script" or program running on the computer, typically using a technique called common gateway interface, or CGI. The bulk of most any CGI program is verifying that the user entered valid data. Entry validation is something VBScript can do, and it can do it very easily, thus making CGI programs much easier to write and implement.

Use VBScript for Multimedia Effects

An oft-cited use of VBScript is for special effects. With VBScript you can easily add dynamic sound to your page, such as a different sound effect for night or day. And, using Internet Explorer's other features, you can use VBScript to achieve animation, color effects, and more.

VBScript gives you greater control over the graphical elements of your page. For instance, you can use VBScript to resize an image intelligently. This is useful if you have a solid-color GIF. You can use VBScript to expand or contract the size of the GIF, as it appears in Netscape Navigator. Possible uses include bar charts, colored divider lines (no more plain <HR> horizontal rules!), and more.

Using VBScript in an HTML Document

A VBScript program consists of one or more *instructions* (also referred to as *code* or *commands*) included with the *HTML markup tags* that form your Web documents.

When Internet Explorer encounters a VBScript instruction, it stops to process it. For example, the instruction might tell Netscape to format and display text and graphics on the page. Unlike most other programming languages, VBScript programs are not in separate files. Instead, the VBScript instructions are mixed together with the familiar HTML markup tags you've come to love, like <H1>, <P>, <IMG>, and the rest.

Consider the very basic HTML document. It simply renders a heading and some text on the page.

```
<HTML>
<HEAD>
<TITLE>This Is a Basic Document</TITLE>
</HEAD>
<BODY>
<H1>This Is a Basic Document</H1>
<P>This is a pretty basic document.</P>
</BODY>
</HTML>
```

Though there is no rational reason for doing so, you can use VBScript to insert the text you see above. Here's how to use VBScript to insert the heading.

```
<HTML>
<HEAD>
<TITLE>This Is a Basic Document</TITLE>
</HEAD>
<BODY>
<SCRIPT LANGUAGE="VBScript">
Document.Write "<H1>This Is a Basic Document</H1>"
</SCRIPT>
<P>This is a pretty basic document.</P>
</BODY>
</HTML>
```

Using VBScript in Your Own Pages

Because VBScript is embedded in the HTML document, you can use any text editor or Web page editor to write your VBScript programs. The only requirement is that the editor must allow direct input. Web page programs that let you insert only a given set of HTML markup tags cannot be used because they don't allow you to insert the VBScript code.

You can try the example to see how VBScript works. Retype the example exactly as you see it. When done, save the document as *sample.htm*. Close the file (if necessary), and start Internet Explorer. In Internet Explorer open the sample.htm file.

How VBScript Uses the <SCRIPT> Tag

Internet Explorer needs to be told that you're giving it VBScript instructions; these instructions are enclosed between <SCRIPT> tags. Within the script tag you can have only valid VBScript instructions. You can't put HTML tags for Internet Explorer to render inside the <SCRIPT> tags, and with the exception of form "events," you can't put VBScript instructions outside the <SCRIPT> tags. The following is allowed:

```
<HTML>
<BODY>
<H1>Here's VBScript-generated text!</H1>
<SCRIPT LANGUAGE="VBScript">
Document.Write "Hello there!"
</SCRIPT>
</BODY>
</HTML>
```

But these are not allowed:

```
<!--No script tags around the VBScript instruction-->
<HTML>
<BODY>
<H1>Here's VBScript-generated text!</H1>
Document.Write "Hello there!"
</BODY>
</HTML>

<!--HTML markup tags inside the script tags -->
<HTML>
<BODY>
<H1>Here's VBScript-generated text!</H1>
<SCRIPT LANGUAGE="VBScript">
<H1>Here's VBScript-generated text!</H1>
Document.Write "Hello there!"
<P>
</SCRIPT>
</BODY>
</HTML>
```

Note the use of the LANGUAGE="VBScript" identifier. This is important. In current versions of Internet Explorer, the default scripting language is JavaScript, not VBScript (the reason: JavaScript was the first to market, so it is the default language; this helps ensure consistency). If you leave off the LANGUAGE attribute, Internet Explorer will think you want to run a JavaScript program instead; your program could terminate prematurely because of an error condition.

A Real-World Use of VBScript

Obviously, you don't use VBScript to insert the text that HTML can otherwise do all by itself. I used the example above because it's simple and demonstrates the basic VBScript concept of embedded scripts in an HTML page.

VBScript is ideal for making your Web pages "smart." Here's an example. Suppose you want to change the graphic depending on whether it's day or night. VBScript has a rich selection of date-oriented functions, one of which returns the current hour, as set by the user's computer. Here's how that basic document uses VBScript instructions to programmatically select the right GIF for the time of day:

```
<HTML>
<HEAD>
<TITLE>This Is a Basic Document</TITLE>
</HEAD>
<BODY>
<H1>This Is a Basic Document</H1>
<P>This is a pretty basic document.</P>
<SCRIPT LANGUAGE="VBScript">
Dim nowDate
nowDate = Hour(Now)
If ((nowDate > 5) And (nowDate < 18)) Then
        Document.Write "<IMG SRC='http://mydoamin.com/day.gif'>"
Else
        Document.Write "<IMG SRC='http://mydomain.com/night.gif'>"
End If
</SCRIPT>
</BODY>
</HTML>
```

This example uses a VBScript *If* statement to determine the time of day. The *If* statement does one thing if the *expression* is true or another if the expression is false. If the hour is greater than 5 A.M., but less than 6 P.M., it's daylight. So, VBScript inserts an image (<IMG>) tag using the DAY.GIF image. If the current time is not between these hours, it is nighttime, and VBScript inserts the NIGHT.GIF image.

HTML alone lacks any decision making, so this example is a perfect job for VBScript. The page contains the basic HTML tags to render the document and VBScript for any tasks that require "thinking."

Understanding the Use of VBScript Objects

You've probably heard of *object-oriented programming*. It's a style of programming in which software is created using self-contained modules. Each module is designed to take a certain type of data and do something with it. The term "object-oriented" comes from how the data is viewed: as an object. Even though object-oriented programming is more difficult than the traditional "procedural" programming (like BASIC and C), the result is usually easier to maintain and fix. Almost all major software products released today are written using object-oriented techniques.

VBScript uses *objects*, but it is not an object-oriented programming language. It's strictly procedural, which means you don't have to learn anything about object-oriented programming. Objects are used in VBScript to represent "things." The document as viewed in the Internet Explorer browser is a "thing." The fill-in form that you see on the browser page is a "thing." The hypertext link you click on to go to another URL is a "thing."

Objects are best viewed as a total entity to make programming easier. Objects are composed of *properties*, which is stuff that belongs to that object. As in real life, not all objects have the same properties. A good example of a VBScript object is the document that you view in the Netscape Navigator window. The document has many properties, including the background color, the text color, and the title. When you work with VBScript, you uniquely identify the properties you want as belonging to a certain object. You don't just say "change the color of the background to green"; VBScript won't have the slightest idea what you're talking about. *What* background? Rather, to change the background of the document, you must specify the document object.

VBScript uses a special syntax for the object-property relationship. You use the object name (in this case, document), a period, and the property name, which is bgColor. Put them together and you have:

```
Document.bgColor
```

This is enough to tell VBScript what object you want to work with and what property of that object you want to change or test. For example, want to change the background of the document? That's easy. The following instruction changes the background color to black:

```
Document.bgColor = "black";
```

Test this for yourself. Here's a short script that sets the background according to the time of day. It uses Document.bgColor to set the background color and fgColor to set the foreground (text) color. The page is rendered black-on-white for the daytime and white-on-black for the nighttime. We'll use the color names for this example, rather than the #nnnnnn color triplet values you may be used to. Both are valid with Internet Explorer.

```
<HTML>
<HEAD>
<TITLE>This Is a Basic Document</TITLE>
<SCRIPT LANGUAGE="VBScript">
Dim nowDate
nowDate = Hour(Now)
If ((NowDate > 5) And (nowDate < 18)) Then
      Document.bgColor = "white"
      Document.fgColor = "black"
Else
      Document.bgColor = "black"
      Document.fgColor = "white"
End If
</SCRIPT>
</HEAD>
<BODY>
<H1>This Is a Basic Document</H1>
<P>This is a pretty basic document.  It doesn't have much of anything in it.
Just a heading, this text, and a graphic of some line.</P>
</BODY>
</HTML>
```

Table 15.1 lists VBScript's main objects, briefly described, in alphabetical order.

Table 15.1 VBScript's Main Objects

Object	Description
anchor	A target (that is, destination) for a hypertext link. Anchors always belong to the document object.
anchors	An array (list of variables sharing a common function) of the anchors in a document.
button	A push button in a form. Buttons always belong to the form object.

Continued

Table 15.1 *Continued*

Object	Description
checkbox	A check box in a form. Check boxes always belong to the form object.
document	Contents of a window.
form	A form in a document.
forms	An array of forms in a document.
frame	A window that is divided into many panes.
frames	An array of frames in a "parent" window.
hidden	A hidden (nonvisible) text box in a form. Hidden boxes always belong to the form object.
history	A list of pages the browser has visited. History always belongs to the document object.
link	A hypertext link. Links always belong to the document object.
links	An array of links in a page.
location	The URL of the current document. Location always belongs to the document object.
navigator	Information about the browser.
options	An array of all the items in a selection list (see select).
password	A password text box in a form. Password boxes always belong to the form object.
radio	A radio button in a form. Radio buttons always belong to the form object.
reset	A reset button in a form. Reset buttons always belong to the form object.
select	A selection list in a form. Select lists always belong to the form object.
submit	A submit button in a form. Submit buttons always belong to the form object.
text	A text box in a form. Text boxes always belong to the form object.
textarea	A textarea (multiple line) box in a form. Text areas always belong to a form object.
window	A browser window. Window is a top-level object.

Understanding VBScript Properties

Properties are behaviors of objects. Here are VBScript's main properties, listed by group. Many properties can be both retrieved and set using VBScript; that is, you can use the property to determine the current state of an object, and you can change the value of the property to make the object change. But other properties are read-only, meaning that you can read the value contained in them, but you can't directly change them.

Browser Info Properties

The browser info properties return settings in the Navigator object; see Table 15.2.

Document Info and Appearance Properties

The properties for document appearance return and change the look of the document. Additional properties for document info return current information about the document. These properties are listed in Table 15.3.

Table 15.2 Browser Info Properties

Property	What It Does
appCodeName	"Code name" for the current browser
appName	Application name for the current browser
appVersion	Version number of the current browser
userAgent	The user agent string sent from the browser to the server

Table 15.3 Document Info and Appearance Properties

Property	What It Does
alinkColor	The color for active links in the document
anchors	List of all anchors in the document
bgColor	Background color of the document
cookie	Semi-permanent storage of textual information
defaultStatus	Default text of status bar
fgColor	Text color of the document
forms	List of forms in the document
lastModified	The date the document was last modified
linkColor	The color of unvisited links in the document

Continued

Table 15.3 *Continued*

Property	What It Does
links	A list of links in the document
location	The complete URL of the document
referrer	The URL of the referring (linked from) document
status	The current text of the status bar
title	The title of the document
vlinkColor	The color of visited links in a document

Forms Properties

The properties of the Form object return (and some change) form elements, including the form itself, and all controls (also called "widgets") in the form; see Table 15.4.

Table 15.4 Forms Properties

Property	What It Does
action	Destination URL for a form
defaultChecked	Default selection state of a check box or radio button
defaultSelected	Default selection of an option list
defaultValue	Default value of text box or text area
checked	State of a check box or radio button in form
elements	List of form elements in the document
encoding	MIME encoding format for a form
form	Parent form object
index	A specific option in a selection list within a form
length	The number of items in the list
method	Posting method for a form (get or post)
name	The name of a form object
options	A list of options in a selection list within a form
selected	Current state of a check box or radio button
selectedIndex	The selected option in a selection list within a form
target	The name of the targeted form

Table 15.4 *Continued*

Property	What It Does
text	The text of an option in a selection list within a form
value	The text of a text box or text area

Link and Anchor Properties

The properties of the anchors and links arrays return and change aspects of links (<A HREF=...>) and anchors (<NAME=...>); see Table 15.5.

Window URL Properties

The URL property returns or changes the current document URL; see Table 15.6.

Window and Frame Properties

The window and frame properties turn and change aspects of the browser windows and the frames within the windows. All window and frame properties, listed in Table 15.7, are typically used as read-only.

Table 15.5 Link and Anchor Properties

Property	What It Does
hash	Text following the hash (#) symbol in a URL
host	The hostname:port portion of a URL
hostname	The host and domain (or IP address) of a URL
href	An entire URL
length	The number of anchors or links
pathname	The path portion of a URL
port	The port portion of a URL
protocol	The protocol portion of a URL
search	The search portion of a URL
target	The name of the targeted link

Table 15.6 Window URL Properties

Property	What It Does
hash	Text following the hash (#) symbol in a URL
host	The hostname:port portion of a URL

Continued

Table 15.6 *Continued*

Property	What It Does
hostname	The host and domain (or IP address) of a URL
href	An entire URL
pathname	The path portion of a URL
port	The port portion of a URL
protocol	The protocol portion of a URL
referrer	The URL of the referring (linked from) document
search	The search portion of a URL

Table 15.7 Window and Frame Properties

Property	What It Does
frames	Array (list) of frames in the window
length	The number of frames in a window
name	The name of a window object
parent	The parent window or frame
self	The current window or frame
top	The top browser window
window	Current window or frame

Understanding VBScript Methods

Closely related to objects are methods. A *method* is something you can do with an object. Like properties, methods are contextually tied with the object to which they belong, and not all objects have the same methods. Think of a method as an action that causes the object to change or respond in some way. Consider that window and desk lamp again. A valid method for the window might be to open and close it. A valid method for the lamp might be to turn it off and on.

You've already seen a VBScript method at work: Document.Write. Write is a method of the Document object. It causes VBScript to send HTML output to the document. Whenever you want to insert text or tags in the document, use *Document.Write*. Similarly, the document property has methods to open a new document, to close a document, and much more.

In many ways, methods can be considered VBScript "commands," as they cause something to happen to an object. There are dozens of methods, each one contextually related to the object it serves. Here is a list of VBScript methods and functions separated by category.

Document Methods

The document methods listed in Table 15.8 let you open, close, and write to a document window.

Form Methods

Form methods, listed in Table 15.9 allow you to interact with form objects. These objects include text boxes, radio buttons, and check boxes. (In Netscape 2.0 many of these methods are broken, depending on the platform.)

History Methods

The history methods, listed in Table 15.10, let you change the URL of a window or frame using previously visited URLs.

Table 15.8 Document Methods

Method/Function	What It Does
clear	Clears the window
close	For a document, closes the output stream; for a window, closes the window
open	Opens a document or a window
write	Writes text to a document or window
writeln	Writes text to a document or window with new line character appended

Table 15.9 Form Methods

Method/Function	What It Does
blur	Removes focus from a text, textarea, and password form control
click	Simulates click on a form button (push button, radio button, checkbox)
focus	Sets focus to a text, textarea, and password form control
select	Selects the text inside a text, textarea, and password form control
submit	Submits a form to a server

Table 15.10 History Methods

Method/Function	What It Does
back	Loads to the previous URL from the history list
forward	Loads the next URL from the history list
go	Loads a URL from the history list

User Interface Methods

User interface methods, listed in Table 15.11, let you interact with the user with a variety of message boxes (additional user interface methods are available under the Form category).

Window Methods

Use the window control methods, listed in Table 15.12, when you need to interact with the browser window—typically to change the URL of the current window or to move back and forth in the history list.

Table 15.11 User Interface Methods

Method/Function	What It Does
MsgBox	Displays a message box with OK button
InputBox	Displays a message box prompting the user for text entry

Table 15.12 Window Methods

Method/Function	What It Does
clear	Clears the window
clearTimeout	Clears a previous set timer (using setTimeout)
close	For a document, closes the output stream; for a window, closes the window
open	Opens a document or a window
setTimeout	Sets a timer

Understanding VBScript Statements

Statements are programming commands. You've already been introduced to the *If* statement. There are others, including *Dim*, *While*, and *For*. Statements are used to construct the thinking and doing portion of your VBScript programs.

The primary VBScript statements are listed in Table 15.13 in alphabetical order.

Understanding VBScript Event Handlers

VBScript also supports something called an *event handler*. An *event* is a condition generated by the browser when some action takes place—usually the result of something the user did. For example, when the user clicks a button in a form, it generates a "click event." VBScript picks up this event and will tell you about it, if you wish.

You can always tell an event handler by its name: All start with the word "on." There are relatively few event handlers, and even fewer still are used to any degree. The most common are onClick, onLoad, and onMouseOver. The majority of the event handlers are used in conjunction with forms.

Table 15.13 VBScript Programs

Statement	What It Does
comment (')	Inserts a comment that is not interpreted by VBScript as a command
Call	Calls a user defined function or subroutine
Do...Loop	Repeats a block of statements while a condition is True
For	Repeats a series of instructions one or more times
For Each	Repeats a group of statements for each element in an array or collection
Function	Defines a user-created function or object
If...Else...End If	Tests if an expression is true or false
Rem	Same as a ' comment
Select Case	Executes one or more statements, depending on the value of an expression
Sub	Defines a user-created subroutine
While...Wend	Repeats a series of instructions until an expression proves false

Note that several of the event handlers, as listed in Table 15.14, deal with "focus." *Focus* occurs when the flashing insertion point is placed in a form control, such as a text box, text area, or selection list.

Authoring Programs in VBScript

Like all computer programming languages, VBScript insists that you format things in a specific way. Otherwise, VBScript cannot interpret what you want to do, and it will display an error as it gives up in despair. Here are some basic programming fundamentals you'll want to keep in mind as you learn and use VBScript.

Understanding Case Sensitivity

If you're familiar with JavaScript, you may notice that VBScript uses the same object model for the browser program. In Javascript, the names of the objects, and properties and methods of the objects, are case sensitive. In VBScript, these same object names, properties, and methods are not case sensitive (in keeping with the tradition of the BASIC language). That is, Document.Write is the same as document.write in VBScript. In JavaScript, using the capitalization Document.Write generates an error.

Furthermore, VBScript's case-insensitivity extends to variable names as well. You can define a variable named myVar and reference it using any capitalization you wish—myvar, myVAR, and so forth. Even though you use different capitalizations, VBScript will know you mean the same variable.

Table 15.14 Event Handlers

Event Handler	What It Does
onBlur	Triggers when focus leaves a text box, textarea, or selection list
onChange	Triggers when text changes in a text box, textarea, or selection list, and focus leaves the control
onClick	Triggers when a form button or hypertext link is clicked
onFocus	Triggers when focus is set in a text box, textarea, or selection list
onLoad	Triggers when a document has been completely loaded
onMouseMove	Triggers when the mouse moves
onMouseOver	Triggers when the mouse passes over a hypertext link
onSelect	Triggers when text is selected in a text box or textarea
onSubmit	Triggers when a form has been submitted to a server
onUnload	Triggers when a document is about to be unloaded

Saving in Text Format

VBScript is contained in the same document as the HTML used to define a Web page. As such, all VBScript programs are in text-only format. You can use most any word processing, text editing, or HTML editing program to write VBScript programs, as long as the program saves in text-only format.

Always Put VBScript Code Between <SCRIPT> Tags

As you read earlier in this chapter, the VBScript interpreter built into the browser is designed to ignore any text unless it is placed within <SCRIPT> tags. Material within the <SCRIPT> tags is considered for VBScript's use only. You don't put any HTML markup tags in there.

To start the tag you insert:

```
<SCRIPT LANGUAGE="VBScript">
```

The LANGUAGE attribute is *not* optional. To end the tag you insert:

```
</SCRIPT>
```

Example:

```
<SCRIPT LANGUAGE="VBScript">
MsgBox "Welcome to VBScript!!"
</SCRIPT>
```

This short script is executed as the browser loads the page.

Use Quotation Marks

Quotes are always used to define strings of text. Without the quotes VBScript will mistake the text for something else, like the name of a variable or object. Use the double-quote character to define a string. Remember to use the same character to start and stop the string; see Table 15.15.

Insert a Comment in a VBScript Program

Comments are notes designed for human readers. VBScript ignores the comment because it knows it doesn't contain anything worthwhile for it. You might use a comment to help remind you of what you did to make that great new feature work

Table 15.15 Use of Quotation Marks

Allowed	Not Allowed	Why It's Not Allowed
"Hello"	Hello	No quotes at all
"Hello"	"Hello	No ending quote

or to document a procedure for someone else trying to use your script. You may use either the Rem keyword or the ' character to define a comment on a line.

Here are some examples:

```
Rem This is a comment
MsgBox "Welcome to VBScript!" 'This is a comment
```

Hide VBScript Code from Non-VBScript Browsers

Not all Web browsers understand VBScript. This can be a problem if you need your Web documents to be viewable with non-VBScript browsers. The natural tendency of browsers is to ignore an HTML tag it doesn't understand. Any text outside the tag is rendered, and is visible, in the browser screen.

To prevent non-VBScript browsers from printing your VBScript code, enclose it in HTML comments. The HTML comment tag begins with <!-- and ends with -->.

```
<SCRIPT LANGUAGE="VBScript">
<!-- Hide this code from "old" browsers
Document.Write "Hello there!"
' stop hiding-->
</SCRIPT>
```

VBScript Example

VBScript is a favorite for Web page creators because it can create dynamic page content with little or no programming fuss. A good example of using VBScript for dynamic page content is the clock script shown below. This script displays the current time using a set of GIF numbers: 0 through 9, the colon separator, and an A.M. or P.M. indicator. The GIFs to use are selected by VBScript according to the time.

```
<HTML>
<HEAD>
<TITLE>VBScript Digital Clock</TITLE>
<SCRIPT LANGUAGE="VBScript">
<!--
Dim Temp
Dim CurHour
Dim CurMinute
Dim AmPm
Call setClock

Function setClock()
OpenImg = "<IMG SRC=dg"
CloseImg = ".gif HEIGHT=21 WIDTH=16>"
CurHour = Hour(Now)
CurMinute = Minute(Now)
```

```
17  If (CurHour >= 12) Then
18      CurHour = CurHour - 12
19      Ampm = "pm"
20  Else
21       Ampm = "am"
22  End If
23  If (CurHour = 0) Then
24       CurHour = "12"
25  End If
26  If (CurMinute < 10) Then
27       CurMinute = "0" + CurMinute
28  Else
29       CurMinute = CurMinute
30  End If
31  CurHour = CurHour
32
33  For Count = 1 to Len(Curhour)
34       Temp = Temp + OpenImg + Mid(CurHour, Count, 1)+CloseImg
35  Next
36
37  Temp = Temp + OpenImg + "c" + ".gif HEIGHT=21 WIDTH=9>"
38
39  For Count = 1 to Len (CurMinute)
49      Temp = Temp + OpenImg + Mid (CurMinute, Count, 1)+CloseImg
41  Next
42
43  Temp = Temp + OpenImg + Ampm + CloseImg
44  End Function
45
46  //-->
47  </SCRIPT>
48  <BODY>
49  <H1 ALIGN=CENTER>The VBScript Clock</H1>
50  The current time is:
51  <SCRIPT LANGUAGE="VBScript">Document.Write(Temp)</SCRIPT>
52  </BODY>
53  </HTML>
```

The following describes the function of the program.

- Line 4 uses the <SCRIPT> tag to define VBScript as an in-line scripting language to use, and Line 5 begins a browser comment, using the <!-- characters, to prevent the script text from appearing on browsers that do not support VBScript or understand the <SCRIPT> tag.
- Lines 6 through 9 define variables used later in the script. Line 10 calls the setClock user-defined function, which is found on lines 12 through 44.

- Lines 12 through 44 define the setClock function. Notice that the function ends with an End Function statement. All of the commands within these characters are construed as being a part of the function.
- Lines 13 and 14 define the text to use for the beginning and ending of the string for formatting the <IMG> tags. Each <IMG> tag requires the source of the image and the < and > characters.
- Lines 15 and 16 gets the current hour and minute from the user's computer. The CurHour and CurMinute variables contain the current hour and current minutes, respectively.
- Lines 17 through 22 determine if it's a.m. or p.m. VBScript returns the hour in 24-hour format, but the clock uses 12-hour format. If the hour is between 0 and 11, it's A.M.; if it's 12 to 23, it's P.M.
- Lines 33 through 35 constitute a For loop, which determines which GIF image to use for each digit of the hour. The <IMG> tag for each GIF is added—otherwise known as "concatenated"—to the Temp string to build one long string of <IMG> tags.
- Line 37 adds the <IMG> tag for the semicolon to the Temp string.
- Lines 39 through 41 constitute a For loop, which determines which GIF image to use for each digit of the minute.
- Line 43 adds the <IMG> tag for the a.m. or p.m. indicator to the Temp string.
- Lines 46 and 47 end the VBScript script section.
- Lines 48 through 53 constitute the HTML portion of the document, which displays a heading and some basic text. Also included is an additional <SCRIPT> tag container, which is used to output (using the Document.Write method) the content of the Temp variable.

The Temp variable is the key to the clock script. It is used to hold the <IMG> tags that display the full time. Not including the path of the images or other attributes except for the image source, the content of the Temp variable may look like the following, after being processed by the setClock function:

```
<IMG SRC="dg1.gif"><IMG SRC="c.gif"><IMG SRC="dg3.gif">
<IMG SRC="dg2.gif"><IMG SRC="am.gif">
```

The time displayed in this case is 1:32 A.M.

Chapter

16

An Introduction to C Programming

C is a high-performance, general-purpose language. A compiled C program is fast and compact, ready for the operating system to execute. Unlike an interpreted language, C programs do not require an additional runtime interpret program or special environment. Because the compiler generates instructions native to the target operating system and CPU, no further interpretation or parsing is needed. Your operating system will execute a compiled C program with the same efficiency as many of its own utilities and commands.

Much of C's syntax may be recognizable to you after reading the other chapters in this book (including those on Java and JavaScript), as most of these other languages borrow concepts from C.

This chapter serves as a quick introduction to C and discusses important aspects of C programming, including its core elements, variable assignments, expressions, and statements. The following chapter provides hands-on, real-world demonstrations of using C for Web programming.

Note that all of the example programs in this chapter are meant to be illustrative only; they are not meant to be typed into a text editor and run as-is on your Web server. The examples are meant as code snippets so you can see how a concept being discussed relates to the actual practice of C programming. You may want to read this chapter and the next before you attempt to run any of the examples. Then come back to this chapter and try out some of the examples in a functional Web program.

Introduction to C

C is widely available, found on every major modern platform including UNIX, Windows, Macintosh, OS/2, and MS-DOS. The language is defined by an ANSI standard, which means that you can write platform-independent code to execute on many different operating systems and platforms.

C provides a large library of routines for a variety of tasks such as reading and writing files, arithmetic, and text manipulation. You can also build reusable libraries of your own routines.

Of central importance is the C compiler. The C compiler is a utility that translates the human-readable text of the C language into a natively executable program. Some platforms include a C compiler with the operating system. If your system (such as MS-DOS or Microsoft Windows) does not include a compiler, several implementations are available. Microsoft and Borland International are the leading commercial vendors of C implementations for the PC with their Visual C++ and Borland C++ packages. UNIX vendors like Sun offer C compilers for their platforms as well.

A noncommercial alternative is the excellent GNU compiler from the Free Software Foundation. In addition to versions for most flavors of UNIX, this compiler has been converted (called "ported") to MS-DOS and Windows NT. This compiler can be downloaded directly from the Internet, and it is often installed on servers used by customers of Internet Service Providers (ISPs).

Some compiler packages like Visual C++ and Borland C++ provide an Integrated Development Environment (IDE) that integrates the compiler with an editor. In an environment like this you would normally compile your program directly from the editing screen by choosing a menu option like "build."

Other packages such as GNU provide only command-line utilities. To compile your program with gcc, the GNU compiler, you would issue a somewhat cryptic command such as:

```
gcc myprog.c -o myprog.exe
```

This command compiles the source file named myprog.c and creates a program named myprog.exe. The -o option specifies the name of the program.

What Makes Up a C Program?

Most programs written in C are actually composed of many files, even though the final result may be a single executable program. The typical C program is composed of one or more source files, functions you have defined or obtained in library files from others, various programming statements, and more. Here is a rundown of what makes up a C program.

Source Files

A C program may be divided into one or more source files. Source filenames traditionally end with the .c file extension. The source files contain the functions, directives, statements, and variables that comprise C programs. The C compiler will translate these individual source files into one executable file.

Functions

Functions are the building blocks of C. Functions are subprograms that carry out a specific task. Every C program contains at least one. On most platforms, you must provide a primary function named "main" to serve as the entry point for your program. For graphical Microsoft Windows programs, this function must be named "WinMain." C is a case-sensitive language, so "Main" or "MAIN" would not work. What this function actually does is up to you; its purpose is provide a starting point for your program. This is an example of a minimal C program:

```
/* a do-nothing program */

void main()
{
}
```

The "void" keyword specifies that the function "main" does not return a value. The function body, enclosed in braces, is empty in this example. The first line of this example is a comment. Comments are enclosed within a pair of "/*" and "*/" delimiters and are ignored by the C compiler.

Functions may in turn call other functions—functions that you provide or those found in a library such as the C Runtime Library, or *RTL*. A library is a collection of functions compiled from one or more source files. Unlike other languages like Perl and BASIC, C has no dedicated input/output statements like "print." This functionality is provided through functions in the RTL. The runtime library contains a large number of functions for many common programming tasks. The RTL functions are accessed in the same way as functions that you write.

C functions, like the other languages in this book, accept parameters and may optionally return a value. Unlike BASIC, Pascal or FORTRAN, there is no distinction between functions that return a value and those that do not.

You can eliminate duplicate code by placing frequently used functionality into separate functions. Functions also reduce complexity by enabling you to divide your program into distinct, logically contained units. Generally speaking, functions should be designed to carry out a single task with a minimal number of parameters. Functions should be given names that reflect the tasks that they perform.

Function definitions include two parts, a *header* and a *body*. The header, also known as a prototype, specifies the return-type, function name, and parameter declarations. The function body is enclosed in braces and includes the declarations and statements that constitute the actual function. Function names must begin with either a letter or an underscore ("_") but may contain any combination of letters, numbers, and underscores. For example:

```
int myfunc( int a )

{
        return a * 2;
}
```

Here we have defined a function named myfunc. The header specifies that this function accepts a single integer type parameter and will return an integer type value. The function body is enclosed in braces, and in this example consists of a single statement. This return statement defines the value returned by the function: in this case it is the value of the parameter a multiplied by two.

Before you can call a function, you must declare at least the header. If the function you wish to call has been previously defined in the same source file, then the function is "visible" and you may call it from within any function defined after it. If the function definition appears later in the file, you must place a copy of its header before the location from which you wish to call the function. You must do this because the C compiler processes your source files line by line and must have seen at least the header of the function, with or without the function body, before you may call that function.

If the function you wish to call is defined in another source file or a library, the header must still be declared. Headers, or prototypes, specify the attributes of a function without defining what the function does. These attributes enable the compiler to check the number and types of parameters used when attempting to call that function, regardless of where the function is actually defined. Often these declarations are placed in separate source files, known as "header files" for convenience. The header file can then be referenced by any source files that wish to call the declared functions.

One of the most popular RTL functions is the printf function:

```
#include <stdio.h>
void main()
{
     printf( "Hello." );
}
```

This sample program prints the text "Hello." on the screen. The printf function is a powerful formatting routine in the RTL. The prototype for printf is in the source file stdio.h, one of many standard "header" files provided with the compiler. The #include directive shown here inserts the contents of stdio.h into this source file, before the call to printf.

The printf function returns a value indicating the number of characters output. Because this value is not used in this example, it is simply discarded.

The definition of the main function contains the body of the function enclosed in braces and includes the executable statements necessary to carry out the given task.

Statements

As with most computer languages, statements are the fundamental elements of a C program. A statement is a specific program operation to be executed. Compared with other languages, C provides a relatively small number of statement types. Statements are provided only for controlling the flow of program execution. All other functionality is provided by functions. This makes C portable and easily extendible through function libraries as the language itself is not encumbered with specific platform or I/O behaviors.

C statements always end with semicolons. Statements are not confined to individual lines; they can span as many lines as needed because C ignores "white-space" characters such as spaces, tabs, and line breaks. The common convention, however, is to place individual statements on single lines where possible to enhance readability.

Statements may be grouped together into functions or compound statement blocks. Enclosed in braces, statements blocks are subprograms within functions that may include local variable definitions of their own.

Statement types include assignment, conditional branching, and looping. Assigning a value to a variable, testing the result of an expression, or calling a function are examples of what can be done in an individual statement. Following are the major C program statement types you should know.

Null Statement

A *null statement* is an empty statement that contains only a semicolon. No action results from a *null* statement. It is mainly used in situations where a statement body is syntactically required, but no action is needed.

Expression Statement

The *expression statement* consists of a valid C expression of any type. The most common usage is to perform assignment or a function call. An *expression* statement does not alter the flow of execution; the statement is executed and control is passed to the next statement.

The basic assignment operator is =. For example:

```
i = j * 2;
```

This statement assigns the result of an arithmetic expression to the variable named i.

In C, the assignment operation yields a result value, the value that was assigned. This enables you to refer to the result of an assignment within an expression. For example:

```
i = j = a + b;
```

Here the result of the expression, a + b, is assigned j. The result of this assignment is the value that was assigned to j, and this is in turn assigned to i.

A function call is a form of the *expression* statement:

```
i = alpha( j * 2 );
```

A function named alpha is called with a single parameter; the result of an arithmetic expression and the return value from alpha are assigned to i. If we did not need the return value from alpha, we could discard it as in the following:

```
alpha( j * 2 );
```

This is also a form of the *expression* statement; assignment is not required.

if Statement

The *if statement* conditionally executes a statement based on the result of an expression. If *expression* is true (nonzero), the first *statement* is executed; otherwise, it is skipped. *Expression* is the condition you wish to test, and it must be enclosed in parentheses.

The syntax of the *if* statement is as follows:

```
if ( expression )
        statement
else
        statement
```

In C, an expression is said to be true if it evaluates to a nonzero value. *Statement* can be any valid statement body; if it consists of multiple statements they must be enclosed in braces.

The else clause is optional; use it to specify an alternate statement to execute if *expression* is false (zero). The else clause and the second *statement* are skipped over if *expression* is true. For example:

```
if( i == 0 )
     printf( "zero" );
```

```
else {
     j = I;
     printf( "nonzero" );
}
```

In this *if* statement, the value of the variable i is tested to see if it is equal to zero. If so, printf will print the word *zero*. Otherwise, the value of j will be set to the value of i and *nonzero* will be printed. Note that the equality operator '==' is different from the assignment operator '='. Braces are needed around the statements in the else clause because there are more than one. Braces are not necessary around the statement body in the if clause as there is only a single statement.

The if and else clauses and *statements* together all form a single statement that can be used anywhere a statement body is expected.

You can test more than one expression by nesting ***if*** statements. For example:

```
if( i == 0 )
     printf( "zero" );
else {
     if( i < 0 )
          printf( "less than zero" );
     else
          printf( "greater than zero" );
}
```

If the value of i is nonzero, it is tested again to see if it is less than zero. Technically, the braces are not necessary because the second *if* statement and its associated else clause form a statement body. The braces and indentation clarify the intent here.

Switch Statement

The *switch statement* handles more complex branching conditions. Unlike the *if* statement, control is transferred based on the specific value of *expression*, not just whether it is zero or not.

The syntax for the *switch* statement is:

```
switch ( expression ) {
        case constant-expression : statement
        case constant-expression : statement
        .
        .
```

```
        .
        default: statement
}
```

Switch evaluates a single *expression* that results in one of several possible values. Control is then transferred to the *case* statement whose *constant expression* matches this value. If no matching *case* statement is found, control is transferred to the optional default statement if present; otherwise, the body of the *switch* statement is skipped. The *switch* statement may include any number of **case** statements; however, each case statement must have a unique *constant-expression* value within the switch statement. Switch is often used to branch based on the content of a variable or the result of a function call.

As in the *if* statement, *expression* must be enclosed in parentheses. Following the *expression* are a series of alternatives enclosed in a block. Each alternative starts with a "case-label" consisting of the case keyword, followed by a *constant-expression* value, then a colon. Variables cannot be used for *constant expression.* The default alternative contains only the keyword "default" followed by a colon because there is no specific value associated with it. For example:

```
switch( ch ) {
     case 'A':
          j = 1;
          break;

     case 'B':
          j = -1;
          break;

     default:
          j = 0;
}

print( "%d", j );
```

In this example, the value of the character variable ch is evaluated. If the value of ch is "A," the statements following the first case label are executed. The variable j is assigned the value 1, then the *break* statement transfers control out of the switch statement to the following statement, print. Without the *break* statements, control would "fall through" to the statements following the next case label. Even though falling through case labels is sometimes desired, forgetting the *break* statements is a common C programming mistake.

Back to the example, if the value of ch is "B," then the *switch* statement executes the statements following the second case label. The variable j is set to –1 and control again passes out of the switch statement to the printf. If the value of ch is neither "A" or "B," execution moves to the statement following the default label and j is set to 0. No break is necessary at this point because the end of the switch block has been reached.

This example uses the formatting abilities of printf to print the value of the integer variable j. The first parameter to printf is a character string that optionally may contain formatting information. Whenever printf encounters a percent sign, it formats the next input parameter according to the type information following the percent sign. The %d specifies an integer type variable. printf recognizes many formatting codes; consult your compiler documentation for specifics.

While Statement

The *while statement* is a looping mechanism that repeats a statement zero or more times as long as *expression* is true (nonzero). As before, *expression* must be enclosed in parentheses. *Expression* is evaluated before the loop *statement*, or body, is executed. If *expression* is initially false, the loop body is not executed at all. The syntax of the *while* statement is as follows:

```
while ( expression ) statement
```

Here is an example of the *while* statement in a simple C program.

```
#include <stdio.h>

void main()
{
      int I;

      i = 1;
      while( i < 100 ) {
            printf( "%d\n", i );
            i *= 2;
      }
}
```

This program prints the numbers that are a power of 2 and less than 100. Note the "escape sequence" used in the print format string. Escape sequences begin with a backslash and are used to represent nonprinting characters, in this case a newline. The printf function does not automatically end lines with newline characters; you must add them yourself, as in this example. Also note the special assignment operator *= used in the loop body. This is simply a more efficient way of expressing i = i * 2.

Do Statement

The *do loop* is an inverted while loop with the conditional *expression* moved to the end of the loop body. The *expression* is evaluated after the loop body executes. The syntax of the *do* statement is:

```
do statement while ( expression );
```

Unlike the while loop, do loops always execute at least once. When *expression* evaluates false (zero), the loop is terminated and control passes to the next statement. A do version of the previous while example yields the same result:

```
do {
      print( "%d\n", i );
      i *= 2;
} while( i < 100 );
```

In this version of the while example, the *do* statement will execute at least one iteration of the loop body even if i initially contains a value equal to or greater than 100.

For Statement

The *for statement* executes the loop *statement* a specified number of times. The for loop contains three types of expressions: initializing, conditional, and modifying; all of them are optional. Semicolons separate the different expression types and must always be present. The syntax for the *for* statement is as follows:

```
for ( init-expression ; cond-expression ; mod-expression ) statement
```

You may have more than one *init-expression* or *mod-expression* separated by commas. The *init-expression(s)* can initialize any variables used in the loop body. The *cond-expression* functions as it does in a while loop; the for loop body will execute while *cond-expression* evaluates to a value of true (nonzero). If *cond-expression* is initially false, the *statement* loop body is not executed at all. If omitted, *cond-expression* is assumed to be true and the only way to terminate the loop is through a *break* statement. After each iteration of the loop, any *mod-expressions* are evaluated and the process begins again by evaluating *cond-expression*. For example:

```
for( i = 1; i <= 10; i++ )
     print( "%d\n", i );
```

This statement prints the numbers 1 through 10. The loop variable i, used in both the *cond-expression* and *mod-expressions,* is initialized with a value of 1. Next, the *cond-expression* is evaluated, and if the value of i is less than or equal to 10 (which it is in this example), the loop body will execute. After each iteration of the loop body, the value of i is incremented via the increment operator ++, and the *cond-expression* is evaluated again. While i is less than or equal to 10, the loop body will execute and i will be incremented.

Return Statement

The *return statement* terminates execution of a function and optionally returns a value to the caller. The *return* statement is optional in functions that do not return a value, but it should be present in functions that do return a value. The syntax of the *return* statement is as follows:

```
return expression;
```

Return statements can appear anywhere within a function, but it is considered good programming practice to have only one exit point from each function. The *return* statement is the only way to return a value from a function. For example:

```
int AddTwo( int i )
{
     return i + 2;
}
```

This example defines a function named AddTwo that accepts an integer parameter and returns its value plus two.

Break Statement

The *break statement* terminates execution of the enclosing *switch, while, do,* or *for* statement in which it appears and transfers control to the following statement. Its syntax is as follows:

```
break;
```

A *break* statement is allowed only within these four statement types. The statement consists only of the "break" keyword followed by the semicolon. Break is commonly used to exit from a *switch* statement after executing a particular case selection. When used inside of a loop statement *(while, do,* or *for)*, the loop is terminated prematurely. Within nested loops, the *break* statement terminates only the loop statement containing it; any outer loops are unaffected.

```
#include <stdio.h>

void main()
{
     int I;
     for( i = 50; i < 100; i++ ) {
          if( ( i % 23 ) == 0 )
               break;
     }
     print( "%d\n", i );
}
```

This program prints the first number between 50 and 99 that is evenly divisible by 23. The *break* statement terminates the loop and transfers control to the following printf statement when the first evenly divisible value of i is encountered. The modulus operator % returns the remainder of the division of the first operand, i, by the second, 23. This expression is placed within its own set of parentheses to ensure that it is evaluated before the equality operator ==. The braces enclosing the loop body are not strictly necessary in this example as the body consists of a single statement, the *if* statement. They are useful in clarifying the boundary of the loop body and will help you avoid the mistake of omitting them should another statement be added to the loop body in the future.

Continue Statement

The *continue statement* is similar to the *break* statement and is used only within the loop statements *while, do,* and *for.* The syntax for continue is:

```
continue;
```

Like break, it interrupts the execution of the loop body. But instead of terminating the loop like break, continue skips the remaining statements in the loop body and passes control to the next loop iteration.

```
#include <stdio.h>

void main()
{
     int i, j;
     for( i = 1, j = 0; i <= 10; i++ ) {
```

```
        if( ( i % 2 ) == 0 )
            continue;

        printf( "%d\n", i );
        j += I;
    }
    printf( "\n%d\n", j );
}
```

This program prints the odd numbers between 1 and 10 along with their sum. During the loop body, if **i** is evenly divisible by 2 the *continue* statement transfers control to the next loop iteration, skipping the following printf and addition statements. The += operator is a more convenient way of expressing j = j + i. Notice that the *for* statement includes two initializing expressions, one each for i and j, separated by a comma.

Summary of Statement Types

The variety of statements in C causes some confusion to beginning programmers, so let's review them and how they are used (see Table 16.1).

Table 16.1 Statement Types

Statement Type	Description
null	Empty statement body with only a semicolon present
expression	Any valid C expression terminated with a semicolon
if	Conditional execution of a statement body based on the truth (nonzero-ness) of an expression, optionally followed by an alternate statement
switch	Execution of one in a series of alternate statements based on the value of an expression
while	Repeatedly executes a statement while an expression evaluates to a nonzero value
do	Inverted while loop with test following the loop body
for	Repeatedly executes a statement a fixed number of times
return	Terminates execution of a function optionally returning a value
break	Terminates execution of a *switch* statement or loop body and executes the next statement
continue	Skips remainder of loop body and proceeds to next loop iteration

Table 16.2 Data Types

Declaration	Type of Value Stored
char	ASCII character values
int	Integral or whole numbers
float	Real decimal numbers
double	Larger decimal numbers

Variables

As you first read in Chapter 4, variables provide storage in memory for values that may change while your program is running. Variables in C must be explicitly declared with a name and *data type* before usage. Declaring a variable associates a variable name with data type information. Defining a variable instantiates a variable of the declared name and type and allocates space for it. Declaration and definition usually occur within the same statement, and they may be accompanied by initialization to a specific value.

Basic Data Types

A data type specifies the type of value that a variable may contain. The basic data types in C are int, float, char, and double (see Table 16.2).

The char and int types are known as *integral,* or *integer* types. The float and double types are known as "floating-point" values as the placement of the decimal point is not fixed.

Variations of these basic types are available through the use of "type qualifiers." C has four of these qualifiers—short, long, signed, and unsigned. These qualifiers are a source of confusion to some, so read the following carefully (maybe even twice!).

The short and long qualifiers affect the size of int variables and thus the range of possible values they can store. The ANSI standard does not specify the storage requirements for variables. The amount of storage used is implementation-specific and may vary between platforms. The standard requires only that long use at least as much storage as short. On many machines such as the Intel x86, a short int requires 2 bytes of storage and long increases the size to 4 bytes. Without a short or long qualifier, the default size of int on many modern platforms is long (4 bytes). A notable exception is the 16-bit MS-DOS/Windows platform where by default int is short (2 bytes).

The long qualifier may also be used with the double type. As with the int type, the long qualifier may increase the size of the double type.

The signed and unsigned qualifiers apply only to the integral types int and char. By default, int and char variables store “signed” values. A signed value may be either negative or nonnegative, and normally it uses one bit of storage to indicate the sign. The signed qualifier is usually redundant; it explicitly states that a variable is signed. The unsigned qualifier specifies that the variable contains only nonnegative values. By utilizing the bit normally reserved for the negative sign, unsigned variables can represent larger nonnegative values.

When appearing by itself, short means short int, and long means lont int. unsigned means unsigned int, and signed means signed int (or int). Table 16.3 illustrates variations of the basic types and the range of values they may contain on a 32-bit Intel x86 platform.

Table 16.3 Variations of Data Types

Type	Synonyms	Size (bytes)	Range of Values
char	signed char	1	–128 to 127
unsigned char		1	0 to 255
short	short int, signed short, signed short int	2	–32,768 to 32,767
unsigned short	unsigned short int	2	0 to 65,535
int	signed, signed int	4	–2,147,483,648 to 2,147,483,647
long	long int, signed long, signed long int	4	–2,147,483,648 to 2,147,483,647
unsigned long	unsigned long int	4	0 to 4,294,967,295
float		4	+/– 3.4E 38 (7 digits)
double		8	+/– 1.7E 308 (15 digits)
long double		10	+/– 1.2E 4932 (19 digits)

The size of operator returns the number of bytes required to store a particular type. The following program prints the number of bytes used to store different types:

```
#include <stdio.h>

void main()
{
     printf( "int:%d  short:%d  long:%d\n",
          size of( int ),
          size of( unsigned short int ),
          size of( unsigned long int ) );

     printf( "float:%d  double:%d  long double:%d\n",
          size of( float ),
          size of( double ),
          size of( long double ) );
}
```

This sample program consists of two statements each calling printf. Each printf call has a format string in the first parameter that includes literal text along with format codes for integer values. The remaining parameters are the result of the size of operator when invoked with different data types. This program generates the following output when compiled with Microsoft Visual C++ (version 4.2):

```
int:4  short:2  long:4
float:4  double:8  long double:8
```

When compiled with a DOS version of the free GNU C compiler (version 2.7.2), the output is slightly different:

```
int:4  short:2  long:4
float:4  double:8  long double:12
```

This shows that the GNU compiler uses 12 bytes to store long double values compared to 8 bytes used by the Microsoft compiler.

The following are a few examples of variable declarations:

```
int i, j;
long int l = 0;
char ch = 'A';
long double salary;
```

In this example two signed integer type variables i and j are defined, and a long int l is defined and initialized with a value of zero. Because and j are not initialized, their values are unpredictable until they are assigned values. A character type variable ch is defined and initialized with an "A." Single character values are enclosed in single quotes; as we will see a little further on, multiple character "strings" are enclosed in double quotes. The salary variable is declared as a very large floating-point variable.

Enumeration Types

The *enumeration type* specifies a set of named integer constants. This is one way to easily associate meaningful names with constant values. Declaring an enumerated set of values creates a new data type. This new data type is capable of representing only those values included in the enumerated set. Enumeration types may contain only integer values. For example, you could not create an enumerated set of floating-point values. Enumerated sets are declared using the enum keyword. An enum declaration consists of the enum keyword, an optional "tag," and the enumerated values enclosed in braces. The declaration statement must be terminated with a semicolon:

```
enum weekday {MON, TUE, WED, THU, FRI};
```

Here we have declared a set of values to represent the days Monday through Friday. This declaration creates a new data type named weekday capable of representing only these values. Although not required, capitalization of the constant names can improve readability of your code by differentiating them from variable names and other language constructs. By default, the first item in the list has a value of 0. Each following item is implicitly assigned a value one greater than its predecessor. In this example, MON has a value of 0. TUE has a value of 1, and so on, ending with FRI having a value of 4. At this point we have only declared a new type with the tag weekday. No variable of this type has yet been defined.

```
enum weekday day;
```

This example defines a new variable named day. Its type is weekday, the tag of our previously declared enumerated type. This tag refers to a specific enumerated set. You may combine the type and variable declarations into one statement:

```
enum weekday {MON = 1, TUE, WED, THU, FRI} day;
```

The tag weekday could be used again to define another variable of this type. The variable day may contain only a value from the set MON through FRI. It cannot represent any other value. Because day is not initialized in this example, its value is unpredictable until it is assigned a value. Notice that the default value assignments have been overridden by explicitly stating a value. MON will now have a value of 1, TUE is automatically assigned the value 2, and so on, ending with FRI having a value of 5. Any or all items in the list may have explicitly assigned values.

Enum variables are used like any other variable. They may be assigned a value:

```
day = WED;
```

But only a value from the enumerated set from which they are declared. Because enumerated sets contain only integer values, enum constants or variables may appear anywhere an integer value is expected:

```
enum {MON = 1, TUE, WED, THU, FRI} day = MON;
int i = WED;  /* initializing an int with an enum value */

i = day + 1;  /* i is now 2, MON + 1 */
```

The enum variable day is initialized in this example. The integer variable i is initialized with a value from the previously declared set of enumerated values. Note that enumerated set in this example has no tag name, so you could not declare another enum variable of this type in another statement. The variable i is then set to the value of an expression involving an enumerated value.

Arrays

An *array* is a collection of one or more variables of the same type stored in consecutive memory locations. The first element of a C array has the subscript, or "index" value, of 0. Similar to the arrays of other languages in this book, C arrays are subscripted using square brackets ([]). An array declaration includes the type and number of elements:

```
int a[3];
```

This defines an array named a with space for three integer values. The individual elements of this array would be accessed as follows:

```
a[0];
a[1];
a[2];
```

Note that while a contains three elements, a reference to a[3] would be erroneous. Because the index values of C arrays begin at 0, the maximum index value is one less than the number of elements in the array. Unlike some other languages, C is unforgiving and makes no attempt to ensure that your array index values are correct. If you refer to an array element with an index value that is out of range, you will access memory outside the bounds of the array. Serious program bugs may be introduced if you are not careful with array subscripts.

An array element may appear anywhere a value of that type is expected. For example:

```
double numbers[3];
double amount = 2.5;

numbers[0] = amount;
amount = numbers[0] * 2;
```

The first element of the numbers array is assigned the value of a double variable named amount. amount is then assigned the result of a floating-point expression involving an element of the numbers array.

Like other variable types, arrays may be initialized when declared. Array initializations are enclosed in braces:

```
int a[3] = { 1, 3, 5 };
```

The individual element values are separated by commas. When initializing an array as part of its declaration, you may omit the size from the declaration:

```
int a[] = { 1, 3, 5 };
```

Note that the brackets (although empty) must still be present to indicate that a is an array. The compiler counts the number of elements in the initialization and will automatically allocate enough memory to store them.

C arrays may be declared with more than one dimension:

```
int a[2][3] = { { 1, 2, 3 }, { 10, 30, 30 } };
```

This statement creates a two-dimensional array and initializes its six (2 dimensions * 3 elements per dimension = 6) elements. Note that the subscript for each dimension is enclosed in a separate pair of brackets. The following program displays the index and value of each element in this array:

```
#include <stdio.h>
```

```
void main()
{
     int i, j;
     int a[2][3] = { { 1, 2, 3 }, { 10, 30, 30 } };

     for( i = 0; i < 2; i++ )
          for( j = 0; j < 3; j++ )
               print( "[%d][%d]: %d\n", i, j, a[i][j] );
}
```

This program utilizes two for loops. The outer loop cycles through each value of the first dimension, while the inner loop cycles through each value of the second dimension and prints the element indexed by the values of the loop counter variables i and j. This program generates the following output:

```
[0][0]: 1
[0][1]: 2
[0][2]: 3
[1][0]: 10
[1][1]: 30
[1][2]: 30
```

Character Strings

You may noticed by now that C does not have a basic type for storing multiple-character strings. A character string in C is simply an array of characters. The following is a declaration for a character string:

```
char str[10];
```

This declares an array named str of type char, with room for 10 characters. In C, character strings are terminated with a "null" character. The null character has a value of 0 and marks the end of a string. The C compiler automatically adds a null character to the end of string constants. String constants are enclosed in double quote marks; single character values are enclosed in single quotes. The following example initializes a character array variable with a string constant:

```
char str[] = "abc";
```

The str array is defined to have four elements. The first three elements (index values 0, 1, and 2) contain the character values "a," "b," and "c." The fourth element (index value 3) contains the terminating null character required in character strings. When the array size is not explicitly specified, the compiler allocates space for the number of characters in the initializing string and automatically adds an extra element for the terminating null.

Structures

Structures are also collections of variables stored consecutively in memory. Unlike arrays, however, the elements, or "members," of a structure may be of different types. Structures are declared using the struct keyword. A structure declaration lists the member variables enclosed in braces. Like an enum declaration, you may include a tag to identify the structure declaration.

```
struct day {
     int day_number;
     char abbrev[4];
};
```

In this example, a struct type named day is declared. This structure contains two member variables, an integer day_number and a string of three characters with room for the terminating null. The declaration does not define a variable; it provides a "template" for creating variables of this type. Once the structure type has been declared, a variable of this type may be defined as follows:

```
struct day weekday;
```

As with an enumerated type, the type declaration and variable definition may be combined:

```
struct day {
     int day_number;
     char abbrev[4];
} weekday;
or further to:

struct {
     int day_number;
     char abbrev[4];
} weekday;
```

In this last example, the struct declaration does not contain a tag, so no other variables of this type may be created in other statements.

Like arrays, structure variables initializations are enclosed in braces:

```
struct day {
     int day_number;
```

```
    char abbrev[4];
} monday = { 1, "Mon" };
```

The first item in braces initializes the first member variable of the structure and so on. A compact declaration of an array with initialization would look like this:

```
struct {
    int day_number;
    char abbrev[4];
} twodays[] =
  { { 1, "Mon" }, { 2, "Tue" } };
```

This complicated-looking declaration defines an array of structures named twodays. The twodays array contains two elements; each is a structure containing a day_number and an abbrev. This declaration initializes the array with values for the two structure elements.

The members of a structure variable are identified by using the "member-of" operator ".". Structure members are referenced by the name of the structure variable, the member-of operatator and the member name. Using our day example, weekday.day_number refers to the day_number member of the structure variable weekday.

As with arrays, structure members may appear anywhere a value of that type is expected. For example:

```
int i;
struct {
    int day_number;
    char abbrev[4];
} monday = { 1, "Mon" };

i = monday.day_number;
monday.day_number = 5;
```

The integer variable i is assigned the value of a member of the monday structure variable. This integer member variable may be used anywhere an integer type is expected, such as the assignment shown here.

Scope and Visibility of Variables

As first introduced in Chapter 4, a key characteristic of variables is *scope*, otherwise known as "visibility" or "lifetime." Local variables are visible (accessible) only within the function in which they are defined. Functions cannot access the local variables defined within other functions unless the variable is passed as a parameter. You can further restrict a variable's visibility by placing it inside a compound statement block.

By default, local variables cease to exist upon exiting the function or statement block in which they are defined. Also known as "automatic" variables, they are allocated storage space upon entry into the function. This space is reclaimed when exiting the function, so that automatic variables do not occupy memory while not in use. Automatic variables cannot "remember" their value between invocations of the enclosing function.

You can override this behavior with the static "storage class" specifier. Placing the keyword "statis" before a local variable declaration specifies that the storage space for the variable is allocated when your program starts and remains until the program ends. This enables the variable to maintain its value for the duration, or lifetime, of your program.

```
void alpha( int parm )
{
        int a;

        a = parm * 2;
}

void beta()
{
        static int b = 0;
        b = b + 1;
        alpha( b );
}
```

This example defines two functions, alpha and beta. The automatic variable a defined in the alpha function is visible only within alpha and cannot be accessed from within function beta or anywhere else outside alpha. Each time alpha is executed, a new a is created and contains an unpredictable, somewhat random value until the assignment statement sets its value to the result of the parameter parm multiplied by two. Upon exiting the function alpha, a ceases to exist and its value is discarded.

In contrast, the local variable b defined in beta is created once and initialized with a value of 0. The variable b is visible only within beta, but the static storage class specification enables it to maintain its value even after exiting beta, for the duration of the program. Each time beta is called, the current value of b is incremented and passed as a parameter to alpha.

Global variables are declared outside any function definitions, and they exist for the entire duration of your program. Like functions, these variables are visible to any function defined in the source file after the point at which the variable is declared. Let's add to the previous example:

```
void alpha( int parm )
{
      int a;

      a = parm * 2;
}

int myvar;

void beta()
{
      static int b = 0;
      b = b + 1;
      alpha( b );
}
```

The global variable myvar has been defined after the function alpha, but before beta. Myvar may be accessed within beta, but not within alpha. This is because the C compiler will not have seen the declaration of myvar before processing the function alpha.

Global variables may be accessed from other source files. To access a global variable defined in another source file, you must declare it using the keyword "extern." This informs the compiler that the variable is already defined and space has been allocated for it elsewhere. You may optionally restrict the visibility of a global variable to the source file in which it resides. When used in the declaration of a global variable, the keyword "static" specifies that the variable is not accessible by functions in any other source files. Unlike local variables, the keyword "static" has no effect on the lifetime of global variables. Global variables exist and maintain their value for the duration of your program.

```
/* main.c */

int public;
```

```
void main()
{
}

/* two.c */

extern int public;
static int private;

void two()
{
}
```

This example illustrates two separate source files, main.c and two.c, each containing a function. The global variable public is defined in main.c and is declared extern in two.c. This variable is accessible to both functions main and two even though these functions reside in separate source files. The global variable private, declared in two.c, is not accessible by the function main from main.c as the visibility of this variable has been restricted to two.c by the keyword "static."

Variable declarations provide another opportunity for the compiler to spot errors in your programs. The compiler will inform you if a variable is used in the wrong context such as attempting to assign character data to a numeric variable.

Operators

C is a compact language that includes few key, or "reserved," words. One reason that C offers so much flexibility with so few reserved words is the large number of operators that it recognizes. You will recognize most of the operators as the same used by other languages in this book.

Arithmetic Operators

Table 16.4 lists C's arithmetic operators.

Table 16.4 C's Arithmetic Operators

Operator	Description
+	Addition
–	Subtraction
*	Multiplication

Table 16.4 C's *Continued*

Operator	Description
/	Division
%	Modulus or "remainder"

The modulus operator may not be as familiar as the others. This operator returns the remainder of the division of two expressions. For example:

```
remainder = 7 % 3;
```

The variable remainder would receive a value of 1, the remainder from the division of 7 by 3.

```
result = 7 / 3;
```

Here result would be 2, the result of the division. Because both expressions (the 7 and 3), or "operands," are integer values, integer division is performed and the remainder is discarded.

Relational Operators

These operators compare two operands and return an integer value of 1 if the specified relationship is "true"; otherwise, they return 0. In C, any expression that evaluates to 0 is considered to be "false". Any other value is recognized as true.

Note that the equality operator == has a different meaning than the assignment operator =. The equality operator compares two operands and returns true if they

Table 16.5 C's Relational Operators

Operator	Description
<	Less than
<=	Less than or equal
>	Greater than
>=	Greater than or equal
==	Equal
!=	Not equal

Table 16.6 C's Logical Operators

Operator	Description
&&	Logical AND
||	Logical OR
!	Logical NOT

are equal. The assignment operator assigns the result of an expression to a variable and returns that value.

Logical Operators

These operators listed in Table 16.6 are used to form more complex logical conditions.

For example:

```
if( ( this == that ) && ( here != there ) )
        print( "true" );
```

If the variables this and that are equal but the variable here does not equal there, the print is executed. Both conditions must be true for the AND operator to return a true result. Contrast this with the OR operator, where only one of the two conditions must be true. Notice that the individual relational expressions are parenthesized to specify that they should be evaluated before the logical AND operator (&&).

The logical NOT operator may be used to reverse the logical value (truth) of any expression. For example:

```
int value = 0;
if( !value )
     print( "value is zero" );
```

The NOT operator converts any nonzero expression to zero and converts a value of 0 to 1. The NOT operator is a "unary" operator as it operates on only one operand.

Bitwise Operators

Bitwise operators are most often used to interact with hardware or low-level APIs. They manipulate the individual bits of integer values. The logical operators mentioned above are interested only in whether their operands evaluate to nonzero. The

Table 16.7 C's Bitwise Operators

Operator	Description
&	AND
|	OR
^	Exclusive OR
<<	Left shift
>>	Right shift
~	Complement

bitwise operators listed in Table 16.7 operate on all of the individual bits that constitute the values of their operands. Each bit contains a value of either 1 or 0. A bit is said to be "set" if its value is 1.

The bitwise AND operator & combines the bits of two integer values, the result having only those bits set that are set in both operands. Think of this as the "intersection" of two sets of values, where each "set" is the collection of the bits of an operand.

Truth tables were introduced in Chapter 4, but they bear repeating here. Table 16.8, a "truth" table, illustrates the results of the AND operator for a single bit.A result bit is set only when both of the corresponding input bits are set.

The bitwise OR operator | also combines two values, but it sets a result bit if that bit is set in either operand. This is similar in concept to the "union" of the two bit sets, as shown in Table 16.9.

Table 16.8 C's Bitwise AND Operator

Operand1	Operand2	Result
0	0	0
1	0	0
0	1	0
1	1	1

Table 16.9 C's Bitwise OR Operator

Operand1	Operand2	Result
0	0	0
1	0	1
0	1	1
1	1	1

Table 16.10 C's Exclusive OR Operator

Operand1	Operand2	Result
0	0	0
1	0	1
0	1	1
1	1	0

The exclusive OR operator ^ differs from the OR operator in that a result bit is set only if the corresponding bits in the operands are unequal, as shown in Table 16.10.

The shift operators move, or shift, all of the bits of an integer value. The left operand is shifted by the value of the right operand.

The complement operator returns the bitwise opposite of its operand. The value of each bit is reversed. Like the logical NOT operator, the complement operator is a "unary" operator.

Assignment Operators

The assignment operator = stores the value of an expression to a variable. C conveniently provides a number of special assignment operators that combine other operations with assignment, as listed in Table 16.11.

Table 16.11 C's Special Assignment Operators

Operator	Description
+=	Addition
-=	Subtraction
*=	Multiplication

Table 16.11 ***Continued***

Operator	Description
/=	Division
%=	Modulus
&=	AND
|=	OR
^=	Exclusive OR
>>=	Right shift
<<=	Left shift

Each of these operators performs the indicated operation and stores the result in the left operand. For example, instead of writing

```
i = i + 2;
```

you can write

```
i += 2;
```

Both of these statements have the same effect.

Increment and Decrement Operators

These are unary operators that increase or decrease a value by 1. Like the special assignment operators, they modify the value to which they are applied; see Table 16.2.

For example,

```
i++;
```

is the equivalent of:

```
i = i + 1;
```

Table 16.12 C's Increment and Decrement Operators

Operator	Description
++	Increment
--	Decrement

These operators may appear on either the left or right side of a value. When appearing on the right side as above, the current value of the operand is returned before it is incremented. When used in this context, the operator is referred to as a "postfix" operator. When placed before the operand, its value is first incremented and the new value is returned. An operator used in this context is a "prefix" operator. For example:

```
i = 3;
j = i++;
```

In this example j would be assigned the value 3 because the i current value of i is used before incrementing.

```
i = 3;
j = ++i;
```

Here the value of i is incremented before its value is returned, so j would now be 4.

Conditional Operator

The conditional operator consists of two symbols, ? and :, separating three expressions. This operator is a simplified way of writing an *if* statement, and it looks more like a statement than an operator. If the first expression evaluates true, then the result of this operator is the value of the second expression; otherwise, the value of the third expression is returned.

```
i = j > 0 ? 1 : -1;
```

Here the variable i receives either a value of 1 or –1, conditional upon the value of j. If j is greater than 0 the result of this conditional operator is 1; otherwise it is –1.

Operator Precedence

When two or more operators are encountered within a statement, the compiler must decide which to evaluate before others. This is known as the *order of evaluation.* As in other languages, operators have different levels of significance, or "precedence."

Operators having the highest precedence are evaluated first, followed by any remaining operators in order of their precedence.

Operators having equal precedence are evaluated from left to right. You may override the normal order of evaluation by enclosing expressions in parentheses. Table 16.13 lists the groups of operators in descending order of precedence.

Table 16.13 C's Operator Precedence

<table>
<tr><th>Operators</th><th>Type</th></tr>
<tr><td>[]</td><td>Array element</td></tr>
<tr><td>()</td><td>Function call</td></tr>
<tr><td>. -></td><td>Structure element access</td></tr>
<tr><td>!</td><td>Logical NOT</td></tr>
<tr><td>~</td><td>Bitwise complement</td></tr>
<tr><td>–</td><td>Negative sign</td></tr>
<tr><td>++ --</td><td>Increment/decrement</td></tr>
<tr><td>& *</td><td>Address-of and indirection (pointers)</td></tr>
<tr><td>sizeof</td><td>Size in bytes</td></tr>
<tr><td>* / %</td><td>Multiplicative</td></tr>
<tr><td>+ –</td><td>Additive</td></tr>
<tr><td><< >></td><td>Bitwise shifts</td></tr>
<tr><td>< > <= >=</td><td>Relational</td></tr>
<tr><td>== !=</td><td>Equality</td></tr>
<tr><td>&</td><td>Bitwise AND</td></tr>
<tr><td>^</td><td>Bitwise exclusive OR</td></tr>
<tr><td>|</td><td>Bitwise OR</td></tr>
<tr><td>&&</td><td>Logical AND</td></tr>
<tr><td>||</td><td>Logical OR</td></tr>
<tr><td>? :</td><td>Conditional</td></tr>
<tr><td>= *= /= %=
+= -= <<= >>=
&= |= ^=</td><td>Simple and special assignment</td></tr>
</table>

Where two or more operators are grouped together in this table, they all have the same precedence level. For example:

```
i = 1 + 2 * 3;
```

Here i would be assigned a value of 7. Even though the addition operator is the first operator to appear in this statement, the multiplication operator will be evaluated first because it is of higher precedence.

```
i = ( 1 + 2 ) * 3;
```

Now i would receive the value 9 because the normal order of evaluation has been changed by the parentheses.

In general it is a good idea to use parentheses to explicitly state the desired order. There is no penalty for unneeded parentheses.

Advanced Topic: Pointers

Pointers are one of the most powerful constructs of the C language. Pointers are special variables that contain memory location information, or "addresses," instead of normal values. A pointer typically contains the address of some other variable, and it is said to "point to" the location of other variable.

As with any other data type, pointers must be declared before usage. Pointers are declared by placing an asterisk, the "indirection" operator, before the name:

```
int *ptr;
```

This statement defines a pointer variable named ptr that can point to integer values. A pointer usually has an associated data type that defines how it will interpret the value it is pointing at. In this example ptr will interpret the contents of any address as an integer value.

Pointers that have been defined but not yet initialized are very dangerous. Because the pointer has not yet been assigned a specific address, it could be pointing anywhere within your program. Even worse, on some platforms it may point to a location outside of your program, perhaps within another running program or within the operating system itself. Take great care to properly initialize pointers before using them.

Examples of Defining Pointers

You can assign the address of any variable to a pointer of the same type via the "address-of" operator. Here is an example.

```
int i;

int *ptr;

ptr = &i;
```

Here we have defined a normal integer variable i and a pointer that points to integer values named ptr. The & operator returns the address of the variable i, which is then assigned to the pointer ptr. ptr now contains the address where the value of i is stored.

You can access the contents of the address stored in a pointer. This is known as an indirect reference, or "dereferencing" the pointer. The indirection operator * returns the value at the address stored in a pointer variable:

```
int i, j;
int *ptr;

i = 3;
ptr = &i;
j = *ptr;
```

In this example two integer variables i and j are defined, along with a pointer variable ptr. The variable i is assigned the value 3. The pointer variable ptr is then assigned the address of i through the "address-of" operator. ptr now points to the location where the value of i is stored. This value may now be accessed through either the variable i or the pointer ptr. The last statement assigns the value found at the address referenced by ptr to another integer variable j. Dereferencing the pointer ptr is the same as directly referring the variable i because ptr is now pointing to the same location.

You can just as easily use a pointer to change a value:

```
*ptr = 5;
```

This statement stores the value 5 in the location pointed to by ptr. The presence of the indirection operator * specifies that the value is stored at the address referenced by ptr and not in the ptr pointer variable itself.

Pointers are often used to access array elements. For example:

```
int a[3] = { 10, 20, 30 };
int *ptr;

ptr = &a[0];
print( "%d\n", *ptr );
```

This example defines an array named a of three elements and initializes their values. The pointer ptr is declared as a pointer to integer values. ptr is then assigned the address of the first element in the a array. We could refer to subsequent elements of this array by using the appropriate index values. The last statement uses print to display the integer value stored at the address referenced by ptr. The indirection operator * references the value to which ptr points; in this case 10, the value of the first element of the a array.

The name of an array is actually a pointer. When appearing without a subscript in square brackets, an array name points to the "base," or first element of that array. The previous example could be simplified to this:

```
int a[3] = { 10, 20, 30 };
int *ptr = a;

print( "%d\n", *ptr );
```

Here we have initialized the pointer ptr with only the name of the array a. Because the array name is itself a pointer to the base of the array, ptr now points to the first element of this array.

Pointers can be manipulated to access different array elements without resorting to using the address-of operator. Because pointers are normally associated with a data type, the compiler knows how much space an item of that type occupies in memory. This enables you to perform simple arithmetic on pointer variables. Let's build on the previous example:

```
ptr += 1;
```

The pointer ptr would now reference the location of the next (second) element of the a array. The ptr variable was previously declared as a pointer to integer values. The compiler knows how much space an int occupies, and thus how far to move ahead to access the next int value. A common operation is to access all elements of an array:

```
#include <stdio.h>

void main()
{
      char astring[] = "Hello";
      char *ptr = astring;

      while( *ptr ) {
            printf( "%c\n", *ptr );
            ptr++;
      }
}
```

This program prints each character of the astring array on a separate line. The pointer variable ptr is declared to point to char values, and it is initialized with the base address of the astring array. The *while* statement will execute as long as the current value pointed to by ptr is nonzero. Recall that character strings are terminated with a value of 0. When the 0 value is encountered at the end of astring, this while loop will stop executing. In the loop body, ptr is dereferenced in the call to print to access the current value to which it points. The last statement in the loop body increments the pointer so that it contains the address of the next element of the array.

The loop body could be simplified to a single statement combining the dereference and increment operators:

```
print( "%c\n", *ptr++ );
```

The postfix form of the increment operator allows the dereference operator in this statement to receive the current address contained in ptr before it is incremented to the next location.

Any operation involving array subscripts can also be done using pointers. It is slightly more efficient to sequentially access array elements with a pointer rather than with array subscripts. Subscripts can be convenient when you need to access the elements of an array in a random or nonsequential order.

Pointers as Function Parameters

In C you may pass parameters to functions either by "value" or "reference." When a parameter is passed by value, the function receives a copy of the parameter value. This copied value is similar in scope and visibility to a local automatic variable and will not exist after the function returns. Because this is only a copy, any changes made to this value are discarded when the function returns.

When passed by reference, however, the function receives a pointer to the actual parameter value. Because the function has the address of the actual parameter value, the function may modify this value through the pointer. For example:

```
#include <stdio.h>

void param_test( int byvalue, int *bypointer )
{
     byvalue *= 2;
     *bypointer *= 2;
}

void main()
{
     int i, j;

     i = j = 2;
     param_test( i, &j );
     printf( "i:%d  j:%d\n", i, j );
}
```

This program will print values of 2 for i and 4 for j, even though they are initialized with the same value and have the same multiplication operation performed on them. The function param_test accepts two parameters; the first by value and the second as a pointer. Each is multiplied by 2 via the multiplication-with assignment operator. Because the parameter byvalue receives only a copy of the parameter value, the underlying variable i in the calling function main is unaffected. The second parameter bypointer receives a pointer, the address of the actual parameter value. The change made using this pointer does affect the underlying variable j in main.

Compiler Directives

Directives are commands for the “preprocessor” to execute. The preprocessor is a phase of compilation that occurs before processing any executable statements. Preprocessor directives are processed before the C language translation of your source code. They do not become part of your compiled program. Unlike C language declarations or statements, preprocessor directives are not terminated by semicolons. They are generally only allowed to appear on a line by themselves.

#include

The most common directive is #include. This command instructs the compiler to insert the contents of the specified file at the current position in the source file during compilation. The actual source file is not modified. This is how header files for commonly used or runtime library functions are processed:

```
#include <stdio.h>
```

stdio.h is the header file containing prototypes for input/output routines in the runtime library. When the filename is enclosed in angle brackets, the preprocessor searches only the standard directories or "include path" for the file. The include path is the list of directories the compiler has been configured to search for header files. If enclosed in double quotes, the compiler will first search the current directory before resorting the include path. It is common practice to enclose all system header files in angle brackets while enclosing your own header file names in double quotes.

#define

The #define directive performs text substitution. The most common use of this directive is to associate meaningful names with constants. For example:

```
#define MAX_BUFFER_SIZE 32
```

This associates the literal text "32" with the symbolic name "MAX_ARRAY_SIZE". Note that the syntax of #define does not accept a '=' between the name and value, nor does it require a semicolon at the end of the line. Every time the symbol "MAX_BUFFER_SIZE" is found in source code (after the point at which this #define appears), the preprocessor will replace it with the text "32".

```
char buffer[MAX_BUFFER_SIZE];
```

This statement declares a character array buffer of 32 elements. If we later decide to increase the size of all buffers in our program, we would need only to change this #define directive.

A common error when using #define is to mistakenly terminate the line with a semicolon. This would result in all occurrences of "MAX_ARRAY_SIZE" being replaced with “32;”. This extra semicolon would cause syntax errors during the C language translation phase of compilation.

Unlike enum types, #define can be used to create constants for types other than integer. For example:

```
#define PROGRAM_VERSION "My Program 1.0"

print( "%s\n", PROGRAM_VERSION );
```

Subsequent versions of this program would need only the PROGRAM_VERSION #define changed to reflect the current version. %s is the printf format code for character strings.

Symbolic names created with #define do not have an associated data type. The #define directive is a simple text substitution mechanism.

Chapter

17

Using C for Web Programming

This chapter demonstrates a few common Web programming tasks. Included are a program that prints the current date and time, a graphical counter, and a pair of programs that process HTML form variables.

Please refer to your compiler documentation for a more thorough explanation of the runtime library functions used in this chapter.

If you are new to programming in C, be sure to first read Chapter 16, "An Introduction to C Programming." This chapter serves as a quick introduction to C and discusses important aspects of C programming, including its core elements, variable assignments, expressions, and statements.

Displaying Date and Time

This program gets, formats, and prints the current local time. It is intended for use with the Server-Side Include (SSI) mechanism, first discussed in Chapter 8. The source code is in the file ssidate.c:

```
#include <stdio.h>
#include <time.h>

#define MAX_BUF_SIZE 64
```

```
5
6     int main()
7     {
8          char tmpbuf[MAX_BUF_SIZE];
9          time_t currtime;
10         struct tm *ptoday;
11
12         printf( "Content-type: text/html\n\n" );
13
14         time( &currtime );
15         ptoday = localtime( &currtime );
16
17         if( ptoday->tm_hour < 12 )
18              printf( "Good Morning." );
19         else if( ptoday->tm_hour < 18 )
20              printf( "Good Afternoon." );
21         else
22              printf( "Good Evening." );
23
24         strftime( tmpbuf, MAX_BUF_SIZE,
25              "%I:%M %p on %A, %B %d, %Y", ptoday );
26
27         printf( "  Local time is %s.\n", tmpbuf );
28
29         return 0;
30    }
```

- Lines 1 and 2 include header files containing function prototypes and data type declarations from the runtime library. stdio.h contains the prototype for the printf function. time.h contains prototypes for the time, localtime, and strftime functions as well as the data type declarations for the time_t and struct tm types.
- Line 4 defines a constant that is later used to specify the maximum size for buffer arrays. Line 6 begins the function main that most C programs must have. Lines 7 and 28 are the enclosing curly braces required of all functions.
- Line 8 defines a character array, or "buffer," that will temporarily contain the formatted date and time. The previously declared MAX_BUF_SIZE constant specifies the size of this array.
- Line 9 declares the variable currtime of type time_t. time_t is a data type declared in the time.h header file. Line 10 declares a pointer to a tm structure type, which is also declared in time.h.

- Line 12 is the first executable statement of the program. This statement prints the "MIME header" required of all CGI (Common Gateway Interface) programs. MIME (Multipurpose Internet Mail Extensions) headers describe the type of data contained in the document body that follows. Headers must be separated from the document body by a blank line, thus the two newline characters in this statement. In this program the header specification "text/html" informs a Web browser (Netscape, Mosaic, et al.) that the data that follows is text and should be interpreted as HTML. If the contents of this header are visible in a Web browser, then this header is not required for SSI programs on your server and you should remove or disable this line.

- Line 14 retrieves the current system time via the time function from the runtime library. The time is expressed as the number of seconds elapsed since midnight of January 1, 1970 ("time zero" for Unix). The time function stores this value in the location specified by its lone parameter, currtime in this program. This function call demonstrates the passing of a parameter via a pointer. The address of the currtime local variable is passed so that this variable can receive a value from the function.

- Line 15 invokes the localtime function in the runtime library to convert the time into a more usable form and translate it into the local time zone. The localtime function accepts a pointer to a time_t value, translates this value, and returns a pointer to a struct tm type containing the results. This pointer points to a static tm structure inside the runtime library, which has been filled with translated information from the currtime variable. Unlike the time function, localtime does not modify the value of its parameter.

  The tm structure is an interesting creature. It contains members that represent the components of a time and date value.

```
    struct tm {
  int tm_sec;      /* seconds (0 to 59) */
  int tm_min;      /* minutes (0 to 59) */
  int tm_hour;     /* hour (0 to 23) */
  int tm_mday;     /* day (1 to 31) */
  int tm_mon;      /* month (0 to 11) */
  int tm_year;     /* year (since 1900) */
  int tm_wday;     /* day of week (0 [Sunday] to 6) */
  int tm_yday;     /* day of year (0 to 365) */
  int tm_isdst;    /* daylight savings time indicator */
};
```

- Line 17 begins an if block to print the appropriate greeting for the current local time. The two *if* statements test the value of the hour member (tm_hour) of the tm structure at which ptoday points. Note that the "pointer-member" operator -> is used because ptoday is a pointer. If the hour member tm_hour is less than 12 (noon), the time is assumed to be in the morning. Otherwise, if the hour is less than 18 (6:00 P.M.) it is assumed to be afternoon. If neither of these conditions are true, than it must be later than 6:00 P.M. and it is evening. The printf function is used to print the appropriate greeting.
- Line 24 utilizes the strftime runtime library function to format the current local time into a character string. This statement is continued on line 25. The strftime function accepts four parameters: a character array to receive the formatted time, the size of this array, a "format" string similar to that used by printf, and a pointer to a tm structure containing the time value to be formatted.

Note that we have used a constant to declare the size of the tmpbuf array and to specify the length of this array when passed to strftime. If it later becomes necessary to handle a longer string, the change will be made in only one place (the #define). This way you won't risk forgetting to increase the value passed to strftime, or worse, the size of the array.

As with printf, the format string used by strftime may contain formatting codes preceded by percent signs '%'; all other characters are included in the output. Table 17.1 lists the more commonly used format codes utilized by strftime.

Table 17.1 Format Codes of strftime

Code	Description
%A	The full weekday name (Friday)
%a	The abbreviated weekday name (Fri)
%B	The full month name (October)
%b	The abbreviated month name (Oct)
%c	Full date and time appropriately formatted for the locale
%d	The day of the month, zero-padded to two characters (04)
%H	The hour (0–24), zero-padded to two characters (15)
%I	The hour (1–12), zero-padded to two characters (03)

Table 17.1 *Continued*

Code	Description
%j	The day of the year, or Julian day, zero-padded to three characters (278)
%M	The minutes, zero-padded to two characters (30)
%m	The month (1–12), zero-padded to two characters (10)
%p	A.M. or P.M.
%S	The seconds, zero-padded to two characters (05)
%w	The day of the week (0–6) (5)
%X	Full time appropriately formatted for the locale
%x	Full date appropriately formatted for the locale
%Y	The year, zero-padded to four digits (1996)
%y	The year (00–99) of the century (96)
%Z	The time-zone abbreviation (PDT)

- Line 27 prints a second sentence that includes the formatted time string. You may recall that the printf function formats a list of parameters according to the codes embedded in the format string, the first parameter. The %s format code is used to insert the contents of the tmpbuf character string. Some of the more popular format codes that printf recognizes are listed in Table 17.2.

Table 17.2 Format Codes of printf

Code	Parameter Type	Description
%c	char	Single character
%d, %i	int	Signed decimal integer
%u	unsigned int	Unsigned integer value
%x	unsigned int	Unsigned integer in hexadecimal format, base 16
%f	double	Real number in decimal format
%p	pointer	Memory address in hexadecimal format
%s	char *	Null-terminated character string

The printf function recognizes several other format codes as well as additional formatting information. See your compiler documentation for more information.

- The last line, 29, exits the main function and terminates the program, returning a value of 0 to the operating system. A value of 0 indicates that the program executed without error. Even though many compilers do not require it, some (like GNU) may generate a warning if you do not declare main to return an integer-type value.

The following command compiles this program with the GNU C compiler:

```
gcc ssidate.c -o ssidate
```

This command invokes the GNU gcc compiler and specifies the name of the source file (ssidate.c). The -o option uses the argument that follows to name the executable program. The DJGPP port of gcc will automatically add the .exe extension required for MS-DOS programs. See your documentation for instructions on using other compilers.

The HTML file ssidate.shtml demonstrates use of this program:

```
1	<HTML>
2
3	<HEAD>
4	<TITLE>SSI Date Example</TITLE>
5	</HEAD>
6
7	<BODY>
8
9	<H1>SSI Date Example</H1>
10
11	<HR>
12
13	<!-#exec cgi="/cgi-bin/ssidate" -><P>
14
15	</BODY>
16	</HTML>
```

- Line 13 contains the SSI directive that invokes the ssidate program. This example uses the cgi method of executing the program, but you may find the cmd method more convenient. Note that this example expects to find the ssidate program in the common cgi-bin directory; you will need to modify this line to specify the correct path for your server. You may also need a special extension like .shtml to get your server to parse the SSI directives. Check your Web server documentation or contact your webmaster or service provider for details.

A Graphical Counter in C

This program maintains and displays a running count of page accesses. The counter is displayed as a graphical image using the X Bitmap, or XBM, format. The XBM format is easy to generate and consists of readable text that is similar in appearance to C code. This program also demonstrates a set of routines from the runtime library for accessing files. While the last program performed all of its processing in the main function, this program is divided into a few separate functions. The source code is contained in a single file named xbmcount.c:

```
#include <stdio.h>
#include <stdlib.h>
#include <string.h>

#define NUM_DIGITS 10
#define NUM_ROWS 10
#define NUM_BORDER_ROWS 2

unsigned char digit_bits[NUM_DIGITS][NUM_ROWS] = {
      {      0x3c, 0x66, 0x66, 0x66, 0x66,
             0x66, 0x66, 0x66, 0x66, 0x3c,  }, // #0
      {      0x30, 0x38, 0x30, 0x30, 0x30,
             0x30, 0x30, 0x30, 0x30, 0x38,  }, // #1
      {      0x3c, 0x66, 0x60, 0x60, 0x30,
             0x18, 0x0c, 0x06, 0x06, 0x7e,  }, // #2
      {      0x3c, 0x66, 0x60, 0x60, 0x38,
             0x60, 0x60, 0x60, 0x66, 0x3c,  }, // #3
      {      0x30, 0x30, 0x38, 0x38, 0x34,
             0x34, 0x32, 0x7e, 0x30, 0x78,  }, // #4
      {      0x7e, 0x06, 0x06, 0x06, 0x3e,
             0x60, 0x60, 0x60, 0x66, 0x3c,  }, // #5
      {      0x38, 0x0c, 0x06, 0x06, 0x3e,
             0x66, 0x66, 0x66, 0x66, 0x3c,  }, // #6
      {      0x7e, 0x66, 0x60, 0x60, 0x30,
             0x30, 0x18, 0x18, 0x0c, 0x0c,  }, // #7
      {      0x3c, 0x66, 0x66, 0x66, 0x3c,
             0x66, 0x66, 0x66, 0x66, 0x3c,  }, // #8
      {      0x3c, 0x66, 0x66, 0x66, 0x66,
             0x7c, 0x60, 0x60, 0x30, 0x1c,  }, // #9
};

void PrintBorderRows( int width, int invert_bits )
{
      int row, i;

```

```
        for( row = 0; row < NUM_BORDER_ROWS; row++ ) {
            for( i = 0; i < width; i++ )
                printf( "0x%02x, ", invert_bits ? 0xff : 0x00 );

            printf( "\n" );
        }
    }

    void PrintDigits( const char *pdigits, int invert_bits )
    {
        int len = strlen( pdigits );
        int row, digit;

        printf( "Content-type: image/x-xbitmap\n\n" );
        printf( "#define xbm_width %d\n#define xbm_height %d\n",
            len * 8, NUM_ROWS + ( NUM_BORDER_ROWS * 2 ) );
        printf( "static char xbm_bits[] = {\n" );

        PrintBorderRows( len, invert_bits );

        for( row = 0; row < NUM_ROWS; row++ ) {
            for( digit = 0; digit < len; digit++ ) {
                int digit_value = pdigits[digit] - '0';
                unsigned char bits = digit_bits[digit_value][row];
                if( invert_bits )
                    bits = ~bits;

                printf( "0x%02x, ", bits );
            }
            printf( "\n" );
        }

        PrintBorderRows( len, invert_bits );

        printf( "};\n" );
    }

    unsigned long GetCount()
    {
        unsigned long count = 0;
        FILE *counter_file;
        const char *pname;

        pname = getenv( "PATH_TRANSLATED" );
        if( pname != NULL ) {
            counter_file = fopen( pname, "r+" );
            if( counter_file != NULL ) {
```

```
83                  if( fscanf( counter_file, "%lu", &count ) ) {
84                       rewind( counter_file );
85                       fprintf( counter_file, "%lu", ++count );
86                  }
87                  fclose( counter_file );
88             }
89        }
90
91        return count;
92   }
93
94   #define INVERT_BITS 1
95
96   int main()
97   {
98        char digits[11];
99        unsigned long counter_value;
100
101       counter_value = GetCount();
102       sprintf( digits, "%06lu", counter_value );
103       PrintDigits( digits, INVERT_BITS );
104
105       return 0;
106  }
```

- Lines 1 through 3 include the standard header files required before using the I/O and string manipulation functions from the runtime library.

- Lines 5 through 7 define a few constant values. NUM_DIGITS is the number of characters (the digits 0–9) that will have graphical representations. NUM_ROWS is the number of rows of pixels that constitute each digit. NUM_BORDER_ROWS is the number of blank "filler" rows of pixels that will be displayed above and below the graphical digits.

- Lines 9 through 30 define and initialize a two-dimensional array containing the pixel patterns for each of the 10 (NUM_DIGITS) decimal digits that may appear in the counter graphic. Each digit is 8 pixels wide and 10 pixels (NUM_ROWS) high. The values representing the rows of pixels that compose each individual digit are enclosed within separate braces.

  These values are coded in hexadecimal base-16 format. Hexadecimal, or "hex," values are preceded with '0x' to indicate that they are base-16 values. The decimal base-10 numbers that you are used to seeing are composed of digits in the range 0–9. Hex numbers include the digits 0–9 representing the corresponding decimal values, plus the digits A–F. "A" represents the decimal value 10, "B" equals 11, and so on with "F" equal to decimal 15. Hexadecimal is simply a more compact way of representing binary data. The individual pixels of an XBM graphic are either black or transparent. This means that only one bit of storage is required for each pixel. Because each digit in our graphic is eight pixels wide, the individual row values fit nicely into the char data type, which is eight bits in size, or one byte. The unsigned qualifier ensures that all eight bits are available for data representation with none reserved to indicate the negative sign.

- Lines 32 through 42 define the function PrintBorderRows, which outputs blank rows that pad the top and bottom of the graphic. Line 32 declares the function to accept two integer-type variables, width and invert_bits. The width parameter specifies the number of digits to be displayed in the graphic. The invert_bits parameter instructs this function to display the blank rows as either transparent or solid. Line 34 defines a couple of local integer-type variables, row and i.

- Lines 36 through 41 compose a for loop that will execute once for each row. Recall that the *for* statement may include three expressions to control loop iteration:

```
for ( init-expression ; cond-expression ; mod-expression )
```

- The *for* statement on line 36 sets the value of row to a starting value of 0 in the initializing expression row = 0. The conditional expression row < NUM_BORDER_ROWS determines whether the loop should execute the next iteration by checking to see if the current value of row is less than the value of NUM_BORDER_ROWS.

  NUM_BORDER_ROWS is a constant, "2," defined on line 7. The modifying expression row++ increments the controlling variable row after each iteration, which affects the conditional expression.

- Line 37 is another for loop nested within the loop body started on line 36. This loop will iterate for the number of times specified by the function parameter width and uses another local variable i to control loop execution. Because the body of this loop consists of only the single statement on line 38, it is not necessary to enclose it within braces.

- Line 38 uses the printf function to output the actual pixel values. Pixel values in the XBM format are encoded in hexadecimal format just like hex values in C. The format specifier "0x%02x, " includes the literal text "0x" and ", " in addition to the hex formatting code "x." The "02" between the percent sign and the "x" are optional fields that provide additional formatting information. The "2" specifies the minimum number of characters that will be output. The "0" specifies that leading zeros will be added as necessary to reach the minimum field width of 2. For example, a value of 3 would be formatted into "03," while a decimal value of 32 would be formatted into "20."

The actual value passed to printf for formatting is the result of the conditional operator. Recall that the conditional operator consists of a logical expression followed a question mark "?" and two values separated by a colon ":". If the first expression is true, then the result of this operator is the first value, which is located between the "?" and the ":". Otherwise, the result is the second value, which is found after the ":". In this case the conditional expression consists of only the variable invert_bits. Remember that in C, any nonzero value is evaluated as "true" in a logical expression and 0 evaluates to "false." So, if the value of invert_bits is nonzero, the hexadecimal value "ff" (equivalent to the decimal value 255) is passed to printf; otherwise, a value of 0 is used.

- Line 40 outputs a newline character at the end of each row. Line 41 closes the for loop body, which began on line 36, and line 42 closes the PrintBorderRows function body. To recap, this function outputs a row of blank or solid pixels for the width of each digit in the output graphic and repeats for each row in the border.
- Line 44 begins definition of the function PrintDigits, which outputs the pixel patterns that represent the digits of the counter value. This function accepts two parameters. The first parameter, pdigits, is a pointer that points to the character string array containing the digit characters. The const modifier prevents this function from inadvertently modifying the digit string through this pointer. The second parameter invert_bits is an integer-type value that specifies whether to invert the pixel patterns. The pixel pattern values in the digit_bits array will display black digits over a transparent background. If the invert_bits parameter is nonzero, these pixel values will be inverted so that the background is black and the digits are transparent. This produces an image that looks like the odometer on a car's dashboard.
- Line 46 declares and initializes the integer-type variable len, which represents the number of characters in the string of digits. This variable is initialized with the return value from the strlen function. The strlen function is one of many string manipulation routines in the runtime library and is declared in the include file

string.h. This function returns the length of a character string by counting the number of characters before the terminating null (0) character. Line 47 declares two more integer-type variables that will be used in this function.

- Line 49 prints the MIME header that lets a Web browser know how to interpret the data that follows. The MIME type for XBM graphics is "image/x-xbitmap." Again, note the two newline characters required to separate the headers from the document body. The http server will generate an error when attempting to run your CGI program if you forget the extra newline character after the last header.
- The statement split across lines 50 and 51 prints lines separated by a new-line character to describe the width and height of the XBM graphic. One of the properties of the XBM format is that it is usable as C source code. The width and height are formatted to look like C #define statements. Each digit will be eight pixels wide, so the width of the entire graphic is the number of digits times eight. For aesthetics, the program adds extra rows above and below the graphic digits. The height of the graphic will be the number of rows composing the digits (NUM_ROWS) plus the number of border rows (NUM_BORDER_ROWS) times two (above and below).
- Line 52 prints a line that indicates that the pixel patterns will follow. This line looks like the beginning of a C array declaration, including the opening brace.
- Line 54 calls the previously defined PrintBorderRows function to output the blank filler rows above the digits. The first parameter passed is the variable len, which contains the number of characters (digits) that will appear in the output graphic. The second parameter is the value that was passed into this function (PrintDigits), which indicates whether to invert the pixel values.
- Line 56 begins a for loop that will execute once for each whole row of pixels to be output. The variable row will contain the current row number for each iteration.
- Line 57 begins a nested for loop that will execute for each digit within the current row. Line 58 declares the local variable digit_value and initializes it to the numeric value of the current digit. Local variables may be declared at the beginning of any block enclosed in braces. This variable is visible and exists only with this statement block, the body of the for statement that began on line 57. The current digit character pdigits[digit] is converted to its numeric equivalent

by subtracting the ASCII value of the zero digit. For example, assume that the current digit character is "3." The ASCII value of the character "3" is 51, and the ASCII value of the character "0" is 48. Subtracting 48 from 51 yields the value 3, the numeric value indicated by the character "3." This statement assumes that the pdigits array contains only numeric characters.

- Line 59 declares and initializes another local variable bits to hold the pixel bits for the current row of the current digit. This variable is of the same type, unsigned char, as the digit_bits array. The value of the loop counter variable row and the previously calculated digit number digit_value are used as indices into the digit_bits array.
- Line 60 begins an *if* statement that will execute only if the value of the invert_bits parameter is nonzero. The body of this statement on line 61 uses the bitwise complement operator to reverse the value of all bits in the bits variable.
- Line 63 outputs the pattern of bits for the current row of the current digit, which is contained in the bits variable. Line 64 closes the inner for loop that began on line 57.
- Line 65 prints a newline character at the end of each row. Because this statement appears outside the inner loop in lines 57 through 64, it is executed only once per iteration of the outer loop, which began on line 56. Line 66 closes the outer loop.
- Line 68 calls the PrintBorderRows function a second time to output the blank filler rows below the graphic digits. Line 70 prints the ending line of the XBM graphic. This output contains a brace to match the one generated by line 52. Line 71 closes the body of this function.
- Line 73 begins definition of the function GetCount, which maintains the running counter value in a file. This function opens the counter data file, reads the current counter value, updates this value and writes it back to the file, then closes the data file. This function does not accept any parameters but returns an unsigned long integer-type value, which indicates the updated counter value. The unsigned long data type enables this program to handle over 4 billion hits.
- Line 75 declares a local variable to hold the counter value and initializes it with a value of 0. Because the Web browser will be expecting only a graphical image from this program, we can't output any textual error messages to describe any errors encountered while attempting to update the data file. If this function

encounters any errors, it will return the value 0 to indicate that something went wrong. Line 76 declares a pointer variable for the FILE data type. This variable will be used to operate on the counter data file.

- Line 77 declares a pointer that will point to the name of the data file. The const modifier specifies that this pointer cannot modify the value to which it points. Line 79 attempts to obtain the name of the data file from the CGI environment variable named "PATH_TRANSLATED." The http server will create this environment variable for CGI programs if the URL used to access the program contains "extra path information." This information is found after the name of the CGI program but before any CGI parameters.

  For example, the URL http://www.my-domain.com/cgi-bin/xbmcount.cgi/mydir/counter.dat contains the extra path information "/mydir/counter.dat" after the program name "xbmcount.cgi." The server will translate this virtual path information into a fully qualified path appropriate for local access to the file on your system. The counter data file must reside in a directory somewhere under the "document root" directory on your server for this scheme to work. For example, if the document root directory on your server is "/web/htdocs" (or "c:\web\htdocs"), then the extra path information "/mydir/counter.dat" would be translated to /web/htdocs/mydir/counter.dat (or "c:\web\htdocs\mydir\counter.dat") and placed in the "PATH_TRANSLATED" environment variable.

  The getenv routine in the runtime library searches the environment for a variable with the specified name and, if found, returns a pointer to its value. If no variable is found for the requested name, the "NULL" value is returned. NULL is most often defined to be 0 in one of the standard header files. This is an address that is not valid, commonly used to indicate that an operation failed.

- Line 80 checks the pointer variable pname to see if getenv returned NULL. If pname is not NULL, the following statement block is executed; otherwise, it is skipped and the GetCount function will return a counter value of 0.

- Line 81 opens the counter data file via the fopen routine in the runtime library. The fopen routine accepts two character string parameters, which specify the name of the file and the "access mode." The access mode determines the types of operations you may perform on this file. Common mode values recognized by fopen are listed in Table 17.1.

Table 17.1 Common Mode Values Recognized by fopen

Mode	Description
r	Read-only access. The file must already exist.
w	Creates a new file, allowing write access. Any existing file will be overwritten.
a	Appends to an existing file, or creates a new file, allowing write access. Existing data is preserved, and new data is added at the end of the file.
r+	Both read and write access are allowed. As with "r" the file must already exist.
w+	Same as "w"; allows additional read access.
a+	Same as "a"; allows read access as well.

This fopen call on line 81 requests read/write access with the "r+" mode. The fopen function returns a FILE pointer, which is assigned to the counter_file local pointer variable for further use. The fopen call will fail by returning a value of NULL if the file cannot be found or is inaccessible by the user that the http server runs as. You will probably need to explicitly set the permissions for your counter data files so that they are accessible by the http server user.

- Line 82 checks this pointer to see if the fopen call succeeded. If the counter_file pointer is not NULL, then the following statement block is executed; otherwise, it is skipped and the function will return a counter value of 0.
- Line 83 reads the current counter value. The fscanf function reads data from a file according to a format string. This function is similar to printf except that instead of outputting variables according to the format string, fscanf inputs values to variables using the format string. For each format code found in the format string, fscanf attempts to read in a variable of the specified type.

The first parameter in the fscanf call on line 83 is the file pointer previously obtained from the fopen call. The second parameter is the format string, and it specifies the "%lu" format to input an unsigned long data type. The 'l' in this format code explicitly modifies the unsigned 'u' type to handle a long unsigned variable. The third parameter is the address of the variable count, which will receive the input value.

The fscanf function returns the number of items that were successfully read in. Line 83 tests this return value to ensure that the counter value was successfully read. If fscanf returns 0, the following statement block is skipped, the file is closed, and the GetCount function will return a counter value of 0.

- Line 84 resets the file's "current position" back to the beginning of the file. The current position in a file is the point at which the next read or write operation will take place. When a file is first opened, its current position is set to the beginning of the file (unless opened with "a" or "a+", in which case the current position will be at the end of the file). After reading the counter value from the file in the previous statement, the current file position was moved past the characters composing the counter value. The rewind call is necessary to reset the current position back to the beginning of the file before updating the counter value in the next statement. The only parameter to rewind is the file pointer obtained from fopen.

- Line 85 writes the incremented counter value back to the file. The fprintf function operates similarly to printf except that the formatted output is directed to a specific file. The first parameter is a file pointer, and the format string is in the second parameter. Note that the count variable is incremented with the prefix increment operator. This means that count will be incremented before its value is passed to fprintf to update the data file.

- Line 86 closes the *if* statement block from line 83.

- Line 87 closes the file. The fclose function ensures that any changes made to the file are committed and that system resources associated with the file are released. Note that fclose, as well as the other file operations in this function, is called only if the fopen call succeeds. Also note that even if the fscanf call should fail for some reason, fclose will still be called.

- Line 88 closes the *if* statement that began on line 82, and line 89 closes the *if* statement from line 80. Line 91 returns the counter value that is stored in the local count variable. If all went well, count will contain the updated counter value; otherwise, it will have the value of 0 with which it was initialized.

- Line 92 closes the body of the GetCount function. Line 94 defines another constant value named INVERT_BITS. Set this value to 0 for black digits over a transparent background. Define it to a nonzero value for a graphic with a black background and transparent digits.

- Line 96 begins the definition of the main function. Line 98 defines a character array digits of 11 elements. This array will hold the individual digits of the counter value. Line 99 defines a local variable counter_value to hold the counter value. The digits array is large enough to contain all of the digits of the maximum unsigned long value, over 4 billion, plus a terminating null character.

- Line 101 invokes the previously defined GetCount function to obtain the updated counter value and assigns this value to the variable counter_value.

- Line 102 formats the value of counter_value into the digits character string using the sprintf function from the runtime library. This function is nearly identical to the fprintf function used in GetCount; the only difference is that sprintf directs its output to a character string while the output of fprintf is sent to a file. The first parameter to sprintf is the address of a character array to receive the formatted output. The format string is in the second parameter, with any values to be formatted in the third and subsequent parameters. The format string used here, "%06lu", formats an unsigned long value to a minimum of six characters, adding leading zeros as necessary to reach six digits. You are free to change this format to use fewer or more digits. Recall that the PrintDigits function uses the strlen function to determine the actual number of digits used without making any assumptions about the width of the graphic.

- Line 103 invokes the previously defined PrintDigits function to convert the character string obtained in the previous statement to an X Bitmap. Line 105 terminates the main function, as well as the program, and returns a value of 0 to the operating system. The last line of this file closes the main function.

The following command line compiles this program with gcc, the GNU compiler:

```
gcc xbmcount.c -o xbmcount.cgi
```

This command specifies an extension of ".cgi," which some servers may require. Ask your system administrator or ISP what is appropriate for your server. You must use the extension ".exe" on MS-DOS or Windows platforms.

The HTML file xbmcount.html demonstrates usage:

```
<HTML>

<HEAD>
<TITLE>XBM Graphic Counter</TITLE>
</HEAD>
```

```
6
7      <BODY bgcolor="#99CCFF">
8      <H1>XBM Graphic Counter</H1><HR><P>
9
10     You are visitor number
11
12     <IMG src=
13      "http://your-server.com/cgi-bin/xbmcount.cgi/your-dir/ctr.dat"
14      align="bottom"><P>
15
16     </BODY>
17
18     </HTML>
```

Graphic counters are displayed in an HTML document using an <IMG> tag. Lines 12 through 14 illustrate this use. You will have to modify the URL shown on line 13 to refer to your server, the location of this program ("/cgi-bin/xbmcount.cgi" shown here), and the location of the counter data file ("/your-dir/ctr.dat" shown here) on your server.

CGI Variable Parsing Examples

This program prints the field values submitted from an example HTML form. As discussed in Chapter 5, field values are normally submitted to a CGI program via either the http "POST" or "GET" method. This program presents a set of reusable functions for finding and parsing CGI form variables. These functions make it easier for you to write programs that handle field values submitted by HTML forms.

Utility Functions Header

Unlike the previous programs, this one is built from multiple source files. The first source file cgiutil.h contains constant definitions and function prototypes for the CGI utility functions:

```
#define METHOD_GET 1
#define METHOD_POST 2

const char *cgiGetEnv( const char *pname,
     const char *pdefault );

int cgiRequestMethod( const char *method_type );
```

```
 8
 9      int cgiGetInput( char *buffer, int max_buffer );
10
11      int cgiFindVar( const char *cgi_input,
  const char *var_name,
12              char *value, int value_size );
13
14      int cgiGetNextVar( const char *cgi_input,
  char *var_name,
15      int name_size, char *value, int value_size );
```

- Lines 1 and 2 define constant values representing the two http methods, "GET" and "POST." The remaining lines are prototypes for the functions that are available in the source file cgiutil.c. Prototypes do not define the body of the function; they specify only the number and types of parameters and return value. This enables the compiler to verify that these functions are called correctly by other source files. Note that prototypes are terminated with a semicolon. The declarations for the functions cgiGetEnv, cgiFindVar, and cgiGetNextVar are split across two lines to fit on the page.

Utility Functions

The source file cgiutil.c contains the definitions of these functions:

```
#include <ctype.h>
#include <stdio.h>
#include <stdlib.h>
#include <string.h>

#include "cgiutil.h"

#define VALUE_DELIM '='
#define CGIVAR_DELIM '&'

int hexvalue( char ch )
{
     return ( ch >= 'A' ?
          ( toupper( ch ) - 'A' ) + 10 : ( ch - '0' ) );
}

char decode( char hex_digit1, char hex_digit2 )
{
     int decoded_char;

     decoded_char = hexvalue( hex_digit1 );
```

```
        decoded_char *= 16;
        decoded_char += hexvalue( hex_digit2 );
        return (char)decoded_char;
}

int scanValue( const char src[], char dest[],
        int dest_size )
{
        int src_pos = 0;
        int dest_pos = 0;
        int done = 0;

        while(!done && src[src_pos] && dest_pos < dest_size - 1 ){
                switch( src[src_pos] ) {
                        case '%':
                                if( src_pos < (int)( strlen( src ) - 2 ) ) {
                                        dest[dest_pos++] = decode( src[src_pos + 1],
                                                src[src_pos + 2] );

                                        src_pos += 3;
                                }
                                else
                                        dest[dest_pos++] = src[src_pos++];
                                break;

                        case '+':
                                dest[dest_pos++] = ' ';
                                src_pos++;
                                break;

                        case VALUE_DELIM:
                        case CGIVAR_DELIM:
                                done = 1;
                                break;

                        default:
                                dest[dest_pos++] = src[src_pos++];
                }
        }
        dest[dest_pos] = '\0';
        return src_pos;
}

const char *cgiGetEnv( const char *pname,
        const char *pdefault )
{
        char *presult = getenv( pname );
```

```
        if( presult != NULL )
            return presult;
        else
            return pdefault;
    }

    int cgiRequestMethod( const char *method_type )
    {
        return !strcmp( cgiGetEnv( "REQUEST_METHOD", "" ),
            method_type );
    }

    int cgiGetInput( char buffer[], int buffer_size )
    {
        int method_type = 0;

        buffer[0] = '\0';

        if( cgiRequestMethod( "GET" ) ) {
            strncpy( buffer, cgiGetEnv("QUERY_STRING", ""),
                buffer_size );

            buffer[buffer_size - 1] = '\0';
            method_type = METHOD_GET;
        }
        else if( cgiRequestMethod( "POST" ) ) {
            int content_len = atoi(
                cgiGetEnv( "CONTENT_LENGTH", "0") );

            if( ( content_len > 0 ) &&
                ( content_len < buffer_size ) ) {

                fread( buffer, 1, content_len, stdin );
                buffer[content_len] = '\0';
                method_type = METHOD_POST;
            }
        }
        return method_type;
    }

    int cgiFindVar( const char *cgi_input,
      const char *var_name,
        char *value, int value_size )
    {
        char *pname_start = strstr( cgi_input, var_name );

        while( pname_start != NULL ) {
```

```
            if( VALUE_DELIM ==
                *( pname_start + strlen( var_name ) ) ) {

                if( pname_start != cgi_input ) {
                    if( *( pname_start - 1 ) != CGIVAR_DELIM ) {
                        pname_start = strstr(
                            pname_start + strlen( var_name ),
                            var_name );

                        continue;
                    }
                }

                scanValue( pname_start + strlen( var_name ) + 1,
                    value, value_size );

                return strlen( value );
            }
            else
                pname_start = strstr( pname_start +
                    strlen( var_name ), var_name );
        }
        return 0;
}

int cgiGetNextVar( const char *cgi_input,
char *var_name,
        int name_size, char *value, int value_size )
{
        static const char *pnextparm = NULL;
        const char *p = cgi_input ? cgi_input : pnextparm;

        if( p != NULL ) {
            p += scanValue( p, var_name, name_size );

            if( VALUE_DELIM == *p ) {
                p++;
                p += scanValue( p, value, value_size );
            }
            else
                *value = '\0';

            if( *p )
                pnextparm = ++p;
            else
                pnextparm = NULL;
```

```
160         }
161         else {
162              *var_name = '\0';
163              *value = '\0';
164         }
165         return strlen( var_name );
166    }
```

- Lines 1 through 4 include header files for the runtime library functions used in this source file. Line 6 includes the file containing the prototypes for the routines in this file. This is not necessary, but it is a "defensive" programming technique. Defensive programming means taking a few additional steps to avert possible mistakes. Including the prototypes in this file guarantees that the prototypes will stay in sync with their accompanying function bodies because the compiler will complain if they do not match.

- Lines 8 and 9 define constant values for the CGI variable and name/value delimiting characters. Recall from Chapter 5 that CGI variable names and their values are separated by an equal sign '=', and these name=value pairs are separated by ampersands '&'. For example:

  ```
  city=Kearsarge&state=CA
  ```

  This input contains two variables, city and state with the respective values Kearsarge and CA.

- Lines 11 through 15 define a function named hexvalue. This function and the two following it are used only within this source file and are not prototyped in cgiutil.h. This function computes the numeric value of a single hexadecimal digit character. The body of this function consists of a single return statement split across lines 13 and 14. A conditional expression is used to handle either an alphabetic or numeric hexadecimal digit.

  If the character parameter ch is greater than "A" it represents a decimal value between 10 and 15. The toupper function from the runtime library converts a single character to uppercase if it is currently lowercase. The ASCII value of the character "A" is subtracted to obtain the ordinal value of this digit. This is the position of this digit within the set of alpha hex digits representing values greater than 10. Adding 10 translates this to the appropriate decimal value. If ch is less than "A" it is assumed to be a numeric digit and is converted as such.

- Lines 17 through 25 define the function decode, which decodes a pair of hex digits. Web browsers will encode many nonalphanumeric characters into a pair of hexadecimal digits preceded with a percent sign before submission to the server. Each individual digit is decoded using the previously defined hexvalue function.
- Line 19 defines a local variable decoded_char to hold the value of the decoded digits. Line 21 assigns the value of the first parameter hex_digit1 to decoded_char variable. Line 22 multiplies this value by 16, the numbering base of hexadecimal numbers. Line 23 adds the value of the second digit hex_digit2 to this value.
- Line 24 returns the value of the two hex digits accumulated in the decoded_char variable. The "(char)" that appears before the variable name is a "type-cast." Type-casting coerces a value to a different data type. Because decoded_char was declared as an integer-type variable, the type-cast is necessary to convert it back to the char type that this function has been declared to return. If decoded_char were to contain a value greater than 127 (the maximum value that a signed char can contain) the excess would be lost.
- Lines 27 through 63 define the scanValue function that parses CGI variable names or values. This function uses the previous decode function to copy decoded input from the src parameter to the dest parameter. For convenience, these parameters are declared as arrays instead of pointers as this function will use array indexing to manipulate them. The dest_size parameter specifies the maximum number of characters that can be safely copied to the dest parameter.
- Lines 30 through 32 define a few local variables. The src_pos variable indicates the current position within the src input array, and dest_pos is the current position within the dest output array. The done variable will be set to a nonzero value to indicate when processing is complete.
- Line 34 begins the main loop of this function. This loop will iterate while the done variable is not set to nonzero, the current input character is not a null character, and the current position within the output is less than the size of the output array. The size of the output array is reduced by one character in this comparison to leave room for the terminating null.
- Line 35 begins a switch statement that branches on the value of the current input character. If the current character is a "%" then execution continues on

line 37. If the current character is a "+" then control is transferred directly to line 48. If the current character is either one of the delimiting characters then execution passes to line 54. If none of the above conditions are true control is transferred to line 58.

- Line 37 begins processing of hexadecimal input. Hex input is preceded by a percent sign "%". This statement first checks to ensure that the input is long enough to contain two more characters by comparing the current position to the length of the input. If so, the following two characters of the input array are passed to the decode function on lines 38 and 39. The decoded result is assigned to the current position with the output array before incrementing the output position with the postfix increment operator "++". Line 41 advances the current position of the input array by three elements to skip over the "%" and the two hex digits that were just processed.

- Lines 43 and 44 handle the unlikely situation that a "%" was encountered, but the input is not long enough to contain the two hex digits that should follow. Line 44 simply copies the current input character to the output array and advances the current position within both arrays. The *break* statement on line 45 transfers control out of the *switch* statement to the next statement. Since the *switch* is the only statement in the while loop body, control passes back to the *while* statement on line 34 for the next iteration.

- Line 48 begins processing of any plus signs "+" encountered in the input array. Plus signs are the encoded equivalent of spaces " ". Line 48 assigns a blank character to the output array and advances the current position. Line 49 advances the current position of the input array to skip past this character. Line 50 terminates the *switch* statement and transfers control back to the *while* statement on line 34 for the next iteration.

- Line 54 handles the presence of either of the delimiting characters in the input. This function doesn't know or care whether it was called to parse a name or a value. It stops when it encounters either delimiter. With no *break* statement after line 52, control falls through to the next case label on line 53. Either delimiting character indicates the end of the current name or value, so processing should terminate at this point. Line 54 sets the done variable to a nonzero value. This signals the while loop on line 34 to stop iterating.

- Line 58 handles all other characters by simply copying the current input character to the output array and advancing the current position within both arrays.

The *while* statement on line 34 will terminate if the end of the input string is reached without encountering any delimiting characters. This loop will also terminate if the output array is filled to capacity.

- Line 61 adds the terminating null character to the output string. Line 62 returns the number of input characters processed. Lines 65 through 73 define the function cgiGetEnv for retrieving environment variables. This function is a safer alternative to the runtime library function getenv. The getenv function returns a NULL pointer if the requested environment variable is not found. A NULL pointer is a pointer containing the NULL value. Because the NULL value is an invalid address, you must remember to check the return value of getenv to avoid using a NULL pointer. The cgiGetEnv function relieves you of this burden by allowing you to specify an alternate value to return if the desired environment variable cannot be found.

  This function accepts two character string parameters. The pname parameter is the name of the environment variable whose value you wish to retrieve. The pdefault parameter specifies a default value to return if the requested environment variable is not found.

- Line 68 uses the getenv function to search for the requested environment variable. The next line checks the value returned from getenv to see if it is NULL. If this value is not NULL, the return value from getenv is returned on line 70. Otherwise, the pdefault parameter is returned on line 72.

- Lines 75 through 79 define the cgiRequestMethod method. This function returns true (nonzero) if the current request method matches the method_type parameter. This enables you to easily determine if a specific http method was used to access your program.

- Line 77 uses the previously defined cgiGetEnv function to get the value of the CGI environment variable "REQUEST_METHOD." The second parameter to cgiGetEnv is the value to return if "REQUEST_METHOD" is not found; in this case it is the empty string "".

  The strcmp function compares two null-terminated character strings. If the strings are equal, strcmp returns 0. If the first parameter is "less than" the second parameter, strcmp returns a value less than 0. Otherwise, the first parameter must be "greater than" the second parameter and a value greater than 0 is returned. The return statement on line 77 compares the value of the

"REQUEST_METHOD" variable obtained by cgiGetEnv with the input parameter method_type. The logical NOT operator ! is used to reverse the value returned by strcmp so that the cgiRequestMethod function returns true if the two strings are equal.

- Lines 81 through 107 define the function cgiGetInput, which gets the CGI input from the location appropriate for the http request method used. Recall from Chapter 5 that CGI input is found in the "QUERY_STRING" environment variable when the "GET" method is used and read from input when the "POST" method is used. The buffer parameter will be filled with all of the form field values in their encoded format. The buffer_size parameter specifies the size of the buffer array so that it is not overfilled.
- Line 83 defines a local integer-type variable method_type to indicate the request method. Line 85 sets buffer to an empty string by placing a null character at the beginning of the string. If no CGI input is found, buffer will appear empty to the caller upon return from this function.
- Line 87 uses the previously defined cgiRequestMethod function to determine if the program was invoked with the http "GET" method. If so, lines 88 through 92 copy CGI input from the "QUERY_STRING" CGI environment variable.
- Lines 88 and 89 use the strncpy function from the runtime library to copy the value of the "QUERY_STRING" environment variable to the buffer parameter. The first parameter to strncpy is the "destination" location to receive the copied characters. The second parameter specifies the "source" location to copy from. The third parameter specifies the maximum number of characters to copy. The strncpy function copies characters up to the terminating null in the source string or the number of characters specified, whichever comes first. If the maximum number of characters is reached, strncpy does not place a terminating null at the end of the destination string. Line 91 anticipates this by unconditionally placing a null in the last position of the buffer array to ensure that this string is always properly terminated.
- Line 92 sets the method_type variable to indicate that the "GET" method was used.
- If the "GET" method was not used, line 94 checks for the "POST" method. If so, lines 95 through 104 read the appropriate number of characters from input into the buffer array.

- The statement split across lines 95 and 96 converts the value of the "CONTENT_LENGTH" environment variable to its numeric value. The atoi function converts a string of ASCII digits to an integer value. Note that the default parameter to cgiGetEnv is 0 so that the atoi function will execute properly in the unlikely situation that "CONTENT_LENGTH" is not found.
- The *if* statement on lines 98 and 99 checks to see if the content length is greater than 0 and less than the size of the buffer array. If so, lines 101 through 103 read the input.
- The fread function on line 101 reads the number of characters indicated by content_len into the buffer array. The last parameter, stdin, specifies which file to read from. stdin is one of a couple of files automatically opened when a C program starts up; you do not explicitly open this file. The stdin file is usually associated with the keyboard, but the http server redirects it when running a CGI program. The fread function does not terminate the input with a null character, so this is done on line 102.
- Line 103 sets the method_type variable to indicate that the "POST" method was used.
- Line 106 returns the value of the method_type variable to indicate which http method was used to submit the form variables.
- Lines 109 through 131 define a function named cgiFindVar. This function searches for a specific form variable contained in a buffer filled with CGI input and retrieves its value. The cgi_input parameter points to the input obtained by the preceding cgiGetInput function. The var_name parameter specifies the name of the requested CGI variable. The value parameter will receive the decoded value of the requested variable if found, and value_size specifies the size of the array to which that value points.
- Line 112 uses the library function strstr to search for the requested name. The strstr function searches for a character string within another string. The first parameter is the character string to search, and the second parameter is the string to search for. If found, strstr returns a pointer to the location of the string within the first parameter; otherwise, it returns NULL. This pointer is saved in the local variable pname_start.

- Line 114 begins a while loop that will iterate as long as the requested name is found within the CGI buffer. The body of this loop checks to see if the name found is a proper CGI variable name. If it is not, the search is performed again until a proper name is found or until the search fails. If the requested name is found, the pname_start variable will not be NULL.

- The statement on lines 115 and 116 checks to see if the character following this name is the value delimiting character ("=") that separates a CGI variable's name from its associated value. If so, the statement block on lines 116 through 130 is executed. If not, then **strstr** found an occurrence of the requested name that is not a proper variable name. The following statement block is skipped and cgi_input will be searched again.

- Line 116 calculates the address of the character that immediately follows the name. The length of the name obtained from the strlen function is added to the address at which the name begins. The result of this operation is an address. This expression is parenthesized to ensure that it is evaluated before the dereferencing operator "*" is applied to it. The dereference operator returns the character at the calculated address.

- Line 115 uses another defensive programming technique to avoid mistaking the assignment operator "=" for the equality operator "==." When comparing two values for equality, the order of the values does not matter. Placing a constant value on the left side will cause the compiler will complain if you inadvertently use the assignment operator "=" in place of the equality operator "==." You cannot assign another value to a constant after it has been defined.

- Line 118 checks to see if the name that was found starts at the beginning of the cgi_input buffer. Because we previously checked the pname_start pointer to ensure that it was not NULL, it is safe to assume that it points to a location at the beginning of or further in the cgi_input buffer. If the two addresses are the same, then the name was found at the beginning of the buffer. In this case it must be a valid CGI variable name because it is followed by the proper delimiting character, as determined in the previous statement. If the addresses are not equal, then the name occurs somewhere later in the buffer and the statement block on lines 119 through 125 is necessary to determine whether this name is a proper CGI variable name.

- Line 119 tests the character immediately preceding the name to see if it is the CGI variable delimiting character ("&") that separates CGI variables from each other. This statement first calculates the address of the character preceding the pname_start pointer by subtracting 1 from it. This expression is also parenthesized to ensure that it is evaluated before the dereferencing operator is applied to it. The dereference operator returns the character at the specified address, which is then compared to the delimiting character. If this character is not a delimiter, then the name that was found occurs either within a variable value or another larger name. In this case, the statement block on lines 120 through 124 performs another search and returns to the top of the while loop.

- The statement spread across lines 120 through 122 assigns the address of the next occurrence of the requested name to the pname_start pointer variable. The strstr function is used again, but this time the search begins after the result of the last search. The starting address is computed by adding the length of the requested name to the address at which it was last found. The *continue* statement on line 124 skips the remainder of the loop body and transfers control back to the *while* statement on line 114.

- Line 128 fetches the value of the requested variable from the cgi_input buffer. We can reach this point only if the preceding statements determined that the variable name that was found is followed by a value delimiting character and starts at the beginning of the cgi_input buffer or is preceded by a CGI variable delimiter. The previously defined scanValue function is used to decode and copy the value of this CGI variable to the value parameter. The first parameter to scanValue is the address at which to begin processing. This address is computed by adding the length of the name to the starting address of the name. This address is incremented by an additional byte to get past the delimiting character. The second and third parameters specify the location to receive the decoded input and the amount of space allocated to hold this value. These values were passed into the cgiFindVar function.

- Line 131 exits this function and returns the CGI value's length via the strlen function. If the value is empty, this statement will return 0.

- The else on line 133 will execute if the variable name that was found is not followed by the appropriate delimiting character, as tested on line 115. In this case, the statement on lines 134 and 135 performs another search in the same manner as line 120. Control then passes back to the top of the while loop on line 114.

- Line 137 returns a value of 0 to indicate that the requested CGI variable could not be found. This statement will be reached only after the while loop beginning on line 114 terminates normally. Line 131 terminates the loop prematurely and exits this function if the variable was successfully located.
- Lines 140 through 166 compose the last utility function in this source file, cgiGetNextVar. This function may be called repeatedly to sequentially retrieve each CGI variable's name and value. Like the previous cgiFindVar function, the first parameter cgi_input contains the CGI input retrieved by the cgiGetInput. The second parameter var_name specifies the location to receive the variable's name. The third parameter name_size specifies the size of this space. The fourth parameter value receives the variable's value, and the value_size specifies the size of this space.
- Line 143 defines a static local pointer variable to remember the last CGI variable processed. Recall that the static keyword specifies that a local variable retains its value between function calls and exists for the duration of the program.
- Line 144 defines a local pointer variable "p" that points to the next CGI variable to be processed. The statement uses the conditional operator to initialize this variable with one of two possible values. If the cgi_input parameter is not NULL, then this value is used. Otherwise, the pointer p is initialized with the previously defined pnextparm pointer. The idea here is that the first CGI variable will be obtained by calling this function with the address of a CGI input buffer in the first parameter. Subsequent calls to this function will pass NULL in place of this buffer. This way the function will use the address remembered in the pnextparm variable to begin processing where it stopped after the previous invocation.
- Line 146 tests the pointer to ensure that it is not NULL. After the last CGI variable has been parsed, pnextparm will be set to NULL to indicate that there is no more input. The following statement block on lines 147 through 160 retrieves the next variable if there is more input.
- Line 147 utilizes the previously defined scanValue function to retrieve the name of the next variable. The current address stored in the pointer p is passed to

scanValue to specify the location at which to begin parsing the variable's name. The var_name parameter is passed to scanValue to receive the variable name, and the name_size parameter is passed to specify the maximum number of characters to store in var_name. The scanValue function returns the number of input characters processed. This value is used to increment the pointer p so that it now points to the first character following the CGI variable name.

- Line 149 checks this character to see if it is the value delimiting character ("="). If so, the variable's value follows. The statement block on lines 150 to 152 retrieves this value.
- Line 150 increments the pointer p past the delimiter. Line 151 calls scanValue again to retrieve the CGI variable's value and increments the pointer p by the number of input characters processed.
- Line 154 sets the CGI variable's value to an empty string if no value was found following the variable name.
- Line 156 checks to see if there is any input left after the last name or value was parsed. After scanValue processes the last name or value, p will point to the terminating null character in the CGI input buffer. If there is more input left to process, p points the CGI variable delimiting character. Line 157 sets the static pnextparm pointer variable to point to the next input character. The current location is first incremented to skip past the delimiting character. The next time this function is called with a NULL cgi_input parameter, it can process the next CGI variable residing at the location stored in pnextparm.
- If there is no more input, line 159 sets pnextparm to NULL. If the cgi_input parameter and pnextparm variable are both NULL, lines 162 and 163 set both the name and value to empty strings.
- The last line, line 165, returns the length of the variable's name to indicate whether a variable was found.

Simple Form Variable Processor

This short program utilizes the functions presented earlier to process a simple HTML form. This program expects the HTML form to contain a few specific elements: an input line named "NAME," a checkbox named "CHKBOX," and a textarea named "COMMENTS." As you will see, the CGI utility functions make it relatively easy to process form variables. The source for this program is in the file formdump.c:

```
#include <stdio.h>

#include "cgiutil.h"

#define BUFFER_SIZE 1000
#define TITLE "Form Variables"

int main()
{
    char input_buf[BUFFER_SIZE], value_buf[BUFFER_SIZE];

    printf( "Content-type: text/html\n\n" );
    printf( "<HTML><HEAD><TITLE>%s</TITLE></HEAD>\n",
        TITLE );
    printf( "<BODY><H1>%s</H1><HR><P>\n<PRE>", TITLE );

    if( cgiGetInput( input_buf, BUFFER_SIZE ) ) {

        printf( "Your name is " );
        if( cgiFindVar( input_buf, "NAME", value_buf,
            BUFFER_SIZE ) )
            printf( "<B>%s</B>.\n", value_buf );
        else
            printf( "<B>missing</B>.\n" );

        printf( "\nThe checkbox is " );
        if( cgiFindVar( input_buf, "CHKBOX", value_buf,
            BUFFER_SIZE ) )
            printf( "<B>checked</B>.\n" );
        else
            printf( "<B>not checked</B>.\n" );

        if( cgiFindVar( input_buf, "COMMENT", value_buf,
            BUFFER_SIZE ) )
            printf( "\n%s:\n<B>%s</B>\n",
                "You entered the following comments",
                value_buf );
        else
            printf( "\nNo comments were found.\n" );
    }
    else
        printf( "No CGI variables found.\n" );
```

```
43
44          printf( "</PRE></BODY></HTML>\n" );
45          return 0;
46      }
```

- Line 1 includes the now familiar header file for I/O functions like printf. Line 3 includes the header file for the CGI utility functions presented earlier. Line 5 defines a constant to represent buffer sizes. Line 6 defines the title that will be displayed in the Web browser.
- Line 8 begins the only function in this file, main. Line 10 declares a couple of character arrays to hold the CGI input and a single variable's value.
- Line 12 prints the MIME header for HTML. Lines 13 to 15 output HTML tags to start the page. The TITLE constant is used for the page title and main heading. The last HTML tag "<PRE>" specifies preformatted text. This was chosen for convenience and minimizes the number of HTML tags necessary in the rest of the output.
- Line 17 calls the CGI utility function cgiGetInput. The first parameter is the local array input_buf, which will receive the encoded CGI input containing all of the variables. The second parameter specifies the maximum number of characters to copy into this array. The cgiGetInput function returns a value that indicates which http method was used to submit the form variables. If no input was found or an unrecognized method was used, the return value will be 0. The body of the *if* statement on lines 19 through 40 will be executed only if CGI input is found.
- Lines 19 to 24 print the value of the CGI variable named "NAME." Line 19 prints the first part of a sentence that will include the value of this variable.
- Lines 20 and 21 attempt to retrieve the value of this CGI variable using the cgiFindVar utility function. The first parameter passed is the array containing the encoded CGI variables obtained by the cgiGetInput function. The second parameter specifies the name of the requested variable. The third parameter is the array in which to place the value of this variable, and the fourth parameter specifies the maximum size of this array. Recall that the cgiFindVar function returns the length of the value. If the variable is empty or cannot be found, this

function returns 0. The *if* statement on line 20 tests the return value of cgiFindVar to see if a value was found for the CGI variable "NAME."

- Line 22 prints the value of the variable if it is found. The value is placed inside an HTML "<B>" tag for emphasis. If no value was found, line 24 prints the word "missing."
- Lines 26 to 31 repeat this process for the variable named "CHKBOX." The word "Checked" is printed if any value was found for this variable; otherwise, the phrase "not checked" is printed.
- Lines 33 through 39 repeat the process again for the variable named "COMMENT." If a corresponding value is found, it is included in the phrase printed on lines 35 to 37. If not, an alternate phrase is printed on line 39.
- The *else* statement on lines 41 and 42 handles the situation where cgiGetInput indicates that no CGI input was found.
- Line 44 prints the closing HTML tags. Line 45 exits the program and indicates to the operating system that this program executed successfully.

The following command line compiles this program along with the CGI utility routines using the gcc compiler:

```
gcc formdump.c cgiutil.c -o formdump.cgi
```

This command compiles the two source files formdump.c and cgiutil.c and combines the compiled output into a single executable program formdump.cgi. As mentioned before, substitute the extension ".exe" on Microsoft operating systems.

The formdump.html file contains two HTML forms that demonstrate this program. One form uses the "POST" method to submit the form variables while the other uses the "GET" method.

```
<HTML>

<HEAD>
<TITLE>CGI Test Form</TITLE>
</HEAD>

<BODY>

<FORM action="http://your-server.com/cgi-bin/formdump.cgi"
```

```
   method="POST">
10     <PRE><CENTER><B>Use POST Method</B></CENTER>
11      Name : <INPUT name="NAME" size=30>
     <INPUT name="CHKBOX" type="CHECKBOX" value="Checked">
     A Checkbox
12     Textarea : <TEXTAREA align="TOP" name="COMMENT" rows=3
    cols=50></TEXTAREA></PRE>
13     <CENTER><INPUT type="submit" value="Post">
    <INPUT type="reset" value="Clear"></CENTER>
14     </FORM><P>
15
16     <HR>
17
18     <FORM action="http://your-server.com/cgi-bin/formdump.cgi"
    method="GET">
19     <PRE><CENTER><B>Use GET Method</B></CENTER>
20        Name : <INPUT name="NAME" size=30>
      <INPUT name="CHKBOX" type="CHECKBOX" value="Checked">
      A Checkbox
21     Textarea : <TEXTAREA align="TOP" name="COMMENT" rows=3
     cols=50></TEXTAREA></PRE>
22     <CENTER><INPUT type="submit" value="Get">
    <INPUT type="reset" value="Clear"></CENTER>
23     </FORM><P>
24
25     </BODY>
26     </HTML>
```

- The unnumbered lines are continuations of their preceding lines. Line 9 begins definition of the first form and specifies the name of the CGI program to receive the contents of this form. You must modify this line to reference the appropriate program location on your server. Line 11 includes tags for the input field "NAME" and the checkbox "CHKBOX." Line 12 defines the textarea "COMMENT." Line 13 defines two push-buttons, one to submit the form and another to clear the form's fields.

- Lines 18 through 23 duplicate this form. The only difference is the method specified in the form tag. This form utilizes the "GET" method instead. Like line 9, line 18 must be modified to reference your server.

CGI Variable Listing Program

This program displays a list of all CGI variables submitted to the program. This information may be helpful while designing HTML forms. Like the previous program this program also uses the CGI utility routines presented earlier in this chapter. Unlike the previous program, however, this program does not expect any specific CGI variables. This program displays the names and values of all CGI variables submitted regardless of their names. The source for this program is in the file vardump.c:

```
#include <stdio.h>

#include "cgiutil.h"

#define BUFFER_SIZE 2048
#define NAME_SIZE 64
#define TITLE "CGI Variables"


int main()
{
     char input_buf[BUFFER_SIZE], name_buf[NAME_SIZE],
          value_buf[BUFFER_SIZE];
     int method = cgiGetInput( input_buf, BUFFER_SIZE );

     printf( "Content-type: text/html\n\n" );
     printf( "<HTML><HEAD><TITLE>%s</TITLE></HEAD>\n",
          TITLE );
     printf( "<BODY><H1>%s</H1><HR>\n<PRE><B>", TITLE );

     if( method > 0 ) {
          if( METHOD_GET == method )
               printf( "GET" );
          else if( METHOD_GET == method )
               printf( "POST" );
          else
               printf( "Unrecognized" );

          printf( "</B> method: %s\n", input_buf );

          printf( "\n<B>Variables:</B>\n" );
          if( cgiGetNextVar( input_buf, name_buf, NAME_SIZE,
               value_buf, BUFFER_SIZE ) )
               do {
                    printf("%s: %s\n", name_buf,value_buf );
               } while( cgiGetNextVar( NULL, name_buf,
               NAME_SIZE,
                    value_buf, BUFFER_SIZE ) );
     }
     else
          printf( "No CGI variables found.<P>" );
```

```
41
42          printf( "</PRE></BODY></HTML>\n" );
43          return 0;
44      }
```

- Line 1 includes the standard library header stdio.h, and line 3 includes the header file for the CGI utility routines.
- Lines 5 through 7 define a few constant values. The INPUT_SIZE constant defines the size of the buffers used to hold the encoded CGI input and individual variable values. NAME_SIZE is the size of an array to hold a CGI variable's name. TITLE will be displayed in the HTML output of this program.
- Line 12 defines character array buffers using the previously defined constants. Line 14 defines and initializes a variable that indicates which CGI method was used, if any. CGI input is retrieved into the input_buf array by this statement as well.
- Line 16 generates the MIME header for HTML output, and lines 17 to 19 output the title and begin the document. Lines 21 through 38 make up an *if* statement block that will execute if any CGI variables were found. The if block on lines 22 through 27 prints the name of the http method by comparing the return value of the cgiGetInput function with constants declared in cgiutil.h. The *else* statement on lines 26 and 27 handles the unlikely event that a method other than "GET" or "POST" was used. If the cgiGetInput function is later extended to handle other method types, this program will continue to function.
- The CGI variables retrieved by cgiGetInput are printed in their encoded form on line 29.
- Line 31 prints a title to accompany the list that follows, which displays the individual variable names and values.
- Lines 32 and 33 attempt to retrieve the first variable and its value via the cgiGetNextVar function. This statement passes the buffer containing the encoded CGI variables, as well as buffers to receive the name and value. If no variables are found in the CGI input buffer, the statement block on lines 34 through 37 is skipped.
- Line 34 begins a do loop, which will execute until no more variables are found in the CGI input buffer input_buf. With the while condition at the bottom of

the loop body, this loop will execute at least once. This is necessary to display the CGI variable retrieved in the previous statement even if there are no more variables found after it. Line 35, the body of the loop, prints the name and value of the last variable retrieved from the CGI input buffer.

- The *while* statement on line 36 is part of the preceding do loop, and it attempts to retrieve the next CGI variable. Each time cgiGetNextVar successfully retrieves a variable, the preceding loop body will be executed. When no more variables are found, this statement will terminate the loop. The first parameter to the cgiGetNextVar function is NULL in this statement so that this function will resume processing where it stopped after the last call.
- The *else* statement on lines 39 and 40 executes if no CGI variables were found, as determined by line 21. Line 42 prints the closing HTML tags, and line 43 ends this program.

Compile this program via the following command line:

```
gcc vardump.c cgiutil.c -o vardump.cgi
```

You can test the output of your HTML forms by substituting the location of this program in the "action" attribute of your "<form>" tag. Alternatively, you can access this program through a URL that includes CGI variables. For example: http://your-server.com/cgi-bin/vardump.cgi?where=here&this=that.

This URL includes variables after the CGI program name vardump.cgi. CGI variables in a URL are preceded by a question mark "?". This example specifies two variables named "where" and "this" with respective values of "here" and "that."

Chapter

18

Guidelines for Adopting Programs and Scripts

Odds are, many of the programs you'll use on your Web server, or as JavaScript, Java, or VBScript programs in your HTML documents, will come from other authors. The Internet is a rich resource in free and nearly free programming examples, and you might as well take advantage of it. Odds are, someone out there has already done the thing you want to do. Why reinvent the wheel if you don't have to?

In this chapter you'll learn the basics of adopting programs and scripts written by other people, including where to find the best programs on the Web.

Matching the Language to the Server

This is one of those "so obvious it doesn't need to be said" topics, but it bear repeating just the same: When adopting a program for your Web server, make sure the program is compatible with your server. This compatibility should extend to the operating system used on the server, as well as the Web server software itself.

A program written in Visual Basic will not work under UNIX, for example. And a C program compiled for a UNIX machine will not run on a Macintosh or PC running NT. Table 18.1 is a short cross-reference list of major program types and the servers on which they are most likely to run. Note that the operating system is the most important element here, not the type of microprocessor. Therefore, there's a difference between NT and DOS Web servers, even though both may use a PC with an Intel microprocessor.

> **NOTE** This book does not cover Web programs written in Visual Basic and AppleScript because they are dependent on a specific Web server platform. It was our intention to concentrate on the most widely used Web programming languages. However, just because the language isn't covered in this book doesn't mean it isn't any good. You are urged to use whatever language best fits your needs.

Adopting Interpreted Language Programs

Programs written using an interpreted language are typically the easiest to adopt to most any server platform (the notable exception to this is AppleScript, which is available only for the Macintosh). The most popular interpreted language used in Web programming is Perl, and this language is among the most widely supported on the Web.

Though Perl was originally created for the UNIX operating system, now every major operating system supports a version of Perl. Each so-called "port" supports

Table 18.1 Program Types and the Servers on Which They Run

Program Type	UNIX	NT/Win 95	DOS	Macintosh	OS/2
Perl	X	X	X	X	X
UNIX shell	X				
C	X	X	X	X	X
Visual Basic		X			X*
AppleScript				X	

* May require additional software support

basic Perl functionality, but this functionality is not identical across all platforms. This is important to remember because it can cause problems in adopting a program written for one operating system for use on another operating system.

The Perl flock (file lock) statement is a good example of basic functionality that differs between operating system versions. The flock statement is fully functional on most, if not all, variations of the UNIX operating system, but it does not function identically in the NT version of Perl that we used for the development of this book (hip's Perl 5.001, see www.hip.com).

The variance in operating characteristics between versions of Perl means that you may have to revise the script as needed for your operating system. This is easier said than done because it requires fairly intimate knowledge of both the source and the destination operating systems, as well as the differences in versions of the programming language. One approach that may help is to try the program as-is and note any differences in operating behavior (be sure to test thoroughly, so you dig up as many potential problems as you can). Most serious compatibility issues will create error messages, which you can use to help you locate those areas of the program that need to be addressed.

Adopting Compiled Language Programs

Programs that are compiled, namely those written in C, are compiled with a target operating system in mind. This means you cannot take a compiled program designed for a UNIX system and run it as-is on a Windows NT system, even if the program has been written with so-called "portable" code (code that is not dependent on any operating system). In order to use the program, you must obtain the source code for it and compile the source code into an executable using a compiler designed for your operating system.

Compiling is usually required even if you are using a UNIX Web server because there are so many different flavors of UNIX. There's Berkeley Unix, Linux, Irix, HP-UX, and over a dozen others. Though each of these flavors is "UNIX," they often differ in important ways. This restricts you from taking a program compiled on one version of UNIX and using it in another.

Furthermore, even programs compiled for a given UNIX flavor often need to be compiled specially because of differences in the version of that particular flavor. Each major version of a particular flavor of UNIX typically requires hat C programs be recompiled for the target operating system. And it is not uncommon for a

Web site administrator to recompile the basic UNIX kernel, which is the main component used by the computer to run the UNIX operating system. This sometimes causes problems when running compiled C programs, requiring that the program be recompiled as well.

The bottom line: If you plan on using a C program on your Web site, odds are you will need to compile it before it can be implemented. Most Web servers already have a suitable C compiler available, such as gcc. Contact the administrator of the Web server if you're not sure what is available for your use. The administrator may prefer to compile the program for you, which is often easier to do than explaining the process to someone who is not familiar with it.

Most C programs that you obtain from the Web come with a Make file, which is an instruction file for the compiler, specifying the default options to use for the compilation. If the C program you get lacks a Make file, look for details on specific command-line options to use when compiling. These instructions are typically provided with the main documentation for the program.

Looking for Portable Code

Portable code is programming that is not dependent on a given operating system platform. Apart from the requirements of compiling for each operating system, C is generally considered to be the most portable language available. It is arguably the most consistent across operating systems, as this is one of the features of C's design. The C language is also the oldest language used on the Web, which means that it's done with most of its fast growth. Unlike most of the Web and the Internet, you should not expect huge changes in the implementation in C.

Still, it is possible to write portable code in other languages, including Perl. The main consideration is that the program not require the use of a facility or option that is part of a given operating system. The *sendmail* program, included as the standard mailing application in many versions of UNIX, is missing in Windows NT, Windows 95, DOS, and the others. If the program you are using requires sendmail and your operating system doesn't support it, the program will need to be revised first. This can be usually be accomplished by substituting the sendmail command with whatever mail program is used on the server.

The lack of sendmail in Windows NT/Windows 95 is a common complaint in Web programming because of the popularity of Web CGI programs that send the content of HTML forms to an e-mail address. The bulk of such CGI programs are written for UNIX and use the sendmail program to do the actual mail transport. But there are other operating system-specific issues to consider as well, including issuing commands that are supported only on one operating system or another. For example, many Web programs for UNIX set file permissions with the chmod command, and this command is not supported by any other operating system.

There are far too many commands and utilities specific to a given operating system to enumerate here. Suffice it to say that you will likely encounter any and all differences as you attempt to implement a program designed for a different operating system. In many cases, you will need to have extensive knowledge of both operating systems, as well as the programming language itself, to fully adopt the program for your use. This is beyond the capabilities of most people, so it is usually better to intentionally adopt those programs that specifically say they are "portable." A number of sites on the Web offer such portable code; see Chapter 20, as well as the sources.htm file on the CD-ROM, for a list of some of the better ones.

Looking for Well-Documented Code

Some programmers delight in making their work as incomprehensive as possible. They use structure and syntax that, while acceptable to the program compiler or interpreter, is very difficult—if not impossible—to read by humans. Those programmers that don't join this practice voluntarily do it unconsciously as they look for ways to shorten and streamline their code. This practice often creates indecipherable code that only the original programmer can understand.

When looking for programs to adopt, try to find those that are written for others to understand and use. This is not always easy because the Internet is full of example programs designed for other programmers. If you are not a programmer intimately familiar with a language, the example will be nearly useless to you. You can only hope that the program runs as-is, without modification. Unfortunately, this is seldom the case unless the programmer uses the exact same server and operating system you do—something you should not count on.

The best Web programs to adopt are those that are written with a basic and consistent syntax and that include extensive documentation, either as a separate file or as comments throughout the program itself. Commented code is perhaps the most common because many programmers add the comments while they are writing or revising the code. The comments not only help others to use their work, but also help remind the programmer of what the code is supposed to do.

As you scour the Web looking for code you can use, be on the lookout for the "well-manicured" programs with copious documentation. Watch for comments inline with the code. If you can reasonably follow along with the code as you read through it quickly, odds are the program will be easier to adapt to your own needs. You may wish to avoid those programs that are simply a dense mass of command lines, as these usually require far more effort to revise. With the amount of free and nearly free examples on the Web, there's seldom a reason to settle for an uncommented, indecipherable example program.

Bear in mind that heavy commenting increases the size of files and can be detrimental to the speed of execution of the program. This applies to interpreted languages, such as Perl and JavaScript, because the interpreter reads the entire file whenever it is executed. In a compiled language like C or Java, the comments are ignored when the program is compiled; the speed of execution is not affected even with heavy use of comments, as the comments aren't part of the compiled version.

If you are adopting an interpreted program, you may wish to make the modifications as required, then strip all but the most important comments from the file (remember not to strip the "#!" comment at the start of Perl and UNIX shell programs; this one must remain in the script).

Understanding Copyrights and Permissions

For the most part, the Internet is a giving community, and a great deal of example programs are provided free of copyright and free of charge. You can use those program on your site without paying a fee or royalty.

Of course, remember that when a program is free, it is typically made available without warranty or support. Respect the time and effort of the author, and don't ask for free assistance in setting the program up or making changes. This is only common courtesy, but you'd be surprised how many people attempt to impose on the goodwill of the authors of free programs by asking for special favors. If you require specific assistance and can't revise the program by yourself, ask about consulting rates or obtain a programmer to do the work for you.

Not all example programs on the Internet are free from both copyright and/or licensing fees. A common practice is for an author to use the GNU copyright license, whereby the author offers the work at no cost but still retains copyright. For users the difference between a program freely available in the public domain and one available via the GNU copyright license is minimal—the program can be freely distributed, used, and modified. The difference between the two is that the GNU license restricts a person or company from adopting an existing program and reselling it (anyone can charge for a program in the public domain, though fortunately there are few people gullible enough to pay for something that is otherwise available for free!).

If you plan on using software offered under the GNU license, read through the license requirements if you're not familiar with it (a copy of it is included at the end of this chapter, for your reference). You will find that, unlike most copyrighted works, you are free to modify the original, and even redistribute the modifications, if you so choose. You are, however, restricted from charging any money for the changes. You must also make sure the copyright notice of the original author remains intact and that the revision is accompanied by a copy of the GNU license.

If you plan only on keeping the software for your own use, you should still keep the copyright notice of the original author, both as a matter of courtesy and as a requirement of the GNU license.

Other example programs available on the Internet are offered for a fee. These programs are typically available as shareware, which is try-before-you-buy software. Though you can download and use the software without paying for it, you are expected to send money if you continue to use the software. Shareware software is sold on an honor system, which works only if those who keep the software register and pay for it. The address for remitting the registration fee is included with the program itself or with the documentation.

Unlike public domain and GNU license software authors, shareware authors typically impose restrictions on how you may revise their work. The nature of Web programming usually requires a certain amount of revision, to make the program compatible with the directory structure of the server, for example. Many shareware authors specifically restrict revising their programs beyond these simple changes, however. If you locate a shareware program you wish to use and it needs a fair amount of revision, be sure to consult the documentation that accompanies the program for any licensing rules. When in doubt, contact the author of the program and ask for licensing specifics. The program should be accompanied by an address for regular mail or e-mail.

Finding Programs You Can Use

By far, the best place to find programs for the Web is the Web itself. There are literally thousands of sites around the world that offer free and shareware Web programs you can use. We list some of these sites in Chapter 20 and in the sources.htm file on the CD-ROM that accompanies this book. But keep in mind that our listings are but the proverbial tip of the iceberg—there are far too many program source sites on the Web to list in a single chapter—and perhaps even an entire book.

The best way to locate Web program sites is to use one of the several free search engines available on the Web. My favorites are AltaVista and Yahoo!, though there are others you may wish to try as well (URLs for these services are provided in the sources.htm file on the CD-ROM). Both AltaVista and Yahoo! offer provide fast and convenient searches, and you can typically find what you want within just a few seconds of entering your search keywords.

For example, to search for Perl examples for UNIX with AltaVista, you might enter *+Perl +UNIX* in the search entry box. This search finds all pages that contain the word Perl and UNIX. You can refine your search by including other keywords and modifiers. For instance, you can find all Perl programs for UNIX that are not counters with the search string *+Perl +UNIX -counter*. Note that capitalization doesn't matter—Perl is the same as Perl and PERL.

Because there are so many program examples on the Web, AltaVista—or whatever search database you are using—will likely return far more entries than you can reasonably visit. In fact, though AltaVista may locate tens of thousands of matching pages, it will display up to the first 200. You can visit the page by clicking on the links provided.

As you use a search service like AltaVista you'll develop work habits to streamline your "surfing" techniques. This will help you locate what you're looking for much more quickly. For example, I prefer to visit as many pages AltaVista supplies, bookmarking all those that look promising (I will often start a new bookmark file for this; both Netscape Navigator and Microsoft Internet Explorer allow for this). Once I've collected a dozen or so good sites, I then go back and investigate further. Those sites that don't yield anything worthwhile are expunged from the bookmark file.

I also find it helpful to avoid downloading programs and other files until I've searched most or all of the other sites on my bookmark list. In this way, I can compare what's available and download only those files that seem to best fit my needs. You may wish to follow this policy as well, or you may find your hard drive filling up with programs and files you end up never using.

When you do download a file, make a notation of where you obtained it. You'd be surprised how many sample program files don't include their own URL or any author or site information. Should you need additional information (like the documentation), you probably won't remember where to look for it. If nothing else, keep a paper notebook handy and jot down the name of each file you retrieve and its URL.

Downloading Single and Multiple Files

Many Web examples consist of just a single file. You download the file either by viewing it and saving it directly in your browser, or by clicking on a link and choosing the Save As button to store the file on your hard disk.

Some program examples consist of many files and are in archive format. The most common format are ZIP and TAR; both of these need separate software to extract the component files. ZIP files are primarily intended for unpacking on DOS and Windows machines; TAR files are intended for use on UNIX systems.

ZIP files are compressed to store more data in a smaller space, so the ZIP is usually smaller than the component files inside. For example, a ZIP file that's 65K in size may actually contains 200K in program and other files. To unzip a ZIP file use PKUNZIP, WinZIP, or another compression program that is compatible with the ZIP format.

Conversely, TAR files are in uncompressed format, even though one TAR file may contain many files. That is, if there are three 10K files, the resulting TAR is

30K. UNIX uses a separate program, such as the compress utility, to compress the TAR file and make it smaller. You know a compressed file when you see a .Z or .z file extension. This file may contain a TAR file or a single regular file.

If a TAR file is compressed, you need to uncompress it first, then untar it. The sequence goes like this (for ease of use, place the file to uncompress in the directory where you want the resulting files):

1. *Uncompress filename.Z*, where filename.Z is the filename you want to uncompress. (Note: some UNIX systems use zcat instead of uncompress.)
2. *TAR xvf filename.tar*, where filename.tar is the name of the TAR file obtained after uncompressing.

> **NOTE** Some UNIX programs are distributed using alternative methods. Two somewhat popular distribution formats are ZIP and rpm. ZIP files can be uncompressed using the gzip program included in many versions of UNIX, most specifically the Linux flavor of UNIX. Rpm files are special distribution packages designed for use with the Red Hat software version of Linux.

Understanding the Process of Modifying Programs

While modifying an existing Web program is not exactly rocket science, the process is made easier by approaching every program you adapt as a collection of small routines. Most of the better Web programs are designed this way, and you can instantly see how the program is constructed and how it should be altered. In addition, the better programs come with copious in-line comments that describe what's happening, so you can follow along with the flow of the code.

An example of a well-written Web program (in Perl) is shown on page 489. This program is a random banner generator, which displays banner images on a random basis. Each time someone visits your page, one of the banners you have previously specified is randomly displayed. Random banner generator programs are somewhat common, and you can find them at a number of sites on the Web. We chose this one because it is cleanly written and expertly documented. This particular version of the random banner generator is from the Selena Sol script repository, at http://www.eff.org/~erict.

Overview of the Banner Generator Program

Here is the random banner generator program in its entirety (it's also included on the CD-ROM). Section numbers have been added for reference purposes.

```
1    #!/usr/local/bin/perl

2    # Name: Selena Sol's Random Banner Generator
#
# Version: 4.0
#
# Last Modified: 07-31-96
#
3    # Copyright Info: This application was written by Selena Sol
#    (selena@eff.org, http://www.eff.org/~erict) having been inspired by
#    countless other Perl authors.  Feel free to copy, cite, reference,
#    sample, borrow, resell or plagiarize the contents.  However, if you
#    don't mind, please let me know where it goes so that I can at least
#    watch and take part in the development of the memes. Information wants
#    to be free, support public domain freeware.  Donations are appreciated
#    and will be spent on further upgrades and other public domain scripts.


4    # Note: Take a look at the sample HTML file located in the sub-directory
# Html...it contains an important line <!--IMG GOES HERE--> which must
# appear in any HTML file you want to display a random banner in.
# Once you have configured the setup variables and the HTML file to the
# specifics of your own server setup, you can try out the random banner
# generator.

5    ########################################################################
#                         Print http Header.                               #
########################################################################

# First tell Perl to bypass the buffer so that information generated by
# the CGI will be sent immediately to the browser. The line $! = 1; does
# this. Then, print out the http header so that we will easily be able to
# debug and so that the browser will not time us out.

    $| = 1;
  print "Content-type: text/html\n\n";

6    ########################################################################
#                         Require Libraries.                               #
########################################################################

# Further, cgi-lib.pl is loaded and the routine ReadParse is used to read
```

```
# and parse any incoming url encoded data.

  require "./random_banner.setup";
  require "$location_of_cgi_lib";
  &ReadParse(*form_data);

7######################################################################
#                         Initialize the Randomizer.                  #
######################################################################

# Then, Perl's randomizer is accessed using the srand command.

  srand (time|$$);


8   ######################################################################
#                         Define Database and Html File to Use        #
######################################################################

# The URL encoded data which may be coming in as form data will be the
# name of the image file that this script should use to find the locations
# of the images as well as the hyperlinks those images are associated
# with. If there was an image file specified in the URL, the script will
# assign that value to the variable $image_database, if there is none, the
# script will use the value of $default_image_list as was defined above.

  if ($form_data{'image_list'} ne "")
    {
    $image_database = $form_data{'image_list'};
    }
  else
    {
    $image_database = "$default_image_list";
    }

# Similarly, the script must determine which HTML file it should display
# with the randomly generated ad.  By default, it will load the HTML file
# defined in  $default_html_file.  However, if the client has specified an
# alternate file to load in the URL string, the script will load that
# instead.

  if ($form_data{'html_file'} ne "")
    {
    $html_file = "$html_directory_path/$form_data{'html_file'}";
    }
  else
    {
```

```
    $html_file = "$default_html_file";
    }

9   ######################################################################
#                        Get the Random Banner and Link.                  #
######################################################################

# Next, the script opens the image file, dying with CgiDie if there is a
# problem opening the image file specified in the URl or defined by
# $default_image_list.

  open (IMAGE_DATABASE, "$image_database") ||
        &CgiDie ("I am sorry, but I was not able to open the image
        databse in the Get the Random Banner and Link routine. The value I
        have  is $image_database.  Would you please check the path and
        permissions.");

# It then goes through the image list file a line at a time and, for every
# line, it gathers the image and the associated hyperlink by splitting the
# line by the pipe (|) symbol.  Further, it pushes the location of the
# image to the list array @imagelist and the associated URL to @url_list.
# Finally, it closees the image list # file.

  while (<IMAGE_DATABASE>)
    {
    ($image, $url) = split (/\|/, $_);
    chop $url;
    push (@imagelist, $image);
    push (@url_list, $url);
    }
  close (IMAGE_DATABASE);

# Now that the script has a list of all the images in the image file, it
# uses Perl's randomizer function to choose one of them at random.  Since
# "@imagelist" is interpreted by Perl as the number of values in the
# array, $random_number is set to be a random (rand) integer value (int)
# from zero to the number of images in the @images array.

  $random_number = int(rand(@imagelist));

# Then, the script takes the number assigned to $random_number and accesses
# the array element in @imagelist that is associated with the number.
# $random_image then becomes the name of one of the images in @imagelist.

  $random_image = $imagelist[$random_number];
  $random_url = $url_list[$random_number];
```

```
10 ###########################################################################
#                       Insert Random Banner Into Page                    #
###########################################################################

# Next, the script opens the HTML file that the client has requested to
# see, using CgiDie if it cannot be opened for some reason.

  open (HTML_FILE, "$html_file") ||
        &CgiDie ("I'm sorry, but I was unable to open the requested
        HTML file in the Insert Random Banner Into Page routine.  The
        value I have is $html_file.  Would you please check the path and
        the permissions for the file.");

# The script then reads through the HTML file a line at a time.

  while (<HTML_FILE>)
    {

# If it comes upon a line which looks like the following:
# <!--IMG GOES HERE-->
# the script knows that it is supposed to replace the line with the
# randomly generated image and the associated hyperlink. So, using the
# "here" method of printing, it replaces the line with the HTML code.
# Remember that since the greater than (>) and less tha (<) symbols
# are Perl special characters and must be escaped if they are to be
# treated as patterns to match for.

    if (/\<!--IMG GOES HERE--\>/)
      {
      print qq!
      <A HREF = "$random_url">
      <IMG SRC = "$image_url/$random_image"></A>!;
      }

# If the line is not the special tag, the script simply prints out the
# line. Thus, every line in the HTML file will be displayed through the
# Web browser except for the special tag line, which will be replaced with
# the <IMG> and <A HREF> tags.

    else
      {
      print "$_";
      }
   } # End of while (<HTML_FILE>)

# Finally, the HTML file is closed and the script exits.

  close (HTML_FILE);
```

Analyzing the Program

The first step in modifying any program is to analyze its component parts. Section 1 of the random banner generator is the "sharp-bang" comment line that indicates the path and name of the Perl interpreter to use. Recall that all good Perl programs begin with this line, and it's often necessary to modify this line to point to the exact location of the Perl interpreter on your machine.

Section 2 describes the program, the version, and the date it was last modified.

Section 3 details the copyright claims of the author. In this case, Selena Sol (which is not the programmer's real name, actually) has not specifically claimed copyright; therefore, the program can be freely distributed and modified (in fact, the author specifically invites use and modification).

Section 4 continues with comments and describes how the HTML file for use with the random banner generator is to be configured. The comment indicates that an example HTML file is provided along with the random generator program—a good example of why it's important to note the URL of all programs you download. With the URL noted, you can return to the site and fetch the example file.

Sections 5 through 10 represent the five main routines of the program (note that user-defined functions are not used; this Perl script runs from start to end, executing each line of code in turn). Each routine is accompanied by a header that describes the purpose of the routine. Many of the routines also include a comment line or two that explains the purpose of the code that follows.

In the case of the random banner generator, the following routines are provided:

- *Print http header.* Bypass the server buffer (often required for this kind of work in Perl), and print the content-type of the HTML page, which is text/html.
- *Require libraries.* The random banner generator needs a separate file cgi-lib.pl (also available at the author's site). The generator program uses one of the functions in that file, ReadParse. By using a library file, common code can be easily shared with any number of programs. The random banner generator also requires a file called random_banner.setup, a setup file that specifies options for the program. This file is likewise available at the author's site.
- *Initialize the randomizer.* The random banner generator uses the Perl srand statement to create a random number.

- *Define database and HTML file to use.* The random banner generator program needs to be told the list of banner images you wish to use, as well as the URLs with which each banner is to be associated.
- *Get the random banner and link.* The actual working portion of the random banner generator opens the list of banners (in the image database file) and locates one of the banners to display.
- *Insert random banner into page.* Finally, the program inserts the image at the proper location in the HTML file. This location is defined with a comment, <!--IMG GOES HERE-->, which can appear anywhere in the body of the HTML file. The remainder of the HTML file is passed on to the browser unaltered.

As you can see, before you can use the random banner generator program, you must prepare several associated documents, in addition to modifying the script as needed for your application. You already know you may need to change the first line of the program so that it points to the directory of the Perl interpreter on your server. Any other alteration is up to you.

For example, you may wish to use a different placeholder comment for the banner image. Instead of <!--IMG GOES HERE-->, you may want to use a shorter comment, such as <!--IMG --> You will need to edit the *if* statement in Section 11 of the program to accommodate the change.

And, of course, you need to edit or create the basic HTML file that contains the <! IMG GOES HERE --> tag, as well as the database of banner images to use.

> **NOTE** Keep in mind that not all example programs you find on the Web are so clearly defined or well documented. If you're new to the process of modifying programs, you may wish to start with a simple one-page script, preferably one that is well documented and doesn't require additional setup or database files. Once you've mastered the basic program, you can tackle the larger jobs.

Getting Expert Assistance

Let's face it: Some modification jobs may be beyond your programming expertise. If this is the case, you'll want to obtain the assistance of a pro who can either steer you through the steps in altering the program or do the job for you. The Web is full of consultants who work on an hourly or per-project basis, and you can often find a consultant who can take on the job immediately (it's a highly competitive business!). As with Web programming examples, you can locate Web programmers using AltaVista, Yahoo!, and other search engines.

Keep the following in mind:

- If you're looking to improve your knowledge of a particular programming language, look for a consultant who can provide "guru help" whenever you need it. The consultant should be prepared to answer your questions and provide sample code, as well as bail you out of the really tough spots.
- If you're looking to get the job done in a short period of time, it's best to look for a consultant who can take over the job completely. Look for a consultant who can revise the program to your specifications (the consultant may have a similar program he or she has previously written, and you may want to consider using this instead).

Avoid the situation where you have a major project to complete, know little or nothing about the programming language you need to use, and have little time to get everything done. This almost always ends in disaster, as all programming languages require a period of adjustment and learning. If you're just starting out with a language, it's best to begin with a simple task, without a deadline (or a very long deadline). That way you won't feel rushed and can fully absorb the learning experience.

Sample GNU License Agreement

Copyright (C) 1989, 1991 Free Software Foundation, Inc.
675 Massachusetts Avenue, Cambridge, MA 02139, USA
Everyone is permitted to copy and distribute verbatim copies of this license document, but changing it is not allowed.

Preamble

The licenses for most software are designed to take away your freedom to share and change it. By contrast, the GNU General Public License is intended to guarantee your freedom to share and change free software—to make sure the software is free for all its users. This General Public License applies to most of the Free Software Foundation's software and to any other program whose authors commit to using it. (Some other Free Software Foundation software is covered by the GNU Library General Public License instead.) You can apply it to your programs, too.

When we speak of free software, we are referring to freedom, not price. Our General Public Licenses are designed to make sure that you have the freedom to distribute copies of free software (and charge for this service if you wish), that you receive source code or can get it if you want it, that you can change the software or use pieces of it in new free programs; and that you know you can do these things.

To protect your rights, we need to make restrictions that forbid anyone to deny you these rights or to ask you to surrender the rights. These restrictions translate to certain responsibilities for you if you distribute copies of the software or if you modify it.

For example, if you distribute copies of such a program, whether gratis or for a fee, you must give the recipients all the rights that you have. You must make sure that they, too, receive or can get the source code. And you must show them these terms so they know their rights.

We protect your rights with two steps: (1) copyright the software, and (2) offer you this license, which gives you legal permission to copy, distribute, and/or modify the software.

Also, for each author's protection and ours, we want to make certain that everyone understands that there is no warranty for this free software. If the software is modified by someone else and passed on, we want its recipients to know that what they have is not the original, so that any problems introduced by others will not reflect on the original authors' reputations.

Finally, any free program is threatened constantly by software patents. We wish to avoid the danger that redistributors of a free program will individually obtain patent licenses, in effect making the program proprietary. To prevent this, we have made it clear that any patent must be licensed for everyone's free use or not licensed at all.

The precise terms and conditions for copying, distribution, and modification follow.

GNU GENERAL PUBLIC LICENSE TERMS AND CONDITIONS FOR COPYING, DISTRIBUTION, AND MODIFICATION

This License applies to any program or other work which contains a notice placed by the copyright holder saying it may be distributed under the terms of this General Public License. The "Program," below, refers to any such program or work, and a "work based on the Program" means either the Program or any derivative work under copyright law: that is to say, a work containing the Program or a portion of it, either verbatim or with modifications and/or translated into another language. (Hereinafter, translation is included without limitation in the term "modification.") Each licensee is addressed as "you."

Activities other than copying, distribution, and modification are not covered by this License; they are outside its scope. The act of running the Program is not restricted, and the output from the Program is covered only if its contents constitute a work based on the Program (independent of having been made by running the Program). Whether that is true depends on what the Program does.

1. You may copy and distribute verbatim copies of the Program's source code as you receive it, in any medium, provided that you conspicuously and appropriately publish on each copy an appropriate copyright notice and disclaimer of warranty; keep intact all the notices that refer to this License and to the absence of any warranty; and give any other recipients of the Program a copy of this License along with the Program.

   You may charge a fee for the physical act of transferring a copy, and you may at your option offer warranty protection in exchange for a fee.

2. You may modify your copy or copies of the Program or any portion of it, thus forming a work based on the Program, and copy and distribute such modifications or work under the terms of Section 1 above, provided that you also meet all of these conditions:

   a. You must cause the modified files to carry prominent notices stating that you changed the files and the date of any change.

   b. You must cause any work that you distribute or publish, that in whole or in part contains or is derived from the Program or any part thereof, to be licensed as a whole at no charge to all third parties under the terms of this License.

c. If the modified program normally reads commands interactively when run, you must cause it, when started running for such interactive use in the most ordinary way, to print or display an announcement including an appropriate copyright notice and a notice that there is no warranty (or else, saying that you provide a warranty) and that users may redistribute the program under these conditions, and telling the user how to view a copy of this License. (Exception: if the Program itself is interactive but does not normally print such an announcement, your work based on the Program is not required to print an announcement.)

These requirements apply to the modified work as a whole. If identifiable sections of that work are not derived from the Program, and can be reasonably considered independent and separate works in themselves, then this License, and its terms, do not apply to those sections when you distribute them as separate works. But when you distribute the same sections as part of a whole which is a work based on the Program, the distribution of the whole must be on the terms of this License, whose permissions for other licensees extend to the entire whole, and thus to each and every part regardless of who wrote it.

Thus, it is not the intent of this section to claim rights or contest your rights to work written entirely by you; rather, the intent is to exercise the right to control the distribution of derivative or collective works based on the Program.

In addition, mere aggregation of another work not based on the Program with the Program (or with a work based on the Program) on a volume of a storage or distribution medium does not bring the other work under the scope of this License.

3. You may copy and distribute the Program (or a work based on it, under Section 2) in object code or executable form under the terms of Sections 1 and 2 above provided that you also do one of the following:

a. Accompany it with the complete corresponding machine-readable source code, which must be distributed under the terms of Sections 1 and 2 above on a medium customarily used for software interchange; or,

b. Accompany it with a written offer, valid for at least three years, to give any third party, for a charge no more than your cost of physically performing source distribution, a complete machine-readable copy of the corresponding source code, to be distributed under the terms of Sections 1 and 2 above on a medium customarily used for software interchange; or,

c. Accompany it with the information you received as to the offer to distribute corresponding source code. (This alternative is allowed only for noncommercial distribution and only if you received the program in object code or executable form with such an offer, in accord with Subsection b above.)

The source code for a work means the preferred form of the work for making modifications to it. For an executable work, complete source code means all the source code for all modules it contains, plus any associated interface definition files, plus the scripts used to control compilation and installation of the executable. However, as a special exception, the source code distributed need not include anything that is normally distributed (in either source or binary form) with the major components (compiler, kernel, and so on) of the operating system on which the executable runs, unless that component itself accompanies the executable.

If distribution of executable or object code is made by offering access to copy from a designated place, then offering equivalent access to copy the source code from the same place counts as distribution of the source code, even though third parties are not compelled to copy the source along with the object code.

4. You may not copy, modify, sublicense, or distribute the Program except as expressly provided under this License. Any attempt otherwise to copy, modify, sublicense, or distribute the Program is void and will automatically terminate your rights under this License. However, parties who have received copies, or rights, from you under this License will not have their licenses terminated so long as such parties remain in full compliance.

5. You are not required to accept this License, since you have not signed it. However, nothing else grants you permission to modify or distribute the Program or its derivative works. These actions are prohibited by law if you do not accept this License. Therefore, by modifying or

distributing the Program (or any work based on the Program), you indicate your acceptance of this License to do so, and all its terms and conditions for copying, distributing, or modifying the Program or works based on it.

6. Each time you redistribute the Program (or any work based on the Program), the recipient automatically receives a license from the original licensor to copy, distribute, or modify the Program subject to these terms and conditions. You may not impose any further restrictions on the recipients' exercise of the rights granted herein. You are not responsible for enforcing compliance by third parties to this License.

7. If, as a consequence of a court judgment or allegation of patent infringement or for any other reason (not limited to patent issues), conditions are imposed on you (whether by court order, agreement, or otherwise) that contradict the conditions of this License, they do not excuse you from the conditions of this License. If you cannot distribute so as to satisfy simultaneously your obligations under this License and any other pertinent obligations, then as a consequence you may not distribute the Program at all. For example, if a patent license would not permit royalty-free redistribution of the Program by all those who receive copies directly or indirectly through you, then the only way you could satisfy both it and this License would be to refrain entirely from distribution of the Program.

   If any portion of this section is held invalid or unenforceable under any particular circumstance, the balance of the section is intended to apply and the section as a whole is intended to apply in other circumstances.

   It is not the purpose of this section to induce you to infringe any patents or other property right claims or to contest validity of any such claims; this section has the sole purpose of protecting the integrity of the free software distribution system, which is implemented by public license practices. Many people have made generous contributions to the wide range of software distributed through that system in reliance on consistent application of that system; it is up to the author/donor to decide if he or she is willing to distribute software through any other system and a licensee cannot impose that choice.

This section is intended to make thoroughly clear what is believed to be a consequence of the rest of this License.

8. If the distribution and/or use of the Program is restricted in certain countries either by patents or by copyrighted interfaces, the original copyright holder who places the Program under this License may add an explicit geographical distribution limitation excluding those countries, so that distribution is permitted only in or among countries not thus excluded. In such case, this License incorporates the limitation as if written in the body of this License.

9. The Free Software Foundation may publish revised and/or new versions of the General Public License from time to time. Such new versions will be similar in spirit to the present version, but may differ in detail to address new problems or concerns.

   Each version is given a distinguishing version number. If the Program specifies a version number of this License which applies to it and "any later version," you have the option of following the terms and conditions either of that version or of any later version published by the Free Software Foundation. If the Program does not specify a version number of this License, you may choose any version ever published by the Free Software Foundation.

10. If you wish to incorporate parts of the Program into other free programs whose distribution conditions are different, write to the author to ask for permission. For software which is copyrighted by the Free Software Foundation, write to the Free Software Foundation; we sometimes make exceptions for this. Our decision will be guided by the two goals of preserving the free status of all derivatives of our free software and of promoting the sharing and reuse of software generally.

NO WARRANTY

11. BECAUSE THE PROGRAM IS LICENSED FREE OF CHARGE, THERE IS NO WARRANTY FOR THE PROGRAM, TO THE EXTENT PERMITTED BY APPLICABLE LAW. EXCEPT WHEN OTHERWISE STATED IN WRITING THE COPYRIGHT HOLDERS AND/OR OTHER PARTIES PROVIDE THE PROGRAM "AS IS" WITHOUT WARRANTY OF ANY KIND, EITHER EXPRESSED OR IMPLIED, INCLUDING, BUT NOT LIMITED TO,

THE IMPLIED WARRANTIES OF MERCHANTABILITY AND FITNESS FOR A PARTICULAR PURPOSE. THE ENTIRE RISK AS TO THE QUALITY AND PERFORMANCE OF THE PROGRAM IS WITH YOU. SHOULD THE PROGRAM PROVE DEFECTIVE, YOU ASSUME THE COST OF ALL NECESSARY SERVICING, REPAIR, OR CORRECTION.

12. IN NO EVENT UNLESS REQUIRED BY APPLICABLE LAW OR AGREED TO IN WRITING WILL ANY COPYRIGHT HOLDER, OR ANY OTHER PARTY WHO MAY MODIFY AND/OR REDISTRIBUTE THE PROGRAM AS PERMITTED ABOVE, BE LIABLE TO YOU FOR DAMAGES, INCLUDING ANY GENERAL, SPECIAL, INCIDENTAL, OR CONSEQUENTIAL DAMAGES ARISING OUT OF THE USE OR INABILITY TO USE THE PROGRAM (INCLUDING BUT NOT LIMITED TO LOSS OF DATA OR DATA BEING RENDERED INACCURATE OR LOSSES SUSTAINED BY YOU OR THIRD PARTIES OR A FAILURE OF THE PROGRAM TO OPERATE WITH ANY OTHER PROGRAMS), EVEN IF SUCH HOLDER OR OTHER PARTY HAS BEEN ADVISED OF THE POSSIBILITY OF SUCH DAMAGES.

END OF TERMS AND CONDITIONS

Chapter

19

Finding and Using Script Repositories

This chapter provides details on several dozen popular Web programming examples available for download on the Web. The vast majority of the programs listed in this chapter are either freeware—they cost nothing—or low-cost shareware. See Chapter 18, "Guidelines to Adopting Programs and Scripts," for more information on using freeware and shareware distributed over the Internet.

The program descriptions that follow are in the program author's own words, as he or she explains what the example program does. So, when you read "I": or "we," it is not the author or publisher of this book, but the author of the program itself.

> **NOTE** In the interest of fairness, the listings in this chapter are in no particular order, either alphabetical or "favorites." When reviewing this chapter you may want to mark interesting scripts for possible download with a marker or highlighting pen. In all cases, the location of the program (or of the introductory page for the program) is provided with each listing.

Various CGI "Goodies"

Available at http://www.eit.com/goodies/software/

The Webmaster's Starter Kit

The Webmaster's Starter Kit, created by Jay Weber in conjunction with the MADE project, simplifies setting up a Web site and also includes several utilities to help you maintain and develop your Web site.

WWWeasel

WWWeasel is a Web publishing tool that includes a full-featured HTML editor and document management capabilities. It was created in conjunction with the SHARE and DICE projects by Niels Mayer, Jay Glicksman, and Jack Hart.

WINTERP

Niels Mayer is the author of WINTERP (Widget INTERPreter), an interactive object-oriented environment for rapid-prototyping and delivering GUI-based applications employing the OSF/Motif widget set, a high-level 2D graphics/animation facility, and support for asynchronous/interactive UNIX subprocesses.

WebPlot

Deepak Nadig is the author of WebPlot, an application that plots the location of the clients accessing your WWW server on a map. Check it out!

Kevin Hughes has created the following World Wide Web utilities for WWW server administrators and users.

- Ewgie is an IRC-like chat and shared whiteboard system.
- Getstats analyzes log output from a variety of HTTP servers.
- Hypermail converts e-mail archives from UNIX mailbox format to cross-indexed HTML files.
- Swish generates searchable indexes of Web sites.
- WWWWAIS acts as an interface between search programs and forms-capable Web browsers.

A Simple CGI E-mail Handler

Available at http://www.boutell.com/email/

Many server administrators have noticed the e-mail- sending forms that are present on our server and on others. Our own e-mail forms are serviced by a simple CGI-compliant C program, based on the postquery program provided in the NCSA httpd 1.1 distribution. It delivers e-mail only to users specified by the maintainer and provides a convenient interface, avoiding the need to "step out of" Mosaic to send short notes.

To use this code, you will need to obtain the file util.c from the NCSA httpd 1.1 distribution. Fortunately, you can also obtain the util.c code here. Save the file to disk after you receive it.

You will also, of course, need a CGI- compliant server, such as the NCSA httpd or the CERN httpd. If you are offering pages over FTP or another access method aside from a true World Wide Web server, you will not be able to use this package. Note that you need access to the cgi-bin directory of your server. (Some administrators configure their servers to allow users to run CGI programs in their public_html directories if they rename the programs to have a .cgi extension.)

LiveCounter

Available at http://www.chamisplace.com/prog/lc/

LiveCounter is a page access counter written in Java 1.0.2 that can display up-to-the-minute access statistics using an animated odometer-like display. It will retrieve page access statistics from the server at specified time intervals and update the client's odometer display. If the access count goes up by more than 1 during the checkups, LiveCounter will keep increasing the odometer's value until it reaches the latest access count. LiveCounter comes with a companion CGI counter, so that even those hits generated from non-Java-enabled browsers can be counted as well.

Its features include the following:

- *Compact.* All required resources are linked into a single 10K class file.
- *Fast.* Runs fast enough to keep up with virtually any server's access statistics.

- *Server Friendly.* Uses a user-configurable time interval to contact the server to retrieve the latest access statistics, so that pages on servers with a slow response time can have a longer idle time in between checkups to avoid any burden to the server.
- *Customizable.* You can customize LiveCounter to display any changing number, not just page access statistics.
- *Smooth Animation.* Even if the time interval in which LiveCounter contacts the server is set to a high number such as 10 minutes, LiveCounter is able to animate its odometer during the idle time until it reaches the latest access count.

Web-Related Software

Available at http://www-genome.wi.mit.edu/~lstein/

CGI.pm

This is a Perl 5 library for handling forms in CGI scripts. With just a handful of calls, you can parse CGI queries, create forms, and maintain the state of the buttons on the form from invocation to invocation. GD.pm A is a Perl 5 interface to Thomas Boutell's gd library that allows you to generate GIF images on the fly.

qd.pl

This is a Perl (4, 5) library for creating Macintosh PICT files on the fly from within CGI scripts. PICT is an object-oriented graphics format that can be manipulated by many graphics programs on the Mac and other platforms. With the netPBM utilities, you can convert PICT into GIF, JPEG, or whatever.

BinHex

This utility allows you to convert UNIX files into Macintosh BinHex files so that you can create Excel spreadsheets, picts, and so on, on the fly and have them downloaded over the Web with type and creator information preserved.

mailmerge.cgi

This is a handy program for processing and mailing out the contents of fill-out forms according to rules laid out in a printmerge-style template file.

random_pict.pl

This is a CGI Perl script for returning a different random in-line image each time it's called. It helps make boring pages a little more interesting.

counter.shtml

This is a minimal server-side include template that prints a count of the number of times a page has been accessed. nph-publish, a Perl CGI script for the Apache server, lets you "publish" HTML files to a Web server using Netscape Navigator Gold and other HTML editors.

Access Counter

Available at http://skpc10.rdg.ac.uk/misc/randomcounter.sht

RandomCounter provides the perfect alternative to all those neat odometers—a short Perl script that introduces a customizable random number onto your page wherever you want (uses SSIs).

Its features include the following:

- Generates a random number every time the page is accessed.
- Has a user-definable minimum, but let's face it, who really cares?
- Appends the ordinals if you want; users can think they're the 801st visitor, rather than visitor number 801 (better English, even if it's a pack of lies !)
- Encourages users to return by offering prizes every so often (a bottle of wine for every hundredth visitor, a Dual Pentium Webserver for every thousandth, but again customizable; define your own prizes or turn them off altogether).
- Is free, environmentally friendly, and less intrusive than the CounterTerrorists—what further encouragement do you need?

The Archive Perl CGI Scripts

Available at http://www.middlebury.edu/~otisg/Scripts/index.shtml

The World-Wide Web CSO/ph

This is a nameserver client written in Perl.

Web2Mail.pl

This is a World Wide Web mail gateway.

URLoRAMA

URLoRAMA will take you to a random link every time you access it. Nothing cool, you already saw that 37 times before, I know, I know, but there is something you don't know—the internal part of this script, the code, is better than the code of other random link scripts.

HyperFinger.pl

This is a WWW-Finger Gateway that even made it to Yahoo!.

MultiMailer

If you have a file containing a list of e-mail addresses you need to mail and you have a file containing the message you want to send to all those addresses (or you create one since you know you can use MultiMailer for this) you can simply call MultiMailer with first argument being the file containing that list of e-mail addresses and the second argument being the file with the message to be sent to all those people.

lottery.pl

This one is just like lotto, except you can't win any $$$.

randGIF

This is a slide show of any GIFs on the Web you want.

WWWhosOn.pl

This is a script that lets you see who is currently logged on.

agents.pl

This analyzes agents_log (NCSA httpd 1.4).

referers.pl

This analyzes referers_log (NCSA httpd 1.4).

Anti-Counter

Available at http://www.cs.wisc.edu/~jenner/anti-counter.html

This is a faux counter script.

CGIWrap

http://wwwcgi.umr.edu/~cgiwrap/

CGIWrap is a gateway program that allows general users to use CGI scripts and HTML forms without compromising the security of the http server. Scripts are run with the permission of the user who owns the script. In addition, several security checks are performed on the script, which will not be executed if any checks fail.

Hitch-Hackers Cgi ToolKit

Available at http://amadeus.ccs.queensu.ca/cgihacks/hacks.html

CGI programming provides an exciting dimension to the Web Services that you provide. For Unix systems it also provides a method of including system resources, like telnet and mail, to your services. The benefits can be truly exciting.

Available selections at the site include the following:

- The basic forms menu technique
- The user authorization demo
- Linx URL page builder
- NCSA security admin tools
- Other CGI resources

CGI Applications

Available at http://www.comvista.com/net/www/cgi.html

CGI applications are the real meat of your WWW server. They provide all of the spiffy features that aren't worth adding to the server because not everyone wants them (and the server should just focus on HTTP). They include the following:

- *Map processing*. For imagemap processing on the server
- *Electronic mail and fax*. For sending electronic mail or FAXes from forms
- *Active pages*. For creating pages or inserting data on the fly
- *Form processing*. For processing form pages
- *Dbase interface*. For enabling database search and updates via the Web
- *Text searching*. For searching files on your server
- *URL redirection*. For redirecting users to other pages and servers
- *Administration*. For administering your server over the Web
- *Other CGIs*. For all kinds of purposes
- *CGI Shells*. Source code for writing CGI applications in various computer languages

CGI Scripts ... To Go!!

Available at http://www.virtualville.com/library/scripts.html

Available at the site are the following:

- Animators
- Automated WWW page generators
- Bulletin boards
- Chat scripts
- Comments pages scripts
- Counters
- Dynamic links (add links)
- Environment variable scripts
- File upload
- Form mail

- Guestbooks
- Height/width tag inserters
- Phone directory
- Random number generators
- Shopping carts
- Web-based e-mail
- WWW page editors

Animators

Program: Animate 0.91

Author: Home Pages, Inc.

Description: Use this script to show simple frame-by-frame, server push, GIF animations.

Type: Freeware

Language: Perl

Program: pull_cgi.pl

Author: John Donohue

Description: This script allows you to create client pull animations.

Type: Freeware

Language: Perl

Automated WWW Page Generators

Program: Create-A-Page Version 0.9

Author: ThotMedia, Inc.

Description: With this script, new HTML authors can have WWW home pages automatically created by filling out a simple form.

Type: Freeware

Language: Perl

Bulletin Boards

Program: WWW Board Version 2.0 ALPHA 2

Author: Matt Wright

Description: This script allows visitors to your Web page to post comments and follow-ups. A working demo of this script is also available.

Type: Freeware

Language: Perl

Chat Scripts

Program: The Chatterbox Version 0.9

Author: ThotMedia, Inc.

Description: This script allows a number of users to communicate with each other in a centralized forum.

Type: Freeware

Language: Perl

Comments Scripts

Program: Comments Script

Author: Matt Kruse

Description: This script allows users to leave comments on a visited page.

Type: Freeware

Language: Perl

Program: Virtualville's Comments Page

Author: ThotMedia, Inc.

Description: This script is a variation on Matt Kruse's comments script.

Type: Freeware

Language: Perl

Counters

Program: Counter Version 1.1.1

Author: Matt Wright

Description: Use this script to show a textual count of the number of visitors to a page.

Type: Freeware

Language: Perl

Program: Counter

Author: Matt Kruse

Description: Another textual script counter.

Type: Freeware

Language: Perl

Program: Count Release 2.2

Author: Muhammad A Muquit

Description: This is a graphical counter that simulates a digital display.

Type: Freeware

Language: Perl

Dynamic Links

Program: Free For All Link Page Version 2.1

Author: Matt Wright

Description: This script allows visitors to your Web page to add URLs to a designated page on the fly. A working demo of this script is also available.

Type: Freeware

Language: Perl

File Upload

Program: Virtual Webwerx Form-Based Upload CGI Version 1.0

Author: James K. Boutcher

Description: This script allows users to upload files via a Netscape Navigator 2.0+ browser.

Type: Freeware

Language: Perl

Form Mail

Program: FormMail Version 1.5

Author: Matt Wright

Description: Use this program to send an e-mail message containing data received from a form.

Type: Freeware

Language: Perl

Program: Form Mailer

Author: Matt Kruse

Description: Use this program to send an e-mail message containing data received from a form.

Type: Freeware

Language: Perl

Guestbooks

Program: Guestbook Version 2.3.1

Author: Matt Wright

Description: Use this program to keep track of who visits your WWW site.

Type: Freeware

Language: Perl

Program: The Walk of Fame

Author: ThotMedia, Inc.

Description: This script is a variation on Matt Wright's guestbook script.

Type: Freeware

Language: Perl

Height/Width Tag Inserters

Program: FixIMG Version 1.3

Author: Patrick Atoon

Description: This script figures out the height and width of images and then adds the appropriate tags to your HTML documents. This allows the text in your pages to be viewed first while the images are still loading.

Type: Freeware

Language: Perl

Phone Directory

Program: phone.pl

Author: John Donohue

Description: This script allows you to search for a person (substring) in a flat-file phone directory. The script then returns the results matching the search criteria.

Type: Freeware

Language: Perl

Random Number Generators

Program: random.pl

Author: John Donohue

Description: This script generates pseudo-random numbers.

Type: Freeware

Language: Perl

Shopping Carts

Program: Vend

Author: Andrew Wilcox

Description: This is a basic catalog script.

Type: Freeware

Language: Perl

Program: MiniVend

Author: Mike Heins

Description: This is a basic catalog script based on Vend.

Type: Freeware

Language: Perl

Web-based E-mail

Program: The WWW Post Office Version 0.9

Author: ThotMedia, Inc.

Description: This program emulates an e-mail system using a World Wide Web browser as the interface.

Type: Freeware

Language: Perl

CGI Scripts for Fun

Available at http://www.netamorphix.com/funcgi.html

The Keirsey Temperment Sorter

The Keirsey Temperament Sorter by David Keirsey is a personality test that scores results according to the Meyers-Briggs system (the actual Meyers-Briggs test is a professional instrument and may be administered only by a licensed practitioner).

Groan

Angus McIntyre is a freelance consultant in knowledge-based systems, interface design, natural language processing, communications, and multimedia. He maintains the Serious Road Trip Site, which is a registered British charity with a focus on children. Angus has written several cool CGI Perl scripts, one of which is called Groan. Groan is a kind of glorified fortune cookie script, and Angus has several incarnations of it at his site. Groan is a Perl script to generate random text from simple RTN grammars.

Tabloid Headlines

This is a round-up of today's current events as seen by the tabloids.

The War of the Worlds

This offers some alternative opening paragraphs for the classic novel by H. G. Wells.

AutoPeeve

An automatic peeve generator, for anyone who'd like to post to alt.peeves but isn't sure he or she can master the style. (Warning: This may be offensive to some readers.)

Browser Matcher

Drea Leed is the Webmaster for the Indiana University Law School and Law Library (IU is where I went to school, too!). She has written a bunch of creative scripts, which you can read about on her resume. Drea has also created a site called the SimConsultant. It's definitely a little weird, with a couple of other wacky scripts in evidence, one that gives you the Excuse Of The Day. The best page of the site is the fun "Literature of the Consultant" list of links. If you have ever been a computer consultant (or at least looked like one) you should check out these links! One of her fun Perl scripts is called Browser Matcher. It sends people with particular browsers to particular places. Now you can be sure that all those people surfing into your java-shockwave-frames combo are using Netscape Navigator 2.0 or better! You can view the script source here. If you want to see what browser you are using, click here!

Web Utilities

Available at http://www.zonecoaster.com/

Editpage

This script allows users to edit their Web pages through their browser windows.

Search

This is a simple search engine script for regular people.

Homepagemaker

This script allows users to fill out a form and have a home page automatically generated and saved in their home directories.

Survey

This versatile survey script allows you to administer a survey using any form you like. Results are stored in a text file and are retrieved, sorted, and presented to you, how you want, when you want.

Guestbook

This guestbook script allows you to make guestbooks that look nice, to have multiple guestbooks, or to have multiple users use the same script.

Chat

This is a chat progam for multiple users. This program requires a frames-capable browser.

Redirect

This is a simple redirection script...nothing much. You can turn it into a random link generator if you want.

Addlink

This script allows visitors to your site to add their links to a page you specify.

Examples of Perl CGI Scripts

Available at http://www.panix.com/~wizjd/test.html

These are meant as examples that programmers may find useful. I have not tried to make these "plug, and play" CGIs that are easy for nonprogrammers to install on their home pages. You need to be familiar with the system your Web server runs on in order to get these to work.

- A Clickable Image Map without "imagemap.c"
- "Juggling" Variables (state info) between pages
- Generate a random number, forces the browser to rerun script each time by including variable "extra path" info
- Search for names in a phone book, and add names to the phone book
- An example of a self-scoring questionnaire, using radio buttons and list boxes
- An example of using client pull with CGI scripts, to do an animation (a pumpkin that breaks into a grin)
- An example of a jump box (list box to jump to other pages)

CGI Example Scripts

Available at http://www.virtualcenter.com/scripts2/DownloadScripts.html

The following scripts are currently available for download.

Classified Ad

An easy-to-use classified ads system for users to read and post classified ads to an unlimited number of topics.

Guestbook

An update to the traditional guestbook program. Now let your visitors paint their message on your graffiti wall. New version 2.0 gives you the option to ignore any html commands the user enters in the text. It no longer needs cgi-libs.pl and is fully self-contained.

Voting Script

This is a simple voting script that allows users to vote an any number of topics.

Message Forum

This is an easy-to-set-up message forum system that allows users to post, read, and reply to messages in an unlimited number of forums.

News Bulletin

This script makes it easy for you or your guests to post news bulletins. It also allows you to delete bulletins at any time.

Interactive Chat

Now you can easily and quickly set up an interactive chat system on your Web site and allow users to talk to each other live. This script is very small and easy on your system. It can handle any number of visitors.

Order Processing

This is an easy-to-use order processor that processes users' orders, tabulates them, and provides the user with an online receipt.

Free CGI

Available at http://www.webcom.se/projects/freeware/

Upload

Uploading files via HTML has been out for a while but never as fast and secure as this. Upload version 2.0 is out!

Dirlist

I wrote this handy little script when we wanted to read a directory and display the content as a listing. You can even add unique descriptions to each file.

Redirect

There has been a lot of requests about this one, so here it is. The URL ReDirector from WebCom Sweden, about to change your way of surfin'...or?

Guestbook

Yes, here it is, the only guestbook you'll need. There is a installation guide and some "how-does-it-work" info included in the ZIP file.

Public Domain CGI Scripts

Available at http://www.eff.org/~erict/Scripts/

Selena Sol's Form Processor

This script can be used to process all of your HTML forms. By adding special hidden tags to your forms, you direct the script as to how the form should be processed (that is, where it should be e-mailed to, and so on).

Selena Sol's Guestbook

This is just your basic guestbook script, somewhat modified from Matt Wright's original version.

Selena Sol's Basic Animation Scripts

This link demonstrates various methods of text and graphics animations. Selena Sol's Random Banner Generator 4.0(Last ModifiedAugust 15, 1996). It is your standard random banner generator. What else can I say—just what we need, more advertisements! Scripts will be available when I have a chance to put them in a text directory.

Selena Sol's Slide Show

This is your basic slide show.

Web Store

Web Store is the culmination in the online shopping scripts. It merges both the electronic outlet HTML and database versions and adds all new routines for error handling, order processing, encrypted mailing, frames, and other goodies. This is a beta test; please send comments.

Selena Sol's Multiple-Choice Grader

This script allows you to create your own multiple-choice exams on the Web and, if you create an answer key database, it will grade the answers submitted by a user.

Selena Sol's Classified Ad Manager

This application manages a classified ads database, allowing people to barter, trade, and sell their stuff.

Selena Sol's Mailing List Manager

This script provides a user interface for browsers to add their names to your mailing list as well as a Web-based administrator's interface so that you can send mass mailings to those who have signed your list.

Selena Sol's Database Manager

This application allows one to maintain (add, modify, delete) multiple flat-file databases from the Web using one script. It also uses file locking routines to prevent more than one person from modifying the database at the same time and incorporates the latest authentication routines.

Selena Sol's Database Search Engine

This application allows you to search through multiple databases based on keywords submitted by users. This example searches the database managed by Database Manager above.

Selena Sol's Fortune Cookie

This is your basic fortune cookie script, with automatically changing fortunes. This routine can easily be incorporated into any HTML page by outputting the page from a script or by calling it with SSI.

Selena Sol's Groupware Calendar

The groupware calendar allows multiple users to view, add to, modify, and delete from a shared calendar. However, though clients can all see all of the scheduled events, only the poster of a message can modify that message. The newest features include the ability to manage multiple calendars with multiple user bases and events from one script.

Selena Sol's Time and Date Script

This one is pretty self-explanatory, really. The only thing of note is that the time and date are displayed in a user-friendly way, not in UNIX mumbo jumbo.

Matt Wright's Freeware Scripts

Available at http://www.worldwidemart.com/scripts/

Guestbook

As the first program to be introduced on MSA, the Guestbook has undergone many changes. This version allows users who visit your site to add their name, e-mail, URL, location, and comments to a single file. Newest entries will appear at the top of the Guestbook, making this script like a registry of those who have visited your site.

Free for All Link Page

The Free for All Link Program allows visitors to your site to add their favorite site or their home page to your list of URLs. There are several categories, and you can feel free to change them or add new ones. Every time a URL is submitted, it is added to the top of the link list for that category.

WWWBoard

Although WWWBoard is still in an Alpha release stage, and may stay that way for a while, it is much more stable than version 1.0 of this message system. WWWBoard comes with a WWWAdmin program to allow for the easy removal of old posts. WWWBoard is a threaded message board that allows for in-depth discussions.

Counter

Odometer-style graphical counters seem to be the newest craze on the Web, or one of the most overused, depending on how you look at it. This Counter program will allow you to use any set of digits on the Net, provided they are all the same height and width. It comes with many features including transparent capabilities, color frame specification, interlaced image capability, and a logging program to view who is visiting your page. It requires a compiled C program called Fly to run correctly.

TextCounter

If you have server-side includes capability and are looking for an easy to use and simple to set up text counter, MSA's TextCounter may be the solution for you. It can be set up to be used by an individual or a whole system, and the newest version allows for file locking and padded counts. Once the script is set up, adding a text counter to a new page is as simple as placing the SSI call into your HTML page.

Simple Search

Even if Simple Search isn't the most efficient search tool on the Internet, if you have a site consisting of only a few hundred documents it can get the job done. Simple Search allows for Boolean and/or switches and case-sensitive or -insensitive searches, and it will return a list of HTML pages that match the query supplied by a user.

FormMail

Looking to set up a feedback form, but don't know where to begin? FormMail allows you to write any form, and as long as a few simple hidden configuration fields are added, the results of the form will be mailed back to you. This script can also be installed and used systemwide or by a single user. You can have the form send the results to multiple recipients and specify how you want the information sorted as it comes into your mailbox.

HTTP Cookie Library

HTTP Cookie Library is a Perl 4 and 5 compatible library that allows you to easily use persistent client state HTTP cookies by allowing you to get the cookies from the environment, prepare cookies, set cookies, and change the expiration date, domain, and path all with easy subroutine calls.

Random Image Displayer

Tired of the same background or in-lined images every time you load your Web page? The Random Image Displayer allows you to specify certain images to be randomly displayed on your Web page, either as a background image or an image in-lined in your Web page.

Server-Side Includes Random Image Displayer

The Server-Side Includes Random Image Displayer is basically an extension of the basic Random Image Displayer. Although it does require the use of server-side includes, this version of the Random Image Displayer allows you to have alt text displayed for each image and a link that corresponds to that image, making it perfect for an advertisement rotation program.

Random Link Generator

Want to let users visit a random Web page on your site? Or one of your favorite Web pages on the Internet? The Random Link Generator will take users of your Web page to a random site on the Internet, choosing from a list of URLs that you can define.

Random Text

Wish to display random quotes, words, phrases, or other snippets of text on your pages? If so, this script takes a plain text file and a specified delimiter and will randomly choose phrases out of it and put them on your Web page. It requires server-side includes.

TextClock

TextClock is a Perl CGI script that is meant to be run from server-side includes. When this script is implemented, it can be used to show browsers several variations of the current time and/or date.

Animation

Animated GIF capability in the newest browsers has made this server push animation script almost obsolete. However, if you have a set of images that you wish to animate on the Web, simply download this program, plug in the names of the images, and fire up Netscape Navigator to watch your images be animated on the screen!

Countdown

How long do we have to wait until the year 2000? This countdown program will tell down to the second how long until a certain event will occur. This script can be implemented by a single user or systemwide, and it allows you to specify the date to which you wish to count down.

Credit Card Verifier—By Spider

The Validator verifies all 13- and 16-digit Visa Cards, 16-digit MasterCards, 16-digit Novus (Discover) cards, and 15-digit American Express cards.

Book 'em Dan-O—By Spider

Book 'em, Dan-O is a readily configurable, easy way to log the time of the visit, the visitor, where he or she came from (when used as an SSI), and what browser he or she was using. All great data to better refine your site! It is configurable as a server-side include or as a "redirect," while logging the visitor.

Central Script Repository

Available at http://www.selah.net/cgi.html

CGI scripts available here include the following:

- *MailForm.cgi, by Todd Kuebler (todd@wolfenet.com).* Language: Perl. This is a handy mailform CGI script that is easily customizable. It includes To:, Cc:, and Bcc:.
- *W3OClock, by Dan Austin (Invented Worlds).* Language: C. This is a nice clock that is customizable to your tastes. Right now, only NetScape Navigator users can view it properly. The clock updates itself at an interval set by you (default = 60 seconds) on the viewer's screen.

- *Guestbook.cgi, by Matt Wright (mattw@worldwidemart.com).* Language: Perl. This is a very nice guestbook script that is easily customizable by you. It features the ability to place the form and the guestbook on the same or different pages. You can e-mail any additions to the guestbook to whomever you choose. You can set the LASTDATE an entry was made, and so on. This script builds the guestbook with the last entry displayed first, but it would be easy to build it with oldest to newest.

- *PickMail.cgi, by Rod Clark (rclark@aa.net) with minor changes by ITM Services.* Language: Perl. PickMail.cgi lets the viewer select a name, partial name, or user name, and their full name and e-mail address is returned with the e-mail address fully displayed and parsed as a mailto: function. The PickMail.cgi program searches /etc/passwd or any other /etc/passwd-like file (we suggest you at least create a clean copy of passwd for PickMail to search with).

- *Logger.cgi, by Rod Clark (rclark@aa.net).* Language: Perl. Logger.cgi is a simple script that keeps a log of everyone who “hits” your page, keeping the information in one file (or more, depending on how you would like to set it up). Logger stores the user name (if identd checking is activated on your server), domain name, IP address, browser used, page that was hit, and the referring page.

- *Access Counter, by George Burgyan.* Language: Perl. This script keeps track of how many hits a page has received. This counter features multiuser support, cardinal, ordinal, and banner displays, as well as multiple language support.

- *Indexing with SWISH and WWWWAIS, by Kevin Hughes at EIT.* Languages: SWISH, C; WWWWAIS, C. Creating a database so that you have your Web pages and files searched is easy with SWISH and WWWWAIS. Both programs can be compiled with cc or gcc. SWISH is the database program similar to WAIS, but it is much easier to create. It searches your files, with the ability to exclude directories and/or particular files, and creates a database (usually swish.index, but you can name it whatever you want, and you can have as many databases as you want).

- *DGClock, by Muhammad A Muquit.* Language: C. DGClock is a small clock, not unlike W3Oclock, except that is it digital. As well, DGClock can use Netscape Navigator’s client pull, so that the clock can be continuously updated.

The nice thing, though, is that it doesn't have to. Where W3Oclock uses client push and cannot be viewed by those not using Netscape Navigator, DGClock can. It compiles with gcc.Client push, and transparent backgrounds are planned for a future release.

- *Register.pl v1.2, by ITM Services.* Language: Perl. Register.pl is a script that helps you control access to pages within one of your directories. It uses a Perl htpasswd.pl, which is a script that performs the same function as NCSA's htpasswd program to get a user name and password from a user and add that information into a password file compatible with htpasswd. The rest of the information is recorded into a log.
- *RandPic 1.0, by Robert Niles.* Language: Perl. A simple random image generator is demonstrated on this page. You have to be able to use SSI.
- *RandImg 1.0, by Robert Niles.* Language: Perl. This is a simple random image generator that doesn't require the use of SSI. It's not all that great for advertisements, but it's pretty cool for backgrounds and such.
- *FrameChat v1.0, by Pelicore Media Group.* Language: Perl 5. This file contains the complete source code and html files to set up WWW FRAME-CHAT on your server. It requires CGI-BIN access and Perl 5. It runs under Netscape Navigator 2.0.
- *Poll it v1.0, by Jason Berry.* Language: Perl. This is a nice script that allows a visitor to participate in a poll. It is customizable by the owner via a pleasant Web interface.
- *UDload v0.01, by Steve Y. C. Hsueh.* Language: Perl. This is an extremely useful script that allows files to be uploaded and downloaded via a Web browser that supports file uploads (currently Netscape Navigator 2.x and up is the only browser that supports this feature).
- *SimpleCount 1.0, by Robert Niles.* Language: Perl. This is a simple script to keep a count on the number of hits a page receives. The count is in plain text, which can be displayed; if you rather, you can comment out one line and have an invisible counter.
- *BookMark v1.0 by Mike Wilbur.* Language: Perl. This script grabs Netscape Navigator bookmarks and reformats them as a Web page. Netscape bookmarks

are normally an HTML document, but this one goes one further, adding subfolders as separate links.

- *Redirect 1.0, by Robert Niles*. Language: Perl. This is a really simple script that allows a visitor to click on a button that then redirects the visitor to another site. The only neat thing about this script is that it logs the location that the person chose. I wrote this in about 10 minutes because I kept receiving e-mails asking for such a script. This script creates a form containing three buttons, and the request is sent to the script using the method POST. This script can easily be changed to use the method GET—doing so means that you wouldn't have to use a form.
- *Logscribe, by Usama Wazeer and Daniel Cedras*. Language: Perl. Logscribe was originally developed by Matt Kruse under the name Graphical Access Stats, but it has gone through some major changes since. Logscribe is no match to the commercial Web access packages that are out there, but Usama Wazeer and Daniel Cedras put in a lot of effort to make it usable by just about any user who is allowed to run his or her own cgi scripts.
- *Internet Phonebook v1.0, by Robert Niles*. Language: Perl. The Internet Phonebook is a small script that stores names, e-mail addresses, and Web addresses. I wrote this for a book and expanded it because a visitor to this page asked for one, in which all entries are sorted when displayed. It's a nice little script for personal use.

BiblioBasket

Available at http://web.syr.edu/~jlhollin/bib.html

This Perl script enables an interactive sorting of bibliographic citations on the Web. BiblioBasket was based on several scripts by Matt Wright, which can be found at Matt's Script Archive.

CGI/VRML/Java Source Code

Available at http://stripe.colorado.edu/~leonarm/src.html

Guestbook

This guestbook is for people who want some control over what goes into their pages. Entries are put into a database for your inspection before going into the guestbook.

VRML

This script includes my VRML worlds, any associated source, and a tutorial on VRML 2.0, as well as my (old) VRML 1.0 worlds and any associated source.

Web Engineer's Toolbox

Available at http://www59.metronet.com/cgi/

CGI Library includes the following:

- Mailto CGIs
- Image maps
- Counters
- Server-push animation
- Redirects
- Finger

CGI.pm—A Perl 5 CGI Library

Available at http://www-genome.wi.mit.edu/ftp/pub/software/WWW/cgi_docs.html

This Perl 5 library uses objects to create Web fill-out forms on the fly and to parse their contents. It is similar to cgi-lib.pl in some respects. It provides a simple interface for parsing and interpreting query strings passed to CGI scripts. However, it also offers a rich set of functions for creating fill-out forms. Instead of remembering the syntax for HTML form elements, you just make a series of Perl function calls. An important fringe benefit of this is that the value of the previous query is used to initialize the form, so that the state of the form is preserved from invocation to invocation.

Turnkey CGI Program

Available at http://www.webgenie.com/

This program includes the following:

- Banner*Show is a Windows application that makes it simple to generate JavaScript-based rotating banners. No CGI is required!
- CGI*Star is the world's first and most powerful Windows CGI scripting tool. It automatically generates Common Gateway Interface scripts to e-mail the contents of HTML fill-out forms.
- Guest*Star is the all-in-one guestbook creator complete with JavaScript functionality.
- Mail*Wiz sends personalized e-mail messages to customers on your mailing lists.
- Site*Sleuth is the ultimate Web site traffic reporter tool.

UnCGI

Available at http://www.hyperion.com/~koreth/uncgi.html

UnCGI is a front end for processing queries and forms from the Web on UNIX systems. (It can also be run under Windows in some cases; see below.)

http://futures.wharton.upenn.edu/~attau791/webit.html

CGI Scripts

Available at http://www.stars.com/Vlib/Providers/CGI.html

Wog (Web Log)

Wog is a CGI script written in Perl that is designed to create a log similar to a regular Web server log for any Web page or group of Web pages. This should be of use to anyone who has access to running CGI scripts, but who does not have access to server statistics or logs.

Window's NT VB 4.0 32bit CGI Collection

This is a collection of CGI programs for WindowsNT servers.

Webcom Dakommunications

These are free CGI scripts for Windows NT. These scripts are written and tested for Microsoft IIS, but they should work just fine on most Web-servers running NT.

WWW Page Counts

Available at http://sw.cse.bris.ac.uk/WebTools/pagecount.html

This is a program for counting visits to a site.

Forms in Perl

Available at http://www.seas.upenn.edu/~mengwong/forms/

cgi-lib.pl

Steven Brenner's script turns messy input into an associative array of keys and values. It provides two sample functions to print the output.

generic.pl

This is a generic Perl script, similar in spirit to the standard postquery. It calls cgi-lib.pl form.html a generic form calling generic.pl.

GLIMPSE

Available at http://glimpse.cs.arizona.edu:1994/

This is a tool to search entire file systems.

Hukilau Search Engine

Available at http://www.adams1.com/pub/russadam/hukisoft.html

The Hukilau Search Engine is a CGI script written in Perl designed to do a keyword search of all the Web pages in a directory. It is designed to be easy to install, and it is for small to medium sites. The program will search for pages in only one directory, and it will return all pages if the keyword is the same as an HTML tag.

WebEvent

Available at http://bio.bu.edu/WebEvent/

WebEvent is an interactive online group calendar program that allows individuals or groups to share event (calendar) information via the World Wide Web. WebEvent runs on UNIX platforms using PERL and a flat database.

EarthWeb Chat

Available at http://chat.earthweb.com/

This is a Java-driven chat program.

Microsoft Site Builder

Available at http://www.microsoft.com/sitebuilder/

This is Microsoft's generic home for a number of Web- and server-related tools and program examples.

Gamelan Program Index

Available at http://www-a.gamelan.com/index.shtml

This index covers the following topics:

- Arts and entertainment
- Business and finance
- Educational
- How-to and help
- Miscellaneous

- Multimedia
- Network and communications
- Programming in Java
- Publications
- Related technologies
- Tools and utilities

Yahoo! Internet-related Pages

Available at http://www.yahoo.com/Computers_and_Internet/Internet/World_Wide_Web/

These pages cover the following topics:

- ActiveX
- Announcement services
- Authoring
- Best of the Web
- Books
- CGI—Common Gateway Interface
- Chat
- Databases and searching
- HTML
- HTTP
- Image maps
- Information and documentation
- Java
- JavaScript
- Programming

- Security
- Servers
- Tutorials
- Virtual Reality Modeling Language (VRML)

JavaScript Information

Available at http://gmccomb.com/javascript/

This is the support site for my book, *JavaScript Sourcebook*.

wtools Collection

Available at http://www-ece.engr.ucf.edu/~mav/Projects/wtools/

wtools is a collection of programs that are intended to help in administrating a Web site. It includes the following programs:

- *waccess*. This is an access_log analyzer and a sample script.
- *wchat*. This is a simple Web chat program and a sample script.
- *wboard*. This is some sort of a messaging board and a sample script.
- *wcount*. This is an access counter and a sample script.

SlideShow

Available at http://www.cs.cmu.edu/~lenzo/SlideShow.html

SlideShow is a Perl synchronized Web presentation scripts package.

WebScript

Available at http://webscript.netgravity.com/webscript/

WebScript images are dynamically generated images containing text in various fonts, sizes, styles, and effects. This type of image reference is ideal for applications that call for specialized text images based on dynamic data, like counters and forms.

JemTek CGI

Available at http://www.camtech.com.au/jemtek/cgi/lib/

JemTek CGI is a C library designed to simplify the creation of dynamic World Wide Web (WWW) applications. Dynamic applications are possible via the Common Gateway Interface (CGI), which provides an interface for running applications under an information server in a platform-independent manner. JemTek CGI is designed to be compatible with any CGI-enabled HTTP server.

WWW Protocol Library for Perl

Available at http://www.ics.uci.edu/pub/websoft/libwww-perl/

libwww-perl is a library of Perl packages/modules that provides a simple and consistent programming interface to the World Wide Web. This library is being developed as a collaborative effort to assist the further development of useful WWW clients and tools.

Java Applets

Available at http://www.javasoft.com/applets/

A Java applet is a Java program that can be included in an HTML page, much as an image can be included. When you use a Java-compatible browser to view a page that contains a Java applet, the applet's code is transferred to your system and executed by the browser. (For detailed information on how to include an applet in an HTML page, refer to the description of the applet tag.)

WebForms

Available at http://www.q-d.com/wf.htm

WebForms lets you create your own WWW forms that you can link to your home page, allowing you to accept orders for your products, conduct surveys, or do anything you can think of that requires a response from your users! WebForms consists of two modules combined into one amazing program.

CGI Slide Show

Available at http://www.ncsa.uiuc.edu/SDG/Software/XMosaic/CCI/cci-slide-show.html

CCI Slide Show is a program that reads a list of Uniform Resource Locators (URLs) and presents each in succession using NCSA Mosaic for the X Window System (version 2.5 or greater), as in a slide show.

Web Page Counter

Available at http://www.behold-software.com/counter/

This script creates a counter on your page using HTML via the <img src> method. It runs under Windows NT or 95 (32-bit) Console Application. It uses standard CGI (which is different from Windows CGI). It must be installed on your server.readme.txt. It supplies a complete description of all features. This file is included in the ZIP. Install notes: These are notes about how to install on all the different servers. Examples: Various example sites using various HTTP servers and processors.

Chapter

20

HTML Primer

Need a reminder of how to use an HTML tag? Found a tag that's new to you? This chapter reviews the most commonly used HTML tags as they are applied in Netscape Navigator 2.0 and above, as well as Internet Explorer 3.0 and above. This is not an exhaustive list of HTML tags by any means, but the following represents about 95 percent of the tags you'll use in your pages.

The chapter is divided into these major sections:

- Typical HTML document
- Anchor element
- Block elements
- In-line elements
- Image element
- List elements
- Form elements
- Frameset elements
- Table elements

A Typical HTML Document

While there is really no such thing as a "typical" HTML document, there is a typical structure to one. This structure follows and is referred to as an example throughout the chapter. The structure is shown with indenting, though such indenting is completely optional.

```
<HTML>
   <HEAD>
          <TITLE>This is the title</TITLE>
   </HEAD>
   <BODY>
      The body of the document goes here.
   </BODY>
</HTML>
```

Anchor Element

The anchor element performs the hypertext function of HTML pages. Without anchors you could not click on a link and be transported to another destination within the Internet. The anchor element comes in two general forms: a NAME tag that indicates a named anchor (or target) in a document and an HREF (HREF stands for *hypertext reference*) tag that indicates a link to some other document or a location elsewhere in the same document.

Because of the dual nature of the anchor element, it is sometimes referred go as an "anchor" and sometimes as a "link." It's an *anchor* when used with NAME and a *link* when used with HREF.

The "anchor" form of the anchor element is:

```
<A NAME="link_to_this_spot">...optional text here...</A>
```

This element creates a target anchor—a link points to this anchor. You can include optional text between the <A> and </A> tags. The text appears in standard body format and does not take on the customary appearance—color and underline—of a link anchor. This type of anchor is similar to a bookmark in a word processor. It marks a spot in the document to go to.

The "link" form of the anchor element is:

```
<A HREF="link_to_another_spot ">...optional text here...</A>
```

This element creates an anchor meant to reference another document or an anchor in the same document (it can even reference another document and an anchor within that document).

The optional text is the "click text" or label text—the text that you click on to activate the link. Though the text is shown here as optional, you must include something between the <A> and </A> tags so you can click on the link to activate it. An image or a combination of an image and text, can be enclosed between the <A> and </A> tags. If an image is used, the image becomes "hot"; that is, clicking on the image activates the link.

Though not often used, an anchor can be both a link and a target destination simply by using both NAME and HREF in the same anchor:

```
<A NAME="link_to_this_spot" HREF="link_to_another_spot">Click here</A>
```

Acceptable HREF Entries

When using the anchor element as a hypertext link, you must specify a valid URL or anchor name after the HREF attribute. Enclose the text in quotes. A typical URL is: http://www.anywhere.com/mypage.html.

When you click on an anchor that contains this for the HREF attribute, the browser program links to the mypage.html document at the location http://www.anywhere.com. Other valid URLs include FTP (file download) sites, local files on your own computer's hard disk drive, newsgroups, Telnet, and target (named) anchors. When using the latter, prefix the anchor name with a # symbol, as in:

```
HREF="#anchor_name"
```

This links to a bookmark anchor elsewhere in the document. You can also combine a URL to another document and an anchor within that document with the following technique:

```
HREF="http://www.anywhere.com/mypage.html/#bookmark_name"
```

Acceptable NAME Entries

With the exception of the # (hash) character, there is virtually no limit to the text you can use for the NAME attribute in an anchor. However, it's best to keep the name short. To maintain consistency, avoid spaces and capitalized characters (however, much of this is personal taste). Examples are shown in Table 20.1.

Table 20.1 Acceptable NAME Entries

Good	Not So Good
anchorname	#anchorname
contents	Contents
tableofcontents	Table of Contents
my_references	MyReferences

Examples of Actual Anchor Tags

Here are some examples of anchor tags as used in working HTML pages.

- Bookmark anchor to a table of contents:

```
<A NAME="contents"><H2>Table of Contents</H2></A>
```

- Link anchor to the table of contents of a document:

```
See the <A HREF="#contents">Table of Contents</A> for more
information.
```

- Link anchor to another document on the Web:

```
Visit<A HREF="http://www.anywhere.com/ugly.html">the ugliest page on
the Web</A> to see some bad examples of HTML page design.
```

- Link anchor to a specific bookmark in another document on the Web:

```
See the<A HREF="http://www.anywhere.com/ugly.html/#contents">table of
contents for the ugliest page</A> on the Web.
```

Remember that images can be used in place of, and in addition to, the text used between the <A> and </A> tags. See the entry for the <IMG> element elsewhere in this chapter for more information.

HTML Block Elements

Block elements literally "block" text in an HTML document, for the purpose of rendering in a special format. They are called block elements because they work with blocks of text and often cannot contain other block elements, or they are restricted in the type of other block elements that can be included.

<ADDRESS>

The address element defines text in a document that you want to display as a mailing or Internet address. Most browsers render this text in italics or some other special way. The address element serves to provide a visual cue that the text within it should be given special consideration.

Address is an HTML block element and therefore contains paired tags: <ADDRESS> and </ADDRESS>. The syntax of the address element looks like this:

```
<ADDRESS>address goes in here</ADDRESS>
```

Quite often you want to include a mailing address, complete with the usual line breaks between the name, address, city, and so forth. This is accomplished within the address block with the use of
 (line break) tags. Following is a typical example of the address element.

```
<ADDRESS>
John Doe & Associates<BR>
John Doe, President<BR>
123 Main Street<BR>
Anytown, US 12345<BR>
</ADDRESS>
```

<BODY>

The body element encloses all of the text and tags that are meant to be displayed in the document. In reality, most Web browsers display text outside the body element, but they may not always behave this way in the future. It's a good idea to include the body element in all your Web documents, if for no other reason than consistency.

Body is a block element and therefore consists of a start tag, <BODY>, and an end tag, </BODY>. Between these tags go all the other formatting and tags you want displayed in your document. See the "Typical HTML Document" example earlier in this chapter to see how the body element is used.

The <BODY> tag accepts a number of attributes. These attributes are used to control the overall appearance of the background and text of the document (though the user has the option to ignore these attributes and stay with the default choices). These attributes include the following:

- Background color
- Text color

- Link color
- Visited link color
- Active link color
- Wallpaper

These attributes may be used alone or in conjunction with any of the others.

Specifying a Background Color

The background color can be set for a Web page with the BGCOLOR attribute. The color is specified using an "RBG triplet" (see "Deciphering RGB Triplet Values," later in this chapter). The value for an all-black background is #000000; the value for an all-white background is #ffffff. The default medium gray is specified as #0c0c0c. The following example creates a red background:

```
<BODY BGCOLOR="#ff0000">
```

Specifying a Foreground Color

The foreground color sets the color of text. Normally the text is black, but it can be changed to any other color. As with the background, the foreground color is specified using an RBG triplet (see "Deciphering RGB Triplet Values," later in this chapter). Use the TEXT attribute to change the foreground color. The following example creates green text:

```
<BODY TEXT="#00ff00">
```

Specifying Link Colors

You can choose colors for the three kinds of links: new (never-before-visited), visited, and active. The color for each is specified as an RBG triplet or as a valid color name, such as "white," "black," or "cadetblue" (see "Deciphering RGB Triplet Values," later in this chapter). The attributes are listed in Table 20.2.

Table 20.2 Link Color Attributes

Link Type	Attribute
New link	LINK= #nnnnnn
Visited link	VLINK=#nnnnnn
Active link	ALINK=#nnnnnn

Here are some examples:

```
<BODY LINK="#ff1494">   (makes pink)
<BODY VLINK="#ffd700">  (makes yellow)
```

Specifying a Wallpaper Graphic

If you're not satisfied with a solid color background you can cover the background with "wallpaper," a small graphic that is repeated as needed to fill the entire background area. Most wallpaper images are small 1-by-1 GIF or JPG graphics files—the smaller the better, so they don't take a long time to transmit to the user's computer.

To specify a wallpaper image use the BACKGROUND attribute, along with the name of the graphic file you wish to use. This can be the filename alone if the file is included in the same directory as the HTML document currently viewed, or it can be in a different directory or even on a different server. The following example specifies a background file called BG.GIF:

```
<BODY BACKGROUND="bg.gif">
```

If you wish to use a graphic not contained in the same directory as the current HTML file, include a URL path. Use an absolute or relative URL, as needed. Here's an example using an absolute URL:

```
<BODY BACKGROUND="http://anywhere.com/mypages/bg.gif.">
```

Specifying Multiple Background Options

Feel free to combine background attributes as desired. For example, to specify a white background and blue text, use the following:

```
<BODY BGCOLOR="#ffffff" TEXT="#0000ff">
```

Ordinarily, if you specify a wallpaper image your background color setting is ignored. This is true if the wallpaper graphic is not transparent. The background color will show through if the image is transparent (it can be made transparent using the transparency option in many advanced graphics programs).

> **NOTE** If you specify one <BODY> tag element, such as foreground color or text color, you should specify them all. Otherwise, your unique color setting may conflict with default settings made by the user.

<BLOCKQUOTE>

The blockquote element defines text in a document that you want to display as a large segment of "quoted" text, such as from a book or magazine article. Most browsers render this text in a special way, usually as standard text with indenting. The blockquote element serves to provide a visual cue that the text within it should be given special consideration.

Blockquote is an HTML block element and therefore contains two paired tags: <BLOCKQUOTE> and </BLOCKQUOTE>. The syntax of the blockquote element looks like this:

```
<BLOCKQUOTE>Text goes in here</BLOCKQUOTE>
```

Most often, blockquoted text is rendered with indenting on the right and left, as shown in Figure 20.1. The effect of the blockquote is most obvious with lots of text.

Figure 20.1 Blockquoted text appears indented from, and, on some browsers, in a different font than, the body text.

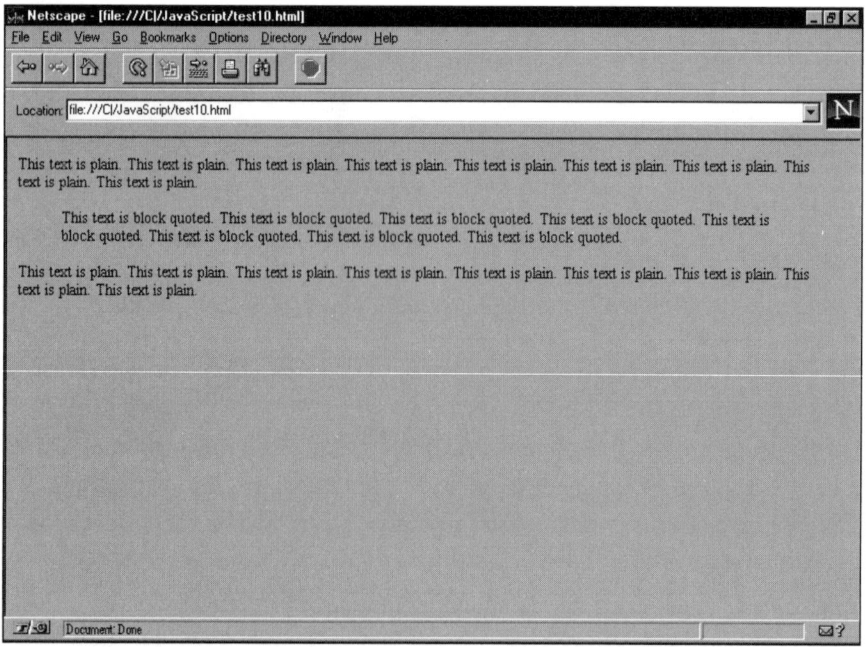

You can use blockquote to create some indented special effects. For example, suppose you are writing a Hollywood screenplay and want to use the standard script format, where character names are centered, and dialog appears indented from the left and right margins. The text for "action" descriptions spans from margin to margin. You can accomplish this by nesting several blockquote elements within one another. Nesting four blockquote elements like this:

```
<BLOCKQUOTE><BLOCKQUOTE><BLOCKQUOTE><BLOCKQUOTE>
Text goes here
</BLOCKQUOTE></BLOCKQUOTE></BLOCKQUOTE></BLOCKQUOTE>
```

Character names are formatted with the <CENTER> tag to center them.

<CENTER>

The center element centers text and images between the visible window margins of the browser. It is used entirely for cosmetic purposes and goes a long way toward improving the looks of Web pages.

Center is an HTML block element and therefore contains two paired tags: <CENTER> and </CENTER>. The syntax of the center element looks like this:

```
<CENTER>Centered text goes in here</CENTER>
```

Once you turn centering on it remains on until you turn it off with the </CENTER> tag, so be sure to switch it off when you're done using it. Remember that centering affects all text and images, as well as tables and forms.

The line break element starts text or graphics on a new line. It acts like a hard return in a word processor, where pressing Enter begins another line. To insert a line break use <BR>. The <BR> tag is used by itself and has no end-tag.

Note that the <BR> tag inserts a line break without extra spacing before or after the line. If you want to add extra spacing between text use the <P> tag instead.

Browsers understand a small assortment of attributes for the <BR> tag. These attributes relate to how text wraps around images. Use the CLEAR attribute in the <BR> tag to indicate how you want the text to flow around the image:

- Use CLEAR="left" to break the line and move down vertically until the left margin is clear of the image.
- Use CLEAR="right" to break the line and move down vertically until the right margin is clear of the image.
- Use CLEAR="all" to break the line and move down vertically until the left and right margins are clear of the image.

<FONT>

The font element lets you change the color and size of individual text (it has no effect on the size of the font used in headings, form buttons, and other elements). The font element is not supported by all browsers, but it is supported by most of the modern ones, such as Netscape Navigator or Internet Explorer. The text appears normally when viewed on a browser that does not understand the font element.

The attributes for the <FONT> tag are listed in Table 20.3.

Font is an HTML block element and is normally used with paired tags: <FONT> and </FONT>. The syntax of the FONT element looks like this:

```
<FONT SIZE=value>Text go here</FONT SIZE>
```

Substitute value with size of the font you want to display, with 1 being the smallest and 7 being the largest. The default is 3. For example, to set the font size to 5 (two steps larger than the default), use:

```
<FONT SIZE="5">Text go here</FONT SIZE>
```

When the browser reaches the </FONT> tag, it reverts to the default font size.

Note that the user can select the default size for body text as a setting in the browser. The values used with the font element are relative, so that even if the user has selected a large font already, specifying a larger font in a font element produces even larger text. You should take this into account when changing the size of font to any great extent, especially when making fonts very small. For example, it's possible

Table 20.3 <FONT> Attributes

Attribute	What It Does
SIZE	Sets the size of the text that follows
COLOR	Sets the color of the text that follows

for the user to choose an 8 point font for regular text. If you reduce the font size to 1 with the font element, that text will be impossibly small when viewed in the browser. Therefore, you should avoid using font size values smaller than 1 and greater than 5.

You can also assign a relative size value, which helps to ensure that the font size actually displayed is not overly large or small. To specify a relative size place a + or – symbol before the font value, as in:

```
<FONT SIZE="+2">Text go here</FONT SIZE>
```

This example increases the size of the body font by two steps. Conversely, you can specify a smaller font by using a negative number, as in:

```
<FONT SIZE="-1">Text go here</FONT SIZE>
```

This decreases the size of the body font by one step. See Figure 20.2 for an example of an assortment of font sizes.

Figure 20.2 The <FONT> tag can be used with the ASIZE attribute to specify an absolute or relative size for text.

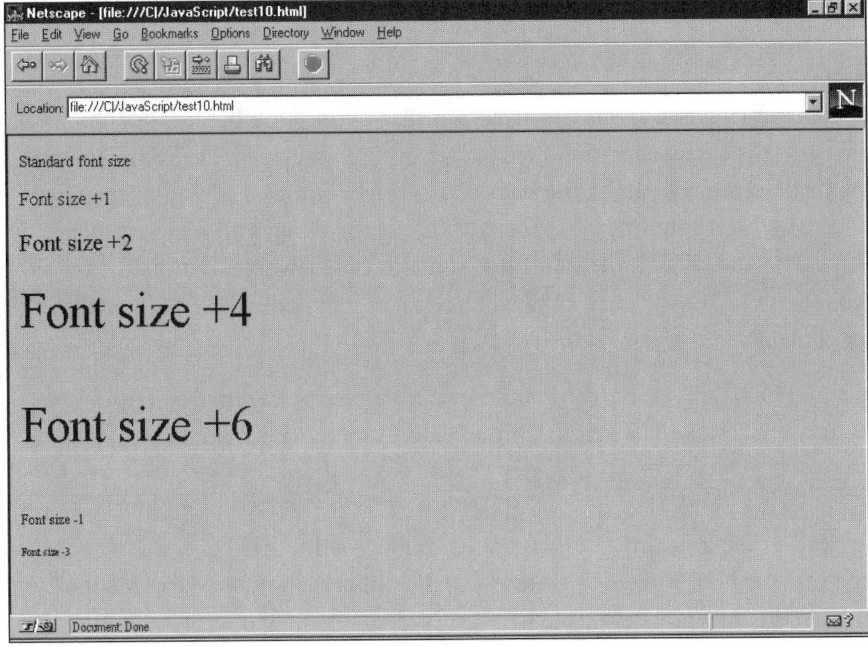

Setting the Overall Font Size

While the font element is designed to be used with paired tags, you can leave off the </FONT> end-tag if there is no need to revert to the standard font size. For instance, this sets the font size value to 4 for the remainder of the document:

```
<FONT SIZE="4">Text follows, with no end-tag...
```

Setting a Base Font

The open-ended method of setting a font size is not the preferred method to use. Rather, if you wish to set a default body text font size for the entire document, use the <BASEFONT> tag, as follows:

```
<BASEFONT SIZE=value>
```

As with the <FONT> tag, use a value from 1 to 7 for the basefont font size.

Setting Font Color

Also use the <FONT> tag for setting the color of specific text. The color for each is specified as an RBG triplet or as a valid color name, such as "white," "black," or "cadetblue" (see "Deciphering RGB Triplet Values," later in this chapter).

```
<FONT COLOR="#ff1494">This is pink text!</FONT COLOR>
<FONT COLOR="pink">This is also pink text!</FONT COLOR>
```

<HEAD>

The head element encloses special information that defines the HTML document. This information is enclosed within its own set of tags, such as <TITLE>. The tags within the head element describe the data. Currently few tags are used in the head element. Of particular importance is the <TITLE> tag, along with any comments that are stored in the HTML file, but not shown in the viewer. Additionally, the head contains the tag that identifies JavaScript as an embedded language used in the HTML document.

Head is an HTML block element and therefore contains two paired tags: <HEAD> and </HEAD>. The syntax of the head element looks like this:

```
<HEAD>Additional tags go here</HEAD>
```

As the head element is almost always used to enclose the <TITLE> tag, which defines the title of the document (the title usually appears in the caption for the browser window). A typical example is:

```
<HEAD><TITLE>This is the title of the document</TITLE></HEAD>
```

An HTML document that contains JavaScript or VBScript uses the <SCRIPT> tag, also contained within the head element. Here's a bare-bones example, formatted onto separate lines for easy reading:

```
<HEAD>
     <TITLE>HTML document with JavaScript</TITLE>
     <SCRIPT LANGUAGE="JavaScript"></SCRIPT>
</HEAD>
```

Comments regarding the construction of the document are also typically included in the head element, using <!- -> comment tags. Though the head is the usual place for comments, they can be placed anywhere in the document. The text contained in the comment tag is ignored by the browser.

```
<HEAD>
   <!--This is a document that contains JavaScript-->
   <TITLE>HTML document with VBScript</TITLE>
   <SCRIPT LANGUAGE="VBScript">
</SCRIPT>
</HEAD>
```

> **NOTE** Many older browsers use a simplified technique for terminating a comment. The comment is terminated as soon as the browser encounters the first > character. This means that a comment such as:
>
> ```
> <!--This is a comment for the <HEAD> tag -->
> ```
>
> will insert the text tag --> into the browser.

<H1> through <H6>

HTML supports headings to separate the text of a document. These headings are numbered 1 through 6, with heading 1 being a "top-level" heading for main sections of a document, and heading 6 being a lowly subheading for minor sections. Few HTML documents use more than the first two or three headings.

The basic syntax for all six heading levels is the same, except for the number that defines the level. As headings are block elements, they consist of a starting tag,

<H*x*>, and an ending tag, </H*x*>). The *x* is a number from 1 to 6. Here's an example of a top level (level 1) heading:

```
<H1>This is a main heading</H1>
```

By definition, a heading appears on a line by itself, so any text that follows it will begin on a new line. All browsers add extra spacing to the top and bottom of the heading to make it stand out in the text. Figure 20.3 shows an example of how all six heading levels look in Netscape Navigator. You will notice that each heading level is rendered in a slightly different format.

How to Use Headings Effectively

One of the bug-a-boos of Web page design is proper use of headings. A lot has been written on this subject, and most any book or reference describing good print layout design is also applicable to Web page design.

Figure 20.3 The six levels of headings and how they compare.

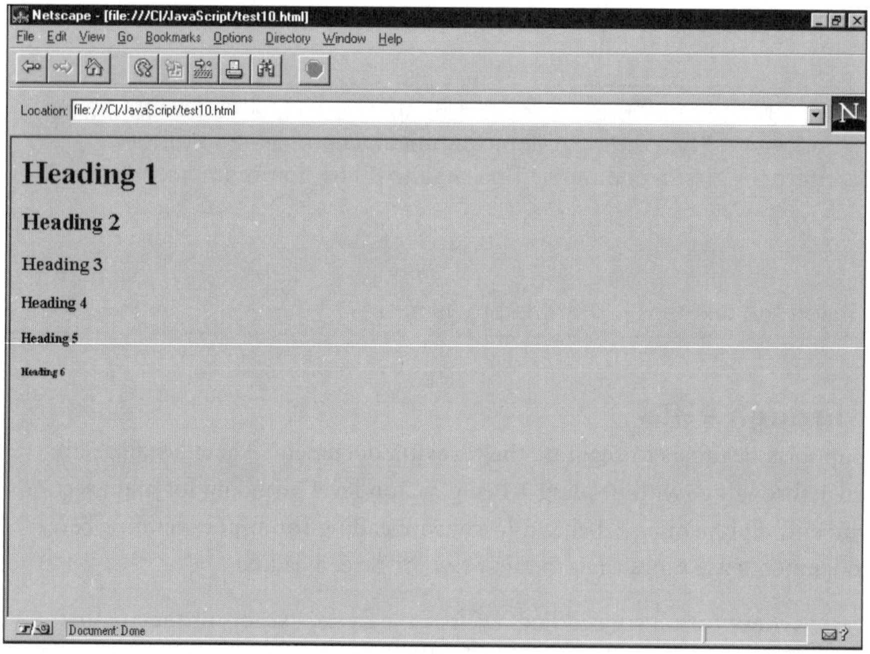

Of most importance is that the headings should convey a hierarchy. Avoid using a level 1 heading and following it with a level 3 heading. Readers are accustomed to using the relative size of headings to help convey the structure of a text—main headings, subheadings, sub-subheadings, and so forth.

Though not a rule, headings are typically applied so that there are at least two headings of each level in a section. For example, if you have one level 2 heading in a section, you should have at least one more. Again, this helps denote structure to the reader. A typical good heading structure might go like this:

```
Main heading 1
        Subheading 1
        Subheading 2
Main heading 2
        Subheading 1
        Subheading 2
Subheading 3
```

Whereas this heading structure is deemed lacking:

```
Main heading 1
        Sub heading 1
Main heading 2
        ...
```

When possible avoid inserting a subhead immediately following the next higher level. Insert at least one sentence of plain text to separate them.

Finally, many Web pages uses the first level head, <H1>, for the main title or banner at the start of the document (often, but not always, the same as the document title, which is defined using the <TITLE> element). Level 2 headings are then used as the main headings within the document.

Using Other Elements with Headings

By design heading elements are meant to stand alone, and they cannot often mix other HTML elements with a heading. There are notable exceptions.

- You may use all or part of the heading text as the "click text" of an anchor. Example: <H1><A HREF="url">This is a heading</A></H1>
- You may add italics and other character attributes to the text of a heading. Example: <H1>This is a <I>heading</I></H1>.

- Most browsers add extra space for formatting following the </Hx> end tag. To add a horizontal line with only a small space between it and a preceding heading, include the <HR> tag within the heading definition. Example: <H1>This is a heading<HR></H1>.
- Conversely, if you want more space between the heading and the horizontal line, place the <HR> tag outside of the header definition. Example: <H1>This is a heading</H1><HR>.
- The same technique mentioned in the above two items can also be applied to horizontal lines added before the heading. Examples: <H1><HR>This is a heading</H1> and <HR><H1>This is a heading</H1>. Figure 20.4 shows some examples.

<HR>

The horizontal rule element inserts a margin-to-margin line across the page and is used to optically separate areas of the page (no, there is no built-in vertical rule ele-

Figure 20.4 Creative placement of the <HR> tag within the <Hx> heading tags yields various spacings.

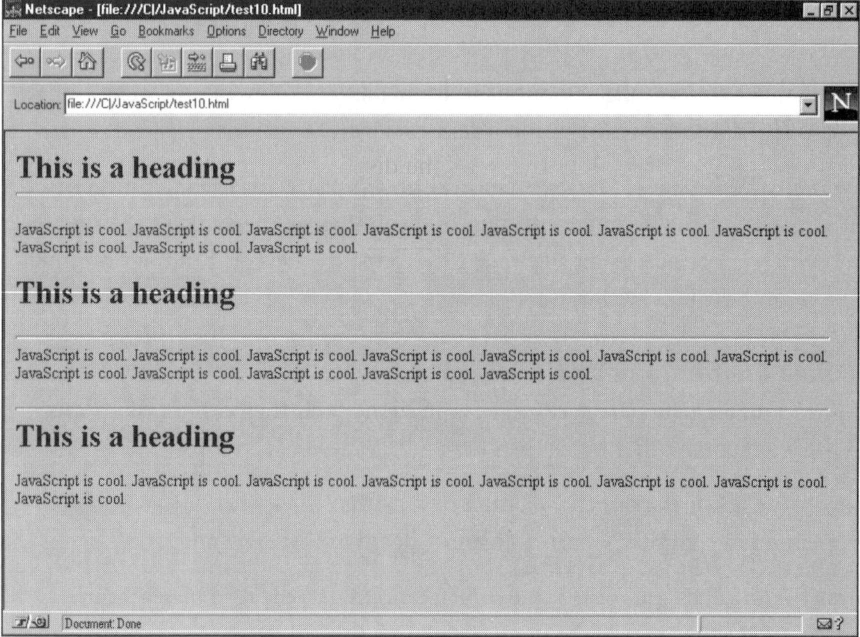

ment, though this would be a good idea). The horizontal rule element is a simple stand-alone tag (there is no end-tag). To insert a horizontal tag use <HR>. The actual appearance of the rule depends on the browser. Navigator renders the rule with a 3D appearance, but some other browsers use a simple black line.

Navigator also adds a number of options to the <HR> tag. These options set the width and size of the rule, as well as its shading.

- Use the *SIZE* attribute to set the thickness of the rule. The default is roughly two pixels.
- Use the *WIDTH* attribute to set the width of the rule. You can use either actual pixels or percentage. Because browsers are used at different screen resolutions, it's almost always better to rely on the percentage measurement.
- Use the *NOSHADE* attribute to tell Navigator that you do not want the rule to be rendered in 3D.
- Use the *ALIGN* attribute to align the line to the left, center, or right. Valid parameters are "left," "right," and "center."

Table 20.4 lists some examples.

Note that Navigator renders a one-pixel rule as a simple black line, whether or not you use the NOSHADE attribute.

By default all browsers add a new line after each horizontal rule. You cannot remove this line break, but you can increase the distance between rules if you are

Table 20.4 <HR> Definitions

Example	Definition
<HR SIZE=5 WIDTH=50%>	Size of 5 pixels, 50 percent width
<HR SIZE=10 WIDTH=100%>	Size of 10 pixels, 100 percent width
<HR SIZE=3 WIDTH=300>	Size of 10 pixels, 300 pixels width
<HR SIZE=1 WIDTH=33%>	Size of 1 pixels, 33 percent width
<HR SIZE=2 NOSHADE>	Size of 2 pixels, no shading
<HR SIZE=2 ALIGN=1"center" WIDTH=33%>	Size of 2 pixels, no shading

inserting more than one. Use either a <P> or <BR> tag after the <HR> tag to increase the spacing, like this:

```
<HR><BR>
<HR>
```

<HTML>

The HTML element defines the text and tags within it as conforming to the HTML specification. All the text and formatting are included in separate sections of the same document.

HTML is a block element and therefore contains two paired tags: <HTML> and </HTML>. The syntax of the HTML element looks like this:

```
<HTML>
...everything else goes in here
</HTML>
```

See the "Typical HTML Document" example earlier in this chapter to see how the body element is used.

<META>

The <META> tag provides "extra" information—called metainformation—for the server. A common use for the <META> tag is providing keywords for cataloging the document. A "search robot" (a program that roams the Web looking for pages to catalog) reads the content of the <META> tag and stores it.

The <META> tag—which is placed in the <HEAD> structure— is traditionally used with three attributes, though as the tag has no specific application, additional attributes may be added. These attributes are as follows:

- *NAME.* Provides the name for a keyword.
- *HTTP-EQUIV.* Provides an equivalent HTTPd (Web server) header. The most commonly used application of HTTP-EQUIV is for "client-pull," where the browser automatically fetches a URL.
- *CONTENT.* Provides the content for a named keyword or HTTP-EQUIV action.

The following example provides two keywords for cataloging the document:

```
<META NAME="Author" CONTENT="Gordon McComb">
<META NAME="Subject" CONTENT="Stuff">
```

The following uses the “client-pull” method to fetch another URL 10 seconds after the current document has been loaded:

```
<META HTTP-EQUIV="Refresh" CONTENT="10; http://mydomain.com/home.htm">
```

<NOBR>

The no break element tells the browser to render the body text without wrapping each line at the right margin. You would not normally do this without a good reason, except for certain special effects and when you don’t want a stream of characters broken up. The no break element is not provided in all browsers (but is in Netscape Navigator), so use it with caution.

No break is a block element and therefore contains two paired tags: <NOBR> and </NOBR>. The syntax of the no break element looks like this:

```
<NOBR>text you don't want broken up</NOBR>
```

See also the <WBR> word break element for an associated tag you can use with no break.

<P>

The paragraph element ends the current body text and starts a new line. It also adds extra spacing at the start of the new paragraph, to help set it off from the rest of the text. To insert a new paragraph use <P>.

Note that the <P> tag inserts a new paragraph and line break with extra spacing. If you want the line break but without the extra spacing use a line break (<BR>) instead.

Often, the <P> tag is used by itself, though HTML does specify an end-tag, </P>. The following structure is perfectly acceptable to most all browsers, where each <P> tag starts a new paragraph:

```
This is a line of text<P>
This is another line<P>
And yet another line
```

But Web browsers are getting more picky, and one day they may require (or at least prefer) the following structure. So best start using it now. This example is rendered exactly the same as the previous example.

```
<P>This is a line of text</P>
<P>This is another line</P>
<P>And yet another line</P>
```

Netscape Navigator and Internet Explorer support several <P> tag attributes, all of which are part of the HTML 3.0 specification:

- *ALIGN=center*. Aligns the paragraph in the center
- *ALIGN=right*. Aligns the paragraph to the right
- *ALIGN=left*. Aligns the paragraph to the left (default)

For example:

```
<P ALIGN=center>
```

<PRE>

Web browsers try to be as conservative as possible, and they remove any extra spaces, tabs, and hard returns contained in the source HTML document. That means you can't normally use spaces, tabs, and hard returns to format your text. However, if strict formatting is absolutely required, you can usually obtain it with the preformatted text element. When a browser encounters this element it respects most of the formatting found inside.

Preformatted text is an HTML block element and therefore contains two paired tags: <PRE> and </PRE>. The syntax of the preformatted element looks like this:

```
<PRE>text and formatting goes here</PRE>
```

You're free to include extra spaces and hard returns in a preformatted text element; however, some Web browsers, particularly older ones, continue to ignore some formatting, such as extra hard returns. As Figure 20.5 shows, the formatting is carried through and is displayed, rather than ignored, which is the usual behavior for Web browsers.

Note that some browsers use a different font for the text inside a preformatted text element. The font is usually monospaced and is used to indicate that the text is of a special nature.

<SCRIPT>

The <SCRIPT> tag is used to enclose runnable script, such as JavaScript. The <SCRIPT> tag is used with an end tag, </SCRIPT>. In a JavaScript-compatible browser, text between these tags is interpreted as executable code, rather than document content. In a non-JavaScript-compatible browser, the <SCRIPT> tag is ignored and the script text is rendered in the browser. For this reason, it is advisable to

Figure 20.5 Formatting is preserved for text in a <PRE> tag.

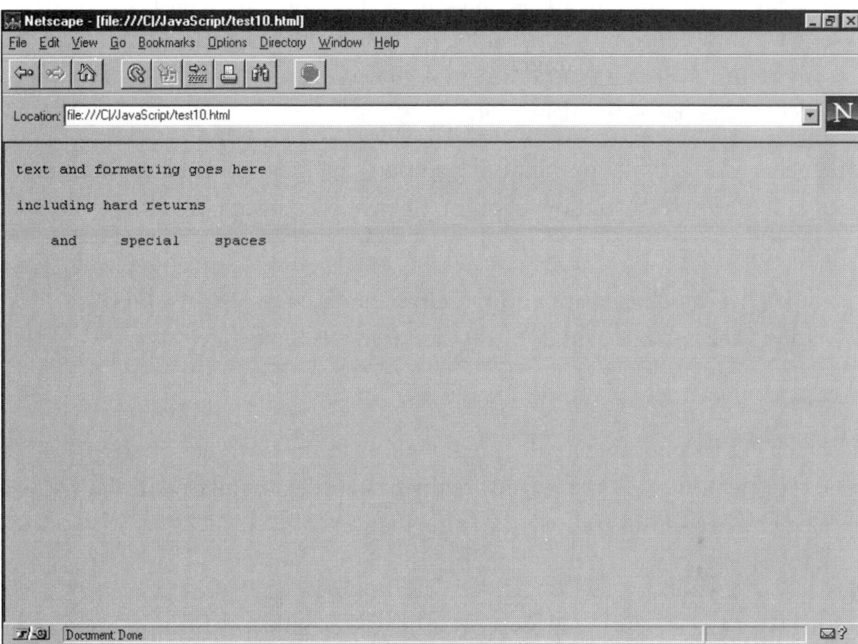

place HTML comments at the beginning and end of the script code to help prevent this text from appearing in the browser.

As used with Netscape Navigator 2.0 and above, the <SCRIPT> tag accepts a LANGUAGE attribute. For JavaScript this attribute is set to LANGUAGE="JavaScript." As used with Internet Explorer, the LANGUAGE attribute can be JavaScript, or VBS, which stands for VBScript, the native scripting language built into Internet Explorer.

For example:

```
<SCRIPT LANGUAGE="JavaScript">
<!-- Hide script text from most non-JavaScript browsers
document.write ("Hello JavaScripters!");
//-->
</SCRIPT>
```

<TITLE>

The title element defines the title of the document file. This title typically appears in the browser's window caption. Additionally, if you save the page as a bookmark (so you can easily return to it at a later date), most browsers use the title—rather than the actual URL of the page—to identify it.

The title element is actually optional. If you don't include a title either nothing will appear in the browser's window caption, or the name of the browser is placed there instead.

Title is an HTML block element and therefore contains two paired tags: <TITLE> and </TITLE>. The syntax of the title element looks like this:

```
<TITLE>This is the title of the document</TITLE>
```

While the <TITLE> tag can actually go anywhere in the document (most browsers accept this), the <TITLE> tag is really designed to be placed in the <HEAD> element. See <HEAD> for more information.

<WBR>

The word break element tells the browser that it is acceptable to break a body of text formatted with the <NOBR> (no break) element, so that the text can be more naturally formatted if needed. The word break element is not provided in all browsers (but is in Netscape Navigator), so use it with caution.

Word break uses just one tag; there is no end-tag. Place the tag at the spot where you want to allow the browser to break the line.

```
<NOBR>text you don't want broken up<WBR>except where permitted</NOBR>
```

See also the <NOBR> no break element.

HTML In-line Elements

In-line elements are those that modify the appearance of text, typically body text. For example, the bold element adds bolding to characters, whereas the underline element adds underlining. In most cases—and assuming a modern browser such as Netscape Navigator 2.0—in-line elements can also be used in conjunction with other in-line elements (bolding and italics, for example) and within many block elements, such as headings. Note that you don't always see a visible difference. You won't notice anything if you add the bolding element to heading text because heading text is already bolded.

For example, this works with most browsers:

```
<H2><I>This is italicized</I></H2>
```

All in-line elements have paired tags: the first tag turns on the character attribute, and the second tag turns it off. Be sure to include the end-tag for all in-line elements start tags or else your Web documents will not be rendered properly.

There are two forms of in-line elements: *physical* and *logical*.

- The physical in-line elements are bold, underline, and italics. They are called physical elements because they are designed to have the same effect in all browsers, no matter what personalization settings the user has adopted.
- The logical in-line elements include emphasis, strong, and citation (there are others as well). They are called logical elements because their effect is determined by browser settings. Depending on the features of the browser, users can turn off formatting for logical elements or change the default formatting.

Which do you use: physical elements or logical elements? It depends. If you absolutely want to convey text using a particular format, such as bold, use a physical element. But if you merely want to set off text in some special way, without worrying about what that format actually is, use a logical element.

Table 20.5 Physical and Logical Elements

Element	Start-tag	End-tag	Type
Bold	<B>	</B>	Physical
Citation	<CITE>	</CITE>	Logical
Code	<CODE>	</CODE>	Logical
Emphasis	<EM>	</EM>	Logical
Italics	<I>	</I>	Physical
Keyboard	<KBD>	</KBD>	Logical
Sample	<SAMP>	</SAMP>	Logical
Strong emphasis	<STRONG>	</STRONG>	Logical

Continued

Table 20.5 *Continued*

Element	Start-tag	End-tag	Type
Typewriter	<TT>	</TT>	Logical
Underlined	<U>	</U>	Physical
Variable	<VAR>	</VAR>	Logical

The elements do the following:

- Bold renders the text in boldface.
- Citation specifies a citation (like a bibliographic entry) and is typically rendered as italics.
- Code specifies a code segment (like programming code) and is typically rendered as monospaced.
- Emphasis specifies emphasized text and is typically rendered in italics.
- Italics renders the text in italics.
- Keyboard specifies a series of keyboard steps and is typically rendered as monospaced.
- Sample specifies a sequence of literal characters (such as stuff you're supposed to type in response to a prompt) and is typically rendered as monospaced.
- Strong emphasis specifies strongly emphasized text and is typically rendered in boldface.
- Typewriter specifies a sequence of literal characters (such as text you see displayed by the computer or printed on a page) and is typically rendered as monospaced.
- Underlined renders the text underlined.
- Variable specifies a variable name (like a variable in a program) and is typically rendered as italics.

Remember that the rendering of logical elements is completely up to the browser and the user's settings within the browser.

HTML Image Element

Despite consisting of nothing more than text, HTML documents can still display full-color graphics. This bit of magic is actually sleight of hand: The graphic (called an image in Web parlance) is not actually a part of the HTML document. Rather, the HTML document merely "points to" a binary image file, stored elsewhere on the computer. In truth, the image doesn't even have to be in the same computer as the HTML document. The image can be located on a different computer, halfway around the world.

The HTML specification supports one element for images, and this is the <IMG> tag. This one element does quite a bit of work. It not only defines the filename of the image to use, but it can optionally specify text to use if the browser does not display graphics. It can also specify the alignment of the image relative to other images or text and the desired size of the image.

The syntax of the basic <IMG> is:

```
<IMG SRC="url">
```

where "url" is a properly constructed URL for the image file. The URL can be absolute or relative. This is an example of <IMG> that uses an absolute URL:

```
<IMG SRC="http://www.anywhere.com/myfiles/myimage.gif">
```

These examples show how to use an <IMG> tag with a relative URL:

```
<IMG SRC="myimage.gif">
<IMG SRC="./myimage.gif">
<IMG SRC="myfiles/myimage.gif">
<IMG SRC="../myimage.gif">
```

Note that the URL is relative to the HTML document that contains the <IMG> tag. If the image is located in another directory (or another computer altogether) you should provide enough information so that the browser can locate it.

Specifying Alternate Text

Not all browsers are equipped to display graphics. And while most modern browsers are graphics-aware, some users intentionally turn graphics display off. This substantially reduces the time it takes to load a page when using a dial-up

Internet connection and a slow modem. Therefore, it's advisable to include "alternate text" with the image for those who are image-challenged. This alternate text is encoded within the <IMG> tag, so that it always stays with the image.

Use the ALT attribute inside the <IMG> tag to specify alternate text. Here's an example:

```
<IMG SRC="../myimage.gif" ALT="This is the myimage.gif graphic">
```

Note that the alternate text does not appear unless the browser does not display the image. The alternate text is not used as a caption for the image.

Specifying Alignment

Images are considered "in-line" because they are treated just like text characters. That means you can intersperse images with text, and the browser will take care of making sure everything flows properly. This technique is handy when you want to add small icons to the text, such as a little button or a miniature graphic that says "New."

Most images are taller than the text that surrounds them, however. The normal behavior of most browsers is to place the bottoms of the image flush with the bottom of the text that surrounds it. But you can change this behavior if you want a different alignment. The most common alignment choices, understood by all browsers that display images, are these:

- *Bottom.* Aligns the text to the bottom of the image. This is the default.
- *Middle.* Aligns the text to the middle of the image.
- *Top.* Aligns the text to the top of the image.

Figure 20.6 shows examples of all three kinds of alignment types. Notice that the middle and top alignments place only one line of text beside the image. While it's ugly and probably not what you wanted, this is the way it was designed to work.

Modern browsers provide for additional alignment choices:

- *Left.* Aligns the text to the *right* of the image. If there is more than one line of text, the additional lines are also aligned to the right until the text clears the image.
- *Right.* Same as left, but the text is placed on the *left* side of the image.
- *Texttop.* Same as top, except that the text is aligned to the tallest characters in the line.

Figure 20.6 Use the ALIGN attribute in the <IMG> tag to align text to the top, middle, or bottom of an adjacent image.

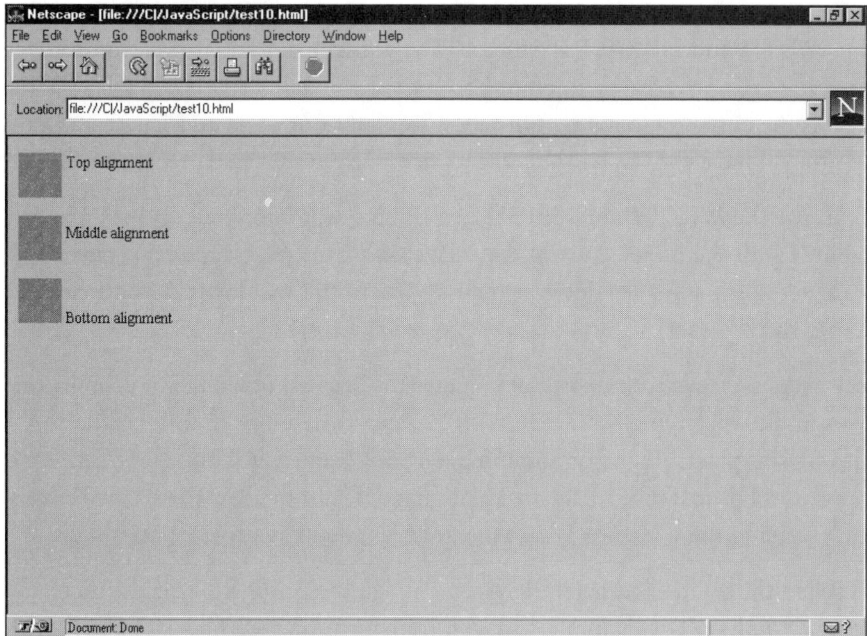

- *Absmiddle.* Same as middle, but more accurately places the middle of the line of text to the middle of the image.
- *Absbottom.* Same as bottom, but more accurately places the bottom of the line of text to the bottom of the image.
- *Baseline.* Same as bottom.

You may use only one alignment at a time. The syntax is:

```
<IMG SRC="myimage.gif" ALIGN="alignment">
```

Replace "alignment" (keep the quotes) with any of the alignment options specified above. For example, to use the left alignment and alternate text, use:

```
<IMG SRC="myimage.gif" ALT="Alternate text1" ALIGN="left">
```

Sizing the Image

Browsers ordinarily display images in their "natural size." If an image is 100 pixels by 100 pixels, for example, that's how big it is when rendered on the browser's screen. But you can change the size of the image if you want it smaller or larger by using the WIDTH and HEIGHT attributes. These attributes are also useful in that when used the browser creates an empty box for the image, then fills the box with the image as the entire page loads. This cues users of your page and lets them know how long they'll have to wait as the image loads.

You can use the WIDTH and HEIGHT attributes separately or together. Follow the attributes with the dimensions of the image, in pixels (Netscape Navigator will tell you the size of the image—look at the title bar in the window—if you load the graphic into the browser).

- Specifying just the width *or* height changes the size of the image in proportion. For example, specifying WIDTH="100" sizes a square image to a height and width of 100 pixels. If the original image is not square, it is sized in relative proportion. For instance, if the original image is 400 pixels wide by 100 pixels high, changing the width to 100 pixels reduces the image to 25 pixels high.
- Specifying the width *and* height lets you change the proportion of the image in any way you like. For example, you can transform that 400 by 100 pixel image to 200 by 200, 500 by 150, or anything else.

Here's an example of the WIDTH and HEIGHT attributes:

```
<IMG SRC="myimage.gif" ALT="Alternate text1" HEIGHT="100" WIDTH="100">
```

> **NOTE** Using the HEIGHT and WIDTH attributes is a good idea, even if you don't want to intentionally make an image larger or smaller. Providing these attributes allows Netscape Navigator to load all the text of the page, leaving just the right amount of space for the images. To the user it will appear as if your pages load faster.

Adding and Removing Image Borders

Images you display in your Web pages don't normally have borders (unless they are included inside an anchor element, as detailed below). You can add a border if you wish using the BORDER attribute. The value used with the BORDER attribute is the size of the border, in pixels. The following example places a border of about five pixels around the image.

```
<IMG SRC="myimage.gif" ALT="Alternate text1" BORDER=5>
```

Images placed inside hypertext elements normally have a 2- or3-pixel colored border, so the user can distinguish it as a hypertext link. If desired, you can remove this border, but remember that if you do, your users may not be aware that the image serves as a link. To remove the border use 0 as the BORDER value:

```
<IMG SRC="myimage.gif" ALT="Alternate text1" BORDER=0>
```

Controlling the Spacing Around Images

Most browsers insert spacing around images so that the surrounding text maintains a comfortable distance. The VSPACE and HSPACE attributes can be used to control the spacing around the image. As their names imply, VSPACE controls the spacing above and below the image, whereas HSPACE controls the spacing to the left and right of the image. Values are in pixels, where 0 butts the text against the image or very close to it. The default is a spacing of approximately 2–3 pixels. Following is an example of wide spacing:

```
<IMG SRC="myimage.gif" ALT="Alternate text1" HSPACE="10" VSPACE="10">
```

Embedding an Image Inside a Hypertext Link

You don't need to stick with words for the "click text" in a hypertext link (the "click text" is the text that appears colored and underlined and that you click to activate the link). You can alternately use an image for the click text or both and image and text. Merely place the <IMG> tag between the <A> and </A> hypertext link tags, as follows:

```
<A HREF="another.html"><IMG SRC="another.gif"></A>
```

If you'd like text to appear with the image, include it before or after the <IMG> tag:

```
<A HREF="another.html">Click here!<IMG SRC="another.gif"></A>
```

Figure 20.7 shows some examples of images used in hypertext links. Notice the example where the "Click here!" text is centered beneath the image. This formatting was accomplished using tables, described under "HTML Table Element," in this chapter.

Figure 20.7. Use images with hypertext links to create active buttons and other objects on your page.

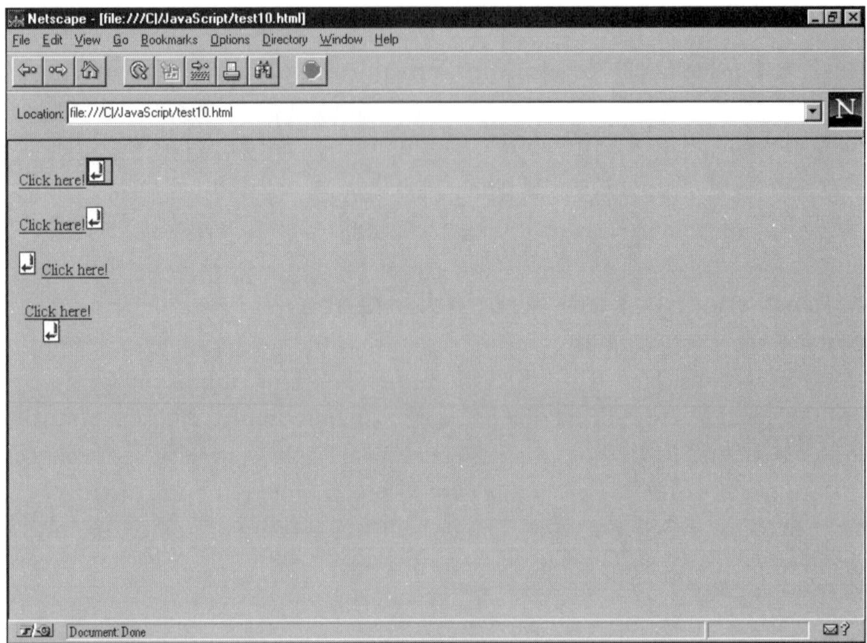

ISMAP Attribute

Some Web pages use a single image as a way to convey a number of hypertext links. A given link is activated depending on where on the image you click. The image is dissected like a "map"; the attribute to activate this feature is logically called ISMAP.

Before you get all excited about using the ISMAP feature be aware that it requires a program running on the server, along with your pages. This program typically conforms to the CGI (Common Gateway Interface) standard and requires a script that you write. Simple adding the ISMAP attribute to a graphic does not automatically endow that graphic with multiple hyperlinking capability.

That said, Netscape Navigator and Internet Explorer support "client-side" image-maps, where the intelligence of the multiple links for the one image is built into the HTML page.

The ISMAP attribute is not used with a parameter. If you wish to use the image as an image map (assuming you've taken care of the CGI script on the server), merely add the ISMAP attribute to the <IMG> tag:

```
<IMG SRC="myimage.gif" ALIGN="left" ISMAP>
```

HTML List Elements

HTML supports a wide variety of lists, including numbered and bulleted lists. The numbers and bullets, as well as the overall formatting of the list, are provided by the browser and aren't included in the text of the document. This provides for more control over the appearance of the list, and it speeds up the rendering of the page on the browser's screen.

There are three general forms of lists: ordered (numbered), unordered (bulleted), and definition. The HTML specification also allows for something called menu lists and directory lists, but these are functionally the same as unordered (bulleted) lists. See Figure 20.8 for an example of the three types of HTML lists.

<DL>

The definition list element creates a "glossary" type of format; the typical use is to render terms and their definitions. The terms appear flush left, and the definitions are indented under the words.

Definition list is an HTML block element and therefore contains two paired tags: <DL> and </DL>. These tags define the start and end of the list, respectively. Inside these tags go additional tags—<DT> for term and <DD> for definition. For each <DT> you should have a corresponding <DD>, but there is no steadfast rule that says you must do this. In fact, some interesting formatting is possible when using just the <DD> tags inside a definition list.

The syntax of the definition list looks like this, when tags for the terms and definitions are also added. This example has been formatted for clarity; the formatting is optional.

```
<DL>
<DT>Term 1
     <DD>Definition 1.
<DT>Term 2
     <DD>Definition 2.
```

```
<DT>Term 3
     <DD>Definition 3.
</DL>
```

Note that there is no end-tag for the <DT> and <DD> tags. Also note that if the text following <DD> spans more than one line, the extra lines are also indented. This preserves the unique formatting of the definition list.

The <DL> description list element supports a variant called COMPACT that is meant to make the formatting of the list more compact. In reality, however, the COMPACT attribute has little effect in most cases, and you probably never need to use it. If you do, the syntax is:

```
<DL COMPACT>
```

Figure 20.8. The most commonly used HTML lists are ordered, unordered, and definition.

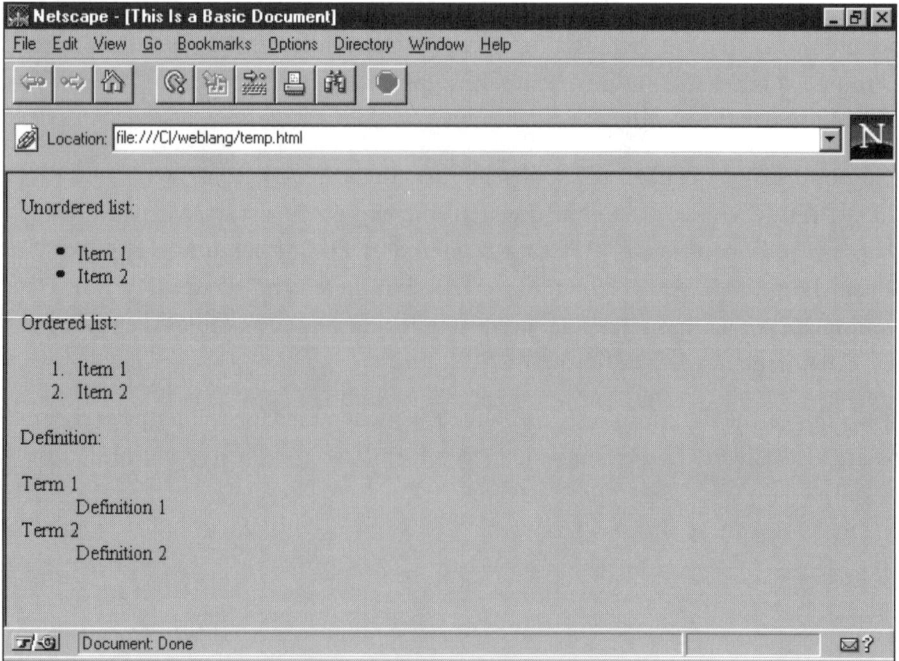

<OL>

Ordered lists are numbered lists. Each element of the list precedes with a number. The browser formats the list with the number so you don't have to. The browser also adds appropriate indention and tabbing to make the list look clean.

Ordered list is an HTML block element and therefore contains two paired tags: <OL> and </OL>. These tags define the start and end of the list, respectively. Inside these tags go additional tags, specifically <LI> for each list item. The end of the list item can be marked off with an </LI> tag, though this is optional. For consistency you may want to get in the habit of providing the </LI> tag.

The syntax of the ordered list looks like this, when tags for the list items are also added. This example has been formatted for clarity; the formatting is optional.

```
<OL>
     <LI>This is the first item.</LI>
     <LI>This is the second item.</LI>
     <LI>This is the third item.</LI>
</OL>
```

You can create multiple-level lists by adding additional <OL> tags (be sure to end each <OL> structure with a matching </OL>). The following example creates a two-level list, as shown in Figure 20.9. You can create lists with as many as seven levels.

```
<OL>
   <LI>This is the first item.</LI>
   <LI>This is the second item.</LI>
   <OL>
   <LI>This is an item in the second level</LI>
      <LI>So is this</LI>
</OL>
   <LI>This is the third item.</LI>
</OL>
```

Netscape Navigator and Internet Explorer allow you to specify the type of number to use. This is done with the TYPE attribute, which is specified in the <OL> tag. Five types of numbering are allowed:

- *TYPE="1"*. The default numbering scheme, where the list is ordered with Arabic numerals (1, 2, 3,...).
- *TYPE="A"*. The list is ordered with uppercase alphabetic characters (A–Z).

- *TYPE="a"*. The list is ordered with lowercase alphabetic characters (a–z).
- *TYPE="I"*. The list is ordered with uppercase Roman numerals (I, II, III...).
- *TYPE="i"*. The list is ordered with lowercase Roman numerals (i, ii, iii...).

<UL>

Unordered lists are bulleted lists. Each element of the list starts with a bullet. The browser formats the list with the bullet so you don't have to. The browser also adds appropriate indentation and tabbing to make the list look clean.

Unordered list is an HTML block element and therefore uses paired tags: <UL> and </UL>. These tags define the start and end of the list, respectively. Inside these tags go additional tags, specifically <LI> for each list item. The end of the list item can be marked off with an </LI> tag, though this is optional. For consistency you may want to get in the habit of providing the </LI> tag.

The syntax of the ordered list looks like this, when tags for the list items also added. This example has been formatted for clarity; the formatting is optional.

Figure 20.9 You may nest <OL> tags to create multiple level lists.

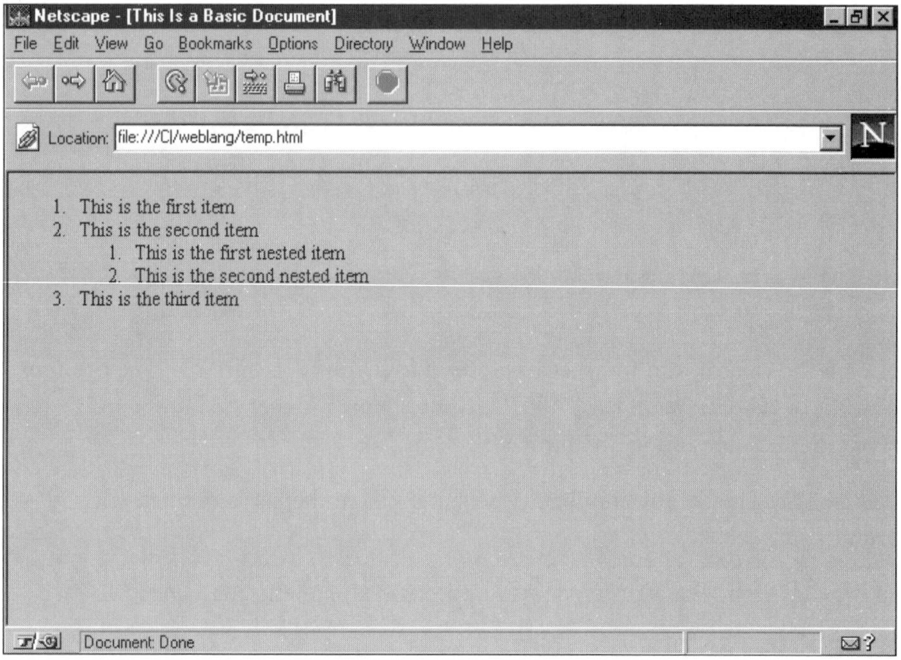

```
<UL>
     <LI>This is the first item.</LI>
     <LI>This is the second item.</LI>
     <LI>This is the third item.</LI>
</UL>
```

You can create multiple-level lists by adding additional <UL> tags (be sure to end each <UL> structure with a matching </UL>. The following example creates a two-level list. You can create lists with as many as seven levels.

```
<UL>
   <LI>This is the first item.</LI>
   <LI>This is the second item.</LI>
   <UL>
   <LI>This is an item in the second level</LI>
      <LI>So is this</LI>
</UL>
   <LI>This is the third item.</LI>
</UL>
```

Many browsers, such as Netscape Navigator, allow you to specify the type of bullet to use. This is done with the TYPE attribute, which is specified in the <OL> tag. Three types of bulleted are allowed:

- *TYPE="disc"*. Bullets appear as a round, hollow disc.
- *TYPE="circle"*. Bullets appear as a circle.
- *TYPE="square"*. Bullets appear as a square.

Combining List Types

Most Web browsers will let you combine the three common list types to produce embedded lists. For example, you can place an unordered list as a second level to an ordered list. Merely add the appropriate start- and end-tags, furnish the list items, and the browser will do the rest. Here's an example (see the result in Figure 20.10):

```
<UL>
   <LI>This is the first item of the unordered list.</LI>
   <LI>This is the second item of the unordered list.</LI>
   <OL>
   <LI>This is the first item of the ordered list.</LI>
      <LI>This is the second item of the ordered list.</LI>
</UL>
   <LI>This is the third item of the unordered list.</LI>
</UL>
```

Figure 20.10 List types can be combined. Here, an ordered list is shown nested inside an unordered list.

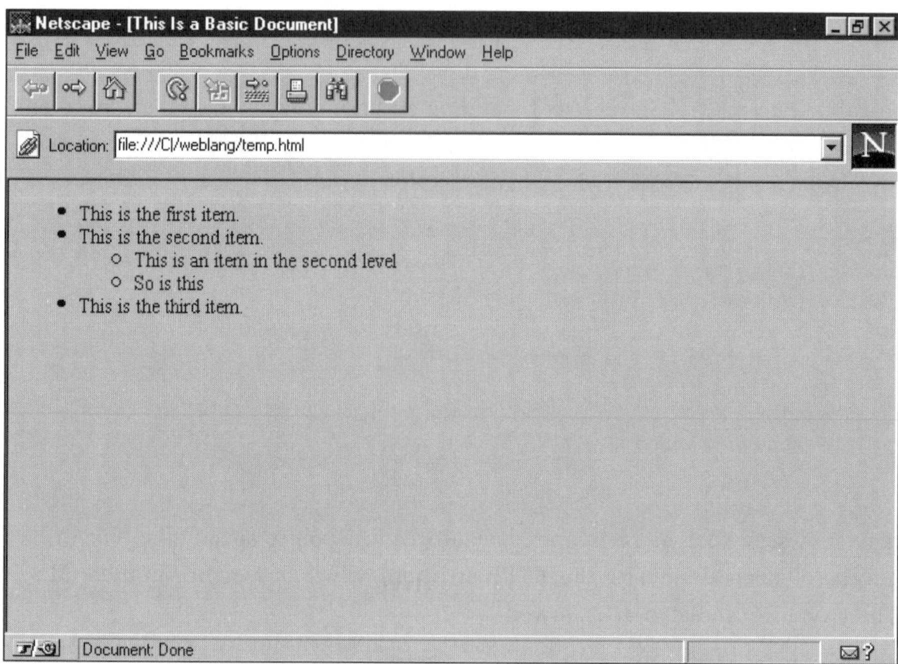

Formatting for the Other List Types

As mentioned above, the HTML specification defines two other list types: directory and menu. With one exception, most browsers render these the same as unordered lists. The syntax for the menu list is as follows. The list appears the same as an unordered (bulleted) list.

```
<MENU>
   <LI>This is the first item.</LI>
   <LI>This is the second item.</LI>
   <LI>This is the third item.</LI>
</MENU>
```

The syntax for the directory list is as follows. The list also appears the same as an unordered (bulleted) list. At one time the directory list formatted text in multiple columns, but few modern browsers render the list in this way.

```
<DIR>
   <LI>This is the item 1.</LI>
```

```
   <LI>This is the item 2.</LI>
   <LI>This is the item 3.</LI>
</DIR>
```

Interesting Tidbits Regarding Lists

There are some useful tips and techniques you can employ with list tags to create special effects. Do note that not all of these techniques work with all browsers, but they do in Netscape Navigator and Internet Explorer. Examples of the techniques are shown in Figure 20.11.

Indenting with <DD>

One very useful trick is to use a <DD> tag by itself to insert indented text. For example:

```
<DD>This is indented text.
```

(Unfortunately, you cannot add extra <DD> tags to add more indenting.)

Figure 20.11 Combining list tags in creative ways produces special formatting.

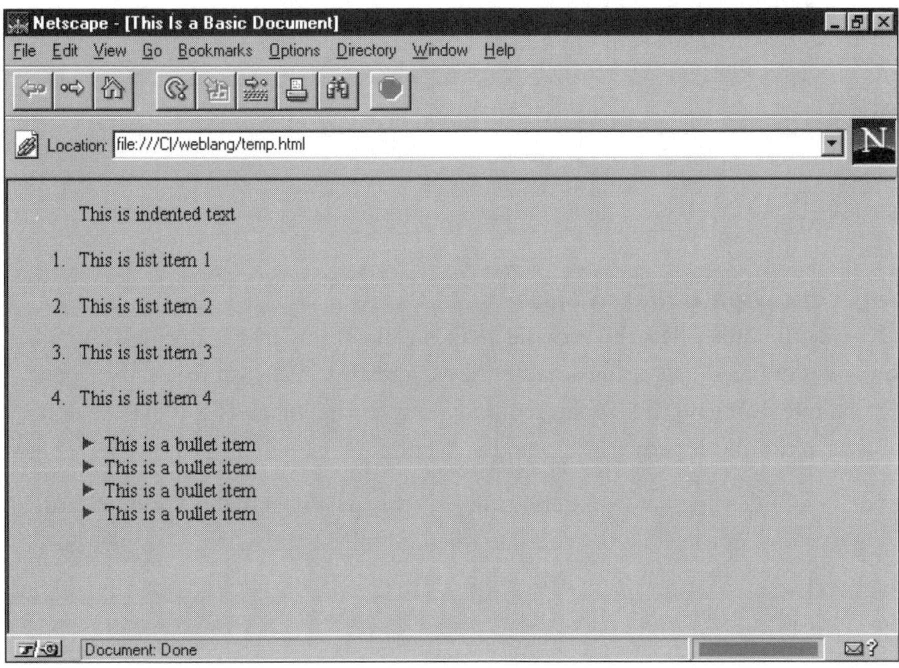

Adding Extra Space Between List Items

Ordinarily each list item is separated by just a line break. If you want more spacing between the lines, add <P> tags after the list items or a pair of <BR> tags. Examples:

```
<OL>
   <LI>This is list item 1</LI><P>
   <LI>This is list item 2</LI><P>
   <LI>This is list item 3</LI><BR><BR>
   <LI>This is list item 4</LI><BR><BR>
</OL>
```

Adding More Indenting to Ordered and Unordered Lists

You can easily add more indention to the beginning of ordered and unordered lists by preceding the <LI> tag with a <DD> tag. For example:

```
<DD><LI>This is an indented list item.</LI>
```

"Nested-in" List

Normally ordered and unordered lists start at level 1 (using the numbering and bullet choices for that level), with one indent. You can create empty nests that force the browser to choose the number and bullet styles for a lower list. To create an empty nest insert multiple <OL> or <UL> tags to define the list (or course, be sure to counter these tags with an equal number of </OL> and </UL> tags). Example:

```
<UL><UL><UL>
   <LI>This list is level 3</LI>
   <LI>This list is level 3</LI>
   <LI>This list is level 3</LI>
</UL></UL</UL>
```

Making Your Own Bulleted Lists

After a while the bullet lists the browser makes can get downright boring. Try making your own bulleted lists using small bullet-shaped images. Just about any image will do, as long as it's no taller than the body text. If the image is too big the text will not wrap around it properly.

To create a bullet list, define a definition list (this part is actually optional) and place <IMG> tags at the start of each line for the bullets. Here's an example. Be sure to add a space between the <IMG> tag and the text.

```
<DL>
   <DD><IMG SRC="ball1.gif"> This is a bullet item
   <DD><IMG SRC="ball1.gif"> This is a bullet item
   <DD><IMG SRC="ball1.gif"> This is a bullet item
   <DD><IMG SRC="ball1.gif"> This is a bullet item
</DL>
```

If you want to add more space between the image and the bullet, use the VSPACE attribute in the <IMG> tag to increase the spacing on the left and right of the image. For example:

```
<DL>
   <DD><IMG SRC="ball1.gif" HSPACE="5"> This is a bullet item
   <DD><IMG SRC="ball1.gif" HSPACE="5"> This is a bullet item
   <DD><IMG SRC="ball1.gif" HSPACE="5"> This is a bullet item
   <DD><IMG SRC="ball1.gif" HSPACE="5"> This is a bullet item
</DL>
```

HTML Form Elements

Forms allow your Web documents to interact with the user. Forms contain all the familiar trappings of a graphic user interface like Windows, including text entry boxes, push buttons, radio buttons, check boxes, and list boxes.

In the past, forms were intended to be used with special software on the server that processed the user's input. This is still possible, but new technologies such as JavaScript make it possible to process form input and manipulate the document while on the client computer. No information need be traded between the server and the client.

The following description of the form elements include just the standard HTML specifications.

<FORM>

The form element defines the actual form. Inside the form are placed the various "controls," such as push buttons and radio buttons.

Form is an HTML block element and therefore contains two paired tags: <FORM> and </FORM>. The syntax of the form element looks like this:

```
<FORM>Additional tags and text go here</FORM>
```

The <FORM> tag is optionally used with the following attributes. These attributes tell the browser how to submit the form to a server.

- *NAME*. The name of the form
- *METHOD*. The submission method, either POST or GET
- *ACTION*. The URL for submitting the form (the form is sent here)
- *TARGET*. The window or frame name where the form output (from the CGI program) should be placed
- *ENCTYPE*. The encoding format of the form

Example:

```
<FORM NAME="myform" ACTION="http://mydomain.com/cgibin/form/"
METHOD=get>
```

<INPUT>

The input element defies various types of input controls for the form. These controls are as follows:

- *Checkbox*. Selects or deselects an option
- *Button*. Creates a push button with any text on it
- *Submit*. Creates a special "Submit" button to submit the form to the server
- *Reset*. Creates a special "Reset" button to return the controls to their default values
- *Text*. Creates a text entry box to enter a line of text
- *Hidden*. Creates a hidden text field that can contain data but does not appear in the browser
- *Password*. Creates a text entry box for storing a password. Text the user types does not appear in the box.
- *Image*. Creates an "image button" that when clicked submits the form and passes the X/Y coordinates of the mouse to the server

Except for the reset and submit types, form controls support the following optional attributes.

checkbox and radio

- *NAME*. Name of the control
- *VALUE*. Unique value for control when form is submitted
- *CHECKED*. Initial checked state

button

- *NAME*. Name of the control
- *VALUE*. Text of the button

text, password, hidden

- *NAME*. Name of the control
- *VALUE*. Initial text
- *SIZE*. Width of the text box
- *MAXLENGTH*. Maximum allowable characters

image

- *NAME*. Name of the control
- *SRC*. Source for image

The following example creates a text box and a Submit button.

```
<INPUT TYPE="text" NAME="textbox" VALUE="">
<INPUT TYPE="submit">
```

<SELECT>

The select element defines a selection list in the form. The list contains one or more options. By sizing the list you can display it as a "drop-down" box or as a standard select box. Scroll bars appear on the right of the list if there are more options than can be shown at one time. Selection lists can provide for single or multiple choices. The attributes for a select list are as follows:

- *NAME*. Name of list
- *SIZE*. Size of list (number of rows to display)
- *MULTIPLE*. Specifies multiple choice

One or more <OPTION> tags are placed in a selection list. The <OPTION> tags accept the following attributes:

- *SELECTED*. Default selection
- *VALUE*. Value of item when form is submitted

The following example displays a selection list with three items:

```
<SELECT SIZE=3>
<OPTION SELECTED VALUE=1>This is item 1
<OPTION VALUE=2>This is item 2
<OPTION VALUE=3>This is item 3
</SELECT>
```

<TEXTAREA>

The <TEXTAREA> tag creates a multiple-line text box. There are three attributes for the textarea control:

- *NAME*. Names the control
- *ROWS*. The height of the control, in lines
- *COLS*. The width of the control, in characters

The <TEXTAREA> tag is always used with its end-tag, which is </TEXTAREA>. Text that you wish to initially appear in the text box can be placed between these tags. Formatting, including new lines, is retained. Example:

```
<TEXTAREA ROWS=4 COLS=40>
This is default text
</TEXTAREA>
```

HTML Table Element

Table elements let you display text and graphics in tabular format. The tables can appear with and without borders, and you can change the width of borders. Various combinations of table elements let you specify an almost unlimited arrangement of columns and rows. See Figure 20.12 for an example of a table you can create with HTML.

Figure 20.12. One of an almost unlimited number of table designs you can create with the HTML <TABLE> tag.

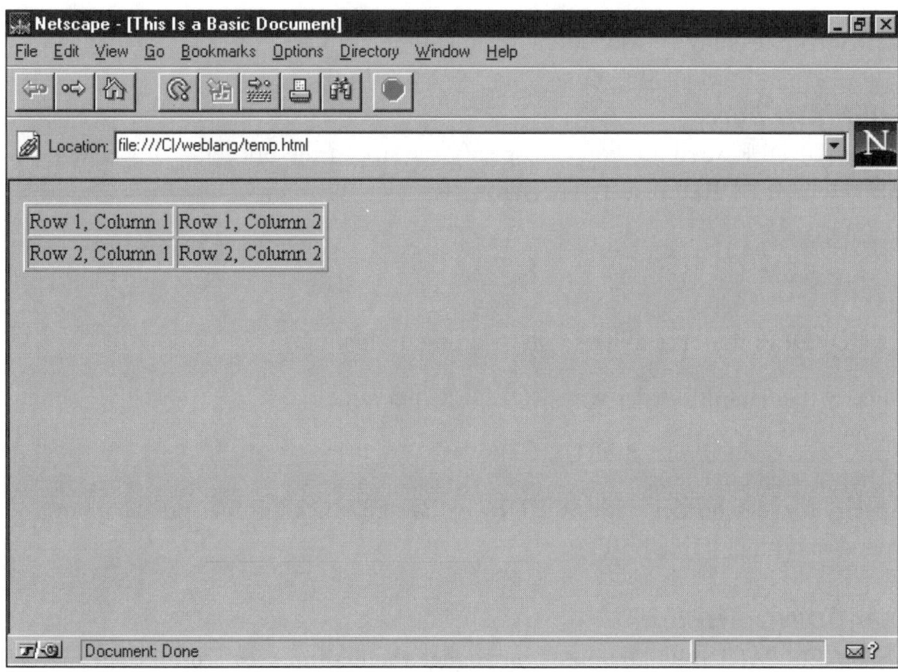

<TABLE>

The table definition begins with the <TABLE> tag and ends with the </TABLE> tag. All of the subordinate table tags must appear between this pair. A one-column, one-row table can be created as simply as this:

```
<TABLE>
     <TD>This is a simple table</TD>
</TABLE>
```

Optional attributes for the <TABLE> tag are as follows:

- BORDER
- CELLPADDING

- CELLSPACING
- WIDTH

These attributes may be used alone or in combination.

BORDER Attribute

With the BORDER attribute you can specify the size of the border, if any. The default value for BORDER is 1. The syntax is

```
<TABLE BORDER>
<TABLE BORDER=x>
```

The BORDER attribute allows you to do the following:

- Specify the default border with BORDER (no value).
- Specify no border with BORDER=0.
- Specify a wider border with BORDER=x, where x is a number greater than 1. Avoid very thick table borders.

CELLPADDING Attribute

With the CELLPADDING attribute you change the margin area within each cell, if any. The syntax is:

```
<TABLE CELLPADDING=x>
```

The CELLPADDING attribute allows you to do the following:

- Specify CELLPADDING=0 for no cell padding.
- Specify the cellpadding amount with CELLPADDING=x, where x is 1 or higher.

CELLSPACING Attribute

With the CELLSPACE attribute you can change the spacing between cells. The syntax is:

```
<TABLE CELLSPACING=x>
```

This attribute allows you to do the following:

- Specify CELLSPACING=0 for no cell spacing.
- Specify the cellspacing amount with CELLSPACING=x, where x is 1 or higher.

WIDTH Attribute

With the WIDTH attribute you can change the overall width of the table (normally, the table appears only as wide as it needs to be to display its contents.

```
<TABLE WIDTH=x>
<TABLE WIDTH=x%>
```

This attribute allows you to do the following:

- Specify the width of the table in pixels with TABLE=x, where x is a positive number.
- Specify the width of the table in a percentage of the total page width TABLE=x%, where x is a positive number.

<TR>

The <TR> tag defines a row within a table. Tables can contain any number of rows that you like. Each row should be marked with a <TR> tag to start and a </TR> tag to end.

```
<TABLE BORDER>
      <TR><TD>This is row 1</TD></TR>
      <TR><TD>This is row 2</TD></TR>
</TABLE>
```

<TD>

The <TD> tag marks the text (or image) within a cell. If you create a table without a <TD> tag pair for a row, the table will appear with a "blank" at that spot.

```
<TABLE BORDER>
      <TR><TD>The row below appears blank.</TD></TR>
      <TR><TD></TD></TR>
</TABLE>
```

Each <TD></TD> tag pair within a row defines a new column. If you want to create a table with more than one column, add more <TD> tags within a row.

```
<TABLE BORDER>
      <TR><TD>Row 1, Column 1</TD><TD>Row 1, Column 2</TD></TR>
      <TR><TD>Row 2, Column 1</TD><TD>Row 2, Column 2</TD></TR>
</TABLE>
```

A number of attributes are supported for the <TD> tag. These are listed in Table 20.6.

Of these attributes the ROWSPAN and COLSPAN are often used to create a wide variety of table formats. With these attributes you can specify that a given column or row should be wider than the standard 1-by-1 size. Here are some examples. All sorts of variations are possible.

```
<TABLE BORDER=2 CELLPADDING=5>
   <TR><TD COLSPAN=2>Spanned</TD><TD>Col 2</TD><TD>Col 3</TD></TR>
   <TR><TD>Col 1</TD><TD>Col 2</TD><TD COLSPAN=2>Spanned</TD></TR>
</TABLE>

<TABLE BORDER=2 CELLPADDING=5>
   <TR><TD ROWSPAN=2>Spanned</TD><TD>Col 2</TD><TD>Col 3</TD></TR>
   <TR><TD>Col 1</TD><TD>Col 2</TD><TD COLSPAN=2>Spanned</TD></TR>
</TABLE>
```

<TH>

Use the <TH> tag to define a heading along the side or top of the table. There are a number of ways to use the <TH> tag, as listed in Table 20.7 (in all cases the closing tag is /TH>):

```
<TABLE BORDER>
     <TR><TH>Column 1</TH><TH>Column 2</TH></TR>
     <TR><TD>Row 1, Column 1</TD><TD>Row 1, Column 2</TR>
     <TR><TD>Row 2, Column 1</TD><TD>Row 2, Column 2</TR>
</TABLE>
```

Table 20.6 <TD> Attributes

Tag	What It Does
<TD ALIGN=val>	Aligns contents in cell as specified; use RIGHT, LEFT, or CENTER for val
<TD VALIGN=val>	Aligns contents in cell vertically as specified; use TOP, MIDDLE, or BOTTOM for val
<TD WIDTH=x>	Specifies width of cell, in pixels
<TD WIDTH=x%>	Specifies width of cell, in percentage of table width

Table 20.6 *Continued*

Tag	What It Does
<TD ROWSPAN=x>	Specifies how many rows cell spans
<TD COLSPAN=x>	Specifies how many columns cell spans

<CAPTION>

The <CAPTION> tag lets you specify a caption for the table. The caption appears centered at the top of the table.

```
<TABLE BORDER>
   <CAPTION>This is the caption</CAPTION>
   <TR><TD>Row 1, Column 1</TD><TD>Row 1, Column 2</TR>
   <TR><TD>Row 2, Column 1</TD><TD>Row 2, Column 2</TR>
</TABLE>
```

HTML Frameset Elements

Starting with Netscape 2.0 and Internet Explorer 3.0, you can divide the document window into many "frames." Each frame can contain different content because

Table 20.7 <TH> Attributes

Tag	What It Does
<TH>	Creates header in cell on top, bold and centered
<TH ALIGN=val>	Aligns header in cell as specified; use RIGHT, LEFT, or CENTER for val
<TH VALIGN=val>	Aligns header vertically in cell as specified; use TOP, MIDDLE, or BOTTOM for val
<TH WIDTH=x>	Specifies width of header cell, in pixels
<TH WIDTH=x%>	Specifies width of header cell, in percentage of table width
<TH ROWSPAN=x>	Specifies how many rows header cell spans
<TH COLSPAN=x>	Specifies how many columns head cell spans

each one can actually be a different HTML document. Frames have a particularly close relationship with JavaScript because the frames are often used for JavaScript output results.

<FAMESET>

The <FRAMESET> tag defines the frames that you want to appear in the window. This tag appears in the "primary" HTML document that the user loads (that is, the URL to your page that uses frame should point to this document). Within the <FRAMESET> tag you define how you want the page divided, using the ROWS and COLS attributes.

```
ROWS="row_height_value_list"
COLS="cols_width_list"
```

For rows, you specify the width of each of the frames, either in pixels or in percentage (or both). For columns, you specify the height of each of the frames, also in pixels and/or percentage. Here are some examples.

```
<FRAMESET ROWS="50%, 50%">
     <FRAMESET COLS="50%, 50%">
```

creates a four-panel frameset, with two rows dividing the document window in half vertically. Two columns divide the document window in half horizontally.

```
<FRAMESET ROWS="200, *">
```

creates a two-panel frameset with the document window divided into two rows. The first row is 200 pixels in height. The * tells the browser to use the remaining width for the second row. No COL attribute is provided, so it is assumed the document window is not divided into columns.

The frameset is ended with the </FRAMESET> tag. This tag appears after any <FRAME> tags that are included.

<FRAME>

The <FRAME> tags specify the actual content of the frames, now that the frameset has been defined.

There are a number of attributes for use with the <FRAME> tag, listed in Table 20.8.

Table 20.8 <FRAME> Attributes

Attribute	What It Does
SRC	The URL of the document you want to place in the frame
NAME	The name identifier you want to use for the frame
MARGINWIDTH	The size of the margin on the left and right of the frame
MARGINHEIGHT	The size of the margin on the top and bottom of the frame
SCROLLING	Specifies if you wish the frame window to have a scrollbar
NORESIZE	Specifies if you wish to allow the user to resize the frame

Following are some examples, shown with the <FRAMESET> tag. See Figures 20.13 through 20.16 for how they look in a browser. (In all cases, the frames are shown empty.)

```
<FRAMESET ROWS="200, *">
     <FRAME SRC="dummy.htm" NAME="frame1" MARGINWIDTH=2>
     <FRAME SRC="dummy.htm" NAME="frame2" SCROLLING="no">
</FRAMESET>

<FRAMESET COLS="130, *">
<FRAME SRC="dummy.htm" NAME="frame1" MARGINWIDTH=1 NORESIZE NOSCROLL>
<FRAME SRC="dummy.htm" NAME="frame2" NORESIZE MARGINWIDTH=0>
</FRAMESET>

<FRAMESET ROWS="*, 100%">
<FRAME SRC="dummy.htm" NAME="text" SCOLLING="no">
  <FRAMESET COLS="150, *">
    <FRAME SRC="dummy.htm" NAME="ctrl" MARGINWIDTH=1 SCROLLING="no">
    <FRAME SRC="dummy.htm" NAME="result" MARGINWIDTH=1>
  </FRAMESET>
</FRAMESET>
```

```
<FRAMESET ROWS="50%, 50%">
   <FRAMESET COLS="50%, 50%">
       <FRAME SRC="dummy.htm">
      <FRAME SRC="dummy.htm">
   </FRAMESET>
   <FRAMESET COLS="50%, 50%">
      <FRAME SRC="dummy.htm">
      <FRAME SRC="dummy.htm">
   </FRAMESET>
</FRAMESET>
```

<NOFRAMES>

Use the <NOFRAMES> tag to provide alternative text for those browsers that do not support the frames feature. Place the text and HTML markup you wish to display between the <NOFRAMES> and </NOFRAMES> tags. Often, this text consists only of:

```
<NOFRAMES>You need Netscape 2.0 or later to view this page!</NOFRAMES>
```

Figure 20.13 Two frames, in two equal rows.

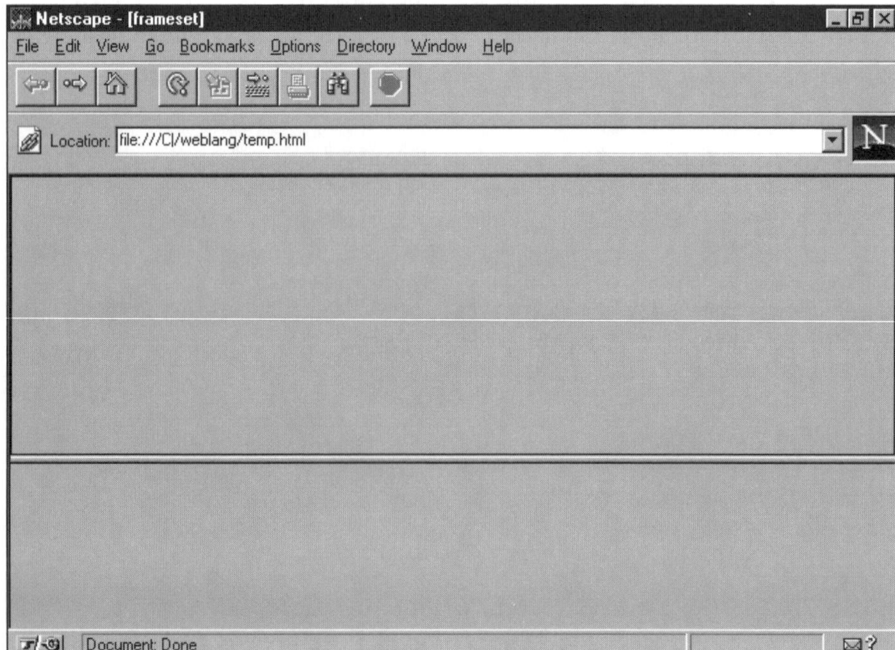

Figure 20.14 Two frames, in columns, with the right column larger.

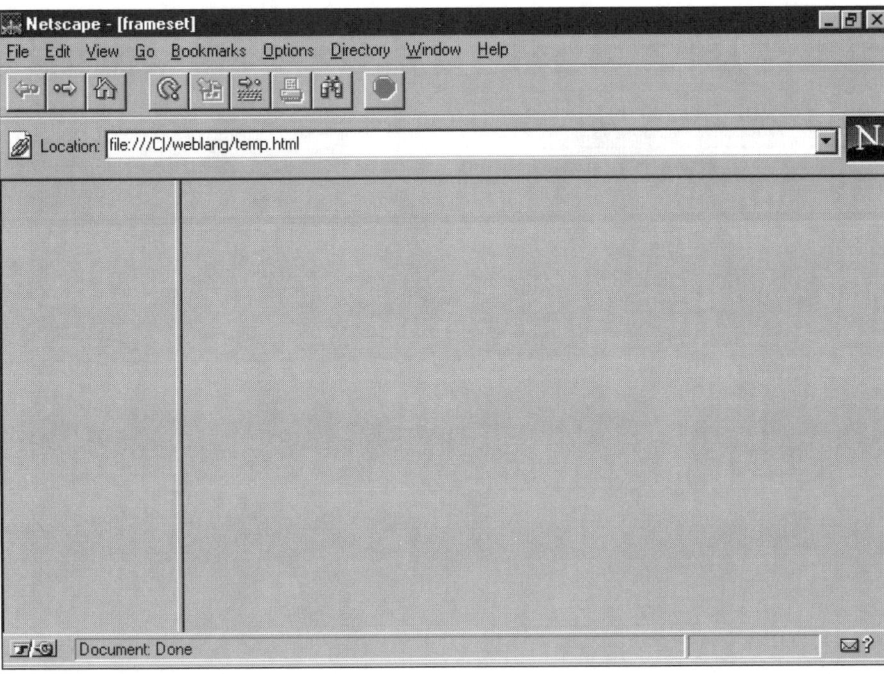

> **NOTE** A scientific calculator or any decimal-to-hex calculator is helpful if you're not familiar with hexadecimal notation. The calculator that comes with Windows can perform decimal-to-hex conversions.

If your page does not require other Netscape 2.+/Internet Explorer 3.0+ features (like JavaScript or VBScript), consider offering a no-frames alternative for your site. You can place the no-frames version within the <NOFRAMES> tag or simply provide a hyperlink to guide people to a completely separate no-frames page.

```
<NOFRAMES>Since your browser doesn't support frames use the
<A HREF="noframes.html">no frame version<A> </NOFRAMES>
```

Deciphering RGB Triplet Values

Modern browsers use three pairs of hexadecimal values to represent the red, green, and blue (RGB) component of colors used for backgrounds and text. Hexadecimal

Figure 20.15 Three frames, with the first frame "hidden" (it contains data).

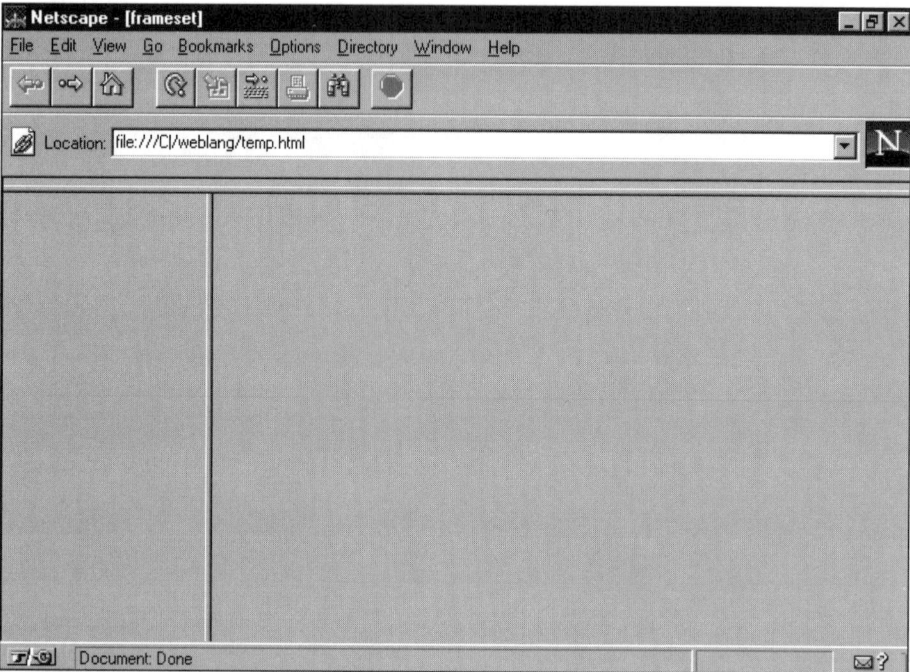

values are base-16 and range from 00 (for 0) to ff (for 255). The typical RGB triplet looks like this:

```
"#00ffoc"
```

The # character is used to prevent leading zeros from being dropped if the value is not enclosed in quotes. Here's how the three values work out:

- 00 is the red component. 00 means no intensity.
- ff is the green component. ff means full intensity.
- 0c is the blue component. 0c means about half intensity.

Table 20.9 provides a more complete list of values for colors supported in Netscape Navigator.

Figure 20.16 Four frames, in window pane fashion.

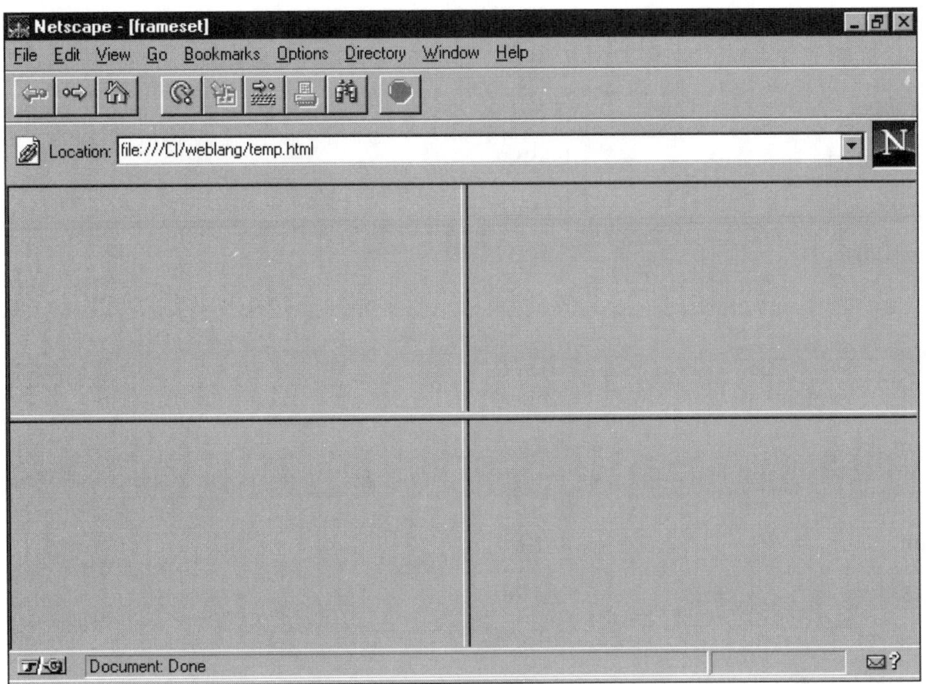

Table 20.9 Navigator-Supported Colors

Color	RGB Triplet
aliceblue	f0f8ff
antiquewhite	faebd7
aqua	00ffff
aquamarine	7fffd4
azure	f0ffff
beige	f5f5dc
bisque	ffe4c4
black	000000
blanchedalmond	ffebcd
blue	0000ff

Continued

Table 20.9 *Continued*

Color	RGB Triplet
blueviolet	8a2be2
brown	a52a2a
burlywood	deb887
cadetblue	5f9ea0
chartreuse	7fff00
chocolate	d2691e
coral	ff7f50
cornflowerblue	6495ed
cornsilk	fff8dc
crimson	dc143c
cyan	00ffff
darkblue	00008b
darkcyan	008b8b
darkgoldenrod	b8860b
darkgray	a9a9a9
darkgreen	006400
darkkhaki	bdb76b
darkmagenta	8b008b
darkolivegreen	556b2f
darkorange	ff8c00
darkorchid	9932cc
darkred	8b0000
darksalmon	e9967a
darkseagreen	8fbc8f
darkslateblue	483d8b
darkslategray	2f4f4f
darkturquoise	00ced1

Table 20.9 *Continued*

Color	RGB Triplet
darkviolet	9400d3
deeppink	ff1493
deepskyblue	00bfff
dimgray	696969
dodgerblue	1e90ff
firebrick	b22222
floralwhite	fffaf0
forestgreen	228b22
fuchsia	ff00ff
gainsboro	dcdcdc
ghostwhite	f8f8ff
gold	ffd700
goldenrod	daa520
gray	808080
green	008000
greenyellow	adff2f
honeydew	f0fff0
hotpink	ff69b4
indianred	cd5c5c
indigo	4b0082
ivory	fffff0
khaki	f0e68c
lavender	e6e6fa
lavenderblush	fff0f5
lawngreen	7cfc00
lemonchiffon	fffacd
lightblue	add8e6

Continued

Table 20.9 *Continued*

Color	RGB Triplet
lightcoral	f08080
lightcyan	e0ffff
lightgoldenrodyellow	fafad2
lightgreen	90ee90
lightgray	d3d3d3
lightpink	ffb6c1
lightsalmon	ffa07a
lightseagreen	20b2aa
lightskyblue	87cefa
lightslategray	778899
lightsteelblue	b0c4de
lightyellow	ffffe0
lime	00ff00
limegreen	32cd32
linen	faf0e6
magenta	ff00ff
maroon	800000
mediumaquamarine	66cdaa
mediumblue	0000cd
mediumorchid	ba55d3
mediumpurple	9370db
mediumseagreen	3cb371
mediumslateblue	7b68ee
mediumspringgreen	00fa9a
mediumturquoise	48d1cc
mediumvioletred	c71585
midnightblue	191970

Table 20.9 *Continued*

Color	RGB Triplet
mintcream	f5fffa
mistyrose	ffe4e1
moccasin	ffe4b5
navajowhite	ffdead
navy	000080
oldlace	fdf5e6
olive	808000
olivedrab	6b8e23
orange	ffa500
orangered	ff4500
orchid	da70d6
palegoldenrod	eee8aa
palegreen	98fb98
paleturquoise	afeeee
palevioletred	db7093
papayawhip	ffefd5
peachpuff	ffdab9
peru	cd853f
pink	ffc0cb
plum	dda0dd
powderblue	b0e0e6
purple	800080
red	ff0000
rosybrown	bc8f8f
royalblue	4169e1
saddlebrown	8b4513
salmon	fa8072

Continued

Table 20.9 *Continued*

Color	RGB Triplet
sandybrown	f4a460
seagreen	2e8b57
seashell	fff5ee
sienna	a0522d
silver	c0c0c0
skyblue	87ceeb
slateblue	6a5acd
slategray	708090
snow	fffafa
springgreen	00ff7f
steelblue	4682b4
tan	d2b48c
teal	008080
thistle	d8bfd8
tomato	ff6347
turquoise	40e0d0
violet	ee82ee
wheat	f5deb3
white	ffffff
whitesmoke	f5f5f5
yellow	ffff00
yellowgreen	9acd32

Netscape Navigator also supports several dozen named colors (Internet Explorer also supports color names, but only a small subset of the ones Netscape supports). The correct appearance of these colors depends on the video settings of your computer. Don't expect all the colors to be rendered properly if your computer displays only 16 or 256 colors.

Appendix

Using the CD-ROM

This book comes with a CD-ROM. It contains all the example program files and applications detailed in the *Web Languages Sourcebook*, as well as numerous freeware and shareware programs and utilities from other authors.

The CD-ROM can be used by IBM-style PCs, the Macintosh, and most Unix computers. Note that most of the programming examples require a specific Web server and programming interpreter or compiler.

The example programs from the book are in uncompressed format and are contained in the examples directory. Open this directory, then open the directory for the type of program you want—Java, C, Perl, and so on. To retrieve a file and use it all you need to do is locate it on the disc and load it into a text editor.

The CD-ROM is divided into several directories. These directories, and their contents, are listed in the *contents.htm* file, located in the root directory of the CD-ROM.

Server and Software Requirements

Hardware and software requirements to use each programming example are detailed in the chapter for that example. However, the general guidelines apply:

Language	Server Operating System
Perl	UNIX, DOS, Windows, OS/2
Shell	UNIX
C	UNIX, DOS, Windows, OS/2

Java, JavaScript, and VBScript programs require a compatible browser. You need one of the following browsers or another browser known to be compatible with each program type:

Language	Supported Browser
Java	Netscape Navigator 2.0 and later
	Microsoft Internet Explorer 3.0 and later
JavaScript	Netscape Navigator 2.0 and later
	Microsoft Internet Explorer 3.0 and later
VBScript	Microsoft Internet Explorer 3.0 and later

The data on the CD-ROM is encoded so that it can be read by IBM PCs and compatibles, Apple Macintosh, Sun workstations, and most machines running the UNIX operating system.

Using the Software

The files included on the CD-ROM need not be copied to your computer's hard disk drive before you can use them. You may instead open the files directly using any text editor. For example, when using the Windows 95 Notepad application do the following

1. Insert the CD-ROM into the CD-ROM drive.
2. In Notepad, choose File, Open.
3. Change to the drive that contains the CD-ROM.

4. Change to the directory that contains the file you want to use.
5. Select the file, and choose OK.

About the sources.htm File

The *sources.htm* file in the root directory of the CD-ROM contains dozens of links you can use to locate resources of interest on the Web. Links are provided for CGI, Perl programming topics, Java, JavaScript, VBScript sources, and more. To use this file, load it into your browser, then click on a link.

User Assistance and Information

The software accompanying this book is being provided as-is without warranty or support of any kind. Should you require basic installation assistance, or if your media is defective, please call our product support number at (212) 850-6194 weekdays between 9 A.M. and 4 P.M. Eastern Standard Time. We can be reached via e-mail at: wprtusw@wiley.com.

To place additional orders or to request information about other Wiley products, please call (800) 879-4539.

Additional support for this book is available at the author's Web site, at http://gmccomb.com/languages/.

Please note that because of the volume of mail received, the author is not able to provide individual support for examples and/or topics not included in this book, nor is he able to provide assistance in modifying the examples.

Index

J

What's on the CD-ROM

The CD-ROM enclosed in the *Web Languages Sourcebook* contains all the example program files and applications detailed in the book, including programs in Perl, C, Java, JavaScript, VBScript, and UNIX shell. It also contains numerous freeware and shareware programs and utilities from other authors such as:

Apache and CERN servers for UNIX, for testing Web programs or for creating a ready-to-go Web site

Complete source and binaries for the gcc C compiler, as well as Perl versions 4 and 5

Sample program in Perl for validating users visiting your Web site

Sample program in Perl for displaying random images (such as banner ads) for each person visiting your Web site

Additional sample programs in Perl for building a Web site shopping card, a guestbook, and a forms processor and more.

Using the Software

This software contains files to help you utilize the models described in the accompanying book. By opening the package, you are agreeing to be bound by the following agreement: